THE RACHEL HABER COHEN EDITION

רפואת השבת

THE HALACHIC GUIDE TO MEDICAL PRACTICE ON SHABBOS

THE RACHEL HABER COHEN EDITION

רפואת השבת

THE HALACHIC GUIDE TO MEDICAL PRACTICE ON SHABBOS

For physicians, caregivers, and the home

Rabbi Michael Chizkiyah

TARGUM/FELDHEIM

First published 2005

ISBN 1-56871-359-2

Published by:
TARGUM PRESS, INC.
22700 W. Eleven Mile Rd.
Southfield, MI 48034
E-mail: targum@netvision.net.il
Fax: 888-298-9992
www.targum.com

In conjuction with
BEIT MIDRASH MA'ALOT KEDOSHIM

Distributed by:
FELDHEIM PUBLISHERS
208 Airport Executive Park
Nanuet, NY 10954

Printing plates by Frank, Jerusalem
Printed in Israel by Chish

For questions and comments the author can be contacted at:
9 Rechov Wasserman, Bnei Brak 51507, tel. 972-3-579-1060

ב"ה

עובדיה יוסף
הראשון לציון
ונשיא מועצת חכמי התורה

OVADIA YOSSEF
RISHON LEZION
AND PRESIDENT OF TORAH SAGES COUNSIL

ירושלים כב שבט תשנ"ה JERUSALEM

לכבוד הרה"ג המפורסם חכו ממתקים וכולו מחמדים, תהלתו בקהל חסדים, שוקד על דלתות תורתינו הקדושה, לילה כיום יאיר כחשכה כאורה כש"ת רבי מיכאל חזקיה שליט"א, בנו של ידידנו רב הפעלים לתורה ולתעודה אוצר כלי חמדה רבי לוי חזקיה שליט"א.

הובאו לפני גליונות הספר "קונטרס הרפואה בשבת", עברתי בין בתריו כמסת הפנאי וראיתי כי ידיו רב לו למשקל ולמטרי במלחמתה של תורה, ואסף כעמיר גורנה מדברי רבותינו הפוסקים ראשונים ואחרונים, חדשים גם ישנים, לאסוקי שמעתתא אליבא דהלכתא, איישר חיליה לאורייתא, כן ירבה וכן יפרוץ.

ולחיבת הקודש אמרתי להעיר על מ"ש בפרק ד' בעינין המחלוקת שבין הרמב"ם (פ"ב מהל' שבת הי"א), לבין הרמב"ן שהובא בדברי הרב המגיד שם, שדעת הרמב"ן צריך שינוי במלאכה לחולה שיש בו סכנה, אם אין שם שום שיהוי, ודעת הרמב"ם אינה כן, שא"צ שינוי אלא ליולדת, שטבעו של עולם הוא, משא"כ שאר חולים שיש בהם סכנה. ומריש הוה אמינא דתליא בפלוגתא אם השבת דחויה היא אצל פיקוח נפש, או הותרה לגמרי, שהרמב"ם לשיטתיה דס"ל שבת הותרה אצל פיקוח נפש, וכמ"ש שם, כללו של דבר שבת לגבי חולה שיש בו סכנה הרי היא כחול וכו', וכ"כ הגאון צפנת פענח (רפ"ב מהל' שבת) בדעת הרמב"ם וכ"כ האבני נזר (חאו"ח סי' תנה אות ה) בדעת הרמב"ם. וכ"כ בשו"ת חסד לאברהם תאומים מה"ת (חאו"ח סי' סז). ובשו"ת דברי מלכיאל ח"ד (סי' טו), ועוד. ולכן כיון שהותרה, כאילו אין כאן שבת כלל, וא"צ שינוי. אבל הרמב"ן אפשר דס"ל ששבת דחויה אצל פקוח נפש. וכמ"ש בתשובת הרשב"א שהובא בב"י (סי' שכח). והיא בסימן תרפט (וע"ע בשו"ת הרשב"א ח"ז סי' שמג). וכן דעת הר"ן ריש פ"ב דביצה (יז). והארכתי בזה בשו"ת יחוה דעת ח"ד (סימן ל), ע"ש, ולהכי ס"ל להרמב"ן שצריך שינוי גם לחולה שיש בו סכנה. ולענין הלכה נראה שהעיקר כדברי הרמב"ם שא"צ שינוי. ושו"ר בשו"ת אבני נזר (חאו"ח סי' קיח אות ד') שכן הסביר בדעת הרמב"ם, וסיים, שהרמב"ן י"ל דס"ל דהשבת דחיוה, ע"ש. ולפי מה שהסביר האבני נזר שם, דה"ט של הרב

המגיד (בפ"ב מה שבת הל' יד) שכתב, שחולה שיש בו סכנה מחללים עליו את השבת לכל צרכיו, אע"פ שאין סכנה במניעת הדבר שעושים לו, משום דס"ל ששבת הותרה לצרכי חולה שיש בו סכנה, לפ"ז גם מרן בש"ע (סי' שכח ס"ד) שפסק כדברי הרב המגיד, וכמ"ש המג"א שם בדעת מרן, יוצא שגם מרן ס"ל ששבת הותרה לגבי פקוח נפש, א"כ גם למרן א"צ שינוי. וצדק בשו"ת אור לציון ח"ב (סי' לו), שצידד להלכה כדברי הרב המגיד אליבא דהרמב"ם שא"צ שינוי בחולה שיש בו סכנה. ומ"ש בכף החיים (בסי' שכח אות עה) להחמיר להצריך שינוי כמ"ש הגר"ז, אינו מחוור להלכה לדידן, שהגר"ז לשטתיה שם דס"ל ששבת דחויה אצל פקוח נפש (ע' בש"ע הגר"ז סי' שכח סעיף יג). אבל לדידן העיקר כסברת הרמב"ם והרב המגיד שא"צ שינוי. והן אמת שיש לדחות ולומר שאף מרן ס"ל כמ"ש בב"י בשם הרשב"א, שהשבת דחויה ולא הותרה, ואעפ"כ יפה פסק כדברי הרב המגיד (בפ"ב הלכה יד) הנ"ל. וכמו שמצינו כן להרדב"ז ח"ד (סי' קל) דס"ל ששבת דחויה ואעפ"כ פסק כהרב המגיד שמחללים שבת גם בדבר שאין במניעתו סכנה לחולה. וכן הוא גם בש"ע הגר"ז הנ"ל, שגם הוא פסק כהרב המגיד בזה, אע"פ שהוא סובר שהשבת דחויה ולא הותרה, וא"כ י"ל כן גם בדעת מרן. (וע"ע בשו"ת חתן סופר סי' לד ודו"ק). ומ"מ לעניין הלכה נראה שהעיקר כד' הרמב"ם שא"צ שינוי בחולה שיש בו סכנה.

ואסיים בברכה יהי רצון שחפץ ה' בידו יצלח ויפוצו מעינותיו חוצה לאסוקי שמעתתא אליבא דהלכתא ולהגדיל תורה ולהאדירה, ברבות הטובה גם עד זקנה ושיבה. בעושר וכבוד בריאות והצלחה ושובע שמחות אמן.

בברכת התורה

עובדיה יוסף

בברכת התורה

עובדיה יוסף

הרב שלום משאש
הרב הראשי
וראש אבות בתי הדין
לירושלים

RABBI SHALOM MESSAS
Chief Rabbi
and Head of Rabbinical Courts
Jerusalem, Israel

הוגש לפני ספר יקר מכל יקר, בשם קונטרס רפואת השבת מעשה ידי אומן, צנצנת המן, הרב הכולל, כל אישורין כולל, גריס באורייתא תדירא, הרב מיכאל חזקיה שליט"א, והוא ספר מלא פרי מגדים, מדיני רפואה בשבת בכל הנושאים השייכים בחולים, שיש בו סכנה, ושאין בו סכנה, אם ע"י גוי, אם ע"י ישראל, לא הניח פינה ועל הכל קבע לו הערות וביאורים למטה להביא מקורות ההלכה כיד ה' הטובה עליו, גם מפלפל ונושא ונותן בהלכה ולהביא ראיות מפי סופרים ומפי ספרים, עד שמסיק לאסוקי שמעתתא אליבא דהלכתא, אסף וקבץ כל הדינים השייכים, ועשה מהם סדר ומשטר נאה ויאה, מפוסקים ראשונים עד אחרונים, לא נמלט ממנו דבר, ישר חיליה לאורייתא, חפץ הייתי להעיר באיזהו מקומן, מרוב העבודות העמוסות עלי מן הציבור והיחיד, שהזמן גרמן, הם מנעו ממני הטוב הזה, ועוד חזון למועד, אי"ה, ואני תפילה, שהרב המחבר יוסיף להתעלות בברכי הלימוד וההוראה, ודבריו יתבדרון בבי מדרשא, וימשיך בדרכו הטובה לחבר ולחדש כאות נפשו, בבריאות איתנא, ונהורא מעליא, אמן.

החו"פ בירושלים עיה"ק בשלהי אלול תשנ"ד לפ"ק
ע"ה שלום משאש ס"ט

הלשכה רחוב החבצלת 12 - ת.ד. 13, ירושלים 91000 טלפון 250606 פקס: 258294
12 HACHAVAZELET ST. P.O.B. 13, JERUSALEM 91000 - ISRAEL TEL. 250606 FAX: 258294

Translation of Rav Chaim Pinchas Scheinberg's letter of approbation:

This most distinguished *sefer* concerning the laws of medical treatment on Shabbos, authored by Rabbi Michael Chizkiyah, is particularly valuable. It treats every topic in an orderly manner, starting with the general and ending with the specific, and it is interspersed with wisdom and highly beneficial remarks.

This most eminent author succeeded in delving deeply into the topics of interest and to elucidate matters that needed detailed explanation. Rabbi Chizkiyah is highly renowned for his expertly presented and numerous lectures, and this *sefer* in Hebrew has been praised profusely.

All that remains is to confer upon him the blessing that his wellspring of Torah learning should spread his wisdom to those who thirst for it.

With Torah blessings,
Chaim Pinchas Scheinberg

Rabbi CHAIM P. SCHEINBERG
Rosh Hayeshiva "TORAH ORE"
and Morah Hora'ah of Kiryat Mattersdorf

הרב חיים פינחס שיינברג
ראש ישיבת "תורה אור"
ומורה הוראה דקרית מטרסדורף

בס"ד

ירושלים סיון תשס"ד

מכתב ברכה

הנה הספר הנכבד מאוד, שרבו פארותיו, "רפואת השבת", שחובר ע"י הרב הגאון ר' מיכאל חזקיה שליט"א הלא הוא יקר ומיוחד. דבר דבור על אפניו, הכללים והפרטים, ושזורות בו בחכמה, הערות מחכימות ומועילות מאוד.

והשכיל המחבר הנכבד, לשדד עמקים ולהרחיב בתבונה ובטוב טעם את כל עניני רפואה והמסתעף, וכבר יצא מוניטין שלו בשיעוריו הרבים, ואתמחי גברא וגם ספרו זה קלסוהו רבים.

לא נצרכה אלא לברכה, יתן ד', ויפוצו מעינותיך חוצה, ותרבה גבולך בתלמידים, ויתקבלו דבריך בבי מדרשא.

בברכת התורה
חיים פינחס שיינברג

בברכת התורה
חיים פינחס שיינברג

רחוב פנים מאירות 2, ירושלים, ת.ד. 6979, טל. 537-1513 (02), ישראל
2 Panim Meirot St., Jerusalem, P.O.B. 6979, Tel. (02) 537-1513, Israel

הרב ש. י. נסים קרליץ

רמת אהרן

רח' ר' מאיר 6, בני-ברק

בס"ד יום ח' חשון תשנ"ז

כאשר הרה"ג מוה"ר מיכאל חזקי' שליט"א חיבר ספר "רפואת השבת" על הלכות שבת הנוגעים לחולים ורפואתם ואסף ובירר דבר דבר וגם ציין מקורו, והדבר הוא לתועלת גדולה לעוסקים בהלכה כ"ש שזה יכול להיות נוגע לפיקוח נפש.

ויהי רצון שיזכה הרב המחבר שליט"א לזכות את הרבים בעוד חיבורים יקרים שרבים יהנו לאורם, מתוך מנוחה שלום ושלוה.

החותם לכבוד עמלה של תורה,
נסים קרליץ

החותם לכבוד עמלה של תורה
נסים קרליץ

יעקב בהגרצ"י **אדלשטיין**
רב דרמת־השרון

JACOB EDELSTEIN
RABBI OF RAMAT-HASHARON
ISRAEL

ב"ה רמת-השרון, יום א' דר"ח חשון תשנ"ז

הן בא לפני הרב המופלג בתויר"ש המאוה"ג חו"ב, ידידינו היקר כמה"ר מיכאל חזקיה שליט"א ובידו החיבור, פרי עמלו, שהעלה על הספר, תוכו רצוף אהבה, פרי מגד מגדנים, בהלכות רפואה בשבת קודש, ומחולק הספר לפי הענינים השונים, לפרקים וסעיפים, דבר דבור על אופניו, כדי שיוכל כל אחד, למצוא בנקל דברי חפץ, את דבר ההלכה שהוא מבקש.

והנה הרב המחבר שליט"א חקר ובירר, העמיק והרחיב בהלכות אלו, והוציא מתח"י דבר מתוקן, כיאות לחבר, בחזקה שכבר איתחזק גברא, על כן אמינא לפעלו יישר כחו. ותועלת גדולה ישנה בחיבור זה, ומומלץ בזה לכל אחב"י כקטון כגדול, לרכוש ספר זה, אשר בודאי יביא ברכה לביתו, כדי לדעת את המעשה אשר יעשון. ושכמ"ה.

הכ"ד הכו"ח לכה"ת
יעקב אלדשטיין

בס"ד

הרב אפרים גרינבלאט
רב ושו"ב במעמפים
מח"ס שו"ת רבבות אפרים ו"ח

Rabbi Ephraim Greenblatt
5556 Barfield Road
Memphis, Tennessee 38120
Telephone (901) 682-3291
Fax (901) 685-0258

הנה ידידי הרה"ג ר' מיכאל חזקיה שליט"א, שלח לי לעיין בכתבים שלו. שעומד להוציא לאור בשם קונטרס רפואת השבת. ועברתי על כל הקונטרס, וראיתי מה שכתב, והכל מסודר היטב וכתב מקור לכל הלכה, ודבריו ראויים לעלות על שלחן מלכים, וניכר שעמל ועבד קשה להוציא לאור דבר שלם ומתוקן לצורך הרבים.

וכבר איתמחי בספרו החשוב על דיני מוקצה, והוא ת"ח גדול, וראוי להתחשב בדבריו שכתב והנני נותן לו הסכמה מלאה על ספרו החדש, ושיזכה להוציאו לאור מיד לתועלת הרבים הנחוצים בזמנינו בעניני רפואה.

והמעיין בספרו יראה וידע ההלכות על בורין, וטוב עשה פה ידידי הרה"ג המחבר שליט"א שמגיש לנו ספר יקר כזה.

והנני מברכו בחותם הברכות, ושיצליח להוציא עוד ספרים חשובים כאלה ואשרי חלקו, וגם אהיה מן הראשונים שארכוש ספרו, ובטוחני מי שיכניס ספרו לביתו יהנה ויפיק תועלת, ונא לרכוש ספרו בכסף מלא, כי השקיע הרבה כסף להוציא לאור חבור זה, ומצוה לבא לעזרתו, שיוכל לשבת בשלוה בלי שום דאגות, ולהוציא עוד ספרים חשובים כאלו, ובזה הנני ידידו הדו"ש הטוב, ושיצליח בכל הענינים, המאחל לו כל טוב.

ולאות כי עיינתי בקונטרס הנני מצרף הערות קצרות.

אפרים גרינבלט

אפרים גרינבלט
רב ושו"ב ומו"צ דפה
מחבר שו"ת רבבות אפרים
על [illegible] חלקים.

הרב אפרים גרינבלט שליט"א
RABBI EPHRAIM GREENBL
MEMPHIS

RABBI Y. ROTH
1556 - 53rd Street
Brooklyn, N.Y. 11219

Tel. (718) 435-1502

יחזקאל ראטה
אבדק״ק קארלסבורג
בארא פארק, ברוקלין, נ.י. יע״א

בעזה״י לסדר כי אני ה' רופאיך תשס״ה לפ״ק

הן הי' למראה עיני ספר רפואת השבת מאת הרב הגאון מוה״ר מיכאל חזקי' שליט״א על עניני רפואה בשבת אשר דבר נחוץ הוא לקבץ כעמור גורנה כל ההלכות שנוגע בזה לעת הצורך לידע את המעשה אשר יעשון וכבר עלה בהסכמה מהרבנים הגאונים שליט״א מאה״ג ת״ח בהדפסה ראשונה על כן גם אנא מצטריפנא בהדייהו שיזכהא השי״ת שחיבורו יתקבל בקרב הלומדים והשי״ת יזכהו לזכות את הרבים ובזכות שמירת שבת קודש נזכה כולנו לישועה קרובה אכי״ר.

הכו״ח לכבוד התורה ולומדי'
יחזקאל ראטה

משה הלברשטאם

מו"צ העדה החרדית

ראש ישיבת **"דברי חיים"** טשאקאווע

מח"ס שו"ת **"דברי משה"**

פעיה"ק **ירושלים** תובב"א

רח' יואל 8 טל. 370514

הן מע"כ הרה"ג יר"ש ומוכתר בנימוסין מוה"ר מיכאל חזקיה שליט"א הראה לפני גליונות ספרו רב הכמות והאיכות אשר בשם "רפואת השבת" יכונה. אשר אסף איש טהור מהשו"ע ופוסקים שמפיהם אנו חיים, וסדרם וערכם בשפה ברורה ונראה היטב כי איתמחי גברא, וקמיע זה מידי מומחה יצא, ותועלת גדולה יפיקו מספרו להנצל מחילול שבת ח"ו בעת בהלה או מצוקת הגוף ונפש ח"ו, אשר השכיל לבאר כל אופן מיחוש גדרו הנכון להלכה. והן למנוע ח"ו חשש סכנה מבלי יודעים.

ואמנם שלא הי' סיפק כמובן לעבור על כל דבריו ממש, אך נאמנים עלי דברי מעכ"ת ידיד ה' וידיד כל בית ישראל, ידיד נעורים הגאון הגדול מוהר"ר יצחק זילברשטיין שליט"א רבה של רמת אלחנן ומח"ס תורת היולדת ועו"ס. שהרבה עמלה של תורה השקיע הרב המחבר הנ"ל שליט"א ומוקימנא ליה אחזקת חבר שלא יוציא דבר שאינו מתוקן מתח"י, ואכן פרי עמלו ויגיעו ניכרים דברי אמת בכל קטע וקטע מדברי ספרו זה החשוב והנכבד מאד.

ואמינא לפעלא טבא איישר כוחו וחילו לאדפוסי אדרא לזכות בו את הרבים והקב"ה ישלח דברו וירפאנו ויחלימנו וכדאי השבת קודש שתצילנו מכל צרה וצוקה נגע ומחלה. ושבת היא מלזעוק ורפואה קרובה לבוא ברוב אונים ואמיץ כח בעזה"י.

ובעה"ח היום יום חמישי לסדר זכור את יום השבת לקדשו.

שנת ויהא לך בה רפואה שלימה לפ"ק

משה הלברשטאם

פעיה"ק ירושלים תובב"א

שמואל אליעזר שטרן
דומ"צ בביד"צ זכרון מאיר
ור"מ ישיבת חוג חתם סופר
רח' הרב קוק 1, בני ברק 51273

RABBI SHMUEL ELIEZER SHTEREN
ZICRON MEYIR BEIT-DIN-ZEDEK
CHUG CHATAM SOFER YESHIVA
RAV KUK 1 ST. BNEY BRAK 51273

ו' שבט תשנ"ז לפ"ק

דבר גדול בעמיו עשה מעלת כבוד ידידנו המפואר האברך המופלג בתורה ובהלכה הרב הגאון מיכאל חזקיה שליט"א, אשר שיכל את ידיו בתבונה ובהשכל לברר וללבן הדק היטב את כל דרכי הטיפול הרפואיים ואת כל המכשירים השונים למיניהם, להורות לעם ה' את המעשה אשר יעשון בשבתות ומועדי השנה. יגיעה רבה ועצומה ועמל מפרך של שנים רבות הושקעה בעבודת קודש זו. עד אשר עלתה בידו מלאכת מחשבת, בטוב טעם ודעת, ערוך ומסודר כשולחן ערוך המוכן ומתוקן לסעודה, והי' פריו למאכל ועלהו לתרופה. כשנכנסתי אל הקודש פנימה קמיה דמרן רבינו בעל שבט הלוי שליט"א אמר לי שאם כי אין ביכלתו לתת הסכמה על הספר מחמת ריבוי המכשירים והתרופות שאינן מסורות לרבים, אך הוא מכיר טובה למחבר שליט"א על האוצר הבלום שזכה לגלות בספרו החשוב וברכת קדשו תלוהו ותנחהו להגדיל תורה ולהאדירה, מתוך בריות גופא ונהורא מעליא.

כעתירת וכברכת
שמואל אליעזר שטרן

יצחק זילברשטיין
רב שכונת רמת אלחנן
בני-ברק

RABBI YITZCHAK SILBERSTEIN
Rabbi of Ramat Elchanan
BNEI-BRAK

בס"ד יום י"ב לחודש הרחמים אלול תשנ"ה

"הנשאל הרי זה מגונה" נאמר רק על הלכות פקוח נפש (משנ"ב שכ"ח ו') "משום שהתלמיד חכם במקומו היה לו לדרוש בפרקא לכל, כדי שידעו כל העם ולא יצטרכו לשאלו".

יפה קיים הלכה זו התלמיד חכם המופלג בתויר"ש מוהר"ר הגאון ר' מיכאל חזקיהו שליט"א שעמל וחקר ותיקן במשך שנים רבות והכין הני הלכתא דפקוח נפש בצורה יפה מאד.

ואנו תפלה שלא תצא תקלה מתחת ידו וילמדו רבים וייראו כי השי"ת הוא מלך החפץ בחיים והזריז להציל הרי זה משובח.

הכו"ח לכבוד התורה ועמליה
יצחק זילברשטיין

יצחק זילברשטיין
רב
שכונת
רמת-אלחנן
בני-ברק ת"ו

Rabbi Benjamin Weiss
Rabbi of the Sanz Congregation
Bnei Brak, Israel

יהונתן בנימין ווייס
רב ביהמ״ד
דחסידי צאנז-קלויזנבורג
בני־ברק

B"H 15 Kislev 5765

Rabbi Chizkiyah's original masterpiece in Hebrew on the issues of medicine on Shabbos has been widely accepted as an authoritative reference work in this field. Many medical professionals have also been learning it in study groups to enhance their understanding of these diverse and complex issues. Since electronic means of halachic consultation (telephone or computers) are not available on Shabbos, it has also become an invaluable handbook for practicing observant physicians seeking urgent answers in real-time situations.

The English version is a refreshing addition to his monumental project. I have had the pleasure and privilege to have carefully gone through every paragraph of both the Hebrew and English versions of this wonderful *sefer*. The translated manuscript was also reviewed by medical professionals knowledgeable in halachah. Special efforts were also taken to ensure the correct translation of the medical terms.

I am confident that the English version will open a new window to a vast audience of English-speaking professionals eager to have immediate access to expert halachic opinions. It will also play a central role in educating a new generation of observant Jewish physicians.

I will conclude my remarks with a prayer that Hashem enable the distinguished author to continue with his wonderful work, diffusing Torah knowledge throughout the Jewish world.

With all due Torah respect,

Yehonoson Benjamin Weiss

B'SD

JOSEPH B. LEIBMAN M.D.

SPECIALIST IN EMERGENCY MEDICI0NE

Senior Attending
Emergency Dept
Tel haShomer Hosp

Residence:
Netivot HaMishpat 52/1
D.N. Modiin
Kiriat Sefer
08 974 1187

I have reviewed the book *The Halachic Guide to Medical Practice on Shabbos* and have found it to be a useful and practical guide. The book has been well researched, and I am impressed with Rav Michael Chizkiyah's efforts to provide accurate information both from a halachic and medical viewpoint.

This book is written in an easy-to-follow format that makes it appropriate for *talmidei chachamim* who wish to increase their knowledge of medical issues on Shabbos, for the practicing physician to be better attuned to the problems he may encounter on Shabbos, and for the layman to better understand and deal with the predicaments that can occur on Shabbos. The book has been translated from Hebrew; nevertheless, it does mention many cases that would be applicable to many communities in the U.S.

I give my blessings to the author — a well-known rabbi in Israel — and congratulate him on increasing the knowledge of the laws of Shabbos and with it the observance of Shabbos. May this result in the bringing of Mashiach tzidkeinu speedily in our day.

Dr. Yosef Leibman MD

ד"ר ליבמן יוסף
מומחה לרפואה דחופה
Specialist in Emergency Medicine
18590 .מ.ר.מ. 30740 .מ.ר

Specialist in Emergency Medicine
Attending Physician Sheba -Tel HaShomer Medical Center
Editor in Chief Israeli Journal of Emergency Medicine

TORAH SCHOOL בית מדרש לתורה

"MA'ALOT KEDOSHIM" "מעלות קדושים"

ע"ש חללי מלחמת יום הכפורים ומערכות ישראל הי"ד

Memory of the Soldiers killed in the Yom kippur War

BEN PETACHIAH ST. 28, BNEI BRAK P.O.B. 1544 ת.ד. רח' בן פתחיה 28, בני ברק

המטרה

השתלמות תורנית גבוהה לאברכים מחוננים והכשרתם למורי הוראה ומנהיגים רוחניים.

מתן מילגות וסטיפנדיות לתלמידים ממשפחות מעוטי יכולת. המשתלמים במוסדות על יסודיים תורניים גבוהים.

החדרת תורה וערכי ישראל בישובי עולים.

קיום רשת שעורי תורה לנוער ולמבוגרים.

☆

AIMS:

To help outstanding Young men acquire advanced Torah Knowledge and prepare them to become Halachic authorities and spiritual leaders.

To award grants and stipends to students from underprivilegd families who are studying in Torah high schools.

To spread Torah study and Jewish values amongst new immigrants.

To maintain a network of evening Torah study sessions for youth.

☆

After the Yom Kippur War, which resulted in the death of thousands of Israeli soldiers, we founded a *beit midrash* in order to share the light of Torah and *mussar* with the public in the merit of the casualties of the Yom Kippur War, *Hy"d*.

With great *siyatta diShmaya*, the *beit midrash* opened its doors on Kislev 5735, accepting young men of exceptional talent who showed potential of finding a place as spiritual leaders, *roshei yeshivah*, and *rabbanim* and disseminate the Torah to the Jewish people, particularly the youth.

Students of the *beit midrash* give classes daily in synagogues and homes after their own studies, and, *baruch Hashem*, they have been very successful, particularly in their activities in the Pardes Katz neighborhood of Bnei Brak.

The topics studied in the *beit midrash* are varied. There are in-depth studies of *seders Nashim* and *Nezikin* and of the practical laws of kashrut and Shabbat. Twice a month students take written tests on the material, and at the conclusion of their studies they are tested by *gedolei Yisrael*, *rabbanim*, and *roshei yeshivah* before receiving *semichah*. With Hashem's help, dozens of graduates completed their studies in the *beit midrash* and went on to start yeshivot and *kollel*s and become community rabbis or educators.

The *beit midrash* has followed the leadership of great Torah leaders of the generation, HaGaon HaRav Yehudah Tzedaka, *zt"l*, and HaGaon HaRav Ben Tzion Abba Shaul, *zt"l*, *roshei yeshivah* of Porat Yosef, who encouraged the students during their visits to the *beit midrash* and lectured there.

ההנהלה: הרב שמואל יונה רח' הרב אלשיך 8, בני ברק טל. 6184960(03) טל/פקס 6188237(03)

THE MANAGEMENT: RABBI SAMUEL YONA 8, Harav Alshich Street, Bnei-Brak. Tel. 972-3-6184960 Tel/Fax 972-3-6188237

חשבון בנק פא"י 1C5-037648

One of the goals of the *beit midrash* is to encourage and assist students to write their own Torah works, and *sefarim* on both halachah and Torah insights have been published by the *kollel* members. Particularly noteworthy are the works of Rav Michael Chizkiyah, *shlita*: his three-volume work *Ketzot HaShabbat* and *Refuat HaShabbat*, which bears the approbations of many Torah leaders as well as prominent medical specialists. This work has now been translated into English as *The Halachic Guide to Medical Practice on Shabbos* and should bring great benefit to the English-speaking public — doctors, medical professionals, and laypeople alike.

The *kollel* supports several charitable endeavors. Ayin Yafah assists needy new mothers with a financial stipend. This fund was established by the philanthropist Mr. David Namdar and his sons Avraham and Moshe, in memory of Yaffa bat Yitzchak, *a"h*.

The *kollel* also established Keren Karmeli, in memory of the righteous woman Mrs. Esther Karmeli, and her son Lieutenant Colonel Ben Tzion Karmeli, *Hy"d*, and Shmuel Karmeli, *z"l*. The fund's purpose is to help students and their families before the holidays with a financial stipend and the distribution of foodstuffs. Before Pesach, approximately 150 families are provided with various items to help them celebrate the festival.

In addition, the *kollel* runs youth groups for girls every Shabbat in which they study the laws of *shemirat halashon* and which provide classes for their mothers as well.

At the head of this holy work stands HaRav Shmuel Nissim Yonah, *shlita*, who spends days and nights working to ensure the success of the beit midrash, sparing no effort to strengthen the *kollel* and help the students learning there. May Hashem repay him and his dear family with strength, health, and success.

A special blessing to those philanthropists who support the endeavors of the *beit midrash* in its efforts. May Hashem send them blessing and success, wealth, honor, and health, and may they merit to bring up their children to Torah, *chuppah*, and good deeds.

Finally, we pray that Hashem grant us and our supporters continued success and that all our deeds should be for the sake of Heaven. May we merit to raise the yoke of Torah everywhere, and may all those who take part in this holy work be blessed. And may the words of the *Tanna* come to fruition: "All who busy themselves with the community should do so for the sake of Heaven, for then the merit of their forefathers assists them and their righteousness endures forever" (*Avot* 2:2). And may we merit to see the redemption and rebuilding of the Beit HaMikdash and eat of the sacrifices, speedily in our days.

קול קורא

אל אחינו היקרים הנדיבים בעם יהיו, אודות בית המדרש "מעלות קדושים" הקיים בבני ברק, אשר לומדים בה אברכים מצויינים בשקידה ובהתמדה, ביראת שמים טהורה וגם מרביצים תורה לקהל בשעות הערב.

היות וביקרנו שם ושמחנו מאד לראות מחזה נפלא זה המאיר את העינים ומשמח את הלב, שב"ה גם בעדות המזרח ישנם ישיבות כאלו, המפיחים רוח חיים בכל הסביבה ומקרבים את אחינו לאבינו שבשמים. וקול התורה בוקע שם כל היום.

אשרי התומך בה ואשרי הזוכה לעזור.

לכן את אחינו אנחנו מבקשים לבוא לעזרת בית המדרש "מעלות קדושים" הנמצאת במצב כספי קשה עקב יוקר החיים.

ונא להשתדל לבוא לקראתה ולתמוך בידי ידידנו הרה"ג שמואל יונה שליט"א, העומד בראש בית המדרש ועושה רבות ללא לאות לקיומו ולשגשוגו.

וזכות תורתנו הקדושה תגן על הנדיבים ועל המשתדלים שיזכו לכל ברכות התורה בהצלחה ובבריאות אורך ימים ושנות חיים.

החותמים בברכה

הגאון רבי יהודא צדקא שליט"א

הגאון רבי בן ציון אבא שאול שליט"א
רבני ישיבת "פורת יוסף" ירושלים

On 7 Adar 5760 (March 14, 2000), the anniversary of Moshe Rabbeinu's passing, Rachel Haber Cohen, *a"h*, left this world at the age of 28. The people she touched, the lives she impacted, the memories she left were extraordinary.

Rachel possessed every conceivable virtue and quality imaginable — charisma, charm, intelligence, compassion for all, and a remarkable inner and outward beauty. All of these attributes joined seamlessly with her unconditional love and loyalty to her parents and brothers. This great love was surpassed only by her love for her only daughter, Esther, who was only four years old at the time of her passing. *Baruch Hashem*, Esther grows daily with the same unique qualities as her mother.

Presently her family is actively involved in perpetuating Rachel's legacy as best as they can — primarily involving themselves in holy projects, including Jewish education, *mikva'ot*, and *chesed* projects of all types.

May Hashem bestow all of the merits of these and other projects for the eternal merit of her precious soul.

לע״נ רחל בת שולמית ע״ה

This book is dedicated in loving memory of

RACHEL BAT SHULAMIT *a"h*
RACHEL HABER COHEN

who will forever be remembered for
her fine character and nobility of spirit.

May the merit of our readers' Shabbos observance
serve as a constant source of elevation to
her precious *neshamah*.

ואלה יעמדו על הברכה

To the supporters of
Beit Midrash Ma'alot Kedoshim

IN ISRAEL

Mr. David Namdar
and his sons **Avraham** and **Moshe**

Mr. Avner Haimoff

Mr. Uri Haimoff

Mr. Yosef Masri
the son of **Mr. Avraham Masri** ז"ל

IN NEW YORK

Mr. David Nissani הי"ו
and his son
Ronen Shimon הי"ו

David Gad ז"ל
ben Nissan and Leah Gad
who passed away on 4 Adar 5762

Dedicated by his wife **Malka**
and their children
Albert, Morris, Steven, and **Dana** הי"ו

The Anshei Shalom Synagogue

The Afghan Jewish Foundation

The Afghan Sisterhood Foundation

The Likrat Kallah Sisterhood Foundation

Shaarei Tova of the Mashad community
The Mashad community of **Great Neck**
Mashad Sisterhood Foundation

Mr. Mirza Aga Kalaty
and his sons **Mashiach** and **Binyamin**

Mrs. Perry Lavian
and her sons **Yehuda, Larry, Moshe, Yitzchak,** and **Efraim**

Mr. Shimon Poldian

Mr. Albert Nachmias

Mr. David Ambalo

Mr. Mordechai Basal

Mr. Yosef Ovadya

Mr. Meyer Siton

Michael Cohen and his family

IN LONDON

Mr. Reuven Cohen Ambalo ז״ל
ben Refael and Zipora
who passed away on the 28 Sivan 5762

Dedicated by his wife, **Devora**
and their children
Yehuda, Ofer, Mina, Ziva, and **Zalcha** הי״ו

Mr. Moshe Betzalel and his wife, **Gila**
and their children **Daniel, Yonatan,** and **Rivka**

IN GENEVA

Mr. Gavriel Tamman and his wife, **Angel**
and their sons **Shlomo, David,** and **Yosef**

Mr. Nissim Gaon
and his son **David** and **Yoel Ersoog**

Contents

Preface to the English Edition

This book originally appeared in Hebrew. After the Hebrew book, *Refuat HaShabbat,* came out, there was a strong demand to translate it into English, since a large segment of the English-speaking world were interested in the halachos of medical care on Shabbos, among them doctors, nurses, hospitals, Hatzalah paramedics, and various medical facilities. Parents, too, who are struggling with questions of medical care on Shabbos and *yom tov* will find this book an invaluable resource.

I thank the team of rabbis who reviewed each and every part of the book, led by Rav Yehonasan Weiss, *shlita*, *rav* of Kehillat Sanz in Bnei Brak, who was involved in every aspect of the translation and who checked it several times until it reached completion.

I also wish to thank the dedicated staff of Targum Press headed by Rabbi Moshe Dombey, *shlita*, particularly Mrs. Suri Brand, who edited and proofread the manuscript, and D. Liff who designed the cover and text of the book.

Finally, I want to thank HaKadosh Baruch Hu for allowing me to publish this book in the English language. May it lead to a greater adherence to the laws of Shabbos observance by the English-speaking public.

Michael Chizkiyah
Elul 5765

Introduction

"*Baruch Elokeinu shebaranu lichvodo*... — Blessed is our God, Who created us for His honor and separated us from those who err, Who gave us the Torah of truth and implanted eternal life within us."

Every moment of a Jew's life is a source and a preparation for eternal life. There is no need to emphasize the urgency and importance of the halachos of saving a life — and specifically in relation to Shabbos. Our Sages say that every *rav* is obligated to be absolutely familiar with these laws. Indeed, the *Talmud Yerushalmi* states (as cited in the *Mishnah Berurah* 328:6) that one who is asked questions concerning the laws of medicine on Shabbos is despicable. The *rav* should have taught the subject so that the people would be familiar with it and not have to ask him.

Unfortunately, not only are laypersons unfamiliar with these halachos, but even scholars often do not know the details of the laws, particularly in view of the many technological advances in medicine.

In its original Hebrew, the book was entitled *Refuat HaShabbat* (The Medicine of Shabbos). While this refers to the laws of medical care on Shabbos, it also makes the point that Shabbos itself brings healing to those who observe its laws. The Sages say, "On Shabbos it is prohibited to cry, may recovery come speedily." In his *sefer Toras HaYoledes* the *gaon* Rabbi Yitzchak Zilberstein, *shlita*, writes, quoting the Chiddushei HaRim:

"The Sages have said that Shabbos came before Hashem and said,

'You have created a mate for each day [Sunday and Monday, Tuesday and Wednesday, Thursday and Friday], but You did not create a mate for me.' God replied, 'The people of Israel will be your mate.' We know that a husband is obligated by his marriage contract for his wife's health needs (see *Even HaEzer* 79). When a woman is under her husband's authority, he is obligated in her health care — but if she rebels against him and refuses his authority, she has not kept the agreement between them and he is not obligated. Therefore we say, 'On Shabbos it is prohibited to cry.' If the people of Israel have not rebelled, by respecting Shabbos and not crying, then 'may recovery come quickly.' Then Shabbos — the 'husband' — is obligated in the healing of its wife, the people of Israel."

Recently a number of books have been published dealing with the issues of medical care on Shabbos, and many of these were very helpful to me. Yet something was missing in these books: a clear and simple presentation of these laws in clear and simple language accessible to both scholar and layman.

The Halachic Guide to Medical Practice on Shabbos examines the halachos of treating illness on Shabbos. The subjects are presented in five sections:

1. *An Overall View* — general principles of medical care on Shabbos. This section discusses general principles of treating illness on Shabbos, in which cases is one exempt from Torah or rabbinic prohibitions, the prohibition against preparing medicines, and the permitted manner of asking a non-Jew to do a *melachah*.

2. *Choleh Sheyeish Bo Sakanah* — life-threatening illness. This section defines what is considered a life-threatening illness, who is authorized to make such a determination, and what one is permitted to do for someone who is dangerously ill.

3. *Choleh She'ein Bo Sakanah* — illnesses that pose no threat to life but cause the patient to be bedridden. This section discusses who is considered an ordinary bedridden patient, the differences between a *choleh sheyeish bo sakanah* and a *choleh she'ein bo sakanah*, and what

may and may not be done for the *choleh she'ein bo sakanah*. It also discusses what equipment may be used and how. The section also discusses cases in which there is danger to a limb (*sakanas eiver*), that of a slightly ill person (*choleh b'miktzas*), and minor aches and pains (*michush*). The section ends with a chart that summarizes what is permitted and forbidden in the case of each of the three categories of illness.

4. *Common Illnesses*. The section includes information from medical sources in order to give readers some understanding of the various bodily systems. In this way a person will gain a greater appreciation for Hashem's wondrous creation, and he will learn how to take better care of his health — and, of course, how to better ensure that Shabbos is kept properly when medical care is necessary.

5. *Medical Equipment and Procedures*. This is by and large a technical section, describing medical equipment and their use on Shabbos. In order to make it more accessible, it begins with an index of medical equipment.

The book includes a detailed index that contains more than 1,500 entries to allow readers to easily find the information they need.

The medical facts found in this book have been taken from respected medical books and journals and were checked carefully by certified medical doctors. They were also checked by Torah scholars specializing in medical questions and halachah.

It must be emphasized that readers should not rely on these facts to make a diagnosis, and all questions must be brought before the appropriate authority, either a doctor or a rabbi. I cannot presume to present the halachah in the manner of the *Mishnah Berurah*, both because of the profundity of the material and my own shortcomings. The halachos were organized after comprehensive study of *Shas* and the *poskim*, both *Rishonim* and *Acharonim*. The final decisions have been brought as delineated by the Chafetz Chaim in his *Mishnah Berurah*, the Kaf HaChaim, the Chazon Ish, and other great halachic decisors. The sources of the halachah generally appear in the notes on the bottom of the page.

Though I have put great effort into creating a high-quality work, perfection is impossible. If anyone finds errors in fact or conclusions, please contact me (through my publisher) so that they can be rectified in future editions.

Here I would like to take the opportunity to extend my thanks to my teacher and rebbe, the *rosh kollel* of Beit Midrash Ma'alot Kedoshim, HaRav Yaakov Peretz Friedman, *shlita*, and my teacher and father-in-law, HaRav Shmuel Nissim Yonah, *shlita*, who invested their time and energy to enable myself and all the members of my *chaburah* to devote our time to Torah study. Throughout the process of putting this book together, they helped me with their advice and counsel and gave me the opportunity to study the halachos of Shabbos in depth. May they and their families be blessed with success in all their endeavors, and may they merit to teach many students to raise their own children to Torah, *chuppah*, and good deeds in peace and tranquillity.

I must also offer my special blessings to the many rabbis and scholars who helped clarify the various sections of the book, giving generously of their time to go over the manuscript. Indeed, dozens of scholars reviewed different parts of the book before its publication, and I benefited much from their advice. I am indebted, too, to the many medical specialists in both Israel and the United States who reviewed the medical portions of the book.

Specifically I wish to thank HaRav Yitzchak Zilberstein, *shlita*, *rav* of Ramat Elchanan and *rosh kollel* of Beis David in Holon; HaRav Shmuel Eliezer Stern, *shlita*; HaRav Moshe Halberstam, *shlita*; HaRav Zev Cohen *shlita*; HaRav Yehonasan Binyamin Weiss, *shlita*; HaRav Yitzchak Yosef, *shlita*; and HaRav Eliezer Greenbaum, *shlita*.

I also want to express my thanks and appreciation to the doctors who worked with me to clarify many different aspects of the book and to check the medical sections. First, my thanks to the dedicated physician Dr. Moshe Shrem, who stood by my side from the beginning of the work until its completion. I also owe thanks to the well-known professor, Rabbi Avraham Sofer, *shlita*, author of *Nishmas Avraham*, and to my friend Dr. Avraham Pinchas. My thanks also to Dr. Yoel First, Dr. Aryeh Gruber,

Dr. Rachamim Beruchim, Dr. Yosef Chadad, Dr. Yosef Liebman, and Dr. Yehoshua Leiman. May the Healer of all people strengthen these devoted and God-fearing doctors so that they can help the unfortunate and bring succor to the ill.

I would also like to thank the professionals, technicians, and engineers for their advice, among them Rabbi Yechiel Melamed, Mr. Yosef Prifaz, Rabbi Avishai Bagad, *shlita*, Rabbi Amram Pisem, Dr. Adina Bar Chaim, and nurses Mrs. Sarah Wieder and Mrs. Rina Cohen.

A special thank you to the faculty of the Tessler Nursing School of Laniado Hospital in Netanya, who helped prepare large parts of the section on common illnesses.

A special acknowledgment to my dear friend Yossi Basson, who assisted me throughout the production of the book. May Hashem grant him and his wife much success in all their endeavors, and may they raise wonderful and healthy children in the way of Torah and pure fear of God.

I cannot begin to express my thanks to my parents, HaRav Levi Chizkiyah, *shlita*, and Mrs. Rivka Chizkiyah, *shetichyeh*, who raised me in the ways of Torah and the fear of God, and to my in-laws HaRav Shmuel Nissim Yonah, *shlita*, and Mrs. Rivka Yonah, *shetichyeh*, who enable us to live in the tents of Torah, and to my brother and sisters and brothers- and sisters-in-law. May Hashem grant them blessings and success in all of their efforts, and may they live long and full lives in good health, with all their desires granted for the good, and may they see *nachas* from all their children.

I will end with a request to the One who dwells on high: Please, Master of the world, bless me and my dear wife, Esther Rut, to raise our beloved sons and daughters in the way of Torah and pure fear of God. May You grant them a heart that understands, success in their studies, and may they merit to dwell all their lives within the walls of the *beis midrash*, toiling in Torah for its own sake. And may I, too, merit to live in Hashem's House all of my days, to behold the sweetness of Hashem and dwell in His palace.

I pray that I never be the cause of anything negative and that I never make an error in halachah by forbidding that which is permitted or permitting that which is forbidden.

May it be His will that in the merit of the holiness of Shabbos and the observance of its laws Torah will not be removed from our midst and from the midst of our children and our grandchildren. And may we merit to see the fulfillment of the prophecy "The world will be filled with the knowledge of Hashem as the water covers the earth," and the arrival of our redeemer, speedily in our days.

Michael Chizkiyah
Adar I 5765

Part 1

An Overall View

Chapter 1
General Principles

1. The advent of new technological advances in the world of medicine have given rise to numerous halachic questions that are encountered with increasing frequency, in particular on Shabbos and *yom tov*.

2. In the field of medicine, it is of the utmost importance to understand clearly which actions involve a *d'oraisa*, a Torah prohibition, and which involve only a *d'rabbanan,* a rabbinical prohibition. In some cases, one is permitted to perform actions that are normally prohibited by Torah law. In other situations, one may only perform actions normally forbidden by rabbinic law, and sometimes even rabbinical prohibitions are not permitted. This section discusses various prohibitions involved in medical treatments and explains which constitute Torah prohibitions and which are rabbinical.

Torah Prohibitions

The following medical situations may involve actions that are forbidden by Torah law on Shabbos and *yom tov*:

3. *Communication.* This includes using the telephone[1] or traveling to the hospital[2] or to a doctor or rabbi for advice.[3]

4. *Diagnoses.* This includes various tests, drawing blood, taking an X-ray, hooking up and operating an ECG monitor, or doing an ultrasound.[4]

5. *Treatment.* This includes administering intravenous injections,[5] setting casts, performing surgery, grinding and mixing medicines,[6] recording medical data,[7] and using various instruments.

Rabbinical Prohibitions

6. *"Grinding herbs."* Even when an action does not involve any specific Torah or rabbinical prohibition, there is a general rabbinical prohibition against any action done for the sake of healing on Shabbos. This was instituted as a decree to prevent one from "grinding herbs" for medicinal purposes (see chapter 2, "The Ordinance against Preparing Medicine").[8]

7. *Asking a non-Jew to perform forbidden labor.* The Rabbis forbade asking a non-Jew to perform any action on Shabbos that the Jew himself cannot perform, whether the act involves a Torah prohibition or a rabbinical prohibition (see chapter 3, "Instructing a Non-Jew to Perform a *Melachah*").[9]

---

1 פרוט האיסורים בשימוש בטלפון בשבת, ובחירת טלפון לשימוש בשבת, עיין לקמן פרק 14.

2 אופן הנסיעה, בחירת נהג ומכונית לנסיעה בשבת, עיין לקמן במערכת חולה שיש בו סכנה פרק 11.

3 יעוץ רפואי או יעוץ עם רב בשבת, עיין לקמן במערכת חולה שיש בו סכנה פרק 13.

4 ויבורר לקמן במערכת מכשירים וטיפולים רפואיים בשבת כיצד להשתמש בכל מכשיר.

5 פרטי הדינים בזריקות יבוררו במערכת הנ"ל פרק 46.

6 ויבורר בכללות להלן בפרק 2 בגזירת שחיקת סממנים. ולקמן מערכת חולה שיש בו סכנה פרק 16.

7 ויבורר לקמן במערכת חולה שיש בו סכנה פרק 15 ניהול והפעלת בית החולים בשבת, חלק פקידות ומזכירות רפואית.

8 ב"י בריש סימן שכ"ח בשם הר"ן, הרשב"א וה"ה.

9 מבואר ברמב"ם פ"ו מהלכות שבת, ובשו"ע סימן ש"ז. ולקמן בפרק 3 נפרט פרטי מקורות ההלכה.

Transgressing Torah Prohibitions in a Manner that Constitutes Only a Rabbinical Prohibition

8. *A forbidden melachah performed by a minor.* If a minor performs any *melachah* that is forbidden by Torah law, he has transgressed only a rabbinical prohibition. In many situations where one wishes to minimize the severity of the action, one may have a minor do it (see chapter 4, "*Melachah* Forbidden Only by Rabbinic Law").

9. *Performing a melachah in an unusual manner.* One transgresses a Torah prohibition only when a *melachah* is performed in the usual manner. Performing it with a *shinui*, a change from the normal manner, turns it into a rabbinical prohibition.[10]

10. *Melachah she'einah tzerichah l'gufah.* If one performs a *melachah* for a purpose other than the normal purpose of the *melachah*, the action is not prohibited by Torah law. However, it does involve a rabbinical prohibition. For example, the normal purpose of digging a hole in the ground is to make use of the hole. If one digs a hole in order to use the dirt, not the hole, the action involves only a rabbinical prohibition. This concept is used extensively in many medical situations (see chapter 4, "*Melachah* Forbidden Only by Rabbinic Law").

11. *A melachah performed by two people.* If two people perform a *melachah* that could have been performed by one, the severity of the action is lessened and in many situations involves only a rabbinical prohibition (see chapter 4).

12. *Gramah.* When a *melachah* is performed in an indirect manner, there are some situations where it is completely permissible and some where the action is permitted to prevent monetary loss or for the needs of a sick person (see chapter 4).

---

10 לקמן בפרק 4 יבורר דין זה בהרחבה.

The Torah's Approach to Treating Patients on Shabbos

13. When it comes to saving a life, Shabbos is no different from any other mitzvah of the Torah. Like any other mitzvah, it is pushed aside when there is danger to life. This is based on Chazal's interpretation of the verse "And you shall guard My statutes and My judgments that are done by a person so that he shall live by them" (*Vayikra* 18:5): " 'so that he shall live by them' — and not die by them" (*Yoma* 87b).

    This teaches that the laws of the Torah are not intended to punish us but are kind and merciful and bring peace to the world. The Torah says of those nonbelievers who say it is forbidden to desecrate Shabbos even in such circumstances that they are then saying, "I have also given you statutes that are not good and judgments that they do not live by" (Rambam, *Hilchos Shabbos* 2:3).

14. Our Sages have classified illness according to levels of severity in terms of what may or may not be done for a sick person on Shabbos. In general, the more serious the illness, the more can be done for the patient. In many cases, the word of the doctor or the patient determines which types of actions are permitted.[11]

15. The five categories of illness are
    a. *choleh sheyeish bo sakanah*, one who has an illness that involves danger to life;
    b. *sakanas eiver*, an illness that is not life-threatening but does involve danger to a certain limb or organ;
    c. *choleh she'ein bo sakanah*, one who has an illness that involves no threat to life or limb, i.e., an ordinary bedridden patient;
    d. *choleh b'miktzas*, one who has a minor illness; and
    e. *michush*, a slight pain or discomfort that does not involve an actual illness.

---

11 ככל שמצב בריאותו חמור יותר, התירו לעבור על איסורים חמורים יותר.

Choleh Sheyeish Bo Sakanah — Life-Endangering Illness

16. An illness that is potentially life-threatening, even where there is only a possibility of a threat to life, is considered "*pikuach nefesh*," i.e., a danger to life. In such a case, it is permitted to desecrate Shabbos to provide all of the patient's medical needs, even if this means a Jew must perform a normally forbidden action.[12]

There are two situations that may not appear to be life-threatening, but our Sages teach us they are included in this category:

17. *Internal injuries.* A wound or inflammation of any internal organ, from the teeth and gums inward, constitutes a threat to life if not properly treated and is therefore regarded as *pikuach nefesh.* Shabbos may be desecrated in order to treat it.[13] Included in this category are wounds or inflammation of any internal organ, such as the heart, liver, spleen, pancreas, and kidneys. The respiratory and digestive organs are also included.

18. *Birth.* A woman who is giving birth is regarded as being in a life-threatening situation from the time she goes into labor until the end of three[14] twenty-four-hour periods,[15] that is, seventy-two hours after giving birth.[16] Thus, all actions that would normally be performed for a woman giving birth may be performed on Shabbos, even if the woman herself states that she can manage without the *melachah* being performed.

    After this seventy-two-hour period until the end of seven days after the birth, *melachah* may be performed for a woman who just gave birth only if she claims to need it. Shabbos should not be desecrated if she declares that she has no need for the given action. If she has not expressed her opinion, we may assume that she has a need, and we are

---

12 שו״ע סימן שכ״ח סעיף ב׳.

13 שו״ע שם סעיף ג׳.

14 שו״ע סימן ש״ל סעיף ד׳.

15 עיי״ש במ״ב ס״ק י׳ דיש בזה מחלוקת ראשונים ואחרונים. אך נראה שפסק כדעת הסוברים מעת לעת שזוהי דעת רוב הפוסקים עיי״ש. ועי״ע בילקוט יוסף שבת ד׳ עמ׳ ש״ו.

16 שו״ע שם סעיף א׳.

permitted to desecrate Shabbos for this reason. That is to say, unless she says outright that she does not need an intervention, we assume she does.[17]

From the seventh to the thirtieth day, a postnatal woman is regarded as a *choleh she'ein bo sakanah*, and the laws relevant to this state apply.[18, 19]

Sakanas Eiver — Danger to a Limb

19. This category applies to an illness which, although not life-threatening, may result in losing the function of a limb, either completely or partially,[20] if not treated.[21] A non-Jew may be asked to do all that is needed, even if it involves an action prohibited by Torah law.[22] A Jew, however, may perform only actions that involve a rabbinical prohibition.

Choleh She'ein Bo Sakanah — A Standard Bedridden Patient

20. This applies to a person who suffers an illness that is not life-threatening. This also applies to someone who suffers an ailment in one of his limbs and is bedridden as a result.[23] A person with a fever is also included in this category.

    A non-Jew may be asked to provide for all the patient's needs even when it involves a Torah prohibition,[24] but a Jew may perform only an action that involves a rabbinical prohibition and only if it is done with a *shinui* (an unusual manner).[25] The patient may take any medicine that is prescribed for him.

---

17 כן מבואר בשו״ע הנ״ל סעיף ד׳ ועיי״ש במ״ב ס״ק י״ד.

18 שו״ע שם סעיף ד׳.

19 במסגרת ספרנו זה לא כתבנו דיני יולדת. ופרטי דין יולדת בשבת כבר נתבארו בהרחבה בטוב טעם ודעת בספר ״תורת היולדת״ להגאון רבי יצחק זילברשטיין שליט״א.

20 עיין בקצות השולחן סי׳ קל״ח סוס״ק י״ח. ובשמירת שבת כהלכתה פל״ג ס״א ובהערה ה׳.

21 שו״ע סימן שכ״ח סעיף י״ז.

22 שו״ע סי׳ שכ״ח סעיף י״ז. פרטי הדינים בהרחבה יבוררו לקמן פרק 28.

23 שו״ע שם.

24 ויבורר בהרחבה לקמן במערכת חולה שאין בו סכנה פרק 22 ופרק 23.

25 יבורר לקמן בפרק 22.

Choleh B'Miktzas — Minor Illness

21. This applies to a person who suffers an ailment or wound, either to a particular limb or to his whole body, but though he experiences pain and discomfort, he is not sufficiently weakened to be bedridden and there is no danger to the affected limb.

A non-Jew may only be asked to perform actions on his behalf that are forbidden by rabbinic law, but a Jew may not perform even such actions on the person's behalf. Moreover, the person may not take medication.[26]

Michush — Slight Pain or Discomfort

22. This category refers to someone who suffers from slight pain and discomfort but has no fever and functions normally, for example, one who has a slight headache, toothache,[27] stomachache, heartburn, or dizziness.[28]

It is forbidden for either a Jew or a non-Jew to perform any forbidden action on his behalf, whether the action involves a Torah prohibition or a rabbinical one (see note 28 below). He may also not take any medication for his illness. Moreover, he may not partake of any food or drink that is not normally taken by healthy people (though a healthy person would be permitted to do so).[29]

---

26 עיין במשנה ברורה סי׳ שכ״ח ס״ק נ״ב, ובשו״ע סימן ש״ז סעיף ה׳. ויבורר דין זה בהרחבה במקורותיו לקמן בפרק 29 ובפרק 30 בעניין חולה במקצת.

27 יבורר בהרחבה לקמן בפרק 34 בעניין מחלות שיניים.

28 שו״ע סימן שכ״ח סעיף א׳. ופרטי הדינים יבוררו לקמן בפרק 31.

29 עיין בית יוסף בשם הר״ן (פרק שמונה שרצים בשם הרמב״ן בספר תורת האדם). וז״ל הר״ן: דכי שרי ע״י א״י ה״מ בחולה שהוא נופל מחמת חוליו למשכב, אבל במיחוש שאדם מתחזק והולך כבריא לא. ולא עוד אלא אפילו דברים שהם מותרים לבריאים, אסורים לו כל היכא שמעשיו מוכיחים שלרפואה הוא מכוון, וזו היא ששנינו ״החושש בשיניו לא יגמע בהן את החומץ״.

Chapter 2

The Ordinance against Preparing Medicine

1. The Sages forbade one to perform any action related to healing on Shabbos. This applies to preparing medication from various herbs, taking medicine, and even using other remedies that do not involve medication,[1] such as massage and exercise with the intention to build up a sweat.[2] (The latter is prohibited because there are medications whose curative functions cause a person to perspire; therefore, all such actions were forbidden, even those that do not involve medication.)
2. This prohibition was instituted in order to prevent one from grinding herbs on Shabbos itself[3] in order to prepare medication. This would constitute a transgression of the Torah prohibition of *tochein*, grinding.

Actions that Are Included in This Prohibition

The following are included in the prohibition against "grinding herbs":

---

1 אבל דברים שהם אמנם לרפואה אך אינם נעשים כלל ע״י סממנים לא נכלל בגזירה זו, וכדלהלן בשם הרמב״ם.

2 עשיית מסז׳, יש מתירים אם אין מגיע עי״ז להזעה, וכשעושה כדי להזיע לכו״ע אסור. עיין בשו״ת אור לציון ח״ב פרק לו אות יב. (ראה להלן הערה 9.)

3 כך פירש רש״י בכמה סוגיות, ברכות דף ל״ו ע״א ד״ה לא יערענו בשמן. ובשבת דף ק״ח ע״ב ד״ה שפיר דמי. ועוד.

3. Taking tablets, syrups, powders, medicinal herbs, and the like, which are not normally ingested unless a person is ill.[4]
4. Eating foods and liquids that are normally consumed only for medicinal purposes.[5]
5. Bathing in mineral springs or in a health spa.[6]
6. Exercise,[7] jogging in order to build up a sweat,[8] physiotherapy, and massage. But if the purpose is not to build up a sweat, these actions are permitted.[9]
7. Applying oils and other liquids for medicinal purposes.[10]
8. Applying bandages or other types of dressings for therapeutic purposes, unless it is done to protect a wound.[11]
9. Administering an enema.[12]

---

4 שו״ע סי׳ שכ״ח סעיף א׳.

5 שו״ע שם סעיף ל״ז.

6 שם סעיף מ״ד.

7 שם סעיף מ״ב, ועיין בט״ז ס״ק כ״ח, וז״ל הרמב״ם פכ״א מהל״ש הלכה כ״ח, ואין מתעמלין בשבת, אי זה מתעמל, זה שדורסים על גופו בכח עד שייגע ויזיע או שיהלך עד שייגע ויזיע, שאסור לייגע את עצמו כדי שיזיע בשבת מפני שהיא רפואה, וכן אסור לעמוד בקרקע דימוסית שבארץ ישראל מפני שמעמלת ומרפאת. עכ״ל.

8 כן משמע מהרמב״ם הנ״ל, וכ״כ בשו״ע סי׳ ש״א סעיף א׳ וסעיף ב׳, ועי״ש במ״ב ס״ק ז׳. ובכפה״ח אות י״ג בשם המג״א ועוד אחרונים. ועי״ש ששיטת הלבוש לאסור אף הליכה כדי להזיע, ורבו החולקים עליו, ועי״ע בשעה״צ שם אות ט׳.

9 בכל הפעולות הנזכרות בסעיף זה אם אין מתכוון כדי להזיע — שרי. התעמלות לשמירת כושר גופני ומסז׳ לחלוץ עצמות, וכמו״כ ריצה ופיזיוטרפיה — כל שאינו מתכוון להזיע שרי (כן כתב בשו״ע סי׳ שכ״ח סעיף מ״ב). ועיין בכפה״ח סי׳ שכ״ז אות טוב ז״ל: ומסופקני שפשוף שעושין ליגעי כח שהם כדי להשיב כוחן אליהן ולבטל עייפותם דדמי קצת לרפואה, ולפרש״י פשיטא דאסור אבל להרמב״ם יש להסתפק. שלטי הגבורים ס״פ חבית כנה״ג בהגה״ט, א״ר. עכ״ל. ועי״ע בשו״ת אור לציון ח״ב פרק ל״ו אות י״ב. והטעם בזה דכל פעולה שנעשית שלא ע״י רפואות מותר לעשות בשבת ואין חשש משום גזירת שחיקת סממנים, אך ה״מ היכא דלא מצי להגיע לאותה תכלית ע״י תרופות, משא״כ פעולות שתכליתם עשויות להגיע ע״י תרופות וסממנים, כגון להזיע, ניתן להזיע ע״י התעמלות וניתן להזיע ע״י תרופות, לכן אסרו חכמים פעולות שמביאים להזעה אם מתכוון להזיע. וכ״כ במ״ב סי׳ שכ״ח ס״ק ק״ל. ועי״ע בילקוט יוסף שבת ד׳ עמ׳ ק״ע שהאריך בזה.

10 שו״ע סימן שכ״ז סעיף א׳.

11 שו״ע סימן שכ״ח סעיף כ״ג. פרוט אופן החבישה המותרת, עיין לקמן בפרק 38 בעניין טפול בחבלות ופצעים.

12 מגן אברהם שם ס״ק נ״ה, וקצות השולחן סי׳ קל״ח ס״ק י״ד. ועי״ע לקמן פרק 41 סעיף 27 שע״י מים בלבד שרי במקום צער.

10. Administering an emetic (medicine that causes vomiting).[13]

Actions Not Included in This Prohibition

The Sages have excluded a number of activities from this decree:

11. Relocation of a dislocated joint.[14]
12. Placing a hot cup on an inverted navel in order to raise it.[15]
13. Swallowing a raw egg to improve one's voice.[16]
14. Placing a metal utensil on one's eye to cool it.[17]
15. Rubbing the legs of an intoxicated person with oil and salt to detoxify him.[18]
16. Since all of the above actions are never performed with medicinal herbs, the injunction against healing on Shabbos does not apply.[19]

---

13 שו״ע שם סעיף ל״ט, ובפרש״י בגמ׳ ישנה סתירה, דבשבת דף קכ״ג ע״א ד״ה אפיקטויזין כתב דאינו אסור משום שחיקת סממנים אלא משום דמתקן גברא. ע״כ. ובדף קמ״ז ד״ה אלא בסם, כתב, דדמי לרפואה וגזירה משום שחיקת סממנים. ע״כ. שו״מ דעמד על כך בגיליון הש״ס.

14 שו״ע סי׳ שכ״ח סעיף מ״ז.

15 שו״ע שם סעיף מ״ג.

16 שו״ע שם סעיף ל״ח בשם המרדכי.

17 שו״ע שם סעיף מ״ו.

18 שו״ע שם סעיף מ״א, ועיין במג״א ס״ק מ״ח.

19 וזה לשון הרמב״ם בפכ״ג מהלכות שבת: ״מותר להעלות אוזניים בין ביד ובין בכלי ולהעלות אונקלי שכל אלו וכיוצא בהם אין עושין אותן בסמנין כדי לחוש לשחיקה ויש לו צער מהם״. (הביאו הטור להלכה בסי׳ שכ״ח עיי״ש.) וכתב הבית יוסף פירוש לדברי הרמב״ם, שמאחר שאינם עושים בסמנים ליכא למיסר משום שחיקת סמנים, וכ״ת אפ״ה ליתסר משום דאיכא טורח והוי כעובדין דחול? לכך כתב ״ויש לו צער מהם״, כלומר ובמקום צער לא גזור רבנן כיון דליכא למיחש לשחיקת סמנים. אמנם, הבית חדש שם תמה על כך, וז״ל: איכא לתמוה הלא כל רפואה אסרו משום שחיקת סמנים דאע״פ שאין רפואה זו בסמנים כלל, מ״מ גזירה משום רפואה אחרת דליתא אלא בסמנים, וגזרו כל רפואה אטו הד. עכ״ל.

Chapter 3

Instructing a Non-Jew to Perform a Melachah

1. The Sages forbade a Jew to ask a non-Jew to perform *melachah* for him on Shabbos, whether the act involves a Torah prohibition or a rabbinical one.[1] This prohibition is known as "*amirah l'akum*." In certain situations, however, a Jew is permitted to instruct a non-Jew to perform a rabbinically prohibited *melachah*, and in some situations, depending on the severity of the patient's condition, it may be permitted to do so even with respect to a Torah prohibition.

For a Patient in a Life-Threatening Situation

2. In general, a non-Jew should not be asked to perform an action for the needs of a person who suffers from a life-threatening illness (*choleh sheyeish bo sakanah*). This should be done by a Jew in order to emphasize the importance of tending to such a person's needs even if it involves performing an act normally prohibited by Torah law.[2] Nevertheless, if a non-Jew is readily available, some authorities rule that one may ask the non-Jew.[3]

---

1 שו״ע סי׳ ש״ז סעיף ב׳, ושם במ״ב ס״ק ח׳ כל דבר שאסור לישראל לעשותו מצד הדין אסור לומר לא״י לעשותו, אבל בדבר שאינו אלא מנהג וחומרה בעלמא שרי לומר לא״י לעשותו (מג״א ושאר אחרונים).

2 שו״ע סימן שכ״ח סעיף י״ב.

3 הרמ״א כתב בסעיף הנ״ל ז״ל: ואם אפשר לעשות ע״י עכו״ם בלא איחור כלל עושין ע״י עכו״ם

For an Ordinary Bedridden Patient

3. A non-Jew may be instructed to supply all the needs of a person who is confined to bed due to a non-life-threatening illness (*choleh she'ein bo sakanah*) or of one who suffers from an ailment that affects his entire body but he is not bedridden (*michush*) — even if this requires the non-Jew to perform a *melachah* normally prohibited by Torah law.[4] For example, a non-Jew may be asked to cook or bake for the patient.

4. It is questionable whether "all his needs" in this context includes spiritual needs, for example, asking the non-Jew to bring him a *sefer* or a siddur in a manner that will require the non-Jew to perform a *melachah*. It is arguable, though, that if he won't have his spiritual needs taken care of, this might have an adverse effect on his overall condition and thus is allowed.

(א״ז) וכן נוהגין אבל במקום שיש לחוש שיתעצל העכו״ם אין לעשות ע״י עכו״ם (תוס׳ ור״ן). ע״כ. מיהו כתב הט״ז ס״ק ה׳ דדיעה זו איתא בש״ג בשם הריא״ז, ול״נ דבר זה תימה דכי היכי דיש איסור לעשות ע״י עכו״ם אם יש לחוש שיתעצל כמה שכתב אח״כ כן ה״נ יש חשש שמא אתה מכשילם לעתיד באם יראו עכשיו שאין עושין רק ע״י עכו״ם יסברו שיש איסור ע״י ישראל ולפעמים לא יהיה עכו״ם מצוי ועי״ז יסתכן החולה במה שימתינו על עכו״ם... נראה לי לומר מה שכתב תרי בבי בגמרא פרק בתרא דיומא אין עושים דברים הללו לא ע״י עכו״ם ולא ע״י קטנים אלא ע״י גדולי ישראל ואין אומרים לעשות דברים הללו ע״י נשים ולא ע״י כותים וכו׳ וכבר נזכר בב״י טעמים לחילוק תרי בבות, ולפ״ד א״ש טפי דתחלה אמר שיש איסור לעשות ע״י עכו״ם שלא יאמרו שיש איסור לעשות ע״י ישראל, ואח״כ אמר מצווה לעשות ע״י גדולי ישראל, וא״א לעשות ע״י נשים וכותים דהיינו אפילו אם הם מזומנים לפנינו והם שומרי שבת אם כן אין שייך מכשול הנזכר כאן ואפ״ה יעשו דווקא גדולי ישראל כדי להורות הלכה למעשה לרבים... ונמצא שיש איסור ע״י עכו״ם ובישראל עצמם יש מעלה לעושה כנלע״ד נכון. והבא לעשות ע״י עכו״ם המזומן — לכל הפחות יגלה לרבים באותו פעם שיש היתר לישראל עצמו אלא שהעכו״ם מזומן כאן. אבל עיקרא דמלתא שלא ישגיח על העכו״ם כל עיקר אם רואה סכנה בבירור ויש אפילו ספק הצלה הזריז הרי זה משובח אם יעשה הוא עצמו כי אע״פ שהעכו״ם לפנינו ועושה ההצלה מ״מ הישראל יעשנה טפי בזריזות ואף שכתב הרמ״א וכן נוהגין אין מזה ראיה דלאו מנהג ותיקין הוא. גם מדברי הר״ן שמביא הב״י משמע כן שכתב שמא יבוא הדבר וכו׳ משמע דחש על העתיד אע״פ שעכשיו אין חשש, ומה שנרשם כאן במראה מקום (תוס׳ ור״ן) הוא טעות המעתיק ואינו אמת בעיקר הדין שזכר הרמ״א בזה כנלע״ד ברור. עכ״ל הט״ז. וכן כתב בשו״ע הגר״ז ז״ל: והעיקר כסברה ראשונה, ואעפ״כ המנהג במדינות אלו כסברה אחרונה, אבל טוב שלא לנהוג כן כי יש חשש שמא יראו עכשיו שאין עושין רק ע״י נכרי יסברו שיש איסור בזה לעולם ע״י ישראל, ולפעמים לא יהיה נכרי מצוי ועי״ז יסתכן החולה במה שימתינו על הנכרי. ועכ״פ הרוצה לעשות ע״י נכרי — יגלה לרבים באותו פעם שיש היתר לישראל עצמו אלא שהנכרי הוא מזומן כאן. עכ״ל שו״ע הגר״ז השייך לענייננו.

4 שו״ע סימן שכ״ח סעיף י״ז, ובמ״ב ס״ק מ״ז.

For a Slightly Ill Person

5. A person who suffers an ailment or injury that does not affect his entire body and does not confine him to bed (*choleh b'miktzas*) may ask a non-Jew to perform a rabbinical prohibition, but he may not ask the non-Jew to perform an action forbidden by Torah law.[5]

6. One who suffers from a minor ailment, such as a cough or headache, but functions in a normal, healthy manner may not ask a non-Jew to perform any forbidden action on his behalf, even if the action only involves a rabbinical prohibition.[6]

---

5 שו״ע סימן ש״ז סעיף ה׳ ועי״ש במ״ב ס״ק כ״א ובכפה״ח אות מ׳. ועיין באורך בביאור דין חולה במקצת לקמן פרק 29 ופרק 30.

6 שו״ע סי׳ שכ״ח סעיף א׳.

Chapter 4

Melachah Forbidden Only by Rabbinic Law

A *melachah* is forbidden only by rabbinic law if it is performed in one of the following ways:

a. With a *shinui*, i.e., in an unconventional manner
b. By a child
c. *She'einah tzerichah l'gufah*, i.e., for a purpose other than the usual purpose
d. By two people concomitantly
e. *Gramah*, in an indirect manner

In an Unconventional Manner

1. A Torah prohibition applies to a *melachah* only when it is done in the usual manner. If it is performed in an unusual way — that is, with a *shinui* — only a rabbinic injunction, which is of lesser severity, applies.[1]

---

1 עיין בספר כלכלת שבת כללי ל״ט מלאכות, ששה תנאים לחיוב על מלאכה מדאורייתא, ובהעדר אחד מהם אינו אלא מדרבנן. בתנאי שלישי כתב ז״ל: שינוי, אינו חייב על המלאכה רק כשיעשה אותה כדרך שרגיל לעשות אותה בלי שינוי, אבל אם שינה בה פטור, וכו׳, וכמו כן הכותב בשמאלו פטור מדאין דרך כתיבה בכך (שבת קג׳ א׳) ונ״ל שדווקא בכותב שדרך לכתוב רק בימין והו״ל שינוי, משא״כ שאר מלאכות, כגון שהדליק נר בשמאלו חייב, מדדרך לעשותו פעם בימין ופעם בשמאל, עכ״ל. עיי״ש. והגמ׳ במסכת כתובות דף ס׳ ע״א הביאה מספר דוגמאות של מלאכה בשינוי, כגון צינור שעלו בו קשקשים ממעכן ברגלו בשבת ואינו חושש מאי טעמא, מתקן כלאחר יד הוא ובמקום פסידא לא גזרו, וכן הביאה הגמ׳ שם דין גונח יונק חלב וכו׳, יבואר להלן.

2. As explained above (see chapter 1, "General Principles"), it is permissible to perform all necessary actions, including those forbidden by Torah law, for the needs of a person in a life-endangering situation (*choleh sheyeish bo sakanah*). Nevertheless, halachic authorities disagree about the manner in which the *melachah* may be performed. Some say it is preferable to perform the action in an unusual manner if time is not of the essence and it will not cause any harm or discomfort to the patient.[2]

In practice, it is certainly preferable to change the way one would normally carry out the procedure as much as possible, as long as it

---

2 בדרכי משה סימן שכ״ח כתב בשם האור זרוע דאף דקיי״ל כהתוס׳ והר״ן דאפילו היכא דאפשר ע״י עכו״ם מצווה בישראל שמא יתעצל הא״י ויבוא לידי סכנה, מיהו כתב דאם אפשר לעשות ע״י שינוי ללא דיחוי עושה. ע״כ. וכן כתב בהגהת שו״ע סימן שכ״ח סעיף י״ב. ובאמת דכמו כן כתב המגיד משנה פ״ב מהל״ש הלכה י״א בשם הרמב״ן, ז״ל: וכתב הרמב״ן ז״ל ושמעינן מיניה דכל צרכי חולה אע״פ שיש בו חולי סכנה היכא דאפשר למעבד לה למלאכה בשינוי שלא יתחלל בה שבת משנין ואין מחללין, והוא שלא יתאחר צרכו של חולה כלל בשינוי זה. ותנן נמי גבי מילה (שבת קל״ג) ונותנין עליה אספלנית וכמון, לא שחק מערב שבת לועס בשיניו ונותן, לא טרף שמן ויין נותן זה בעצמו וכו׳. וש״מ אע״פ שסכנה היא לו אין מחללין את השבת לעבור על דברי תורה אלא עושין המלאכות בשינוי בדבר שהוא משום שבות, ובלבד שיעשה כל צרכו של חולה בזריזות. עכ״ל הרמב״ן. ומלשון רבינו ז״ל נראה שאין חולה שיש בו סכנה בכלל השינוי, אלא החיה, וזהו שכתב הרי היא בסכנת נפשות ולא הזכיר השינוי בחולי שיש בו סכנה, וכתב למעלה כללו של דבר שבת לגבי חולה שיש בו סכנה הרי הוא כחול לכל הדברים. והטעם בזה (החילוק בין יולדת לשאר חולה שיש בו סכנה) נראה מפני שכאב היולדת וחבליה הם כדבר טבעי לה ואין אחת מאלף מתה מחמת לידה, ולפיכך החמירו לשנות במקום שאפשר ולא החמירו בחולה. ודין המילה הוא לפי דעת רבינו מפני טענה אחרת, מפני שהן מכשירין שהיה אפשר לעשותן מערב שבת כמו שהזכיר רבינו פרק שני מהלכות מילה. עכ״ל המגיד משנה. ואמנם בהגהות הגר״א בשו״ע ציין לתוס׳ בפ׳ ר״א דמילה דכתבו ז״ל: לועס בשיניו, אע״ג דאחר מילה חולה שיש בו סכנה הוא מ״מ כמה דאפשר לשנויי משנינן. ע״כ. ובנוסח זה לא יוכל ההה״מ לפרש כדפירש בשם הרמב״ם בהלכות מילה, אלא כדברי הרמב״ן. ודו״ק.

בשו״ת אור לציון ח״ב סי׳ לו אות ג׳ צידד להלכה כדברי המגיד משנה בשם הרמב״ם דבחולה שיש בו סכנה אין צריך לשנות כלל ודלא כדברי הרמ״א, וציין גם לכפה״ח סי׳ שכ״ח אות ע״ד. ואמנם בכפה״ח שם כתב דמש״כ הרמ״א די״א לעשות בשינוי, זה לשיטת הרמב״ן וכתב ה״ה דמדברי הרמב״ם לא משמע כן וכו׳. אך אחר המחילה מכבוד מרן הגאון שליט״א לא כן ס״ל לכפה״ח דמיד באות ע״ה כתב ז״ל עושה ע״י שינוי שאז אין אסור מן התורה, ר״ז אות י״ג, והטעם דכל מה שנוכל לעשות בהיתר לא עבדינן אסורא, ולפי״ז אם ע״י השינוי מתאחר הדבר מעט והחולה אינו נחפז כ״כ במהרה עבדינן ע״י שינוי שהוא איסור מדרבנן כמ״ש לעיל אות ס״ט יעו״ש. ע״כ. ובאות ס״ט כתב ז״ל: אבל במקום שאפשר לעשות לו הרפואה מיד בלי חילול שבת אלא שיצטרכו לשהות שעה מועטת, לא יחללו כדי לעשותה תיכף ומיד בלי שיהוי כלל אם הוא בענין שאין חשש סכנה כלל בשיהוי מעט כזה לפי שהשבת דחויה היא אצל פ״נ ולא הותרה לגמרי וכו׳. עכ״ל. ולכאורה משמע שגם הכף החיים מצדד וס״ל כהרמ״א דכל היכא דאפשר לשנות משנינן.

does not interfere with its effectiveness. However, one who is lenient and performs the action in the normal manner is regarded as acting properly.

3. It was previously stated that one may ask a non-Jew to perform any *melachah* for the needs of a *choleh she'ein bo sakanah*, an ordinary bedridden patient (see chapter 3, "Instructing a Non-Jew to Perform a *Melachah*").[3] However, if this is not possible, either because there are no non-Jews in the vicinity, the non-Jew does not have the expertise to perform the action, or the action must be performed by the patient himself, the Sages permit a Jew to perform the *melachah* in an unusual manner.[4] Therefore, if a sick person requires fresh goat's milk, for example, they permitted the patient to suck the milk directly from the goat. Since the normal manner of extracting milk is by hand or machine, sucking the milk directly from the animal is a change from the normal manner and is therefore permitted.[5]

By a Minor

4. By Torah law, a boy becomes obligated to keep the commandments

---

3 שו״ע סימן שכ״ח סעיף י״ז.

4 מקור דין זה בגמ׳ כתובות דף ס׳ ע״א גבי גונח, וז״ל הגמ׳ שם תניא רבי מרינוס אומר גונח יונק חלב בשבת, מאי טעמא יונק מפרק כלאחר יד ובמקום צער לא גזור רבנן. אמר רב יוסף הלכה כרבי מרינוס. ע״כ. ועיי״ש בתוס׳ ובר״ן ובעוד ראשונים כשיטת הרי״ף דמיירי בחולה שאין בו סכנה ויונק הוי תולדה דדש, ובשינוי מ״מ שרי דבמקום צער לא גזור רבנן. ובר״ן פירש דאף דקיי״ל דעושין כל צרכיו ע״י אינו יהודי, י״ל הכא א״א על ידי נכרי, דרפואת החלב ע״י שינק ישיר מן העיזה חלב רותח. ע״כ. וכ״כ הרמב״ם פכ״א מהלכות שבת הלכה י״ד, היונק בפיו פטור, ואם היה גונח מותר לו לינוק בפיו מפני שהוא מפרק כלאחר יד ומשום צערו לא גזרו ואף על פי שאין שם סכנה. ע״כ. וכ״פ בשו״ע סי׳ שכ״ח סעיף ל״ג.

5 הרמב״ן בספר תורת האדם שער המיחוש (הובא בחידושי הרמב״ן על הש״ס בסוף סדר מועד על מסכת ביצה) סיכם בקצרה דיני חולה בשבת וז״ל השייך לעניינינו: ״מיחוש שאדם חולה ממנו ונופל למשכב ואין בו סכנה התירו משום שבות שאין בו מעשה דהיינו אמירה לארמי, כן התירו בו שבות דמלאכה הנעשית בשינוי. וזהו שאמרו דבר שאין בו סכנה אומר לארמי ועושה, ואמרו לעניו חיה כל ל׳ יום אפילו אמרה צריכה אני אין מחללין עליה את השבת אלא עושה לה ע״י ארמאי בשבת. וזהו אמימר דכחל מארמי. ואמרינן נמי פרק כלאחר יד הוא ובמקום צער לא גזור רבנן, מפני שהן נעשין בשינוי שלא כדרך המלאכות״. עכ״ל השייך לעניינינו. מבואר מדבריו להדיא דחולה שאין בו סכנה מותר לעשות עבורו מלאכה מדאורייתא בשינוי שהיא בכלל איסור מדרבנן דשרי לצורך חולה שאין בו סכנה.

upon reaching the age of thirteen, and a girl becomes obligated at the age

---

כמו״כ הר״ן בפרק חבית גבי דין גונח יונק מעז בשבת הביא דעת הרמב״ן הנ״ל וז״ל: ״והרמב״ן ז״ל כתב בספר תורת האדם דמשום הכי שרינן [גונח יונק] מפני שהוא שבות הנעשה בשינוי שלא כדרך המלאכות״ עכ״ל הר״ן שם. אך מ״מ קשיא לי טובא דהר״ן גופא סיכם את דיני חולה בקצרה בפרק שמונה שרצים, וציין שסיכומו זה הוא לדעת הרמב״ן ז״ל אך השמיט את התירו של הרמב״ן שהתיר לחולה שאין בו סכנה מלאכה בשינוי. ובקצרה אצטט את לשונו בענין חולה שאין בו סכנה וז״ל: אין בו סכנת נפש אלא סכנת איבר — צרכיו במלאכות מדאורייתא נעשין ע״י נכרי ובשל דבריהם אפילו ע״י ישראל. אין בו אפילו סכנת אבר אלא חולי בעלמא צרכיו נעשים על ידי נכרי ואפילו במלאכות של תורה אבל לא ע״י ישראל אפילו בשל דבריהם, וכו׳ זהו דעת הרמב״ן ז״ל בדברים הללו בספר תורת האדם״ עכ״ל הר״ן. הרי שהשמיט התירו של הרמב״ן שכתב דמלאכה הנעשית בשינוי שרי לצורך חולה שאין בו סכנה. וצ״ע.

ועיין במ״ב סי׳ שכ״ח ס״ק ק״ז, וז״ל: היינו דאף דעיקר חליבת הבהמה הוא מדאורייתא משום מפרק דהוא תולדה דדש וכמו שכתבנו בריש סימן שכ״א מ״מ בזה שהוא ע״י יניקה דהוא רק כלאחר יד לא הוי רק איסור דרבנן והתירו בזה, ואף דקיי״ל דבכל חולי שאין בו סכנה אומר לא״י ועושה הכא שאני דרפואה שלו לינק בעצמו [ר״ן]. והנה אמנם במ״ב בהלכות יו״ט סי׳ תצ״ו סעיף ב׳ גבי אב מלאכה אסור לישראל לעשותו ביום טוב שני של גלויות, כתב בשער הציון אות ט׳ וז״ל: ועל ידי שינוי יש לעיין דהנה ביו״ט ראשון בודאי יש להחמיר כיון שהוא מדאורייתא כמו בשבת. [ואף דמצינו שהתירו חכמים לגונח שיונק חלב בשבת משום דהוי מפרק כלאחר יד ובמקום צער לא גזרו י״ל התם דאין דרכו של מפרק בכך לא חשיבה מלאכה כלל וגרע הדבר מסתם שינוי בעלמא] אכן לענין יו״ט שני שהוא דרבנן אפשר שיש להקל לגבי חולי שאין בו סכנה וצ״ע. עכ״ל השעה״צ שם. ולכאורה משמע דס״ל לאסור מלאכה מדאורייתא בשינוי בשבת לצורך חולה שאין בו סכנה. וקשה דזה סותר לכאורה לדבריו בסימן שכ״ח הנזכ״ל וצ״ע. (ובאמת לא ידוע לי מדוע הוקף חלק זה בשער הציון בסוגריים מרובעות [] במקור).

אולם שאר גדולי הפוסקים כתבו כדברינו להדיא כפי המשתמע משיטת הרמב״ן, עיין בנשמת אברהם ח״ד הקדמה לסימן שכ״ח עמ׳ ל״ו בשם שו״ע הגר״ז (סי׳ שכ״ח סעיף י״ט) ובתהלה לדוד (שכ״ח כ״ב) אגלי טל (מלאכת טוחן סעיף י״ח) וקצות השולחן (סימן קל״ד בבדי השולחן) — שכולם בדעה אחת להתיר מלאכה מדאורייתא ע״י שינוי לצורך חולה שאין בו סכנה. והוסיף שם בנשמת אברהם וז״ל: וכותב השמירת שבת כהלכתה בשם הגרש״ז אויערבאך זצוקי״ל דמכיון שכל אלה הגדולים מתירים מסתבר דיכולים ודאי להקל אם אי אפשר ע״י נכרי עכ״ל. וע״ע שם. ובאמת המעיין בדברי הגר״א סי׳ שכ״ח סעיף י״ז בביאור דעת הרמב״ן בסעיף זה מבואר מדבריו כהבנתנו בדברי הרמב״ן, עיי״ש. וע״ע בתורת היולדת פרק כ״ו הערה ה׳ שהביא דעות אלו עיי״ש. כמו״כ עיין באורך וברוחב בענין זה בילקוט יוסף שבת ד׳ עמ׳ צ״ד הערה י״ב, ואכמ״ל יותר.

ואמנם אחרי כתבי כל זה העיר את עיני מו״ר הגאון רבי זאב כהן שליט״א שהרמב״ן עצמו בחידושיו למסכת שבת משמע לכאורה שסתר דברי עצמו, דז״ל הרמב״ן בחידושיו שבת קמ״ד ע״ב בתוך דבריו ״ודאמרינן התם מפרק כלאחר יד איונק והי״ה לחולב שאין זה מפרק הדומה לדש ומדינא מותר היה לחלוב אלא משום שאתי לאחלופי בסחיטה כיון דמלאכה גמורה היא הוו ינקי. ועוד שעיקר רפואת הגונח ביניקת החלב כשהוא רותח, מיהו רש״י נמי פירש שם בדבריו שהחולב מפרק גמור הוא וכן י״ל שאע״פ שהחולב מדבריהם כיון דדמי למפרק וכי אורחיה קעביד אסור, ולא התירו אלא שבות בשינוי דהיינו יונק והכי משמע לישנא דגמרא״. עכ״ל. הרי דחשיב הרמב״ן יונק לשבות בשינוי והיינו שבות דשבות (שינוי באיסור דרבנן). וצע״ג בזה דהרי כל הפוסקים ראשונים ואחרונים סמכו את ידיהם על דברי הרמב״ן בתורת האדם דחשיב יונק כמפרק מדאורייתא אלא כיון שנעשה בשינוי שרי. והנה הוא עצמו גילה דעתו אחרת דחשיב שבות דדבריהם בשינוי וצע״ג. וקשה ליישב בדוחק ולומר דמה שכתב בספר תורת האדם שזה ספר הלכה ויש להתחשב בו יותר ממה שכתב בחידושיו על הש״ס. וה׳ יאיר עינינו בתורתו, אך

of twelve.[6] Therefore if a minor eats a prohibited food or performs a *melachah* on Shabbos, the court has no obligation to stop him.[7]

5. Nevertheless, a parent is obligated to educate his child. He must reprimand him and prevent him from performing actions forbidden by Torah law.[8] Moreover, a parent may not assist the minor in performing even actions that are forbidden by rabbinic law. Therefore, he may not instruct him to perform any forbidden action on Shabbos and *yom tov*, even if it is prohibited only by rabbinic law.[9]

6. However, the Sages permitted instructing a minor to perform *melachah* forbidden by rabbinic law[10] in the case of a sick person or of potential monetary loss.[11] This license has certain limitations, as will be explained.

7. If a *melachah* is to be performed for a patient suffering from a life-threatening illness (*choleh sheyeish bo sakanah*), it is preferable that this be done by an adult Jew.[12] However, if the situation is not urgent, and nothing will be lost in terms of time and effectiveness, it is preferable to minimize the level of Shabbos desecration by instructing a minor to perform the action.

אין לנו אלא גדולי הפוסקים ראשונים ואחרונים שהסבירו בדעת הרמב״ן דשרי מלאכה בשינוי לצורך חולה שאין בו סכנה בדליכא דרכא אחרינא, והכי נקטינן.

6 משנה באבות פרק ה׳ משנה כ״א, בן שלוש עשרה למצוות. וע״ש ברש״י. וע״ע ברא״ש בתשובה כלל ששה עשר אות א׳ הביא דשעורין אלו הלכה למשה מסיני.

7 לשון הרמב״ם פי״ז מהלכות מאכלות אסורות הכ״ז.

8 הרמב״ם שם.

9 שו״ע או״ח סי׳ שמ״ג סעיף א׳.

10 הראשונים דנו בכלל חיוב הקטן במצוות אם הוא מדרבנן או שאף מדרבנן אינו חייב כלל, רק החובה היא לאביו לחנכו למצוות. דעת רש״י בכמה מקומות שאין הקטן חייב במצוות כלל אף מדרבנן ורק אביו מצווה מדרבנן לחנכו. עיין רש״י בברכות כ׳ ע״א לעניין קטן הפטור מק״ש, ובמפורש יותר ברש״י שם דף מ״ח ע״א ד״ה עד שיאכל, וכן ברש״י חגיגה דף ב׳ ע״א ד״ה איזהו קטן, ובעוד מקומות ברש״י. וכ״כ הרמב״ן בחידושיו על קידושין ל״א. וכ״כ הריטב״א במגילה דף י״ט ע״ב, וכ״כ המאירי במגילה שם. וראשונים אחרים סבורים שקטן חייב עכ״פ מדרבנן. עיין בתוס׳ ברכות ט״ו ובדף מ״ח ע״א ד״ה עד, ובמגילה דף י״ט ד״ה ורבי יהודה ובעוד מקומות בתוס׳. וכן דעת הר״ן במגילה י״ט ע״ב עיי״ש. ואכמ״ל עוד בזה.

11 דהנה בשו״ע סי׳ רס״ו גבי מי שהיה בא בדרך וקדש עליו היום והיו עמו חרש וקטן יתנהו למי שירצה, עיי״ש. משמע דבמקום הפסד התירו חכמים לעבור איסור ע״י קטן. ועיי״ש בבאו״ה ד״ה הג״ה ז״ל: ״ומ״מ אכתי קשה אמאי מותר מבעו״י הא תנן [שבת קכ״ח] קטן שבא לכבות אין שומעין לו וכו׳ ואולי י״ל דמה שאמרו שאסור בקטן העושה על דעת אביו הוא רק מדברי סופרים, כיון שאינו מצווהו בפירוש לזה והכא מפני הפסד התירו, ואח״כ מצאתי שכ״כ בשלטי הגיבורים בשם ריא״ז, אך הוא יש לו בעניין זה שיטה אחריתא עיי״ש״ עכ״ל.

12 כמבואר לקמן במערכת חולה שיש בו סכנה פרק 10 סעיף 2.

8. It is best that the forbidden action be performed by a child who is too young to be educated in the laws of Shabbos.[13] But if such a child is not available, any minor under bar or bas mitzvah age may be instructed to perform the action.

9. Even in situations where a minor may be asked to perform an action on Shabbos, it is desirable that the instruction not be given by the minor's father. This is because the verse states, "You shall not do *melachah*, you and your son and your daughter" (*Shemos* 20:10), which implies a special prohibition against a parent instructing his child to perform a *melachah* on Shabbos.[14] It is therefore preferable that another person instruct the minor. If there is no one else available, however, the parent may do so. In such a case, it is better for the mother to instruct the child, since the father has a greater obligation to educate his child than the mother.

For a Purpose Other than the Usual

10. Performing a *melachah* for a purpose other than the usual refers to a situation where a person performs a *melachah* for a purpose that is different from the defined purpose of the *melachah*. For example, digging a hole is a transgression of the *melachah* of *boneh*, building.[15] If, however, one does not need the hole itself but is digging to obtain the dirt he is removing from the ground, the action is classified as a *melachah she'einah tzerichah l'gufah* — the purpose (using the dirt) is different from the purpose that defines the *melachah* ("building," or creating the hole in the ground).[16]

11. Halachic authorities disagree as to whether a *melachah* performed for a purpose other than the usual is prohibited on Shabbos by Torah law or

---

13 עיין בשו״ע סי׳ שמ״ג בהגה ובמ״ב. וע״ע בביאור הלכה סי׳ רס״ו ד״ה יתננו בשם הפרמ״ג.

14 כמבואר כל זה בשו״ע סי׳ של״ד סעיף כ״ה, ועיין שם בשער הציון אות נ״ד. ולכאורה הדבר ברור שלשיטת רש״י ודעמיה הנזכ״ל דכל מצות חנוך על האב והבן מצד עצמו פטור לגמרי, ודאי שלשיטתם עדיף שאדם אחר שאינו אביו יצווהו לקטן. ודו״ק.

15 רש״י ביצה דף ח׳ ע״א.

16 עיין בתפארת ישראל בכלכלת שבת כללי ל״ט מלאכות מה שביאר בפרטי מלאכה שאינה צריכה לגופה. וע״ע במשנה ברורה סי׳ רע״ח ס״ק ג׳. וע״ע בכף החיים שם אות ג׳.

only constitutes a rabbinical prohibition. The majority of *poskim* conclude that it is a rabbinical prohibition.[17]

12. In cases of illness, there are many situations where there is no license to transgress a Torah prohibition, but it is permitted to transgress a rabbinical prohibition, such as for a *choleh she'ein bo sakanah* or where the patient is a non-Jew.[18] Even when transgressing a Torah prohibition is permitted, it is best to minimize the severity of the act if it will cause no delay in the treatment. Thus, there are many situations where the principle of *melachah she'einah tzerichah l'gufah* is utilized.[19]

A *Melachah* Performed by Two People

13. Any action that can be performed by one individual but is instead done by two people together is only forbidden by rabbinic law. For example,

---

17 כתב הרמב״ם פ״א מהלכות שבת הלכה ז׳ ז״ל: כל העושה מלאכה בשבת אף על פי שאינו צריך לגופה של מלאכה חייב עליה, כיצד הרי שכבה את הנר מפני שהוא צריך לשמן או לפתילה כדי שלא יאבד או כדי שלא יישרף או כדי שלא יבקע חרס של נר, מפני שהכיבוי מלאכה והרי נתכוון לכבות ואע״פ שאינו צריך לגוף הכבוי ולא כבה אלא מפני השמן או מפני החרס או מפני הפתילה הרי זה חייב. וכן המעביר את הקוץ ארבע אמות ברשות הרבים, או המכבה את הגחלת כדי שלא יזוקו בהן רבים חייב ואע״פ שאינו צריך לגוף הכבוי או לגוף ההעברה אלא להרחיק ההיזק הרי זה חייב וכן כל כיוצא בזה. וכתב הראב״ד ז״ל, ר״ח ז״ל פסק כרבי שמעון שהוא פוטר מדאמרינן פרק נוטל רבא כר״ש ס״ל דאמר מלאכה שאינה צריכה לגופה פטור עליה עכ״ל. הרב המגיד משנה שם מביא שגדולי הראשונים חולקים על פסק הרמב״ם בזה וס״ל כרבי שמעון שמתיר מלאכה שאינה צריכה לגופה ודלא כרבי יהודה. כן פסקו הרשב״א והרמב״ן, עכ״ל המ״מ. וע״ע בתוס׳ ביצה דף ח׳ ע״א ד״ה ואינו. דפסק מלאכה שאינה צריכה לגופה פטור. עי״ש. וכן מצאתי בתשובות הרשב״א המיוחסות סי׳ רפא דפסק כן, בעניין נר לחולה שיש בו סכנה שמותר להדליק עבורו, ולחולה שאין בו סכנה שפטור אבל אסור. עיי״ש. בשו״ע סי׳ של״ד סעיף כ״ז הביא שיטות שני הצדדים לעניין כבוי גחלת ברשות הרבים, אמנם סתם כדברי המתירים והוסיף ולהרמב״ם אסור בשל עץ. כמו״כ בסימן רע״ח לעניין נר כתב ז״ל: מותר לכבות הנר בשביל שישן החולה שיש בו סכנה. ע״כ. ובב״י שם הביא דיש אומרים אף לחולה שאין בו סכנה פטור אבל אסור משום דס״ל מלאכה שאינה צריכה לגופה פטור. ולכאורה מדסתם ולא פירש משמע דס״ל כהרמב״ם דבמלאכה שאינה צריכה לגופה חייב. וכן משמע בעוד מקומות בב״י שהביא הדברים כפשוטן ולא הכריע דעתו לכאן או לכאן. עכ״ז במקום חולי יש להורות בזה לקולא וכדעת רוב הפוסקים.

18 מבואר לקמן פרק 6 בעניין חלול שבת עבור חולה נכרי.

19 בשו״ת מנחת יצחק ח״א סימן ס״ג הביא בעניין חייל בצבא הגויים שמוכרח להתגלח בשבת ולפניו שתי ברירות: א׳ להתגלח בעצמו ע״י סם. ב׳ להתגלח ע״י עכו״ם בתער. והביא שם דעת הפרמ״ג (בראש יוסף שבת ע״ב) שמלאכה שעושה על כורחו בשבת הוי מלאכה שאינה צריכה לגופה וקיל טפי משאר איסורין דלא שייך בהו פטור דמלאכה שאינה צריכה לגופה. עיי״ש. וע״ע

if one person picks up an object in a private domain and another puts it down in a public domain, or if two people hold a pen and write together, neither have transgressed a Torah prohibition.

14. If a single person cannot perform the action on his own and it is performed by two people, both have transgressed a Torah prohibition, for example, carrying a heavy beam through a public domain. If one of them can perform the action alone and the other cannot, then the one who can perform the action on his own has transgressed a Torah prohibition; the second is only considered to have assisted him and has not transgressed.[20]

15. In general, this exemption of two people performing a *melachah* applies where the *melachah* requires that a certain amount of work to be done and the task is split between the two people. It also applies to a *melachah* that has a start and a finish (such as carrying), where two people participate from beginning to end or where one starts the *melachah* and the other completes it.

    However, halachic authorities disagree as to whether the exemption applies to a *melachah* that involves a minimal action, such as kindling a fire or turning on an electrical appliance. Some maintain that the exemption applies in these situations as well, whereas others hold that in such cases both people are culpable. According to these authorities, it would be preferable for these actions to be performed by one person rather than two.

    In practice, the first view is followed, and we apply the principle of two people performing a *melachah* whenever possible.[21]

בדעת תורה סי׳ רע״ח אריכות דברים בעניין מלאכה שאינה צריכה לגופה עי״ש, ועי״ע בעניין זה בלוית חן סי׳ פ״ג, ובילקוט יוסף שבת ד׳ עמ׳ קפ״ב. ואכמ״ל יותר.

20 לשון הרמב״ם פ״א מהלכות שבת הלכה ט״ו והלכה ט״ז.

21 בשו״ת מנחת יצחק ח״י סימן ל׳ דן בארוכה בגדר הפטור בשניים שעשאוה, ומסיק — ע״פ דברי שו״ת חסד לאברהם — לחלק בין מלאכה שיש בה שעור קצוב ככתיבה (שתי אותיות) או הוצאה שיש בה תחילה וסוף (עקירה והנחה) דבזה שייך הפטור של שניים שעשו (ע״פ הכללים המבוארים ברמב״ם הנ״ל) ובין מלאכה שאין לה תחילה וסוף ואין לה שעור קצוב כבונה וחורש הבערה וכיו״ב ולמעשה רוב מלאכות שבת הנעשות ע״י חשמל כהפעלת מכשירים וכדומה — אין בהם הפטור של שניים שעשו. וכך הסיק המנחת יצחק להלכה דשב ואל תעשה עדיף ובמקום שצריך לעשות מלאכה יעשה על פי הכללים האחרים במלאכות שבת כשינוי או ע״י עכו״ם וכיו״ב, אך לא יעשו שניים את המלאכה.

16. Thus, in any case where one is permitted to perform a *melachah* for the needs of a sick person, it is preferable, wherever possible, for two people to perform the action together (in accordance with the conditions mentioned in paragraphs 14 and 15). In this way, one can minimize the severity of the act.[22]

Gramah — Indirect Action

17. It has become very common, especially in the area of medical procedures, to minimize Shabbos desecration through the application of the principle of *gramah*.[23]

18. Indirect action is defined as an act that does not in and of itself involve

---

ואולם בשו״ת יביע אומר ח״ה חאו״ח סי׳ לב אות ז׳ העלה להתיר חליבה מאשה מינקת לצורך רפואה ע״י שניים שעשאוה שתצטרף עוד אשה לחולבת ויחלבו כאחת ובזה הוי איסור מדרבנן ושרי לצורך חולה או לצורך תינוק באינקובטור עיי״ש. ולא חש לחלק בין מלאכה שיש בה תחילה וסוף או שיש בה שיעור לבין מלאכה שאסורה בכל שהוא.

התפארת ישראל בכלכלת שבת הביא דין ששניים שעשו פטורים וחילק דין זה לכמה אופנים: (א) עשה האחד חצי שיעור ואדם אחר עשה חצי השני כגון שזה עשה עקירה והשני הנחה או שיעור כתיבה שהוא ב׳ אותיות ושיעור אריגה שהוא ב׳ חוטים וכדומה, ועשה זה אחד והאחר עשה השנית בצדה, אע״ג שמבין שניהם נעשה מלאכה שלימה אפילו הכי פטורים. (ב) לא עוד אלא אפילו עשו שניהם ביחד כל המלאכה, כגון שהוציאו שניהם יחד ככר לרה״ר, או שאחזו במזלג ועמרו ביחד, או שאחזו בקנה אחד וכתבו, או שאחזו בנר והדליקו ביחד שניהם פטורים (שבת דצ״ב ב׳) אמנם בזה האופן האחרון יש חילוק דאם אחד יכול ולא השני — היכול חייב, אבל אם שניהם כל אחד יכול — שניהם פטורים, ואם כל אחד אינו יכול — שניהם חייבים (כצ״ל) עכ״ל. משמע מדבריו (מהדוגמא של הדלקת נר) שלא כהמנחת יצחק בשם שו״ת חסד לאברהם הנזכ״ל. ולעולם כל מלאכה הנעשית ע״י שניים הוו בכלל שניים שעשו ופטורים. גם בספר תורת היולדת פרק ה׳ הערה ד׳ האריך בעניין זה ומסקנתו כמו שכתבנו שאין לחלק בין המלאכות ובכל מלאכה הנעשית ע״י שניים כאחד פטורים.

22 ואמנם בשו״ת אור לציון ח״ב פל״ו אות ג׳ כתב שאין צריך לעשות כל שינוי וא״צ לעשות ע״י שניים באופן שמותר לחלל שבת לצורך חולה שיש בו סכנה או לצורך יולדת, עיי״ש. אך מ״מ עיין במש״כ לעיל הערה 2 בעניין מלאכת שבת עשייתה בשינוי, שלא כדבריו.

23 מקור דין הגרמה מובא בגמ׳ שבת (דף ק״כ ע״ב) גבי כיבוי דליקה, והגמ׳ מביאה את הפסוק שנאמר בתורה (שמות כ) לא תעשה כל מלאכה, עשייה הוא דאסור ״גרמה״ שרי. והובא להלכה בשו״ע סי׳ של״ד סעיף כ״ב דכתב ז״ל: תיבה שאחז בה האור יכול לפרוס עור של גדי מצדה האחת שלא תישרף ועושים מחיצה בכל הכלים להפסיק בין הדליקה אפילו כלי חרס חדשים מלאים מים שודאי יתבקעו כשתגיע להם הדליקה — דגרם כיבוי מותר. הגה במקום פסידא (מרדכי פרק כ״ב). וכתב בביאור הלכה שם ד״ה דגרם כיבוי מותר — לאו דווקא כיבוי דהוא מלאכה שאינה צריכה לגופה דאפילו בכל המלאכות הדין כן עיי״ש. וכ״כ החזון איש או״ח סי׳ ל״ח עיי״ש. (ומיהו בשלטי הגיבורים בשבת פרק כל כתבי דף מה [בדפי האלפסי] מסתפק בזה וז״ל: ומסופקני בכל מלאכת שבת הנעשית בלא מתכוון ע״י גרם בפסיק רישיה כי האי דגרם כיבוי אי שרי או דלמא גבי דליקה הקילו. עכ״ל.)

any *melachah*, but after a certain amount of time the action causes a *melachah* to occur on its own.[24]

Certain types of *gramah* are completely permissible, some are permitted only where monetary loss may occur, and others are forbidden in all situations.

19. *A completely permissible gramah*. One may set a timer *before* Shabbos that will cause a light, heater, or fan to switch on or off during Shabbos. This is a classic form of indirect action that is utilized in almost every Jewish household.[25]

20. A *gramah that is permissible to prevent monetary loss.* One is permitted to milk a cow on Shabbos with a milking machine through the use of the principle of *gramah*. The tubes may be attached to the cow's udder on Shabbos (while the electricity is off), and a timer will subsequently switch on the electricity so that the cow can be milked by the machine.[26]

21. *A gramah that is forbidden.* One may not remove oil from a burning oil lamp on Shabbos or *yom tov*. Though he causes the lamp to go out sooner only indirectly, the act of removing the oil itself momentarily weakens the light. (This would not apply, however, to cutting a wax candle in two.[27, 28])

---

24 מקורות בפוסקים בדיני גרמה והגדרתה, עיין בשו״ת זרע אמת ח״א סימן מ״ד מהרש״ם-קונטרס אהבת שלום בסוף ספר מנחת שבת, חזון איש סי׳ ל״ח ויביע אומר ח״ג סימן י״ז.

25 חזון איש שם, ועי״ש באורך על כל ענייני שעון שבת.

26 חזון איש שם ס״ק ד׳.

27 תוס׳ ביצה דף כ״ב ע״א ד״ה והמסתפק, והובא להלכה בשו״ע סי׳ רס״ה סעיף א׳ , וע״ע בביאור הלכה סי׳ רנ״ב ד״ה להשמעת קול.

28 אמנם גם בנר שעווה כתבו התוס׳ שם דאין לחותכו לשניים אלא ע״י האור ולא בסכין. והובא להלכה בסי׳ תקי״ד סעיף ג׳ עיי״ש.

Chapter 5

Life-Threatening Ailments Mentioned in the Talmud

Our Sages define various types of ailments as life-threatening:

1. Internal injuries.[1] This refers to a wound, fracture, or inflammation (abscess) of any internal organ. All internal parts of the body are included in this category, including the mouth and teeth.
2. A wound on the back of the hand or leg (see chapter 38, "Wounds and Dressings").[2]
3. An ailment of the teeth and gums (scurvy), which Chazal call "*tzafidna*" (see chapter 34, "Dental Diseases and Hygiene").[3]
4. A severe eye ailment (see chapter 35, "Diseases of the Eye").[4]
5. Injuries caused by a metal implement,[5] for example, if a rusty nail penetrated the skin or a deep knife cut (see chapter 38, "Wounds and Dressings").
6. A snakebite or the bite of a rabid dog (see chapter 36, "Bites and Stings").[6]

---

1 מסכת עבודה זרה דף כ״ז ע״ב.
2 ע״ז שם, ובשבת ק״ט ע״א.
3 יומא פ״ג ע״א.
4 ע״ז כ״ח ע״א.
5 שם.
6 יומא פ״ג ע״א.

7. Childbirth — the first seven days.[7]
8. A child born in the eighth month of pregnancy (see chapter 6, "For Whom May Shabbos Be Desecrated?").[8]
9. High fever (see chapter 33, "Fever, Hypothermia, and Measuring Temperature").[9]
10. A pregnant woman craving a certain food.[10]
11. An intense, ravenous hunger that causes loss of eyesight (hypoglycemia).[11]
12. Diphtheria.[12]
13. Parasites in the liver.[13]

Other life-threatening situations mentioned in the Talmud include the following:[14]

14. One who sees a child fall into the sea may spread out a net to save him.
15. If a child is locked in a room, one may break down the door to get him out.
16. If a child falls into a pit, one may remove part of the surrounding earth to bring him out.
17. One may extinguish a fire and set up a barrier in front of an approaching fire to save a life.
18. When someone is trapped under a collapsed structure.

---

7 שבת קכ״ח, קכ״ט. במסגרת ספרינו זה לא התבאר דין יולדת.

8 שבת קל״ה.

9 ע״ז כ״ח ע״א.

10 יומא פ״ב ע״א וע״ב.

11 יומא פ״ד ע״ב.

12 שבת ל״ג, ועיין בספר פקוח נפש דף פ״ט ע״ב בשם אוצר ישראל דאסכרא היא חולי שסוכר את הנשימה בגרון, הידועה בשם לרינגל דיפטריה — מחלה זיהומית חיידקי המתבטאת בקרום אפרפר המתיישב על השקדים ומתפשט ומתפתח עד כדי חסימת דרכי הנשימה וללא טיפול מתאים גורם למוות רח״ל.

13 שבת ק״ט ע״ב.

14 עיין יומא פ״ד ע״ב.

Chapter 6

For Whom May Shabbos Be Desecrated?

A Fetus

1. It is permissible to desecrate Shabbos to save the life of a fetus.[1]
2. In this regard, the age of the fetus does not matter. Everything may be done on Shabbos to preserve the fetus even in the first trimester, including the first forty days of pregnancy.

   This may be done only if it is known that the pregnancy will continue and the fetus will be fully viable. If, however, all that can be done is to extend the life of the fetus for a short time, Shabbos should not be desecrated on its behalf. This does not apply to a person who was already born — Shabbos may be desecrated for him even if it means extending his life for only a few more moments.[2]

---

1 הרא״ש במסכת יומא בעניין עוברה שהריחה ביום הכיפורים, הביא מחלוקת ראשונים מה הדין באופן שיש סכנה רק לעובר ואין סכנה למעוברת (אמו) האם גם מחללים שבת עבורו או שלא. יש אומרים שגם עבור עובר מחללים וראייתם מהיושבת על המשבר ומתה שמחללים שבת להציל העובר, ויש אומרים שאין מחללים שבת עבור העובר כשאין בזה צורך עבור האם. והראיה מיושבת על המשבר אינה ראיה בהיות ושם כבר ניתקה השליה והרי הוא (העובר) כמונח בקופסה, משא״כ בשאר תהליכי ההיריון, לכן אין מחללים שבת עבורו. מסכם הרא״ש שאין מקום לוויכוח כלל שאין לך סכנה לעובר שאין בו סכנה לאם ואין לך סכנה לאם שאין בו סכנה לעובר ולעולם מחללים. וכן כתב הרמב״ן בתורת האדם שער הסכנה , כמו״כ פוסק הר״ן שם ומוסיף שעל עובר אפילו בפחות מארבעים יום שאין בו חיות כלל מחללים עליו את השבת.

2 הר״ן ביומא (פ״ב:) וכן הרשב״א בנידה (מ״ד) ס״ל דאף דההורג תינוק רק בן יומו חייב אבל עובר אין חייב, לעניין שמירת מצוות מחללים עליו, אמרה תורה חלל עליו שבת אחת שמא ישמור

A Child Born in the Eighth Month of Pregnancy

3. In the days of Chazal, a baby born during the seventh or ninth month of pregnancy was considered viable. A baby born during the eighth month had no chance of survival, however, and one was not permitted to desecrate Shabbos on its behalf because the baby was considered like an inanimate stone, which is *muktzeh*. Nowadays, Shabbos may be desecrated for any infant, even one born during the eighth month, since today babies born in the eighth month do survive. Moreover, this may be done even for a premature baby born prior to the seventh month if there is the slightest chance of survival.[3]

4. One is obligated to desecrate Shabbos to secure the survival of any child born with a debilitating disease or with a severe anomaly, such as Down's syndrome, even if his chances of survival are very slight.

An Apostate

5. Some halachic authorities rule that one may not desecrate Shabbos to save the life of a Jew who has cast off the yoke of Torah and mitzvos by denying God's existence.[4] Since one of the sources for allowing Shabbos desecration is the axiom "Desecrate one Shabbos for him so that he may observe many more Shabbosos" (*Shabbos* 151b; *Yoma* 85b),

---

שבתות הרבה, הלכך אפילו בהצלת עובר פחות ממ׳ יום שאין בו חיות כלל מחללים כדעת בה״ג, מיהו היכא דידוע שיחיה העובר רק חיי שעה, אף שגבי אדם מחללינן, גבי עובר אין מחללים דאינו בכלל חיים. וע״ע במש״כ המהרש״ק בספר החיים, הובא ביסודי ישורון מערכת פקוח נפש.

3 עיין בחזון איש יו״ד סימן קנ״ה ס״ק ד׳, ובאה״ע סי׳ קט״ו ס״ק ד׳ וז״ל: ״וכמדומה דעכשיו נשתנה הטבע וכפי בחינת הרופאים שהוסיפו השתלמותם אחר ז׳ ונגמרו לחי, והרי נשתנו הטבעים ללדת למקוטעין כמש״כ הרמ״א סי׳ קנ״ו ס״ד בהג״ה״.

עוד כתב שם ז״ל: ״יש טועים וסוברים דהנולד קודם ט׳ הוא נפל ומתיאשין הימנו ואינם זריזים ברפואתו וזו טעות, אלא כל שנגמרו שערו וצפרניו הרי הוא ספק בן קיימא, וליש פוסקים הוא בחזקת ודאי בן קיימא, וחייבין להשתדל ברפואתן, ומחללין עליו את השבת לרפאותו, וכן מעידין עכשיו עובדות רבות דבני ח׳ חיים ומתקיימין״.

4 הפרי מגדים (או״ח סי׳ שכ״ח מ״ז ס״ק ז׳) כתב, פשיטא לי דמחלל שבת בפרהסיה ועכו״ם או מומר להכעיס אין מחללין עליו את השבת. ובכף החיים (שכ״ח אות ח׳) כתב ז״ל עיין שו״ת קול יהודה סי׳ ז׳ באחד שחילל שבת בפרהסיה וחלה אם רשאים לחלל עליו השבת שהיה חולה מסוכן, והאריך בזה והעלה דאין רשאים לחלל עליו שבת רק בעבר על איסור דרבנן יעו״ש. א״ח אות ד׳.

these opinions say this does not apply to a Jew who does not observe Shabbos.

Others maintain that since it is probable that a sick person will take heart and consider repentance, we may desecrate Shabbos on his behalf. Some authorities point out that today most non–Shabbos observers violate Shabbos out of temptation rather than conviction. We are hence commanded to save such Jews and do our utmost to reach out to them and bring them back to the faith of their forefathers.[5]

6. In practice, contemporary authorities[6] rule that we may desecrate Shabbos to save any Jew.[7]

---

5 וכתב החתם סופר (יו״ד סי׳ שמא) ״שקרוב לודאי שסמוך למיתתו בראותו כי מטה ידו, פנה למעלה לאלוקי אבותיו״. עיי״ש ומסקנתו שבדבר כזה אין לדיין אלא מה שעיניו רואות אם נראה שמהרהר בתשובה רשאין לחלל עבורו. היעב״ץ בתשובה (ח״א סי׳ ל) ״שבזמננו בכל תלינן שרובם עושים את זה להשביע יצרן בעבירה או לחימוד ממון בעלמא, ומומר כזה פשיטא שאסור להורידו מחיים אדרבא אנו מצווים להחיותו ולהחזיר אבידת גופו ונשמתו״.

בספר לקוטי הלכות (שכ״ח סעיף ב׳) הביא דעת שו״ת מהר״ם שיק חאו״ח סי׳ ק״מ שחולק על הפרי מגדים, ובמחלל שבת לתיאבון אם נראה לדיין שהרהר בתשובה שפיר מחללין. וע״ע בדעת תורה סי׳ שכ״ח סעיף ב׳ דהביא בשם ח״א להקל דשמא עשה תשובה וזה דבר המצוי, ולא דמי לתוס׳ (פסחים מ״ו ע״ב) בענין הואיל, דהתם מלתא דלא שכיח והכא שכיח. ועיי״ש שהביא גם דעת הפרי מגדים ולא הסיק למעשה ולא כלום.

וכ״כ במשנה ברורה סי׳ שכ״ט ס״ק ט׳ ״ישראל בעל עבירות לתיאבון כל זמן שאין כופר בתורה נראה דמחללין עליו שבת כדי להצילו״. ועיין שם שהוסיף ״אבל אם הוא להכעיס אסור להצילו אף בחול וכ״ש שאסור לחלל עליו שבת בפקוח הנ״ל או בשאר רפואה וה״ה לכל הני דאיתא ביו״ד סימן קנ״ח ס״א וב׳ עיי״ש. וכן הוא בפרמ״ג שמומר לחלל שבת בפרהסיה אין מחללין עליו את השבת״.

6 בשו״ת חלקת יעקב ח״א סי׳ מ״ה כתב דבמחללי שבת שבזמנינו יש להקל והכל לפי ראות הדיין. ועיין בשו״ת ציץ אליעזר ח״ח סי׳ טו, ובח״ט סי׳ יז, דהסיק כשיש חולה לפנינו יש להקל לחלל שבת עבורו עד דידוע לנו שהחולה מומר להכעיס דאז אין מחללין עליו את השבת לכל הדעות. וע״ש שהביא בשם שו״ת פרי השדה חלק ב׳ סימן י״ז, וכן משו״ת מחנה חיים ביו״ד ח״ב סימן ס׳. וע״ע בשו״ת בית יצחק יו״ד קונטרס אחרון להלכות טרפות סימן כ״ט. ובשו״ת מנחת יצחק ח״א סימן נ״ג אות ד׳ ובח״ג סימן כ׳. וע״ע בילקוט יוסף שבת ד׳ עמוד רנ״א.

7 כתב החזון איש (יו״ד סי׳ ב׳ ס״ק ט״ז): דאין דין מורידין אלא בזמן שהשגחתו יתברך גלויה כמו בזמן שהיו נסים מצויין ומשמש בת קול, וצדיקי הדור תחת השגחה פרטית הנראית לעין כל, והכופרין אז הוא בנליזות מיוחדת בהטיית היצר לתאוות והפקרות, ואז היה ״ביעור רשעים״ — גדרו של עולם, שהכל ידעו כי הדחת הדור מביא פורענויות לעולם, ומביא דבר וחרב ורעב בעולם. אבל בזמן ההעלם שנכרתה האמונה מן דלת העם, אין במעשה ״הורדה״ — גדר הפרצה, אלא ״הוספת הפרצה״ שיהיה בעיניהם כמעשה השחתה ואלימות ח״ו. וכיון שכל עצמנו — ״לתקן״ אין דין זה נוהג בשעה שאין בו תיקון, ועלינו להחזירם בעבותות אהבה ולהעמידם בקרן אורה במה שידינו מגעת.

A Non-Jew

7. Since the axiom "Desecrate one Shabbos for him so that he may observe many more Shabbosos" does not apply to a non-Jew,[8] it is, in principle, forbidden to desecrate Shabbos to save a non-Jew with a life-threatening illness.[9]

8. In order not to arouse the wrath of non-Jews, however, halachic authorities rule that one may perform actions forbidden by rabbinic law in order to save a non-Jew.[10] But this still leaves the possibility of arousing the wrath of the nations of the world if they hear that we do not treat sick non-Jews in the same way we treat Jews. This may lead to libel against the Jewish community and cause non-Jews to refrain from treating Jews.

9. Moreover, hospital regulations today require medical staff to treat everyone, regardless of race or religion. A doctor who is found to be negligent in this area would be relieved of his position. Therefore, the ruling is that a Jewish doctor should do what he can to avoid treating non-Jews on Shabbos, such as having a non-Jewish doctor available to see his patients.[11] When this is not possible, he may perform any *melachah*, even those prohibited by Torah law, to provide the necessary care to his non-Jewish patients.[12] His intention should be to protect his job and to protect other Jews who require treatment by non-Jewish doctors so they will be treated properly.[13] Since this is his intention,

---

8 שבת (קנ״א ע״ב) יומא (פ״ה ע״ב). ועיין בבאור הלכה סי׳ שכ״ט ד״ה אלא לפי שעה.

9 בגמ׳ ע״ז (כ״ו ע״א) אמר אביי יכולה לומר דידן דמינטרי שבתא מחללינן עלייהו, דידכו דלא מינטרו שבתא לא מחללינן. וכ״פ ה״ה בפ״ב מהלכות שבת הלכה י״ב עיי״ש.

10 מ״ב סי׳ ש״ל ס״ק ח׳.

11 עיין בשו״ת אגרות משה או״ח ח״א סי׳ קל״א, וח״ד סי׳ ע״ט.

12 שו״ת חתם סופר חו״מ סי׳ קצד. וכן הסכימו גדולי האחרונים עיין בשו״ת ציץ אליעזר ח״ח סימן טו פרק ו׳ ובח״ט סימן יז אות ג׳. וכ״כ בשו״ת מנחת יצחק ח״א סימן נג, עיין מסקנתו שם (אות ג) דהיינו דווקא בחולה שיש בו סכנה, אך בחולה נכרי שאין בו סכנה צריך לדקדק בכל פעם אם הוי איסור מדאורייתא או דרבנן ואם אפשר לאשתמוטי או לא. ועי״ע במנחת יצחק שם סימן ס״ג בביאור דין מלאכה שאינה צריכה לגופה, מש״כ בשם הפר״מ בראש יוסף ובעוד פוסקים עיי״ש. כמו״כ עיין במנחת יצחק בח״ג סימן כ׳. ועי״ע בשו״ת חלקת יעקב חלק ב׳ סימן נד. ובשו״ת משנה הלכות ח״ג סימן מה. ועי״ע בספר הלכה ורפואה ח״א מאמרו של מרן הגר״ע יוסף שליט״א באורך וברוחב.

13 ציץ אליעזר שם והוסיף שכאשר מטפל היהודי בנכרי בשבת עליו להימנע מלקבל שכר עבור

rather than the performance of the *melachah* as such, his action can be categorized as a *melachah she'einah tzerichah l'gufah* (an act that is not performed for its usual purpose), and he may therefore rely on this leniency.[14]

A Person Attempting Suicide

10. It is permitted to desecrate Shabbos for one who attempted to commit suicide. Similarly,[15] Shabbos may be desecrated to save someone who has knowingly placed himself in a dangerous situation and now finds his life threatened.[16]

פעולתו, או שלפחות לא להנות משכר השבת שקיבל מהגוי כגון שיזרוק את הכסף לים וכיו״ב. ובספר שמירת שבת כהלכתה פרק מ׳ הערה מ״ב הביא משו״ת חתם סופר הנ״ל שהשכר יתנהו לצדקה.

14 נזכר עניין זה במנחת יצחק הנ״ל ובציץ אליעזר שם. וע״ע בדעת תורה סימן רע״ה דכל מלאכה שאדם עושה מחמת יראה או מצד חוקי הממשלה ע״פ גזירת המושל — הוי מלאכה שאינה צריכה לגופה. וכ״כ מרן הגר״ע יוסף שליט״א במאמרו הנזכ״ל.

15 אגרות משה חאו״ח סי׳ קכ״ז. וע״ע בילקוט יוסף שבת ד׳ עמוד רסב-רסו.

16 כתב בברכי יוסף (או״ח ש״א ו׳) מעשה באיש אחד שמצא סגולה אחת בספר כתב יד מאדם גדול מהראשונים למי ששתה סם המוות לכתוב לו ותיכף מקיא האדם וחוזר לבריאותו וכו׳ ויהי היום ליל שבת קודש אירע שנערה ישראלית שתתה סם המוות והתחילו לה דבקי מיתה ובא אצל האיש הלז בליל ש״ק וקם וכתב הקמיעא לנערה ותיכף הקיאה ועמדה על בוריה, וביום השבת נודע בעיר כל אשר נעשה ולעזה עליו מדינה דחילל שבת וכו׳ והוא השיב דפקוח נפש דוחה שבת והיו מגמגמין בדבר, אי לזאת שאל האיש אם חטא בזה וכו׳.

והשיב הגאון החיד״א זיע״א לאחר שדן בארוכה דאמנם לא שפיר למעבד הכי, והיינו משום דהוא דרך סגולה, אך לאחר מעשה כיון שכוונתו היתה להצילה ומש״ה לא שאל שהשואל הי״ז שופך דמים ונמצא שהצילה, לא עבר לא על אסורים מדאורייתא ולא אדרבנן, והיינו כיון שעשה רפואה סגולית. אך אם חילל עבורה בחילול רגיל אין כאן בית מיחוש אף שהביאה הצרה על עצמה, לית לן לזרוק אבן אחר הנופל. ועיין עוד במה שכתבנו לקמן פרק 16 הערה 18.

Part 2

Choleh Sheyeish Bo Sakanah

Chapter 7

The Definition of Choleh Sheyeish Bo Sakanah

The category of *choleh sheyeish bo sakanah* (one who has a life-threatening illness) includes:

1. A person who has a condition that, without treatment, will deteriorate into a life-threatening condition.[1]
2. A person in a situation where the slightest possibility of danger to his life exists.[2]
3. A mentally ill person who may endanger himself.[3]
4. A person who is not presently in danger but whose life might be endangered in the near term if he does not receive immediate medical attention.[4]

---

1 כן מבואר במשנה ברורה סי׳ שכ״ח ס״ק י״ז. וע״ע בסי׳ רע״ח בביאור הלכה ד״ה בשביל שישן החולה.

2 כן מבואר בסוגית הגמ׳ ביומא דף פ״ג דאפילו על ספק סכנת נפשות מחללים, ועיין במ״ב סי׳ שכ״ח ס״ק י״ז ובהגהות הגרעק״א.

3 עיין ביסודי ישורון מערכת פקוח נפש. וע״ע בשו״ת ציץ אליעזר ח״ד סי׳ י״ג. ובח״ח סי׳ ט״ו פ״ב ס״ק ה׳.

4 עיין במשנה ברורה סי׳ שכ״ח ס״ק מ״ט ז״ל: כשנפגע אחד מאיברי האדם, והרופאים אומרים שאם לא יטופל ולא ירפאו האיבר, יוכל לבוא לפיקוח נפש הרי הוא כשאר חולי שיש בו סכנה. וע״ע באגרות משה או״ח ח״ג סימן צ״א. וע״ע בספר תורת היולדת סוף פרק א׳ שהאריך בעניין

5. A dangerously ill person who was in intensive care. Even though his situation has improved and he has been removed from intensive care, since he has not yet fully recovered, we must consider the possibility that his situation may worsen if he does not receive proper treatment.[5]

6. Someone with an internal injury, an injury on the back of the hand or foot (see chapter 38, "Wounds and Dressings"), a wound caused by a metal implement, or a woman who has just given birth.[6]

Internal Injuries

7. The term *internal injury* applies to any wound, fracture, or infection that affects any of the body's internal organs, including the teeth and mouth. Included in this category are ailments affecting the respiratory system, the digestive system, the urinary tract, the heart and circulatory system, the liver, the pancreas, and the spleen. If any of these organs is injured, becomes infected, or is affected by any other ailment, the condition is considered life-threatening, and Shabbos may be desecrated in order to treat it, if needed.[7]

זה עיי״ש. מיהו כתב הב״י בשם רבינו ירוחם ז״ל: כתב רבינו ירוחם בחלק ט׳ יש מי שכתב שכל דבר שאין בו סכנה עתה אע״פ שיוכל לבא לידי סכנה אין מחללין עליו אלא שבות דרבנן אבל לא איסור מדאורייתא ע״כ.

והעיר על כך הגרי״י זילברשטיין שליט״א בזה״ל: נ״ל שאפילו בעוד שנים רבות יסתכן מותר כבר כעת לעשות עבורו איסורים כדי למנעו מהסכנה. דהרמב״ם פסק דאסור לתינוק לצום בגלל הסכנה, וכתב החקרי לב ראיתי נערים צמים ולא מסתכנים. השיב לעומתו היד דוד (לר׳ דוד צינזהים) מי יודע אם לאחר שנים רבות יסתכן בגלל צום זה וגם זה נחשב לסכנה. עכ״ל.

5 ביסודי ישורון מערכת פקוח נפש הביא דברי התוס׳ בחולין (ט״ו ע״ב) ד״ה כגון שהיה חולה והבריא, שכתבו שם דטעמא דהשוחט לחולה והבריא אמאי לא חשיב מוקצה אם אמרינן יש מוקצה לחצי שבת, י״ל כיון שרגילות הוא שחוזר לחוליו לא הוי מוקצה ע״כ.

ועיי״ש ביסודי ישורון עוד בעניין זה, ומקור דבריו עיין בספר דעת תורה סי׳ שכ״ח סעיף י״ז. עוד הביא שם ביסודי ישורון את דברי הב״י ביו״ד הלכות מילה סימן רס״ב שהשיב על דברי המהרי״ק בענין תינוק שחלה בחולי שיש בו סכנה שצריך להמתין אחר שהבריא שבעה ימים, אם תוך שבעה עלה חומו במקצת שאין בו סכנה כלל, אי מנינן שבעה מחולי ראשון או מחולי שני? והסיק הב״י שם דודאי מנינן מחולי שני, וטעמו כתב שם וז״ל: כיון שחזרה לו הקדחת בקצת לסוף ב׳ או ג׳ ימים אגלאי מילתא שעדיין לא הבריא מחולי הראשון ואין לשלוח יד בילד עד אחר שבעה ימים להבראתו השנית מכל וכל שהרי זה ספק נפשות והולכים בו להחמיר עכ״ל הב״י שם. ולכאורה יש סמך דחולה שהיה בכלל סכנה כל זמן שלא קם מחוליו לגמרי עדיין מוחזק כחולה שיש בו סכנה. גם בדעת תורה שם הביא ראיה זו עיי״ש.

6 פרוט דיני יולדת לא יתבאר במסגרת ספרנו זה.

7 שו״ע סי׳ שכ״ח סעיף ג׳.

8. However, internal pain or stress that is not related to a wound, infection, or other ailment that affects the internal organs is not considered life-threatening.[8] But when there is the slightest doubt by the doctor or by the patient himself whether an infection or some other ailment exists, it is considered *pikuach nefesh* and one may desecrate Shabbos to travel to the hospital for an examination. For example, severe lower abdominal pain, which might indicate acute appendicitis, justifies emergency evaluation in the hospital on Shabbos.[9]

9. A person does not have to obtain an expert medical opinion to ascertain that he suffers from an internal ailment. If he is in severe pain or believes there is even a slight chance of danger, he may travel to the hospital or seek medical advice without first being examined by a doctor.[10]

10. If it is certain that one who suffers from an internal ailment is not in immediate danger if treatment is delayed until after Shabbos, one may not desecrate Shabbos for him.[11] For example, a person who must receive dialysis every three days due to a kidney ailment may not desecrate Shabbos for it. He should schedule his treatments during the week and thereby avoid Shabbos desecration.[12]

---

8 שו״ע שם, ומגיד משנה פ״ב מהלכות שבת ה״ה בשם הרשב״א.

9 וע״ע בילקוט יוסף שבת ד׳ עמוד רי״ט.

10 שו״ע שם סעיף ד׳.

11 שו״ע שם, ומגיד משנה שם בשם הרמב״ן.

12 בכף החיים סי׳ שכ״ח אות ס״ט כתב שבמקום שאפשר לעשות לו הרפואה מיד בלי חילול שבת אלא שיצטרכו לשהות שעה מועטת, לא יחללו כדי לעשותה תיכף ומיד בלא שום שיהוי כלל, אם הוא בעניין שאין חשש סכנה כלל בשיהוי מועט כזה — לפי שהשבת דחויה היא אצל פקוח נפש ולא הותרה לגמרי. עכ״ל. מזה משמע שלדעת הפוסקים ששבת אכן הותרה כדעת המהר״ם מרוטנבורג ודעימיה מותר לחלל בהאי גוונא. ונראה דמסתבר דגם לדידהו לא יחללו.

אולם העיר לי הגר״י זילברשטיין שליט״א בזה״ל דשיטת הכף החיים בשם שו״ע הגרש״ז ס״ל דאם הותרה מותר לחלל ואין צורך לשהות אפילו זמן מועט. דומיא דעבודה דלמ״ד טומאה הותרה בצבור עושים את העבודה בטמאים ולא מהדרים אחרי טהורים מבית אב אחר, וללישנא בתרא אפילו היכא דאיכא טהורים בההוא בית אב עושים בטומאה כמבואר ביומא (ו:) ויש לעיין בחולה שיש בו סכנה שנחלה בסוף השבת והדבר לא בהול האם ממתינים למוצאי שבת?

יעויין בתוספת יום הכיפורים פ״ד: ד״ה ואין אומרים נמתין שמא יבריא שכתב: ומשמע דאפילו הוא סמוך למוצאי שבת דלא נשאר משבת רק שעה אחת או חצי מחללים. ומתוך תשובת הרשב״א שכתב מרן הב״י סוף סימן קל״ד לא משמע הכי, וצ״ע. ועיין או״ח שכ״ח סי״ד, ועיין ביו״ד במורם ס״ס קנ״ה עכ״ל. מבואר בדבריו דמשמע ליה דאין ממתינים אפילו חצי שעה אלא מחללים שבת. ויתכן דלמ״ד הותרה פשוט שכך הוא. עכ״ל.

Chapter 8

Determining Whether an Illness Is Life-Threatening

1. Whenever a doctor states that an ailment may pose a danger to life, Shabbos may be desecrated, even if the symptoms are only external.[1]
2. Shabbos may be desecrated for any ailment described by the Talmud as life-threatening even if doctors insist that it does not pose a danger to life.[2] But if the doctor says that a danger to life exists, Shabbos may be desecrated even if the Talmud implies that the illness is not life-threatening.[3]
3. If a person states that his life is in danger due to internal pain and there is no doctor available, the patient's opinion may be relied upon to permit Shabbos desecration.[4]

---

1 שו״ע סי׳ שכ״ח סעיף י׳.

2 בכף החיים סי׳ שכ״ח אות י״ג כתב ז״ל: ויש הפרש בצפידנא אפילו החולה והרופא אומרים אין צריך, שקר אומרים כי מקובל ביד חז״ל שסכנה הוא וכו׳ א״א אות ב׳. ע״כ.

ועיין בנשמת אברהם ח״א סי׳ שכ״ח אות י׳ שהביא דעות הראשונים בזה, הרשב״א בתשובה (ח״א סי׳ צ״ח) הרמב״ם (פ״י מהלכות שחיטה הי״ב והי״ג) בענייני טרפות. עוד הביא דברי הריב״ש בתשובה (תמ״ז) ז״ל: אין לנו לדון בדיני תורתנו ומצוותיה ע״פ חכמי הטבע והרפואה, שאם נאמין לדבריהם אין תורה מן השמים חלילה, כי כן הניחו הם במופתיהם הכוזבים, ואם תדין בדיני הטרפות ע״פ חכמי הרפואה, שכר הרבה תיטול מן הקצבים עכ״ל. ועיי״ש באורך וברוחב בעניין זה.

3 בעניין מחלה — שבתלמוד משמע שאין בה סכנה — והרופאים חוששים לסכנה, עיין בכפה״ח סימן שכ״ח אות מ״ח ז״ל: וסמכינן ארופא גוי לחלל שבת אפילו במאי דמשמע מלשון התלמוד שאין בחולה זה סכנה, שעינינו הרואות השתנות הזמנים בכל העניינים האלו. תשובות בשמים ראש סי׳ רנ״ט, פת״ע אות י״ב. עכ״ל. וא״כ כ״ש שנסמוך בזה על רופאי ישראל.

4 שו״ע סימן שכ״ח סעיף ד׳. וע״ע להלן סעיף ח׳.

4. When an internal injury is involved and no doctor is available, anyone, even a layperson, may decide or raise the concern that there is a danger to life and permit Shabbos desecration, even if the patient does not feel that his life is in danger. This is because internal ailments are considered life-threatening even in the absence of a diagnosis.[5] Even where there is a difference of opinion, Shabbos desecration is permitted because of the mere possibility that danger to life is involved.

5. Where no internal ailment or injury is involved, and the patient does not feel that his sickness is life-threatening, someone who is well versed in medicine, or at least in this particular illness, should be consulted. If the medical authority states that even the slightest possibility of danger to life exists, we may desecrate Shabbos to help the patient.[6]

6. If there is no expert available, however, and the patient does not feel that his life is in danger, a layman's opinion does not count when no internal injury is involved.[7] Only if the layman states that he is knowledgeable in that disease may he be relied upon concerning Shabbos desecration when no internal injury or ailment is involved.[8,9]

---

5 שו״ע שם.

6 שו״ע שם סעיף ה׳.

7 כ״כ בב״י (ריש סי׳ שכ״ח) בשם הרמב״ן בתורת האדם. ועפ״ד יש להסיק כפי הטבלה דלהלן:

	במכה של חלל	במכה שאינה של חלל
בסתם	מחללים מבלי להשאל	נשאלים בבקי או בחולה ובלאו הכי אין מחללים
בידוע שיש סכנת חיים	מחללים	מחללים
בידוע שאין סכנת חיים	אין מחללים	אין מחללים
בספק אצל החולה או הרופא	מחללים	מחללים

וע״פ עקרון זה כתב בשו״ע סעיף ד׳ וסעיף ה׳ דיני מכה של חלל, ומכה שאינה של חלל.

8 הטור הביא בשם הר״י, אחר שהביא דין רופא אחד אומר צריך ואחד אומר אינו צריך מחללים, וכתב ר״י שא״צ מומחה דכל בני אדם חשובין מומחין קצת וספק נפשות להקל. והוסיף ע״כ הדרכי משה אות ו׳ וז״ל: וכתב באו״ה הא דסתם בני אדם בקיאים במקצת היינו בסתם ישראל אבל לא בסתם א״י ע״כ. עיי״ש. ואכן דעת ר״י הנזכר הביאו השו״ע בסעיף י׳ בשם יש מי שאומר, אחר שסתם כדעה הראשונה דדוקא ברופא אומר מחללים, וקיי״ל דסתם ויש הלכה כסתם. וכתב עוד שם בביאור הלכה שבאמת לא משמע כדברי ר״י ברמב״ם ובר״ן, אך משום דהוא סכנת נפשות חשש המחבר לדעה זו כמו שסיים בעצמו, וע״כ נראה דאם אפשר לעשות ע״י א״י יעשה ע״י א״י, דבלא״ה יש דעות דאף אם רופא מומחה ציווה לחלל והוא יכול לעשות ע״י א״י דיעשה ע״י אינו יהודי וכדלקמן בסי״ב. ע״כ בבה״ל.

9 כתב המ״ב ס״ק כ״ז דמה שכתב בשו״ע משם ר״י שא״צ מומחה, מ״מ דווקא כשיאמר שמכיר

7. If the doctors disagree whether or not there is danger to life, with one doctor claiming danger and his colleague dissenting, Shabbos may be desecrated, because in matters of *pikuach nefesh* we are lenient in situations of doubt.[10]

8. If a patient feels he needs a particular medication and the doctor says it is unnecessary, we rely on the patient's feelings because he will best perceive if something is wrong.[11] But if the doctor claims that the medication will harm the patient, we heed the doctor's opinion.[12]

באותו חולי כמש״כ סי׳ תרי״ח, וגם אינו נאמן להכחיש המומחה אפילו להקל. [מג״א וא״ר]. הארכתי מעט בהערה 8 והערה 9 בביאור דין זה כדי שלא יקשה בין פסקי מרן השו״ע בסעיפים ד׳ ה׳ ליש מי שאומר בסעיף י׳.

10 שו״ע שם סעיף י׳.

11 מגן אברהם בשם הרדב״ז, והביאו במ״ב סי׳ שכ״ח ס״ק כ״ה, וע״ע בבה״ל שם וז״ל: ולעניות דעתי אין הדברים אמורים אלא כשאומר מרגיש אני חולשה באיבר פלוני על כן יעשו לי תרופה פלונית שמועלת לחולי איבר זה, ובזה ודאי שומעים לו, שלב יודע מרת נפשו שייכא בכל מילי, ואפילו רופא אומר שאין צריך שום תרופה אין שומעים לו, אבל אם המחלה ידועה והחולה אומר שתרופה זו מועלת למחלה זו, והרופא אומר שאנו מועיל, בזה אין סברה לשמוע לחולה לחלל שבת בחינם [ומכל מקום אפשר לומר דהיכי דאומר החולה דידוע לו שטבע גופו להתרפאות ממחלה זו כשנוטל רפואה זו אפשר דשומעין לו דגם בזה שייכות קצת לומר דאדם בקי בגופו יותר ממאה רופאים] אם לא דאיכא חשש שמא תטרף דעתו עליו אם יראה שאינם עושים כדבריו. עכ״ל.

12 ודע דכל מה שאנו אומרים דאם הרופא אומר שתזיק לו הרפואה שומעים לרופא — ה״מ בתרופה אבל אם החולה אומר שצריך לאכול אפי׳ הרופא אומר שהמאכל מזיק שומעים לחולה כמש״כ סי׳ תרי״ח סעיף א׳ ומג״א שם ס״ק ג׳ (כף החיים סי׳ שכ״ח אות מ״ז). ומ״מ כתבו האחרונים דיש פעמים שידוע שהאכילה היא נזק גמור לחולה, כגון חולה שאחרי ניתוח הן במערכת העיכול והן במערכות אחרות — האכילה מסכנת את חייו ודאי — בזה אף אם אומר החולה צריך אני אין שומעים לו כלל. וכל דבר יש לדון בו לגופו.

Chapter 9
Levels of Urgency

1. There are three degrees of urgency for treating a person whose life is in danger:
   a. An extreme emergency
   b. The emergency is not extreme, but treatment cannot be delayed
   c. When treatment can be postponed for a short time

   Determining the degree of urgency will affect the manner in which various actions are performed on the patient's behalf. Also, the patient may exhibit varying symptoms so that his condition may encompass all three levels of urgency.

An Extreme Emergency

2. Examples of "extreme emergency" include loss of consciousness, a heart attack, hypoglycemia, snakebite,[1] ingestion of kerosene or other toxic substances, and a serious road accident. In all these cases, any slight delay may cause irreversible damage, serious deterioration of the patient's condition, or death.

   In such situations, there are absolutely no restrictions, and everything should be done to help the patient as if it were a weekday.[2]

---

1 עיין מה שכתבנו בזה לקמן פרק 36 בשם הגרי״י זילברשטיין שליט״א.

2 שו״ע סי׳ שכ״ח סעיף ד׳ בשם הרמב״ן, ושכ״כ הרמב״ם.

Concerning such situations, our Sages teach, "One who acts quickly is praiseworthy, and one who asks questions is considered to have murdered."[3]

Therefore, as many people as necessary may be employed to hasten rescue operations as much as possible.[4] No calculations should be made as to how to limit the scope of Shabbos desecration, neither the number of forbidden acts or their severity nor whether to employ a Jew or non-Jew. Any such considerations can cause a delay that could endanger the person further.[5]

3. For example, many communities maintain Hatzalah teams, comprised of local Jewish medics, in addition to the regular ambulance services supplied by the city. In emergency situations, both the regular ambulance service and the Hatzalah service can be summoned. The Hatzalah team may travel to the patient even if they know the ambulance will arrive in any case. They should not make calculations to determine whether or not it is actually necessary for them to come. Even if they discover upon arrival that they were not needed, they have still performed a great mitzvah.[6]

When the Emergency Is Not Extreme, but Treatment Cannot Be Delayed

4. Sometimes the situation is not so urgent, and Shabbos desecration can be minimized by making a few calculations without endangering the patient. In such situations, such calculations should be done, and Shabbos desecration should be minimized in all possible ways.[7] This can be done either by minimizing the number of people involved, the number of actions, or the severity of those actions.

5. *Minimizing the number of people.* If it is not an extreme emergency, there is no need to call both Hatzalah and the local ambulance. Similarly, if

---

3 שם סעיף ב׳.

4 שם סעיף ט״ו.

5 כן משמע בשו״ע שם, ועי״ע ברמ״א שם סעיף ט״ז בשם הגהות מרדכי.

6 כן משמע בשו״ע שם סעיף ט״ו.

7 כמבואר שם בשו״ע סעיף ט״ז וברמ״א שם.

Hatzalah knows that an ambulance is on the way, they should not desecrate Shabbos to attend to the patient. Moreover, if treatment can be easily performed by a non-Jew, this is better than a Jew performing it.

6. *Minimizing the number of transgressions.* The *Shulchan Aruch*[8] states that where the doctors prescribe that the patient eat one fig and it is an extreme emergency, if ten people run to procure the fig, they are all exempt from Shabbos observance and receive a reward for their actions, even if the patient has already recovered after eating the first fig. But if it is not an extreme emergency and the patient can wait for a short time, although the fig should be procured as quickly as possible, no more than one person should go to pick a fig for him.

   Similarly, if the doctors have prescribed two figs, and two figs are found, each on a different branch, or three figs on one branch, the branch that contains three figs should be cut. But if one branch contains two figs and another contains three, then only the branch with two figs should be cut.[9] Again, in an extreme emergency, these calculations are not made in order to prevent even the slightest delay.[10]

7. Practical applications: If a machine that has a number of functions, and controls can be set up so that they all begin to function simultaneously immediately upon plugging it in, it should be set up beforehand in order to minimize the number of forbidden actions necessary on Shabbos.

   If one machine can perform a complete blood analysis with one activation, although it includes many unnecessary results, whereas by using two or three machines we can analyze only the necessary parameters, it is preferable to use the one machine that performs many tests. However, in an extreme emergency, where using the more advanced device will entail even the slightest delay in getting the necessary results, two devices should be used if this will speed up the process, even though an extra action is involved.

---

8 סימן שכ״ח סעיף ט״ו.

9 שם סעיף ט״ז.

10 הרמ״א שם בשם הגהות מרדכי.

8. *Minimizing the severity of the desecration.* If an action can be performed in a way that constitutes a rabbinical prohibition rather than a Torah prohibition, this is preferable, as long as it does not involve any delay in the patient's treatment and the situation is not extremely urgent. This can be accomplished either by performing the action with a *shinui*[11] (in an unusual manner), through a non-Jew,[12] or by performing a *melachah she'einah tzerichah l'gufah* (an act that is not performed for its usual purpose).

9. For example, if a person is in critical but stable condition and needs to be monitored by an electrocardiograph (ECG), it is possible to activate the machine with a *shinui*, such as by using one's elbow or the back of the hand.[13]

   Similarly, if the situation is not extremely urgent, different devices can be operated or prescriptions and patient charts filled in by a non-Jew. Even if a Jewish doctor is performing the actual treatment, he can have a non-Jew stand by to assist him in all actions that involve a Shabbos prohibition.[14]

10. Another example: A patient in critical condition must eat *cheilev* (the forbidden fats of an animal, i.e., tallow). There are two possibilities: he can eat the *cheilev* of a kosher animal, where the transgression is normally punishable with *kareis* (excision), or that of a non-kosher animal, where one transgresses a negative commandment that does not incur the severe punishment of *kareis*. It is best to feed him *cheilev* from the non-kosher animal, since he thereby minimizes the severity of the prohibition.[15] It is clear, however, that this applies only when both types

---

11 הרמ״א שם סעיף י״ב, ובמ״ב ס״ק ל״ה. ועיין להלן הערה 12.

12 הרמ״א שם. וזהו לדעת הרמ״א ודעימיה, אך דעת הט״ז דבכל חולי שיש ב״ס עושין החילול דווקא ע״י ישראל ולא ע״י עכו״ם. ונתבאר דין זה בהרחבה לעיל בפרק 3 הערה 3 עיי״ש.

13 עיין לעיל פרק 4 דשם ביארנו דיש מקילים שאין צורך לעשות פעולות אלו בשינוי אלא בכל חולי שיש בו סכנה שמותר לחלל את השבת — מחללין אף בלא שינוי.

14 עיין בביאור הלכה ד״ה כל שרגילים, דמחלק בין פעולה שאם לא יעשו לחולה יסתכן דשרי לכתחילה ע״י ישראל. משא״כ פעולות אחרות שאין במניעתם חשש סכנה אף שהחולה צריך לה — עדיף לעשות ע״י א״י.

15 כן כתב בחידושי הגאון רבי עקיבא איגר ביו״ד סימן ס״ד (ט״ז סק״א). והוסיף על זה הגר״י זילברשטיין שליט״א בזה״ל: וה״ה כשהבשר נתבשל בחלב שיש להעדיף את הבשר הטמא שלא

of food are readily available or there is no increased danger in taking the time to look for the *cheilev* of a non-kosher animal.[16] (This rule is applicable also on weekdays.)

For Which of the Patient's Needs May Shabbos Be Desecrated?

11. All actions necessary to save the life of a critically ill patient and to help him recover may be performed. However, there are many actions that, if not done, will not endanger the patient further but will nevertheless make him more comfortable or fill some of his other needs. May Shabbos be desecrated for such needs that are not essential to his recovery?

    This question is discussed at length by halachic authorities.[17] The conclusions of the *Mishnah Berurah* are as follows:

    a. Even if the situation calls for Shabbos desecration, a Jew may desecrate Shabbos for a person whose life is in danger only if there is a possibility that if the act will not be done, the patient's condition will deteriorate dangerously. But if it is absolutely certain that there is no danger in refraining from a particular action, even though it is being done for the needs of the patient, it should be performed by a non-Jew, as for an ordinary bedridden patient (*choleh she'ein bo sakanah*). It is certainly proper to act strictly, as explained, with respect to Torah prohibitions (*Mishnah Berurah* 328:14).

    b. If there is a possibility that refraining from the act will cause the patient's condition to deteriorate, Shabbos must be desecrated.

    c. If performing the action will improve the patient's condition,

---

נוהג בו איסור זה, דאינו נוהג אלא בבשר טהורה כמבואר בשו״ע יו״ד סי׳ פ״ז סעיף ג׳. ובהגהות חכמת שלמה יו״ד סי׳ ס״ב כתב שחולה הצריך לאכול בשר ואין שם כי אם בהמה טמאה חיה והוא שבת, אם נימא דיש איסור איבר מן החי גם בטמאה אסור להאכילו בעודה חיה, אבל אם נימא דאין בה איסור איבר מן החי אסור להמית את הבהמה יעו״ש ובדרכי תשובה ס״ב ס״ק ט׳.

16 יש לדון אם ידוע לחולה שהמאכל מבהמה טמאה ולא ידוע לו שזה חלב וממילא נפשו קצה בזה (עיין במ״ב סי׳ שכ״ח ס״ק ל״ט על פי דברי הרא״ש).

17 א) כתב הב״י ריש סימן שכ״ח ז״ל מדברי רש״י משמע דלא שרי לחלל שבת בשביל חולה שיש

Shabbos should be desecrated since he is a *choleh sheyeish bo sakanah* (*Bei'ur Halachah*, ad loc., citing the *Meiri*).

d. If the patient requests a certain treatment and the doctor states that the procedure will be ineffective, we may still desecrate Shabbos if there is the possibility that not carrying out the request will have a negative effect on the patient's mental state (based on *Bei'ur Halachah* 328:10, s.v. "*v'rofei*").[18]

When Treatment Is Not Urgent

12. If a person suffers from an internal injury, and we know there is no urgency in treating him, Shabbos may not be desecrated.[19] This is also

---

בו סכנה אלא דווקא בדבר שאם לא יעשוהו לו הוא מסוכן למות בשבילו, אבל דבר שאף אם לא יעשוהו לו אינו מסוכן למות בשבילו אין עושין אותו ע״י ישראל. שבסוף פרק מפנין (קכ״ט:) אהא דאמרינן חולה שאין בו סכנה אומר לא״י פרש״י צרכי חולה שאם לא יעשו לו רפואה זו אין מסוכן למות, ומ״מ צריך הוא לה. (משמע דחולה שיש בו סכנה — היינו חולה שאם לא יעשו לו רפואה זו הרי הוא מסוכן למות, הא לאו הכי חולה שאין בו סכנה מיקרי.) ממשיך הב״י — אבל ה״ה כתב בפ״ב גבי אין עושין מדורה לחולה, דלחולה שיש בו סכנה משמע דלכל צרכיו מחללין ואע״פ שאין במניעת הדבר שעושין לו סכנה. ע״כ.

ב) בדרכי משה שם כתב ז״ל: בהגהות מרדכי פרק מפנין דף קפ״ב ע״ב (בספרים שלפנינו בהגהת מרדכי סי׳ תס״ג וסי׳ תס״ד עיי״ש) האריך בדינים אלו וכתב ״דלא שיאמר שאם לא יעשו לו דברים אלו שימות אלא כל שיודע החולה שהוא שבת ואומר שצריך שאינו יכול לסבול מחמת החולי מחללים וכו׳ וכן משמע לקמן סי׳ תרי״ח״. עכ״ל בדרכי משה שם.

ג) ועיין עוד בראי״ש (יומא פ״ג) דפליג על רש״י שמתיר אכילה ביום הכפורים רק אם יש חשש מיתה בהעדר אכילה, והראי״ש ס״ל שאינו כן אלא כל שאם לא יאכל יגבר חוליו שרי באכילה. וע״ע בספר פקוח נפש סימן ג׳ בגדרי חולה שיש בו סכנה שהאריך בזה ואכמ״ל יותר.

ד) בשו״ע סי׳ שכ״ח סעיף ד׳ כתב וז״ל: מכה של חלל אינה צריכה אומד שאפילו אין שם בקיאים וחולה אינו אומר כלום עושים לו כל שרגילים לעשות לו בחול, אבל כשיודעים ומכירים באותו חולי שממתין ואין צריך חילול אסור לחלל עליו אף על פי שהוא מכה של חלל. עכ״ל. ומקור דבריו הם ברמב״ן בספר תורת האדם.

ה) והנה המשנה ברורה שם בס״ק י״ד ובבאור הלכה ד״ה כל שרגילים האריך לפסוק שלא כהבנת המגיד משנה בדברי הרמב״ן הנ״ל בב״י, וביסס דבריו על פי שיטת רש״י ור״ת ר״י, תוס׳ ישנים תוס׳ פרק מפנין, מאירי שם, רשב״א בתשובה, אור זרוע, ר״ן ורמב״ן.

ו) גם בכף החיים סי׳ שכ״ח הביא דברי הבה״ל הנ״ל. אולם בשו״ת יחוה דעת ח״ד סימן ל׳ ובספר לוית חן סי׳ פ״ה האריך לדחות דברי הבה״ל ולהעמיד דברי מרן השו״ע וכפי שהבין המגיד משנה בשם הרמב״ן. עי״ש באורך מה שהביא משם הגר״ח מבריסק זצ״ל בעניין אכילה לחולה שיש בו סכנה ביום הכיפורים עיי״ש.

18 בעניין חשש טרוף דעת אצל חולה אי חשיב פקוח נפש לעבור עליו איסורים מדאורייתא, ע״ע בזה באריכות בשו״ת מנחת יצחק ח״ד סי׳ ח׳.

19 שו״ע סי׳ שכ״ח סעיף ד׳.

true of a person in a life-endangering situation who requires medication or tests that are not urgent and can be obtained after Shabbos. Desecration of Shabbos to perform these tests or to get him the medication is not permitted.[20]

Examples

13. The Gemara mentions a person who suffers from a heart condition and his treatment is to drink goat's milk every day. Although his life will be in danger if he does not drink it at all, he will not be in any danger if he misses one day. In such a situation, Shabbos may not be desecrated in order to obtain goat's milk for him (*Kesubos* 60a). (He may, however, suck the milk directly from the goat, because this involves performing the *melachah* of milking with a *shinui*, which is permitted.[21])

14. A person who needs dialysis every three days should schedule his treatments on weekdays if possible. However, if for some reason it must be done on Shabbos, it is permissible.

15. A person scheduled to undergo surgery on *motza'ei Shabbos* and must have various tests done prior to the operation should, if possible, be tested after Shabbos. If it will not be possible to perform the tests after Shabbos, they may be performed on Shabbos.

16. The *sefer Nishmas Avraham* states that a person who was cut with an unclean or rusty instrument may be given a tetanus shot on Shabbos. However, if the accident occurred just before the end of Shabbos and delaying the shot for such a short time is not dangerous, the shot should indeed be postponed until after Shabbos.[22] Many physicians hold that a delay of twenty-four hours for a patient who has already had the original tetanus series as a child is not a problem.

---

20 כן משמע גם במ״ב שם ס״ק ט״ז וס״ק ל״ב.

21 באור הלכה סימן שכ״ח ד״ה שממתין בשם הרשב״א והרמב״ן.

22 וכ״כ בשמירת שבת כהלכתה פל״ה סעיף מ׳.

Chapter 10

Procedures: What May Be Done and by Whom

The Rambam states: "When performing these acts we do not employ the services of a non-Jew, children, servants, or women so that they should not become accustomed to taking Shabbos lightly. Rather, they are done by *gedolei Yisrael* and their wise men. It is forbidden to postpone desecrating Shabbos for a person whose life is in danger, as the verse states, 'that a man shall do them [the mitzvos] and live by them' — and not die by them" (*Mishneh Torah, Hilchos Shabbos* 2:3).

The Kesef Mishneh explains that the Rambam means we do not employ the services of a non-Jew or a child to save a life on Shabbos so that bystanders will not say that the Sages were hesitant in permitting Shabbos desecration and therefore only permit using a non-Jew or a child who are not obligated in mitzvos. We are therefore concerned that if no non-Jew or child is available, adults will not wish to desecrate Shabbos to treat the patient. And the reason women or servants should not be employed is "so that they should not become accustomed to taking Shabbos lightly."

The Kesef Mishneh explains the Rambam's words "*gedolei Yisrael* and their wise men" as follows: "*gedolei*" refers to adults, excluding children; "*Yisrael*" excludes non-Jews; and "their wise men" excludes women, who may come to take Shabbos lightly.

The Ran offers another reason women should not be asked to perform the necessary actions. He explains that if someone instructs a woman to do a particular action, she may think he is asking her to perform the action because he doesn't want to desecrate Shabbos himself. She will therefore refrain from performing the action. But she may, according to this explanation, assist males in performing the necessary activities. The Ran cites the *gemara* that permits calling a midwife to deliver a baby on Shabbos (*Shabbos* 128b). This implies that, on the contrary, the desecration *should* be done by a woman. He answers that delivering a baby is usually performed by women, and they are generally more proficient in this area than men. Therefore, in this particular case, they are preferred over men.

In conclusion, we cite the words of the *Ketzos HaShulchan* (135:9): "In our days we allow women to be involved in Shabbos desecration [to save a life], and they even receive training as nurses to attend patients. Since they have been trained to save lives, we are no longer afraid that they may be hesitant or come to take Shabbos lightly. On the contrary, we see that they perform their duties with dispatch."

What Should Be Done in a Life-Threatening Situation

1. One who is confronted with a life-threatening situation is commanded and obligated to desecrate Shabbos even if it means performing actions prohibited by Torah law in order to save the person in danger. One who acts quickly is praiseworthy, and one who asks for a halachic ruling is considered to have shed blood.[1] Even the rabbi who is asked the question is regarded as not having fulfilled his rabbinical duty, because he should have taught this halachah to the entire community so that they would not have found it necessary to ask the question.[2]

   Therefore, every Jew is obligated to call a doctor or drive the patient to a hospital and do everything he can to obtain assistance as

1 שו״ע סי׳ שכ״ח סעיף ב׳ ושם במ״ב ס״ק ו׳ ז״ל: פי׳ אותו האיש שהוא מתחסד ויררא לחלל שבת בחולה כזה כ״א ע״י מורה הרי הוא שופך דמים שבעוד שהוא הולך לשאול יחלש החולה יותר ויוכל להסתכן והרי הכתוב אומר לא תעמוד על דם רעיך.

2 בירושלמי איתא הנשאל הרי זה מגונה פי׳ משום שהתלמיד חכם במקומו היה לו לדרוש בפרקא לכל כדי שידעו כל העם ולא יצטרכו לשואלן.

quickly as possible. Even if the sick person does not agree that others should desecrate Shabbos for him, he should be forced to accept help, because his stringency is simply foolish.[3]

Desecration through an Adult Jew or Non-Jew

2. If the situation is extremely urgent,[4] one should not look for a non-Jew or a child to perform a particular action, nor should he ask a woman or an ignorant Jew. On the contrary, the desecration should be done by a knowledgeable adult male Jew.[5] Whoever personally rushes to help save the sick person's life is more praiseworthy than someone who appoints another to do what is necessary. The person who assists someone whose life is in danger has merited the great mitzvah of saving the life of a fellow Jew. (As to whether there is a preference in calling a Jewish doctor over a non-Jewish one, see chapter 13, "Choosing a Doctor and Seeking Medical Advice," paragraph 8.)

Calling for Help

3. Whenever necessary, one should call for help (such as an ambulance or mobile intensive care unit) immediately when someone's life is in danger. It is even permissible to call more than one agency if one may arrive sooner than the other.

4. When the situation is not extremely urgent and one has time to plan various methods, the following factors should be considered:

   a. who should call for help, and

   b. who should be called.

---

3 באר היטב ס״ק א׳. ושם במ״ב בשם הרדב״ז. וז״ל רבינו יונה באו״ה כלל ס׳ סעיף ח: ״ואם החולה עצמו רוצה להחמיר עליו אחרי שיודע שצריך לכך עליו נאמר ואך את דמכם אדרוש, ואל תהי צדיק הרבה, ולא דמי לדבר הנוגעת בכבוד השם יתברך שכתוב בסמ״ק שאדם יכול לוותר על נפשו, דהתם כתיב ביה ובכל נפשך וגם שואלין ממנו נפשו, ואפילו על השואל אמרו רז״ל ששופך דמו, והרי אפילו ספק נפשות דוחה שבת״ עכ״ל.

4 כפי המבואר לעיל פרק 9 הגדרת חולי בהול.

5 על פי הגמ׳ ביומא דף פ״ג דאין עושין דברים הללו לא ע״י נכרים וכו׳ והובא להלכה בשו״ע סימן שכ״ח סעיף י״ב.

Who Should Call

The possibilities are as follows:

a. A non-Jew
b. A child
c. An adult Jew with a *shinui*
d. Two people together

5. *A non-Jew*. If the situation is not extremely urgent and a non-Jew is available, the best option is to ask the non-Jew for assistance, whether to call the hospital or a doctor, to order a taxi, or to drive the patient to the hospital.[6]

6. *A child*. When a non-Jew is not available, the next best option is to ask a child to call. It is best that the child's parents do not instruct the child to make the call; in a sense, this would be considered as if they themselves are desecrating Shabbos. Rather, one should instruct someone else's child. If there is no other option, it is better for a parent to instruct the child rather than have an adult perform the action, but it is preferable that the mother instruct the child rather than the father. It is also preferable, if possible, to use a very young child who has not reached an age where he can be educated, but where this is not possible, any boy under the age of thirteen or any girl under the age of twelve may be asked.[7]

7. *An adult Jew with a shinui.* When there is no child or non-Jew available, it is permissible and incumbent on any adult Jew to desecrate Shabbos on behalf of the person whose life is in danger. However, where no undue delay will result if the action is done with a *shinui*, this is preferable to performing the action in the normal manner.[8] (See chapter 14, "Using a Telephone on Shabbos," where various suggestions are given with regard to using a telephone with a *shinui*.)

---

6 כמבואר לעיל פרק 3.
7 כמבואר לעיל בפרק 4 בעניין מלאכה ע״י קטן.
8 כמבואר לעיל פרק 4.

8. *Two people.* If two people together perform an action that one person could have done alone, no Torah prohibition has been transgressed, only a rabbinical one. Thus, wherever possible, any Shabbos desecration should be done by two people together since this minimizes the severity of the desecration.[9]

Whom to Call

9. In certain situations, such as when dealing with a chronic condition, it is more important to first call and consult the patient's doctor rather than to take him directly to the hospital. It is permissible to telephone the patient's doctor or even travel to his home for this purpose, especially if the doctor is familiar with the patient's condition. One should then proceed in accordance with the doctor's instructions.

10. If a person is injured, it is preferable to take him to a nearby first-aid facility rather than a more distant hospital if both facilities can provide equivalent care. Similarly, if a licensed paramedic is available nearby, he should be called instead of desecrating Shabbos by unnecessary travel, unless the matter is very urgent and the injury appears to be serious, in which case an ambulance or any other means should be used.

11. It is important to note that an untrained person should not offer help in transporting a person who has suffered an injury where there is the possibility of broken bones or neck injury. Doing so may endanger the person even more. Only people trained in moving an injured person should do so. Many people, unaware of the dangers involved, in spite of the best intentions often do more harm than good and cause irreversible damage, God forbid.

---

9 כמבואר לעיל בפרק 4 בעניין מלאכה ע״י שניים.

Chapter 11
Traveling on Shabbos

1. Many situations require transporting a patient to the hospital on Shabbos. However, not all of these situations call for ambulance service or Hatzalah assistance, such as when the patient is not in urgent need of first aid. Similarly, a doctor who must go to the hospital to treat a patient but has time to plan out the best way possible should attempt to minimize his Shabbos desecration. For example, if there is time to walk to the hospital, he should do so — but not if this will affect his ability to treat the patient in the most efficient manner possible.

   The issue of traveling on Shabbos includes the question of what type of transportation and which drivers are preferable for the trip and whether the driver can be paid and how.

Choosing the Mode of Transportation

2. Rav Yitzchak Zilberstein elaborates on this subject in *Toras HaYoledes* (ch. 13). Here are some of his conclusions:

3. The order of preference for transportation is as follows:

   a. A bicycle, within city limits (for going out of town, a non-Jew should be employed)[1]

---

1 ברכיבה באופניים יש לנתק מראש את הדינמו שלא ידליק את המנורה אם נוסע במקום מואר או ביום.

b. A car driven by a non-Jew — preferable to a bus driven by a Jew who is traveling in any case

c. A horse-drawn buggy driven by a non-Jew

d. A bus driven by a Jew who is traveling in any case

e. A motorcycle — preferable to a car driven by a Jew

f. A car with a diesel engine — preferable to one that runs on gasoline

g. An ambulance — preferable to calling a Jewish taxi service

h. A private vehicle — preferable to calling a Jewish taxi service

i. A car that has fewer pistons, a smaller engine, and fewer lights

j. A manual drive — preferable to an automatic

k. A car with an air-based cooling system — preferable to water-based

l. An observant driver — preferable to a nonobservant one

Questions and Answers

The following questions were brought to Rav Zilberstein:

4. *Question*: If one has to choose between a nearby Jewish taxi service and a non-Jewish taxi that one has to order by phone, which is preferable?

   Answer: If the Jewish taxi driver is traveling to the hospital in any case (for example, if he works for a shuttle service), it is better to use that taxi rather than calling a non-Jewish one. But if the Jewish driver will be making a special trip to the hospital, it is better to order a non-Jewish taxi or ambulance service.[2]

5. *Question*: If there are two local ambulance services, one manned by nonobservant Jewish drivers and workers and the other by non-Jews, the accepted practice, in a non-urgent situation, is to phone the non-Jewish service. The problem arises when the person calling does not

2 עיין תורת היולדת פי״ג הערה י״א. ועיין בשש״כ פרק מ׳ הערה קס״ב בשם הגרש״ז אויערבאך זצ״ל, שאם יש לפנינו מכונית של מחלל שבת המוכן לנסוע עמו, ואין צורך לחפש אחריה, יסיע את החולה בה ולא יטלפן, שהרי העבירה של הנהג תהיה רק אח״כ בשובו לביתו. עיי״ש.

have the telephone number of the non-Jewish service and he can obtain it in one of three ways:

a. He can call Information, which employs Jewish workers (if he is living in Israel), to obtain the number of the non-Jewish ambulance service. This option would require making two phone calls.
b. He can call a non-Jewish hospital or an emergency center that employs non-Jewish operators to obtain the phone number and then dial the non-Jewish ambulance service. This option also involves making two phone calls.
c. He can call the Jewish ambulance service. This requires only one phone call.

Which option should he choose?

Answer: The second option is the preferred one even though two phone calls are needed; the advantage of using a non-Jewish driver outweighs the disadvantage of making two calls. Moreover, calling the Jewish ambulance service will more than likely involve many acts that are unnecessary for the needs of the patient, such as filling out forms and the like.[3] The call should be made with a *shinui.*

Of course, this discussion is relevant mainly in Israel, where the telephone and emergency services are generally manned by Jewish personnel. In countries where these services are staffed by non-Jews, the course of action is straightforward.

Carrying

6. With regard to bringing the necessary forms, records, and money to pay the driver or the doctor,[4] one must take into consideration the prohibition of carrying on Shabbos. This problem exists both when carrying things from the house into the taxi and from the taxi into the hospi-

---

3 כ״כ לי הגרי״י זילברשטיין שליט״א, שאם אפשר להתקשר לנכרי ע״י שנוי, פשוט שצריך לעשות כך, כדי למנוע אח״כ נסיעה ע״י ישראל שיעבור על אלפי הבערות בנסיעתו.

4 עצם טלטול הכסף הוא איסור דרבנן משום מוקצה, והתשלום גם הוא מדרבנן משום מיקח וממכר, דשרי לצורך חולה.

tal, or even carrying articles from one place to another outside. Let us examine how Shabbos desecration can be minimized in this area.

7. Where time is of the essence and an emergency exists, this question should not be considered at all.[5]

8. When there is time to plan out one's actions and there is an *eiruv* around the city or neighborhood, even those who are normally stringent regarding the use of an *eiruv* may be lenient and rely on it if the carrying is for the needs of a sick person.[6]

9. If there is no *eiruv* either in the city or in the vicinity of the hospital, but the hospital grounds are surrounded by a fence or wall and the car enters this enclosed area, there is no prohibition of carrying on the hospital grounds. If the area is not enclosed, the following methods should be employed:

    a. If a non-Jew is available, one should ask the non-Jew to carry the items from the house into the taxi and from the taxi into the hospital. If a non-Jew is not available, one should carry the items with a *shinui*, such as placing them under one's hat or shirt.

    b. When carrying from the house into the car, one should enter the car without stopping. Similarly, when one leaves the car to enter the hospital, he should not stop if he is carrying until he has entered the building.[7]

---

5 כמבואר לעיל בפרק 9 סעיף 2.

6 נושא זה ארוך ומסועף ביותר, אך נצטט קטע מביאור הלכה השייך לכללות העניין. בביאור הלכה סי׳ שמ״ה האריך לבאר מחלוקת מרן השו״ע ומג״א והט״ז דפליגי בהו גדולי הפוסקים ראשונים ואחרונים. וסיים שם בבה״ל וז״ל: מכל זה מוכח שיש להחמיר כדעה ראשונה (אך במקום שיש עוד צד להקל יש לסמוך על הסברה אחרונה, כ״כ האליה רבה עיי״ש), מ״מ אין בנו כח למחות ביד המקילים שהם סומכים על הפוסקים העומדים בשיטת בה״ג ורש״י, אבל כל ירא שמיים בוודאי להחמיר לעצמו שבזמננו יש גם כן רשות הרבים מן התורה וממילא אין לסמוך על עירוב של צורת הפתח דבעינן דווקא דלתות עכ״ל עיי״ש באורך.

7 באופן זה הופכת ההוצאה להיות מדרבנן, כדין הוצאה מרשות היחיד לרשות היחיד דרך רשות הרבים, המבואר בשו״ע הגר״ז סי׳ שמ״ז סעיף ט׳ דהוי שבות בעלמא. ובפרט שעל פי רוב אין מדובר ברשות הרבים ממש אלא בכרמלית, שאז ההוצאה נחשבת כשבות דשבות במקום חולי דשרי כפי המבואר בשו״ע סי׳ ש״ו סעיף ה׳ אף בחולה במקצת.

Paying the Driver

10. There are three situations in which one is confronted with the problem of payment for transportation:

    a. When taking an ambulance

    b. When taking a taxi

    c. When taking a bus

    In general, it is always preferable to convince the driver to wait until after Shabbos for payment. If the driver refuses, or he insists on writing down identification information and the driver is a Jew, it is better to pay him right away so he will not transgress the prohibition of writing on Shabbos.[8] This can be avoided, however, by handing over some form of ID or by giving the driver a blank check with one's name and address to hold as collateral until *motza'ei Shabbos*. If the driver nevertheless insists on immediate payment, one should consider the best way to pay him.

Paying a Bus Driver

11. There are three ways to arrange payment for bus transportation on Shabbos:

    a. paying cash;

    b. paying with a bus ticket, if available (common in Israel, where one pays in advance for a certain number of trips, often with some kind of discount); and

    c. paying with a monthly pass, if available (this refers to a card purchased at the beginning of the month that is shown to the bus driver in lieu of paying cash for each bus trip; one can purchase such passes in Israel).

The ideal way of paying is with a monthly pass, since this does not fit the halachic definition of a purchase.

---

8 בדין אין אומרים לו לאדם חטא כדי שיזכה חברך, יש לדון אם שייך בענייננו.

Paying with cash appears to be preferable to using a bus ticket in which the bus driver punches a hole (as is done in Israel). Since each driver punches a unique hole, this may involve the prohibition of writing on Shabbos.[9]

If one is paying cash, one should, if possible, carry exact change, even if by doing so he will carry a larger quantity of coins or bills, in order to avoid having to accept change from the driver. If this is not possible, he should not accept the change unless he needs it for reasons of *pikuach nefesh*.

If the driver is Jewish, the passenger should request that he not tear off a receipt for him.

Paying a Taxi Driver

12. It is easier to make an arrangement with a taxi driver than with a bus driver, either by depositing with him some identification or a valuable item for collateral. If the driver insists on receiving payment, he may be paid in the same manner as described above regarding a bus driver.

    If the driver is Jewish, it is better to arrange a price in advance rather than using the meter even if one will end up paying more. It is certainly forbidden to ask the driver to print out a receipt, even if this causes a monetary loss to the patient or the doctor who is traveling to perform his medical duties.

    As we have noted, all these limitations apply only to a Jewish driver. If the driver is not Jewish, he may run the meter, but one should still refrain from asking him to print out a receipt.[10]

Paying an Ambulance Service

13. The accepted practice in Israel is to give the ambulance driver identification and to arrange payment after Shabbos. If, in spite of this,

---

9 וכתב לי הגרי״י זילברשטיין שליט״א שאם אפשר לבקש מהנהג שיקרע את המשבצת שבכרטיסיה ולא יעבור איסור רושם זה עדיף על טלטול המעות ותשלום שהוא נראה יותר כמיקח וממכר.

10 מסתבר שאין היתר לבקש קבלה דבזה עושה האינו יהודי מלאכה מדאורייתא לצורך הישראלי ואין בזה כלל צורך החולי. אך מ״מ אם הנהג על דעת עצמו הדפיס קבלה נראה שאין לחוש לאיסור ליקח את הקבלה, אך מ״מ אם אין זה הפסד מרובה לא יטול הקבלה משום מוקצה מחמת חסרון כיס.

the driver insists on being paid immediately and filling out all the usual forms, as is done during the week, one should try the best he can to persuade the driver to postpone filling out the forms until after Shabbos. But if he fails to do so and the driver insists, he should sign with his left hand and not with his usual signature.

Writing a Check

14. Unessential writing should be minimized. Therefore, even if one must write a check, he should not fill in the date or the name of the payee. Also, there is no need for him to fill in the amount in words; just writing in the number is sufficient. If the bank will not accept a check signed with an illegible scribble, he may sign his name unless it is possible to locate the driver after Shabbos to exchange the check for a valid one.

15. If possible, one should avoid tearing the check out of the checkbook. Instead, he should give the recipient the entire checkbook and retrieve it from him after Shabbos. If this is not possible, he should not tear along the perforation but on the check stub itself, being careful to avoid tearing letters.

16. If the driver is not Jewish, one should ask the non-Jew to write out the check and tear it out of the checkbook. The check should be signed in the manner mentioned above (paragraph 13).

Chapter 12
Choosing a Hospital

1. The most competent hospital with the best staff suitable for the particular illness should be used, even if it is farther away from another hospital and traveling there will involve further Shabbos desecration.
2. Of course, if there is no need for a specialist, and a closer hospital offers the same expertise as a more distant one, the closer hospital is preferable.
3. There is a Torah prohibition against traveling more than twelve *mil* (approximately 11.5 kilometers or 7.2 miles) outside the city limits on Shabbos. In view of this, one is permitted to travel that far only if there is a very great need.[1] Therefore, if there is a hospital located less than twelve *mil* away, it is preferable. It makes no difference, in this instance, whether the driver is a Jew or a non-Jew; if one can travel to a closer hospital, it is better. It should also be noted that this prohibition applies only to traveling on the ground (by vehicle, bicycle, or on foot). The prohibition of traveling outside the "Shabbos border" does not apply to air travel.

---

1 דוגמא, יולדת שנרשמה ללידה בבית חולים מסוים, ורגילה ללדת שם ואין לה יישוב הדעת ורגיעה ללידה אלא בבית חולים זה — אף שהוא מרוחק יותר מ-י״ב מיל רשאית לנסוע לבית החולים הרחוק. דוגמא זו היא רק ביולדת שחז״ל למדונו עד כמה יש לחוש לרגיעתה.

4. One should not base the choice of hospitals on monetary considerations. For example, if the patient will receive a refund from his medical insurance from the more distant hospital but not from the closer one, he should still use the closer hospital on Shabbos. But if there are medical considerations, such as the patient's records being accessible in the more distant hospital, which might facilitate his treatment or minimize the need for additional tests, he may base his decision on these factors.

5. A more distant hospital should not be chosen because it meets a higher standard of kashrus or Shabbos observance. The exception to this rule is giving birth. If a woman feels more comfortable in a particular hospital because of any of these factors, she may choose to give birth in that hospital even if it is farther away.

6. All of the above applies whether the driver is Jewish or not. That is, even when using a non-Jewish driver, the more distant hospital should not be chosen because of monetary considerations,[2] and one should be careful not to leave the "Shabbos border" (twelve *mil;* see paragraph 3), unless the circumstances are dire.

---

2 כ״כ לי הגר״י זילברשטיין שליט״א שאף ע״י עכו״ם, לא התירו אמירה לעכו״ם שיעשה מלאכה מדאורייתא בגלל הפסד ממון.

Chapter 13

Choosing a Doctor and Seeking Medical Advice

1. It is difficult to lay down ironclad rules regarding the choice of a doctor, since many factors are involved. Nevertheless, the halachah does give us general guidelines as to what should be considered when choosing a doctor in general and on Shabbos in particular.

2. The first rule is to choose a properly licensed specialist.[1] He should have experience in the patient's illness and good recommendations by others he has treated, even if he doesn't have a world-renowned reputation or expertise in other areas of medicine.[2]

---

1 יש לצטט כאן את דברי הטור ביורה דעה סימן של״ו בעניין רשיון הרופא, זכיותיו וחובותיו וז״ל: ״לא יתעסק ברפואה אא״כ יהא בקי ויודע בחכמה ובמלאכה ולא יהא שם גדול ממנו, אבל כל שאינו יודע בטיב מלאכה זו לא יהא עוסק בה, וכן אם יש גדול ממנו לא יתעסק בה כלל, ק״ו משאר דינים והוראות שבתורה, דהיאך יורה בספק נפשות במקום שיש גדול ממנו. ואם לא נתעסק בה כלל ה״ז שופך דמים ובן גיהנם הוא בוודאי. ואם ריפא שלא ברשות ב״ד והזיק חייב בתשלומים אפילו אם הוא בקי וכ״ש באחד שאינו בקי שאין ב״ד מרשים למי שאינו בקי, אבל אם ריפא ברשות ב״ד וטעה והזיק פטור מדיני אדם וחייב בדיני שמים״. ועיין שם בבית יוסף שמקור דברי הטור הוא ברמב״ן בתורת האדם ושם מחמיר יותר שהגרסא שבידינו ״ואם נתעסק בה כלל שופך דמים הוא בוודאי״, ואמתעסק בה במקום שיש גדול ממנו קאי וכו׳, ולענין הדין מסיים הב״י תרווייהו איתנהו בודאי דזה וזה שופכי דמים הם.

2 בהקשר לזה נצטט מספר תורת היולדת פרק ח׳ בהערה ז״ל: ״במקרים שיש לבצע ניתוח שגרתי כגון שבר או אפנדיציט, נוהגים רבים לפנות לרופא מומחה ומפורסם, טועים העושים זאת, מאחר והרופא הרגיל אף שאינו מפורסם, מסוגל לטפל בניתוחים ביעילות רבה, אף יותר מהרופא המומחה, מאחר ועקב פרסומו עסוק הוא בעבודות מחקר ובדברים הקשים ואינו רגיל כל כך בניתוחים שגרתיים, ולכן בדרך כלל עדיף לפנות לרופא הרגיל לניתוחים אלו״. עכ״ל.

3. Where possible, the rules of modesty require choosing a male doctor to treat a man and a female doctor to treat a woman, especially for obstetrics and gynecology and intestinal ailments.[3] Jewish hospitals should be particularly sensitive to this issue — when possible, male staff should treat male patients and female staff should treat the women.[4]

4. On Shabbos, one must take into consideration two additional factors: distance and Shabbos observance on the part of the doctor. In order to minimize Shabbos desecration in terms of traveling, it is better to see a doctor who lives close by.[5] Also, it is preferable to go to a Shabbos-observant doctor who knows what is permitted and what is forbidden rather than a Jewish doctor who is not observant.[6] Of course, this ap-

---

3 ועיין בטושו״ע יורה דעה סי׳ של״ה סעיף י׳ ז״ל בחולי מעיים אין האיש משמש את האשה אבל האשה משמשת את האיש ע״כ. ונחלקו הפוסקים בטעם הדבר. בדרכי משה כתב דהטעם הוא משום גנאי ופריצות שיותר יש פריצות וגנאי כשהאיש משמש לנקיבה בקינוח ודברים כאלו, מאילו הנקיבה המשמשת לאיש, כי יצרו של איש גדול משל אשה. וכן פרשו בש״ך ובט״ז. וע״ע בברכי יוסף שמבאר החילוק להלכה בין הרהור דאיש להרהור דאשה עיי״ש. ודע דכל הנ״ל היינו מדינא, אבל מגדרי הצניעות ובמיוחד בדורנו בעוה״ר שפרוצים בעריות ובאבזרייהו יש לתקן הדבר והרחק מן הכיעור ומן הדומה לו. וע״ע בהערה ד׳. בספר טהרת הבית הקצר סי׳ י״ב ס״ק צ׳ כתב וז״ל: אשה חולה שצריכה להיבדק אצל רופא מומחה, אם הדבר נחוץ ביותר כגון שהיא חולה ממש, ואין שם אשה רופאה מומחית, מותר להיבדק על ידי הרופא, אפילו אם בודק אותה באותו מקום, אולם אם אין בכך צורך גמור אלא מיחוש בעלמא שאפשר להתגבר עליו, וכן אם יש שם רופאה מומחית הבקיאה בדבר, אסור לה בהחלט להיבדק אצל איש רופא וצריכה לשמור על הצניעות של בת ישראל, שעל זה אמרו חז״ל ולמען תהיה יראתו על פניכם לבלתי תחטאו — זו הבושה. ולכן אסור לנשים ללכת להיבדק בדיקה שגרתית בתקופת ההיריון אצל איש רופא להיווכח בהתפתחות העובר, ובפרט כשיכולות ללכת להיבדק אצל רופאה. ואפילו אם צריכה לשלם לרופאה שכר, ואילו הרופא עושה זאת בחינם, צריכה ללכת אצל הרופאה, ואסורה ללכת אל הרופא. ושומע לנו ישכון בטח. עכ״ל.

4 נצטט את דבריו של ספר ״קצות השולחן״ סי׳ קל״ה ס״ק ט׳ ז״ל: והנה בזמן הזה מסרו הפקוח לנשים ומלמדים אותן בבתי החולים לטפל עם החולים וקורין להם ״אחות בית החולים״ ולהן נמסר להוציא לפועל פקודות הרופאים לעשות זריקות וכל כיוצא בזה, נראה דאין חשש שמא יתעצלו או יפשעו, כיון שנכנסו ביחוד בעול הזה של הצלת נפשות החולים, ועינינו רואות שממלאות תפקידן בזריזות. ברם דא עקא, שבכל בתי החולים אפילו החרדים משרתות אחיות את הגברים החולים, ומה יעשה החולה, הרי הוא שבוי בתוך בית החולים ובעל כרחו הוא נכנע לסדרים שלהם, ויש שנדמה שלחולה הכל מותר, ורק יחידי סגולה אפשר להם להשיג מבוקשם שרק גברים יטפלו בהם, וזו היא אחת מהעבירות שהזמן גרמא וחובה על ראשי הצבור לתקן הדבר. עכ״ל.

5 דדמי למי שיש לו תרופות בתוך ביתו ונוסע לבית מרקחת לקנות את אותן תרופות ודאי שהוי מחלל שבת כדין מי שיש לו תאנה קצוצה לפניו וקוצץ תאנה אחרת — אפילו עבור חולה שיש בו סכנה — דחייב.

6 עיין בנשמת אברהם ח״א עמ׳ קפ״ו שבירר ענין זה בהרחבה ונימק דבריו בשם הגרש״ז אויערבאך

plies only if both doctors are equally competent in treating the patient. But if one of them is more familiar with the patient's case, or if there is some medical reason why that one is preferable, this is the overriding consideration.[7]

5. A doctor should not be chosen on the basis of monetary considerations. For example, if the fee of the doctor who lives close by is not covered by the patient's insurance and the more distant doctor's fee is, he may not choose the more distant doctor because of this. Monetary considerations are not included in *pikuach nefesh* calculations, and one may not desecrate Shabbos for this purpose.[8]

6. Therefore, if the patient must travel to see a doctor on Shabbos, he may not extend his journey in order to see a doctor who charges less.[9]

Choosing a Doctor with a Better Character

7. The *sefer Toras HaYoledes* (ch. 8, responsum 2) discusses the following question, which was asked of *gedolei hador*:

   A person requires an eye operation, and he must choose between two doctors. One is a world-renowned expert at the top of his field, but he is very unfriendly toward his patients and arrogant. The other doctor, though competent, is not known to be as great an expert as the first doctor. However, he is kind and gentle with his patients and does not regard it beneath his honor to consult with his colleagues and to follow their advice.

   The *gedolei hador* responded that it is better to choose the doctor who is humble and has good character traits even if he is not consid-

---

שליט״א, וז״ל: עדיף טפי לעשות המלאכה ע״י שומר מצוות, כי ע״י עבריין שכוונתו רק עבור בצע כסף אע״ג דקעביד מצוה, מ״מ הו״ל כמתכוון לבשר חזיר ועלה בידו בשר טלה שמבואר בקידושין ל״ב תוסי׳ ד״ה דמחיל, דגם ע״ז יש משום לפני עיור עיי״ש. וכתב לי ע״ז הגאון רבי יצחק זילברשטיין שליט״א בזה״ל: יש מקום להעדיף את זה שאינו שומר שבת, מאחר ושומר השבת יפסיד עשה דשבתון כמבואר בדברי רבי שמעון שקאפ זצ״ל, וגם הלב חיים ח״ג פ״ה כתב שהמחלל שבת לצורך פיקוח נפש איבד מצות עשה דשבתון ואילו זה שלא שומר בין כך מאבדם. ועין מש״כ בתורת היולדת פרק נ״ט הערה א׳ ב׳.

7 פשוט כן, וכ״כ בנשמת אברהם שם בשם השש״כ פל״ב סעיף ל״ח.

8 עיין בספר תורת היולדת פ״ח סעיף א׳. ובשש״כ פל״ב סעיף ל״ב.

9 שכל כמה שאפשר למעט ממעטים בחילול שבת.

ered as expert as his colleague; his counterpart's bad traits might cause him to make mistakes and act in an irresponsible manner.

This question has ramifications on Shabbos — it is possible that one may desecrate Shabbos to call on the less expert doctor even if using the more expert but arrogant doctor will not involve such desecration.[10]

A Jewish Doctor versus a Non-Jewish One

8. According to some opinions, it is always better to use a Jewish doctor rather than a non-Jewish one, since the non-Jew may cause harm to the patient.[11] However, in a hospital situation, where Jewish and non-Jewish doctors work side by side, we can assume the non-Jewish doctor will not discriminate against his Jewish patients. Moreover, if the non-Jewish doctor is more competent in treating the illness than his Jewish counterpart, it is preferable to use the non-Jewish doctor.[12] (Also, now-

---

10 עיין שם בתורת היולדת בשם הגרי״י אברמסקי זצ״ל, ששאל מדוע מתעניינים חולים אודות רופאים ומבררים היטב סגולותיהם, ואין מוסרים עצמם לטיפולם טרם קבלו עליהם מידע טוב ונאמן, ואילו העוברים אורחות ימים ונתיבי אויר אינם מתעניינים כלל וכלל על טיבם של רבי החובלים או הטייסים. האם יודעים הם את מלאכתם אם לאו? והשיב, הטייס גם הוא נוסע במטוס ועל כן אין צורך להתעניין אודותיו. ומכאן שרופא המרגיש שהוא עצמו ״נוסע״ עם החולה וקושר גורלו עמו דינו כדין הטייס, ומותר לחלל שבת ולהביאו. עכ״ל.

11 על פי דברי הגמ׳ יומא פ״ג, ״ואין עושים דברים הללו לא ע״י נכרים ולא ע״י כותים ולא ע״י קטנים אלא ע״י גדולי ישראל וחכמיהם״ עיי״ש. וביותר נאמר בגמ׳ במסכת עבודה זרה דף כ״ז ע״ב שכל מכה שמחללים עליה את השבת אין מתרפאים מהן (מרופאים שאינם יהודים). בראשונים על הסוגיה שם, הרא״ש והר״ן ועוד סוכמו הדינים הללו לפי חלוקה זו:

א) חולה שיש בו סכנה אין מתרפאים מהם, משום שיכולים להשתמט שלא הם גרמו לו המיתה, ומסוכן היה ולפיכך מת.

ב) בטיפול שאין בו עניין מיוחד כגון הקזת דם (ריבדא דכוסילתא) — ג״כ אין מתרפאים מהם, משום שאם ימיתו את החולה לא יתלו הדבר במעשיהם משום שברפואה זו אין בה אומנות מיוחדת או מסוכנת ויאמרו כי בלאו הכי הגיע זמנו למות.

ג) אבל בחולה שאין בו סכנה לא מרעים אומנותם ומותר להתרפאות מהם שאין להם במה לתלות, ומשתדלים לרפאות כפי אומנותם.

ובהגהות אשר״י מוסיף שם וז״ל: ונראה בעיני דכל זה בחינם אבל בשכר הכל שרי דחייש להפסדיה דאגריה ולא קטיל ליה, והאי דלא אוקי מתני׳ הכי משום דלא משמע ליה לישנא הכי אבל האמת שבשכר הכל שרי. מא״ז ע״כ.

בעל המאור מחדש עוד דבר, וז״ל: שאם אדם חשוב הוא החולה או שהעכו״ם הוא רופא מומחה, מותר אפילו בדבר שיש בו סכנה. ובלבד שלא יהא העכו״ם שונא, כאותו מין לרבי אבהו. עכ״ל.

12 עיין בב״י סי׳ תר״ח ובמגן אברהם שם ס״ק א׳. ועין עוד לעיל בהערה 11 בסופה מש״כ בשם בעל המאור.

adays, when all doctors require certification, there is no longer any fear that they might harm Jewish patients.[13])

9. If a doctor demands immediate payment, the same rules that apply to paying a driver on Shabbos apply here (see chapter 11, "Traveling on Shabbos").

Getting Medical Advice

10. It is customary for the patient or his relatives to consult other doctors or well-known rabbis before agreeing to a medical procedure or operation. If the patient's life is in danger, and time is of the essence, one may desecrate Shabbos to obtain a second opinion or rabbinical advice.[14]

Desecrating Shabbos to Receive a Blessing

11. Halachic authorities differ as to whether one may desecrate Shabbos to receive a blessing from a tzaddik on behalf of a person in a life-threatening situation.[15] Their conclusion is that one should not desecrate Shabbos for this purpose even when one will only be performing an action that is rabbinically prohibited. As our Sages note, "[On] Shabbos we [refrain from] earnest prayer and trust that healing will come speedily."[16]

    Nevertheless, if there is a possibility that the patient will be very upset if one doesn't seek a tzaddik's blessing, even if one explains to

---

13 וכתב לי הגר״י זילברשטיין שליט״א בזה״ל: כבר כתב הש״ך ביו״ד סי׳ קנ״ה ס״ק ג׳: ״אבל מומחה דהיינו אומן לא מרע לאומנותיה״ ובימינו כל הרופאים שיש להם רשיון ומתפרנסים מעבודתם הרי הם בכלל מומחה ולא מרע לאומנותיה, ופוק חזי מאי עמא דבר. (פרט ליולדת יעוין תורת היולדת פ״ח הערה ה׳) אך אם שניהם שווים יש להעדיף את הישראלי בגלל שמצווה לתת לו להשתכר, וכמבואר במשנה ברורה סי׳ תרמ״ח ס״ה ובשעה״צ ס״ק ע״ו, דכתיב או קנה מיד אמיתך ופרש״י והוא מהספרא ״אם תרצה לקנות קנה מיד אמיתך״. וה״ה בנידוננו.

14 פשוט, וכ״כ בתורת היולדת פט״ו סעיף ב׳.

15 עיין בנשמת אברהם ח״א סי׳ ש״א אות ידי שהביא פוסקים לכאן ולכאן עיי״ש ואכמ״ל בזה.

16 המהרש״ם בתשובה ח״ה סימן רכ״ה כתב וז״ל: עובדא ידענא בעיר מולדתי בזלאטשוב שהיה חולה מסוכן, ובאותו זמן היה מו״ר הגה״ק מוהר״ש אבד״ק בעלז זצ״ל משובתי שבת קודש בבראד והתיר דיין אחד לכתוב ע״י עכו״ם בשבת קודש שם החולה ואמו לשלוח לבראד (כדי שהצדיק יתפלל עליו) והרעיש הגאון מהר״ש קלוגר זצ״ל ופסל את הדיין מלהורות עוד, וכבוד מו״ר הגה״ק הנ״ל נתרעם ג״כ על הכותב וכו׳ ובכל כה״ג אין להקל ובפרט בדור הזה אין להקל מכמה טעמים, ועל כיוצא בזה אמרו שבת היא מלזעוק וכו׳ יכולה היא שתרחם וכו׳ עכ״ל. וע״ע

him that it is forbidden to desecrate Shabbos for this purpose, and his condition will worsen if his request for a blessing is not heeded, one may ask a non-Jew to drive to the tzaddik or send an urgent telegram (if the postal workers are non-Jews).[17]

במנחת שבת סי' פ"ד אות כ"ט. ובשו"ת ציץ אליעזר ח"ד סימן ד' אות י"ז, ובח"ח סימן ט"ו פ"ח אות ז', ובח"ט סימן י"ז פ"ג אות א-ג, ובחלק י"א סימן ס"א אות ד'.

17 כ"כ בנשמת אברהם שם, וע"ע בילקוט יוסף שבת ד' עמוד רכ"ו, דאם אפשר להטעות את החולה שקיימו את בקשתו והודיעו לצדיק — יש לעשות כן, ובמוצאי שבת יודיעו לצדיק ויבקשו את ברכתו.

Chapter 14
Using a Telephone on Shabbos

Note: All of the strategies described in this chapter are to be used only when the situation is not extremely urgent and there is time to work out the best way to proceed. But when time is of the essence, one should not waste time devising strategies, but use the simplest and fastest method.

1. It is permissible to phone a doctor or an ambulance on Shabbos for a *choleh sheyeish bo sakanah* provided that it is necessary and there is no other way to summon help.[1] One may even call when there is doubt whether or not the doctor is at home at that time.[2]

2. It is permissible to call the doctor even if there is time to leave the patient alone and walk to the doctor's home. Since the patient may panic if left alone, it is permissible to desecrate Shabbos to make the telephone call. But if someone else is available to stay with the patient, and the situation is not urgent, it is preferable to get the doctor without desecrating Shabbos in any manner.

3. If a doctor's telephone rings on Shabbos, he may answer it, since the call may be for the needs of a *choleh sheyeish bo sakanah*, a dangerously ill

---

1 פרק זה מבוסס ברובו ככולו על הספרים נשמת אברהם ח״א סי׳ של״ח, וספר תורת היולדת פרק ט׳ — אשר בררו ולבנו עניינים אלו כדבעי, עם תוספת נופך בעזר ה׳ יתברך.

2 נשמת אברהם שם.

person.[3] (Some doctors leave on an answering machine for Shabbos.[4])

4. Using a telephone on Shabbos involves a number of problems. These include:
   a. picking up the receiver to get a dial tone,
   b. dialing,
   c. talking,
   d. hanging up, and
   e. choosing which phone to use.

Picking up the Receiver

5. Picking up the receiver to get a dial tone or using the speakerphone should be done in the order of preference discussed in chapter 10, namely, first by asking a non-Jew, then a child, then through a *shinui* (such as using one's elbow or the back of the hand),[5] and, finally, by

---

3 נשמת אברהם שם בשם שש״כ ועוד, ואמנם בשו״ת ציץ אליעזר ח״ח סי׳ ט״ו פ״ז מחלק בזה דרק אם רוב הפונים אליו בדרך כלל הם שומרי הדת — דבזה משוכנע שהצלצול עבור פקוח נפש — מותר לו בעצמו לענות על קריאת הטלפון, הא לאו הכי אין להתיר לו אלא ע״י גוי או קטן, עיי״ש. אך רבים מהאחרונים חולקים על מגבלה זו ובכל אופן מותר לרופא לענות לטלפון. יעויין בספר הלכה ורפואה ח״ג , וע״ע בספר ליקוטי הלכות סימן שכ״ח סעיף ה׳. וע״ע בשו״ת באר משה ח״ו קונטרס אלקטרי סי׳ נ״ג.

4 שאלה: האם רופא יכול להפעיל מערב שבת בביתו מכשיר ״מזכירה אלקטרונית״ שתקבל שיחות בשבת, ונוסחת ההודעה של המזכירה תהיה כך: ״נא מסור הודעתך ושאלתך מהרופא, באם הרופא בביתו יענה לך מיד״. והרופא שומע את הודעת המטלפן ועושה את השיקול שלו אם הדבר מצדיק חילול שבת יורה לשואל את אשר עליו לעשות, ובאם אין הצדקה — יתעלם מהשיחה.

תשובה: בספר שו״ת ציץ אליעזר (שם) הציע שמוטב אם יהיה לרופא מס׳ טלפון מיוחד לשימוש בעת חולי של סכנה שיתקשרו לטלפון זה ואז יוכל להרים את השפופרת ללא כל חשש. ואכן זו עצה טובה. אך יתכן וגם עצה זו של שימוש ב״מזכירה אלקטרונית״ טובה מאוד שעדיף לשמוע את הבקשה מבלי לעבור על שום איסור.

אלא שעדיין עצה זו לכאורה היא אליה וקוץ בה שאם המטלפן יראה שהרופא לא עונה לשאלתו ודאי יסבור ששאלתו אינה בגדר פקוח נפש ועשוי לבוא לידי סכנה, ומה שהרופא לא ענה לו, באמת הסיבה משום שלא היה בביתו באותו זמן, א״כ מנין ידע המטלפן את אשר עליו לעשות נמצא שאת הרופא תקנתי ואת החולה לא תקנתי. ולכן הודגש לעיל בנוסח ההודעה שאם הרופא בביתו יענה לך מיד, מכאן יסיק המטלפן שאם לא עונה לו הרופא אין זאת אומרת שפנייתו אינה מוגדרת כפקוח נפש.

ואמנם ישנם עוד רעיונות שונות לפיתוח מכשיר זה, אך יש להתייעץ עם טכנאים שונים על כל, ועוד חזון למועד.

5 אופן השינוי: הרמת השפופרת כלאחר יד במרפקו או בגב היד וכדומה, ולאחר שהרים השפופרת ונוצר הקשר יכול להחזיקה כרגיל. ודע שבספר שו״ת אור לציון ח״ב פרק לו אות ג׳ כתב דאין

using two people to pick up the receiver. (After one hears the dial tone, one can hold the receiver in the ordinary manner.)

Dialing

6. Dialing should also be done according to the order of priorities listed in chapter 10. One can dial with a *shinui* by using a toothpick to press the keys or to turn the dial;[6] one should not dial directly with one's fingers. (When using a rotary phone, after dialing one should allow the dial to return to its place by itself and not move it back with one's finger.[7])

Talking

7. Once on the phone, one is not required to consider if each word is really necessary. He may say anything that pertains to the patient, down to the smallest detail, since any detail may affect the treatment and perhaps even save the doctor the need to make a personal visit to the patient. Similarly, when phoning for a taxi, he should be sure to explain in detail how to reach the patient's home.

   At the conclusion of the conversation, it is permissible to say "goodbye" or "thank you," but matters that are not relevant to the patient's care should not be discussed.[8]

Hanging Up

8. At the conclusion of a phone conversation, one normally returns the receiver to its cradle. On Shabbos, there are various rules regarding this

---

צורך בשינוי כלל. וע״ע לעיל פרק 4 הערה 2 משי״כ בזה.

6 החיוג עצמו סוגר ופותח מעגלים חשמליים, ויבואר לקמן בהערה 11 ומשי״כ שיחייג בקיסם, כ״כ בספר תורת היולדת פרק ט׳ ובהערה ד׳ כתב וז״ל: כמבואר בשבת דף ק״מ לגבי שופתא דטומא דהיינו קנה של שום שאם מערבבים ובוחשים בו הוי שינוי, מאחר ובימות בחול בוחשים ביד. עכ״ל.

7 שבזה עצם החיוג נעשה ע״י גרמה, שהרי אין החיוג נוצר אלא כשחוזרת החוגה למקומה, וזו נעשתה ממילא ע״י הקפיץ שבחוגה. וזו סיבה גדולה לשימוש בטלפון עם חוגה. וע״ע בשו״ת מנחת שלמה סי׳ ט׳ שכתב כן.

8 מבואר בנשמת אברהם שם ובתורת היולדת שם.

action, depending on the type of telephone and system being used.

a. In one type of system, if the caller does not hang up, the recipient cannot use his phone. Thus, if the call was made to a doctor or a medical center that must have the phone available for other urgent callers, the receiver must be replaced at the end of the conversation. However, if the recipient has no further need for his phone, the caller should not hang up.

b. In other systems, once the recipient hangs up, the connection is broken after a few moments and the phone can be used again. Where this kind of system is used, it is forbidden for the caller to hang up even if he called a doctor or medical center.[9] This, of course, applies only if the caller does not expect to receive any calls that pertain to the patient's needs. But if he does expect such calls, he is obligated to hang up.

It should be noted that in the second system, if the caller does not hang up, a beeping signal sounds indicating that the phone has not been replaced. Although this may involve the rabbinical prohibition of causing a loud sound, this passive act is much less serious than actively hanging up the phone.[10]

9. When replacing the receiver (when allowed, as explained in the previous paragraph), it should be done in the order of preference described in chapter 10 (non-Jew, child, *shinui*, two people).

---

9 וכ״כ בשו״ת אור לציון ח״ב פרק ל״ו שאלה י״ז. אולם מוקד עזרה ראשונה או רופא חייבים להחזיר השפופרת למקומה כדי לקבל שיחות נוספות, ועי״ע בשו״ת באר משה ח״ו קונטרס אלקטרי סי׳ נ״ג.

10 עוד כתב בנשמת אברהם סי׳ של״ח סעיף א׳ — באופן שאפשר להחזיר את השפופרת כנ״ל באופן הראשון — אם מקבל השיחה מחזיר את השפופרת בראשונה, יש ונדלקת נורה במרכזיה הטלפונית והיא כבה רק אחרי שיחזיר המטלפן את השפופרת למקומה, ולכן מה טוב אם יחזיר המטלפן את השפופרת למקומה בראשונה, ורק לאחר מכן יחזירה מקבל השיחה, משום שאז לא תדלק כל נורה. (שש״כ פל״ב הערה קי״ד). עוד כתב בספר מעשה חושב ח״א סי׳ ב׳ שישנו סוג של מכשירי טלפון שבתוכם נדלקת נורת להט (נגד) שלוהטת לזמן קצר, והיא נועדה למנוע זרימת חשמל גדולה במכשיר ובמרכזיה כאשר קיים מרחק קטן בין מכשיר הטלפון למרכזיה, וככל שהמרחק גדול יותר נחלש להט רגעי זה, וכשקיים מרחק מסוים אין הנורה מתלהטת כלל.

אך לאחר בירור עם מהנדסי טלפון נודע שכיום כמעט ואין מהמכשירים האלו, מכשירים אלו היו בעבר עם חוגה ועם ניצוצות, כהיום המכשירים החדישים (גם עם חוגה) — לא מצוי בהם נורת להט.

Choosing a Telephone

10. Due to the proliferation of different types of telephones today, it is important to know which phones are better to use for placing calls on Shabbos.

11. The following types of telephones are available today:
    a. Rotary phones
    b. Touch-tone phones
    c. Touch-tone phones with redial feature
    d. Touch-tone phones with automatic redial
    e. Touch-tone phones with a flashing light
    f. Touch-tone phones with a screen
    g. Cellular phones with a light
    h. Telephones with a speakerphone feature
    i. Public telephones that work with coins or tokens
    j. Public telephones that work with a credit card or phone card

12. Here are a few general guidelines for using the various types of phones that are available today:
    a. In general, it is best to use simple phones that do not have lights, screens, or play music. However, medical centers, hospitals, or other emergency services that are likely to need the telephone on Shabbos should be equipped with the most advanced telephone system. The more advanced the system, the less Shabbos desecration is involved. For example, a phone with pulse dialing involves more desecration than that with tone dialing.[11]

---

11 יש להבחין בין שתי מערכות שונות המשדרות ומתרגמות את החיוג בטלפון: (א) מערכת הפועלת ע״י שליחת ״פולסים״. (ב) מערכת הפועלת ע״י שליחת ״טונים״.

ההבדל ביניהם: בשליחת פולסים ישנם מספר רב של פתיחת וסגירת מעגלים חשמליים, לדוגמא חיוג הספרה 8 ב״פולסים״ נוצרים 8 פתיחות וסגירות מעגלים חשמליים, וב״טונים״ נוצרת פתיחה וסגירה אחת, וכן על זה הסדר בכל ספרה לפי גודלה נוצרים יותר מעגלים חשמליים בפולסים, ואילו בטונים פעולה אחת בלבד.

מעבר לכך במערכת הבנויה על שליחת ״פולסים״ בחוגה מכנית המעגלים החשמליים נוצרים ע״י מעגלים מכניים הגורמים לניצוצות לעומת המערכת השניה הפועלת ע״י מעגלים

b. Some phones are connected to an internal (PBX) system, and if one wishes to make an outside call, the private system must connect him to the public system. Other phones are connected directly to the outside without having to go through the internal system. If one has to use the phone on Shabbos, it is preferable to use the direct connection rather than going through the internal system to be connected to an outside line.

c. It is better to use a rotary phone, since the rotary phone has no special features. Moreover, some say that phoning with a rotary phone is considered an act of *gramah*.[12]

d. A touch-tone phone with tone dialing is preferable to a phone with pulse dialing (see note 11).

e. There is a great advantage in using a phone with a redial feature since a complete number can be dialed with a single action.

f. Using a phone that has an automatic redial feature where the phone automatically redials until it is answered is even better than using the regular redial feature.

g. It is preferable to use a telephone without any screens or lights. If one must choose between a phone that has a redial feature and also has a screen or light and one that has no screen or light but does not have a redial feature, the latter is preferable.

אלקטרוניים שכידוע לא קיימים בהם ניצוצות. ישנם עוד שינויים מהותיים לגבי עוצמת הזרם בין המערכות הללו — אשר על כן יש להשתדל בכל מערכת שנבנית שעשויה לפעול כמטה חירום ולפעול גם בשבת, הן בבתי חולים, מעונות רופאים, מעונות חולים בדרגת סיכון או אפילו בכל בית מישראל — אם אפשר לצמצם את אפשרות החילול במקרה הצורך — ביצירת קשר טלפוני — ודאי יש לפעול ולבקש התקנה של מערכת הפועלת ע״י שליחת ״טונים״ עכ״פ כאופציה.

יש להעיר שמבחינה זו העדיפות לטלפון לחצנים גדולה יותר אם היא מחוברת ל״טונים״. לעומת טלפון עם חוגה שאינו יכול לפעול ולהתחבר לאופציה של שליחת ״טונים״.

12 לעיל בהערה 7 הבאנו שיטת הגרש״ז אויערבאך שליט״א במנחת שלמה סי׳ ט׳ הסובר שהחיוג ע״י חוגה חשיב לגרמא משום שהחוגה חוזרת למקומה מאליה ואחר שהחוגה חוזרת למקומה מתבצע החיוג. אך ראיתי באנציקלופדיה התלמודית נספח לערך החשמל עמ׳ תש״י בשם ספר מעשה חושב שהמחייג נדון כזורק חץ שהרי בסבבו את החוגה הוא מותח את הקפיץ ובסילוק אצבעו הוא משחרר אותו והרי זה כמותח את המיתר של הקשת וכשהוא מרפה ממנו נזרק החץ על ידו, שאנו דנים את החץ כנזרק מכחו. ע״כ. ולכן כיון שהדבר תלוי במחלוקת, ובנוסף לכך כאמור בהערה 11 לא ניתן לחייג בטלפון עם חוגה ע״י שליחת ״טונים״ נראה דיש להעדיף חיוג ע״י לחיצים — כמובן בתנאי שאינה מדלקת נורות או תצוגה וכיו״ב — אך בלאו הכי ודאי עדיף טלפון עם חוגה רגילה על מכשירים עם נורות ותצוגה.

h. Many phones sound a beep to indicate that the number was pressed correctly. Some have the same sound for each number, while others have a different sound for each number. If possible, one should turn off this feature before Shabbos in order to avoid making unnecessary sounds.

   A phone with a light is more problematic than a phone that makes sounds. Therefore, using a cellular phone, most of which have lights, should be avoided.

i. If one anticipates that he may need to make an emergency call on Shabbos, it is a good idea to enter the phone number of the medical center or doctor in the phone's memory before Shabbos. In this way, only a single key will have to be pressed to make the call on Shabbos. But if using the memory feature will involve a light being turned on, it is better to dial in the ordinary manner.

Connecting a Telephone to a Phone Jack

13. When necessary, one may plug the telephone into a jack on Shabbos. It is preferable to lift the receiver off the hook before connecting the phone.[13] Therefore, if one has a phone that has lights or a screen, one may connect another, simpler phone in order to avoid using the one with the light. However, if after connecting the second phone, the lights on the first phone will light up when the second one is used, the second phone should not be connected. Similarly, if removing the more advanced phone from the outlet can be done without any lights being turned on or off, it is arguable that one may even remove that phone and replace it with the simpler one. (Halachic authorities are undecided on this last point; it is best to consult a *rav* on what to do in such a case.)

14. In Israel, there are two types of phone plugs. One has a narrow pin, while the other is called an "American plug" (RJ-11, 14). Since plugging in the one with the pin causes sparks, the American plug is preferred.[14]

---

13 כאשר יש צורך לחבר מכשיר לתקע, יש להרים את השפופרת תחילה שעם חיבור המכשיר לתקע בפעולה אחת יופעל כבר הטלפון ויחסוך בזה הרמת השפופרת.

14 ובאותו עניין, כשיש צורך לנתק מכשיר א׳ ולחבר מכשיר אחר, יתכן שעדיף לנתק המכשיר בקצה החוט

Public Telephones

15. In general, it is better to use a private telephone rather than a public one. When this is not possible, it is better to use a phone that works with coins or tokens rather than one that uses credit cards or phone cards.[15, 16]

Finding a Phone Number

16. It is permissible to look up a number in a telephone book in order to find the number of a doctor or emergency service.[17]

17. Similarly, one may look in a newspaper to find the number of a hospital or pharmacy or any other emergency service.[18]

18. The question comes up whether, if one cannot find a number in a telephone book or newspaper, it is better to call Information when it is known that Jewish workers will answer (such as in Israel), or should one rather call a non-Jewish hospital and ask for information regarding a certain doctor or phone number.

19. *Answer:* If time is of the essence, it is better to call Information, since one will get a faster and more efficient response. He should politely ask the operator not to give him the number with an electronic message but

---

המחובר למכשיר ולא בקצה החוט המחובר לקיר, ולחבר את הטלפון השני בחוט במחובר כבר לקיר.

15 משום שבטלכרד מפעיל תצוגה, ובחיוג עולה על הצג המספר שמחייג, ובניתוק — מכבה את התצוגה. (ויתכן מאוד שאף במקרה הדחק כשמתקשר ממכשיר טלכרד — אסור לנתק את השיחה גם מחמת כיבוי התצוגה.)

16 עיין בספר תורת היולדת פרק ט׳ הערה ז׳ וז״ל: אם יש רק טלפון ציבורי, וחייבים להשתמש באסימונים, יתכן שניתן למנוע איסור טלטול מוקצה, אם יצבע את האסימונים מערב שבת בצבע זהב כדוגמת תכשיט, ויעשה מהם שרשרת, ויהיו דומים למבואר במשנה ברורה סי׳ ש״א ס״ק קכ״א. עיי״ש. והעיר ע״ז מו״ר הגאון רבי זאב כהן שליט״א בזה״ל: נראה דאם ניכר שהן אסימונים אין ריווח, ואינו דומה למש״כ המ״ב דשם מאחר שהמטבע מזהב או כסף באמת ראוי לתכשיט, משא״כ כאן. וכ״ש במש״כ בפנים שיצבעם בצבע זהב בלי לעשותם שרשרת שלא מהני, ועוד יש לעיין אם בפועל יעשה שרשרת ויצטרך לפרקה בשבת אם אין כאן מלאכת סותר השייך גם בכלי. עכ״ל.

17 דספר טלפונים חשיב ככלי שמלאכתו לאיסור, דשרי לטלטלו לצורך גופו ומקומו, ואין לך צורך גופו גדול מזה. דאפילו שלא לצורך חולה — אם רוצה לחפש כתובת של ידיד וכיו״ב מותר לעיין בספר טלפונים לצורך חיפוש הכתובת.

18 שאסור לעיין בעיתון מסחרי בשבת כמבואר בשו״ע סי׳ ש״ז ובמ״ב ס״ק ס״ג.

to give it to him orally.[19] If the telephone exchange has an automated dialing feature that will automatically dial the number after the caller answers yes, an electronic message is preferable. If time is not of the essence, it is better to phone various non-Jewish places (using a *shinui*) in order to obtain the number.

---

19 יש להעיר, שנכון לבקש מהפקיד במשרד המודיעין שימנע מלהעביר את המספר המבוקש דרך הכריזה האלקטרונית אלא ישמיעו הם את המספר. ויעורר אותם בשפה יפה שיתקבלו דבריו.

Chapter 15

Hospital Administration

1. Administering a hospital on Shabbos involves many different aspects, including professional and routine treatments, patient assistance, security, and hygiene. The hospital staff is often confronted with the need to perform actions that involve Shabbos desecration. In some situations, measures can be taken to avoid desecration; in others, it is possible to employ a non-Jew.

2. In general, all treatments that are directly related to the needs of a dangerously ill patient (*choleh sheyeish bo sakanah*) — whether diagnostic testing or medical procedures — should be performed by expert Jewish doctors even if non-Jewish doctors are present.[1] Of course, if the non-Jewish doctor is more expert than the Jewish doctor, it is preferable that he treat the patient rather than the Jewish doctor.[2]

---

1 עיין לעיל פרק 13 סעיף 8 אם יש להעדיף רופא יהודי על רופא שאינו יהודי וכל המסתעף, וכתב לי הגרי״י זילברשטיין שליט״א דלגבי חילול שבת יש לסמוך על הש״ך הנ״ל שרופא מומחה לא מרע לאומנותיה, ויש לפנות לרופא הנכרי אם הוא באותה רמה של הרופא היהודי וכמבואר ברמ״א בסי׳ שכ״ח סעיף י״ב. ויתכן שגם דברי השו״ע לא מיירי כי אם בוודאי פיקוח נפש ולא בספק. לכן במסגרת בית החולים לא שייך ההסתייגויות המובאות שם, כיון שהרופאים לא מרעים את אומנותם, כמבואר שם מהגמרא במסכת עבודה זרה דף פ״ג, ובשם הגהות אשר״י ובעל המאור.

2 כן מבואר שם בבעה״מ, וההסתייגות היחידה שיש גם אצל רופא מומחה שאינו יהודי היא דווקא אם הוא הדוק בע״ז שלו והחולה שלפניו הוא יהודי המתקנא בו באופן מופגן שאז מוכן הרופא האינו יהודי להרע לו ולאבד אומנותו כמבואר שם.

Hospital services include the following:

a. Medical treatments
b. Nurses and their assistants
c. Medical secretaries
d. Blood banks and laboratory technicians
e. X-ray technicians
f. Maintenance staff
g. Orderlies and ambulance drivers
h. Kitchen staff
i. Cleaning staff
j. Laundry services and sterilization
k. Security

Those working in these areas in the hospital must be on duty on Shabbos, although in many cases it is possible to hire non-Jews. However, there are certain services that can be dispensed with on Shabbos, and there is no need even to appoint non-Jews. These include general hospital administration, accounting, collection of fees and paperwork by admissions staff, and archiving. Since these functions need not be performed on Shabbos, they should be suspended for the duration of the day.

Medical Treatments

3. A Jewish doctor can and should perform any necessary treatment for a *choleh sheyeish bo sakanah*, even when a non-Jewish doctor is readily available, unless the non-Jew is more expert in carrying out the necessary treatment.[3]

4. Similarly, we give preference to a Torah-observant doctor over a non-observant Jewish doctor when they are both equally competent in treating the patient. The reason for this is that the Torah-observant Jew will

---

3 עיין במש"כ לעיל בהערה 1 ובהערה 2 בשם בעה"מ.

be more careful to limit his Shabbos desecration to the minimum necessary for proper treatment (see also chapter 13, "Choosing a Doctor and Seeking Medical Advice," paragraph 4). But if the nonobservant Jew is more expert, he should be given preference.

Nurses

5. If mechanical devices can be used for taking blood pressure, temperature, pulse, and heart or breathing rate, a Jewish nurse may carry out these functions.[4] It should be noted that if Vaseline is used for taking temperature rectally, one may not smear the ointment on the thermometer. Rather, the thermometer should be dipped into the ointment.[5]

   Laboratory tests, drawing blood, X-rays, ECG, oxygen, monitors, ultrasound, or any other diagnostic tool that is needed for a *choleh sheyeish bo sakanah* is permitted. Certain changes can be made to minimize the severity of Shabbos desecration in cases where there is no great urgency. But again, it must be emphasized that if the patient's life is in danger, no calculations should be made to minimize Shabbos desecration, and he should be treated in the same manner as on a weekday.

6. A non-Jew should be employed to record the test results. Similarly, a non-Jew should be the one to turn on the various devices and machines that are needed for the patient's treatment. Although it was previously stated that, even on Shabbos, the needs of a dangerously ill patient (*choleh sheyeish bo sakanah*) should be preferably attended to by a Jew, if a non-Jew can do it without any delay whatsoever, especially when the action is not related directly to the treatment, such as setting up the machinery or recording the results, it is preferable to employ a non-Jew.

   It is a great mitzvah and obligation for the hospital administration to make sure that in every department there are some non-Jewish nurses and doctors on staff to record results and assist in setting up the different devices and machinery on Shabbos. Treatments and other

---

4 בדיקות אלו אינם כרוכים בחילול שבת כלל (ההיינו במד חום כספית ובמד לחץ דם כספית אבל במד חום ובמד לחץ דם אלקטרוני או דיגיטלי יש בזה איסורי תורה), רישום תוצאות הבדיקות להלן סעיף 6.

5 נתבאר דין זה בהרחבה לקמן פרק 26 סעיף 28.

medical needs that do not involve Shabbos desecration should be carried out by Jewish nurses. (See chapters 43–48 for the laws of using equipment that involve Shabbos desecration.)

7. If no non-Jew is available for assistance and the patient is a *choleh sheyeish bo sakanah*, the Jewish medical staff is obligated to do whatever is needed for the patient's welfare, including operating the equipment and recording the necessary information in the patient's file. Nevertheless, if the situation is not extremely urgent, it is best to perform these actions with a *shinui* (see chapter 9, "Levels of Urgency," paragraphs 8–9, and chapter 44, "Operating Medical Equipment on Shabbos").

Medical Secretaries

8. Medical secretaries are constantly performing tasks that involve Shabbos desecration, such as answering the phone, opening patient files, printing stickers, filling out records, and accepting payments. It is proper for a Jewish hospital to hire a non-Jewish receptionist to receive patients and open new files. If this is not possible, a Jewish receptionist may open a new file but only to record the most necessary information: the patient's identification, age, time of arrival, sensitivity to medications, and a short summary of the patient's complaint. This information is crucial to the hospital staff in order to properly diagnose and treat the patient and not to confuse him with someone else. The receptionist should not record the patient's address, type of health insurance, or other information that is not essential to the treatment. However, when the type of health insurance may determine which specialists are called in (i.e., which doctors in the network should be called), this information is considered essential to treatment.

9. Therefore, if no non-Jewish workers are available, special forms should be prepared in advance for use on Shabbos. Where feasible, any necessary writing should be done with the left hand or in a language other than Hebrew (in Israel).[6] Similarly, it is permissible to answer

---

6 עיין לקמן פרק 21 סעיף 6 וסעיף 7 ובהערות שם, ומ״מ כאן כשמדובר בחולי של סכנה — שהותרה הכתיבה, ודאי שיש עדיפות בכתיבה בלועזית על כתיבה בעברית.

the phone, since the call may involve the needs of a *choleh sheyeish bo sakanah* even if it is certain that there will also be calls that do not involve life-threatening situations.

10. *Question:* In a hospital where there are no non-Jewish workers and a new file needs to be opened, there are two options: either the forms can be filled in by hand (which would involve making duplicate copies, increasing the amount of writing needed), or the information may be typed into a computer, as is done during the week, and then, with one keystroke, all the copies can be printed out at one time. Which is the preferred method?

11. The use of a computer involves many prohibitions, both Torah and rabbinic. They are as follows:

    a. Turning on the computer involves a Torah prohibition.

    b. Typing the information into a computer involves a rabbinical prohibition.[7]

    c. Saving the information onto a hard disk involves a Torah prohibition.[8]

    d. Printing out the information involves a Torah prohibition.

12. Some of these prohibitions may be avoided in the following way:

    a. The computer and printer can be left on before Shabbos.

    b. A program with an autosave option can be used for storing information on the hard disk.

    c. The halachic problems involved in printing information on a printer are less severe than those involved in writing by hand (see note 9).

---

7 בספר נשמת אברהם ח״ד סי׳ ש״מ ס״ק א׳ כתב וז״ל: ולגבי שימוש במעבד תמלילים לכאורה אין כאן איסור מדאורייתא במה שמתקתקים ומופיעים אותיות ומילים על מסך המחשב כי האותיות מופיעות על המסך ע״י ירי של אלקטרונים על חומר זרחני אשר מרוח על הדופן הפנימית של המסך ומאיר בצורה של אותיות. וכתב לי הגרש״ז אויערבאך שליט״א ״ירי של אלקטרונים אין זה חשיב מן התורה ככתב אך בהכנסת האותיות לתוך הדיסקט (וה״ה כשמקליטים ברשם קול) יתכן שיש לחשוש לאיסור מדאורייתא של בונה כי הוא עושה בכך כלי״.

8 כמבואר בהערה 7.

13. *Answer:* According to the conditions mentioned in paragraph 12, use of a computer would be preferable, since it is arguable that typing the information into a computer and printing it out is preferable to writing it by hand.[9] As noted, the software should contain an automatic save feature.

Blood-Bank and Laboratory Workers

14. It is permissible to draw blood from a *choleh sheyeish bo sakanah* for analysis. When the situation is extremely urgent, such as when the patient has been in an accident, fallen, or has an urgent medical condition (such as a heart attack), or if he requires emergency surgery (for example, in the case of a suspected aortic aneurysm rupture or ectopic pregnancy), there are no limitations, and one may perform the neces-

---

9 בשאלות ותשובות אגרות משה חלק אבה״ע ח״ד סימן ע״ג אות ד׳ נשאל שאלה דומה לשאלתנו, ננסה ללמוד את העניין, וז״ל: ובדבר רופא שומר תורה שמטפל בשבת בבית החולים עם חולה שיש בו סכנה בשבת ומוכרח לשלח דמו לבדוק בהמעבדה (לאבאראטארי) וצריך לכתוב שם החולה על הנייר שמצורף להכלי שהדם בו כדי שידעו של איזה חולה הוא, ושואל איך יותר טוב.

א) אם לכתוב בשינוי בקיצור שאפשר לידע מזה של איזה חולה הוא — שצריך לעשות מעשה כתיבה על כל אות ואות.

ב) או שיש פס שכתוב בו באותיות בולטות שם החולה, אשר מניחים את הפס תחת נייר ומושכים המכונה ע״ג הנייר, וע״י יוצא דיו מהמכונה ומסמן במקום בליטת האותיות — שאולי נחשב זה למעשה אחת.

ג) או שיש מכונה שעושה הפעולה בחשמל (עלעקטרי) שמעשה האדם הוא רק פעם אחת הדחיקה בכפתור אחרי שהניח שם מקודם את הנייר, אבל ע״י מכונה לא שייך לעשות בשינוי כי כל עשיה מהאדם שהוא מעשה הדחיקה בכפתור החשמל, ומעשה הדחיקה בהעברת המכונה על פס הנייר, ליכא שום חלוק באיזה אופן נעשית מהאדם אם ביד ימין או שמאל ואף ע״י איברים אחרים.

בתחילת תשובתו דן על האופן הראשון והשני, ואח״כ כתב ז״ל: אבל לכאורה היותר נכון הוא דרך שלישי ע״י המכונה שעושה ע״י חשמל. דלכאורה אין שם שום איסור מדאורייתא נעשה ע״י האדם, דמה שהאדם צריך לדחוק על הכפתור הרי בזה לבד אין כאן עשיית מלאכה, כי אף שכל דחיקה בכפתור החשמל מוציא ניצוצות אין בזה שום חשיבות דעשיית אש כל זמן שלא הדליק מהניצוצות שיוצאין איזה דבר. ונודעתי מהמומחין בענין חשמל שאין ניצוצות הללו שיוצאין בשעת הדחיקה בכפתור עושין כלום להחשמל ואין ידוע להם שום צורך בזה. וא״כ מסתבר שאין בזה איסור דאורייתא דמלאכת הבערה בזה שדוחקין על כפתור החשמל שנעשה למלאכה דהוא כחשמל דמעליות (עלעוועטאר) בבתים הגבוהים ובאלו שנעשים בכל מכונות דעשיית מלאכה, וכמו כן הוא ודאי במכונה זו שנעשה לכתיבה שאין שם מלאכת הבערה, ונשאר רק מלאכת כותב שבזה רק בכח ראשון שייך להחשיב מלאכת האדם ממש שיתחשב מעשה הכתיבה מעשה כתיבה דהאדם, אף שכח החשמל עשה זה בעצם אבל לא מה שנכתב בכח שני דזהו רק כח חשמל כתב אך האדם גרם שהוא יכתוב, שודאי אין להחשיב זה עשיה ממש

sary tests just as they would be carried out during the week. But if there is no immediate emergency, one should attempt to minimize Shabbos desecration as much as possible.

15. Here are some suggestions for administering a hospital laboratory on Shabbos:

    a. If it is possible to employ competent non-Jews, this is certainly preferable, since in many instances the laboratory is called upon to test blood samples from patients who do not suffer from life-threatening illnesses.[10]

    b. Certain tests can be performed either on whole blood or serum with the same results. In such cases, it is preferable to use whole blood, since this avoids the need to use a centrifuge to separate the blood, which involves the prohibition of *borer*, selecting. Where there is a need to perform a number of tests on the same sample, some of which need to be performed on serum and others that can be tested either on serum or whole blood, one should centrifuge the entire sample at one time and perform all the tests on serum.

    c. Certain devices can be programmed to print out test results without any additional actions on the part of the typist. Even if, after the results are printed, they have to be stapled onto the patient's file, this is preferable to writing down the information by hand onto the patient's chart.

    d. If the results of a certain test will not be needed until after Shabbos, the test should not be carried out on Shabbos.

דהאדם. ונמצא שאם הנייר היה מונח ברחוק קצת, ואף כשהיה מונח בקירוב, אבל אפשרויות הכתיבה היה בריחוק מקום שלא היו האותיות בתחילת הנייר הרי ליכא אף מקצת מלאכה דכותב מהאדם שדחק בהכפתור ועשה שהחשמל יכתוב. אלא אף לו היו האותיות בתחילת הנייר הרי ג״כ אפשר נכתב רק חצי שיעור אות אחד מכל שורה שאין מצטרפין ואולי גם פחות מאות אחד שליכא אף חצי שיעור. וגם הרי הוא רוצה לעשות בכוונה באופן שלא יהיה איסור כלל אם אפשר, ולכן יניח הנייר רחוק קצת או אף בנייר גדול שמקום הכתיבה יהיה רחוק ולא יהיה בכח ראשון שנמצא שלא יעשה הרופא איסור מלאכה, שא״כ יהיה זה עדיף מכפי שיכתוב בעצמו אף כל הקצור שיהיה אפשר, וכן מסתבר לע״ד לדינא. עכ״ל.

10 שהרי בדיקות אלו כרוכות באיסורי תורה רבים, ובחולה שאין בו סכנה ולא חשש סכנה — אין היתר לישראל לעבור על איסורי תורה כדלקמן פרק 21 סעיף 4 וסעיף 22.

e. Tests that have to be repeated every few hours in order to track the patient's condition may be performed on Shabbos.

f. It is forbidden to test the bilirubin level of a child in order to determine whether or not to perform a bris milah on Shabbos. Such tests are permitted only if there is a medical reason to ascertain whether there is an unusual rise in the bilirubin level. Needless to say, testing the bilirubin level to allow a bris milah scheduled for Sunday is forbidden.

X-Ray Technicians

16. The X-ray department is one of the most active in the hospital, crucial for determining various diagnoses, from broken bones or pneumonia on a regular X-ray to bleeding or stroke on a CT scan. Often it is the X-ray that determines a patient's condition.

17. It is certainly permissible to perform X-rays when there is the slightest possibility of danger to life. However, with proper planning, it is possible to minimize the amount of Shabbos violation:

    a. The hospital can employ non-Jewish X-ray technicians.

    b. If non-Jewish technicians are not available, the hospital can leave the machinery running before Shabbos.

    c. When X-rays are taken, an ID camera is used to photograph the patient's details on the film. This action can be avoided by preparing stickers with the patient's information on it and sticking it onto the film after it has been developed.

    d. The stickers can also be used to label the envelope in which the film is placed rather than writing down the patient's name.

Maintenance

18. Many of the devices used in a hospital are sensitive and require constant maintenance. Technicians must be on hand to repair any malfunction that may develop in the course of their use.

19. It is best to employ non-Jewish technicians and maintenance staff.

20. The technicians should be instructed to repair only equipment that is needed on Shabbos or that hospital regulations demand must always be functionable in case of emergency. But regular maintenance that is not necessary for Shabbos should not be carried out even by non-Jews. Similarly, equipment that broke down should not be repaired on Shabbos if other equipment is available to replace it.

Orderlies and Ambulance Services

21. It is best to use non-Jews for transporting patients from place to place for tests, because the patients must often be taken on an elevator or the transport may involve other acts of Shabbos desecration.

22. If there is no need to transport the patient in an elevator, or if the hospital has a Shabbos elevator, Jewish orderlies may be used.

    All of the above applies only when the situation is not extremely urgent and nothing is lost by delaying moving the patient. But when there is an emergency that requires the immediate transfer of a patient, there are no limitations whatsoever. In such a situation, it is preferable to use a Jewish orderly, even if he must use the elevator or desecrate Shabbos in other ways. He should be diligent in performing this meritorious act and not refrain from doing his part in the patient's treatment.

23. The summoning of an orderly over an intercom should be done by a non-Jew.

24. If a hospital employs an internal ambulance service to transport patients or doctors from one department to another, a non-Jewish driver should drive the ambulance on Shabbos.

25. In certain hospitals, the kitchen is located some distance away from the hospital wards. In such cases, transfer of food on Shabbos should be done manually with carts. If it is necessary to transfer food to the hospital by a motor vehicle, a non-Jewish driver should be employed to do so on Shabbos.

Kitchen Staff

26. It is proper for any Jewish hospital to prepare on Friday all the food that will be needed for its patients on Shabbos and store it in the refrigerator. It is then permitted to warm up the food on Shabbos using a stove that is turned on automatically by a Shabbos clock.

27. If there are patients who require special food that must be prepared fresh, it should be cooked on Shabbos by a non-Jew. If the patient is classified as a *choleh sheyeish bo sakanah*, a Jew is permitted to cook the food for him (see chapter 17, "Cooking," for more details).

28. Every hospital requires hot water to prepare tea or coffee for the patients, staff, and guests. Halachah forbids a healthy person (including doctors and nurses[11]) to benefit from water that was heated on Shabbos, whether it was heated by a Jew for a dangerously ill patient (*choleh sheyeish bo sakanah*) or by a non-Jew for an ordinary bedridden patient (*choleh she'ein bo sakanah*).

29. It is recommended that any Jewish public institution or hospital purchase a Shabbos coffee urn. These are available in Israel with the certification of the Institute for Technology and Halachah and the Tzomet Institute. This type of urn enables doctors, nurses, and other healthy people to use hot water on Shabbos.

Cleaning Staff

30. The importance of maintaining a clean hospital environment, which is vital for the swift and full recovery of the patients, is proven (see chapter 19, "General Assistance for a *Choleh Sheyeish Bo Sakanah*"). Nevertheless, non-Jewish cleaning staff should be employed on Shabbos, since there are many functions in this area that may not be performed on Shabbos under any circumstances.

---

11 וכתב ע״ז הגרי״י זילברשטיין שליט״א בזה״ל: רופא או אחות שהיו ערים כל הלילה וכעת זקוקים לכוס קפה חם נראה שמותר להם לשתות מהמיחם שהפעילו הנכרי בשבת, שהרי מותר לומר לנכרי שיחלל שבת עבור חולה, ויישוב הדעת של הרופא המרגיש צורך לקפה חם הוא צרכיו של החולה.

Laundry Services

31. Laundry may not be done on Shabbos. Therefore, enough linen, sheets, and other necessary supplies should be on hand to supply the hospital's needs for the entire day.

    If Shabbos and *yom tov* fall out on two or three consecutive days and the hospital does not have enough supplies to last the entire period, or if there is an unusual demand and the stock runs out during Shabbos, it is permissible to ask a non-Jew to launder the amount needed for the rest of Shabbos. If the hospital knows in advance that there will not be enough stock to last the entire Shabbos, the washing machines and dryers should be set up in advance to run on a timer.

Sterilization

32. Some of the laundry in the hospital, such as surgical gowns and linens used in maternity and surgery wards, must be sterilized before use. The hospital should plan in advance to make sure there is enough stock to last the entire Shabbos. If there is a shortage, the rules regarding laundry apply (see paragraph 31).

33. Certain hospital instruments must go through a sterilization process before being used. Ideally everything should be prepared before Shabbos. But in time of need, it is permissible to sterilize the instruments on Shabbos. Preferably this should be done by a non-Jew, but if that is not possible, even a Jew can do it.

Security

34. A non-Jewish security service should be used on Shabbos. But if this is not possible, a Jewish security service may be used even if the guards carry weapons.

Chapter 16

Medication for a Choleh Sheyeish Bo Sakanah

In this chapter the following issues will be discussed:

a. Preparing and taking medication on Shabbos

b. Taking approved medication and experimental medication

c. Using amulets and *segulos*

d. Handling amulets and objects related to *segulos*

Preparing Medication

1. It is permissible and obligatory to prepare any medication for a dangerously ill patient (*choleh sheyeish bo sakanah*) even if the preparation entails Shabbos desecration, such as grinding, kneading, or cooking.[1]

2. In time of need, it is permissible for a Jew to travel[2] in a car to bring medication if it is not available where the patient is located. However, if there is no great urgency, it is preferable that a non-Jew drive the car

---

1 ז״ל השו״ע סימן שכ״ח סעיף ב׳ מי שיש לו חולי של סכנה מצווה לחלל עליו את השבת וכו׳ וע״ש עוד בסעיף ד׳ שחולה שיש בו סכנה עושים לו כל שרגילים בחול ממאכלים ורפואות וכו׳ (הרמב״ן בתורת האדם, הובא במ״מ פ״ב מהלכות שבת ה״ב, והביאו המ״ב שם ס״ק י״ד).

2 דלא גרע משאר מלאכות המנויות בשו״ע סי׳ שכ״ח כגון תולש מן המחובר, המבואר בסעיף ט״ו וסעיף ט״ז בעניין קציצת תאנה, או בעניין שחיטה ובישול בסעיף י״ד וכיו״ב.

and the Jew accompany him. If the Jew can travel by bicycle without causing any undue delay, this is preferred.

3. One may prepare medication on Shabbos for a dangerously ill patient only if the patient needs the medication on Shabbos. But it is forbidden to prepare the medication on Shabbos for weekday use. Therefore, if one knows that the patient will not need the medication until after Shabbos and there is time to prepare it once Shabbos ends, one may not prepare it on Shabbos.[3]

4. If a person has the halachic designation of being in danger (*choleh sheyeish bo sakanah*), and he is receiving medication to save his life, may he also be given other medications and therapies for additional medical problems that are not dangerous? An example would be a patient receiving dopamine for low blood pressure who also takes a laxative or a glaucoma preparation. Once he is in danger, can one forgo all limitations on Shabbos observance in treating him, even if some of the procedures are unrelated to the immediate danger to his life? Halachic authorities debate this question and conclude that, unless there is a great need, one should not transgress a Torah prohibition unless it is directly necessary for saving the patient's life.[4]

---

3 עיין בכפה״ח סי׳ שכ״ח אות ס״ז ז״ל אם נודע בברור דנוכל להמתין עד הערב אין לחלל שבת בחינם ואם נצרך לעשות לו הרפואה היום דווקא אבל אינו מוכרח לעשות תיכף רק דנוכל לאחרה עוד איזה שעות, בכזה אמרינן הזריז הרי זה משובח. ואם נצרך לעשות לו הרפואה ב׳ פעמים אחד היום דווקא והשני נוכל להמתין עד לאורתא, עיין בשו״ת יחוה דעת ח״ד סימן ל׳ שכתב דרק מה שצריך לשבת מותר לחלל את השבת ולא להוסיף גם לצורך מוצאי שבת. וע״ע בכפה״ח שם מש״כ בשם הרש״ש במסכת יומא וצ״ע. וכתב ע״ז הגר״י זילברשטיין שליט״א בזה״ל: אם אין עושה מלאכה מדאורייתא כי אם דרבנן צ״ע, שאולי מותר. ויעוין בשו״ת רב פעלים ח״א סימן כ״ז (הובא לקמן פרק כ״ג הערה ז׳). יש לעיין ברופא הזקוק לרשום לחולה מסוכן מרשם של 3 כדורים ליום, האם מותר לו לרשום 9 כדי שיספיקו גם לימות החול? ויעוין בדברינו בתורת היולדת פרק ל״ט הערה י״ט. ובשו״ת ציץ אליעזר ח״ח סי׳ ט״ו.

4 בשמירת שבת כהלכתה פרק ל״ב סעיף נ״ו כתב שמותר לחולה שיש בו סכנה להשתמש בתרופות גם אם אינם הכרחיות להצלתו מהסכנה כגון גלולה להרגעת כאב הבא מן השיניים. אלא שבמקרה זה יש להיזהר שלא לחלל את השבת באיסורי תורה לצורך זה, כגון כתיבת מרשם לתרופות, או נסיעה בשבת לצורך הבאת התרופות. אולם בשו״ת יחוה דעת הנ״ל כתב דכל מה שהוא צורך החולה אף שאינו קשור ישירות עם הסכנה שנמצא בה מותר לעשות לו כל צרכו אפילו במלאכות הקשורות בחילול שבת. עיי״ש. ואמנם על פי הכרעת הביאור הלכה הנזכר לעיל בפרק ט׳ סעיף י״א בעניין לאיזה מצרכי החולה מחללים שבת מבואר שכל שאינו לצורך רפואתו הישירה של החולה אין מחללים על כך את השבת, עכ״פ ודאי לא באיסורי תורה — יש להחמיר

5. If the patient requests a particular medication that the doctor claims is unnecessary, we heed the patient's request, unless the doctor claims the medication will harm him.[5]

6. The rules for preparing medication for a *choleh she'ein bo sakanah*, an ordinary bedridden patient, will be discussed in the section dealing with such illnesses (part 3, "*Choleh She'ein Bo Sakanah*").

Approved and Experimental Medication

7. One is permitted to desecrate Shabbos in order to prepare medication only if it is known to be effective for the patient's condition. This means that a competent doctor has diagnosed that the patient is suffering from a particular condition, and it is known that the medication is effective for treating that condition.[6] If the doctors are doubtful as to whether

---

בכל זה. וכתב לי ע״ז הגר״י זילברשטיין שליט״א שלכאורה נראה לתלות אם יש צורך גדול לחולה דשרי אף מלאכה מדאורייתא, ואם אין בזה צורך גדול יהיה אסור במלאכה, וכמבואר בשעה״צ סי׳ שכ״ח ס״ק י״א שלצורך הרבה מותר אפילו לדעת המחמירים.

5 מגן אברהם סי׳ שכח בשם הרדב״ז (זכרנוהו לעיל פרק 8 סעיף 8 עיי״ש) והביאו במ״ב ס״ק כ״ה. ובביאור הלכה שם ד״ה ורופא כתב ז״ל: עיין במ״ב שכ׳ בשם הרדב״ז וכו׳ ולענ״ד אין הדברים אמורים אלא כשאומר מרגיש אני חולשה באיבר פלוני ע״כ יעשו לי תרופה פלונית שמועלת לחולי איבר זה ובזה ודאי שומעים לו שלב יודע מרת נפשו שייכא בכל מילי ואפילו רופא אומר שא״צ שום תרופה אין שומעין לו. אבל אם המחלה ידועה והחולה אומר שתרופה זו מועלת למחלה זו והרופא אומר שאינו מועיל — בזה אין סברה לשמוע לחולה לחלל שבת בחינם [ומ״מ אפשר לומר דהיכי דאומר החולה דידוע לו שטבע גופו להתרפאות ממחלה זו כשנוטל רפואה זו אפשר דשומעין לו דגם בזה שייכות קצת לומר דאדם בקי בגופו יותר ממאה רופאים] אם לא דאיכא חשש שמא תטרף דעתו עליו אם יראה שאינם עושים כדבריו. והא דאמרינן גבי חיה דעד שבעה מחללין כשאמרה צריכה ומבואר בחידושי הרשב״א דאפילו רופא אומר א״צ שומעין לה מיירי ג״כ באופן זה שהיא אומרת שצריכה חמין לשתות או לרחיצה שמרגשת חולשה באיבריה וכדומה ורופא אומר שלפי חיזוק גווה א״צ אין שומעין לדבריו שלב יודע מרת נפשו, אבל כשהיא מחולקת לאיזה תרופה תועיל אין סברה לשמוע לה. וכן משמע בתשובות הרשב״א ח״ד סי׳ רי״ד כדברינו. עכ״ל הבאו״ה.

6 עיין במגן אברהם סי׳ שכ״ח אות א׳ שכ״כ ע״פ הרמ״א ביו״ד סי׳ קנ״ה סעיף ג׳ בשם האו״ה. וז״ל הרמ״א שם: וכל חולה שמאכילים אותו איסור צריכים שתהא הרפואה ידועה או עפ״י מומחה, (או״ה כלל נ״ט) ואין מתירים שום דבר איסור לחולה אם יוכל לעשות הרפואה בהיתר כמו באיסור — אע״פ שצריך לשהות קצת קודם שימצא ההיתר — מאחר שאין סכנה בדבר. (בית יוסף ותשובות הרשב״א סוף סימן קל״ד) והנה הרמ״א כתב שני דינים:

א) דכל חולה בעינן רפואה ידועה או עפ״י מומחה, ולמד זה מהאו״ה, וז״ל שם כלל נ״ט סעיף ל״ה: השיב מהר״ם (הגהת תשובות מיימוניות פ״ד ממאכלות אסורות) על נכפה אחד שרצה כנעני לרפאותו ולהאכילו שרץ העוף, נכפה הוא חולי גדול וכמכה של חלל הגוף דמי ופעמים שמסתכן ונופל לאש או למים — אם הרפואה ידועה מותר, ואם אין הרפואה ידועה אין בידי להתיר עכ״ל ועיי״ש עוד באורך.

or not the patient's condition has worsened to the point where medication known for its effectiveness will no longer work, it is still permissible to desecrate Shabbos to prepare and administer the medication on the chance that it will be effective. Similarly, if some patients react favorably to the medication but some do not, it is still permissible to desecrate Shabbos to prepare and administer the medication.[7]

ב) כתב הרמ״א דאם אפשר בהיתר לא עושין באיסור אע״פ שצריך לשהות קצת קודם שימצא ההיתר מאחר שאין סכנה בדבר, וכתב בביאור הגר״א שם ס״ק כ״ד וז״ל: ״וז״ש מאחר שאין סכנה בדבר ר״ל בהשהאה, אע״ג שהוא חולה שיש בו סכנה״ ע״כ עיי״ש. משמע דבשני הדינים שהביא הרמ״א מיירי בחולי של סכנה ועכ״ז הצריך שני תנאים: (א) בעינן רק רפואה ידועה. (ב) הקל הקל תחילה בהיתר ולא האיסור עד כמה שניתן. והנה בפרי מגדים א״א אות א׳ תמה על המג״א דבעינן תרופה ידועה וז״ל: ומש״כ שהרפואה ידועה צ״ע דבספק נמי ספק פ״נ להקל. ועין סי׳ תרי״ח, וביו״ד י״ל דמיירי בחולה שאין בו סכנה דאיסור דרבנן אין מתירין בספק כה״ג. ע״כ.

ורבים מן האחרונים תמהו על הפרי מגדים בביאור דברי הרמ״א ביו״ד, שהבין שהרמ״א מדבר על חולה שאין בו סכנה, דזה אינו אלא הרמ״א איירי בחולה שיש בו סכנה וכמבואר לעיל בפשטות. וע״ע בדעת תורה ובתהלה לדוד סי׳ שכ״ח, וע״ע בשערי תשובה או״ח סי׳ תס״ה ס״ק א׳ שפקפק בהבנת הרמ״א עיי״ש. וע״ע בשדי חמד מערכת יום הכיפורים סימן ג׳ אות כ״ד. וע״ע בהערה 7.

וכתב לי ע״ז מו״ר הגר״ז כהן שליט״א בזה״ל: נראה פשוט דכל דברי הרמ״א אינם אלא בדבר שלא ידוע כתרופה, אבל דבר שידוע כתרופה ויש ספק אם למחלה זו הוא יכול להועיל — מחללינן, כי גם זה ספק פיקו״נ, ורק בדוגמת שרץ העוף כוונת הרמ״א שאין זה אפי׳ ספק מאחר שזה לא רפואה ידועה בכלל וממילא לא נחשב ספק לעניין מחלה זו. ולדוגמא אנטיביאטיקה אפילו לדבר שהרופא ללא ניסיון אם למחלה זו היא תרופה, ויש סיבה אפילו רחוקה לתלות שיועיל פשיטא דמחללין שבת. עכ״ל.

7 שו״ע הגר״ז סי׳ שכ״ח סעיף ב׳ (הובא בהרחבה בשדי חמד הנ״ל) כתב וז״ל: ומ״מ אפילו בודאי סכנה אין מחללים אלא ברפואה שהיא ידועה לכל או ע״פ מומחה (כהמג״א) וכשהיא רפואה ידועה אף שאין ידוע אם זה יתרפא בה אם לאו מחללים מספק. ע״כ. ובסי׳ ש״ו בקו״א כתב ז״ל: רפואה שהיא ודאי מרפאת בשאר פעמים אלא שעכשיו בחולה זה אינו יודע אם תועיל לו דמחללין כמבואר בר״ן פ״ד (שמונה שרצים דף מ׳ ע״א בדפי הרי״ף ד״ה ואין אומרים נמתין לו) גבי מחמין להברותו, ואפשר שלזה התכוין הט״ז סק״ה שכתב לחלל ברפואה אפילו בספק כי היכי דלא לפלוג על הרמ״א ביו״ד, ע״כ.

בנוסח זה פשט הגר״ז ספיקו של הפרמ״ג על המג״א דיש ספק אם הרפואה המוצעת היא בכלל רפואה, ובזה לא מחללין מספק. ורק כשהרפואה ידועה למחלה זו אלא שספק אם תועיל לחולה זה במצבו דשמא גבר עליו החולי, וזה מפורש בר״ן הנ״ל דאף אם הרופאים לא בטוחים בודאי שהחמין ירפאו את החולה גם מחללין עיי״ש.

בשדי חמד הנזכ״ל הביא בשם שו״ת עטרת חכמים (אבה״ע סי׳ ל׳) לחלק בין פסק מהר״ם בנכפה לשאר חולה, וז״ל: דצריך לומר דשם לא נאמרה הרפואה באכילת שרץ מפי רופא רק מעכו״ם שלא היה רופא ע״כ לא רצה מהר״ם להתיר על סמך דבריו רק אם ידועה רפואה זו בלעדיו, ודעת לנבון נקל שכל רפואות שעושין במאכלות אסורות שיש עליהם אזהרת כרת או מיתה לחולה שיש בו סכנה אף שידוע ששייך רפואה כזו לחולאת כזאת מ״מ אין להחליט שתהא לרפואת תעלה לאיש ההוא וממילא תמיד ספק בתועלת הרפואה ועם כל זה מותר משום דגם

8. An "approved" medication is one that is known to be effective or has been recommended by a competent doctor.[8]

9. If a patient's condition has not been diagnosed by a competent doctor, treating the patient blindly with experimental medication on the chance that it might be effective is forbidden if it involves Shabbos desecration, unless it is known from previous experience that the medication was beneficial in similar cases.[9]

10. If a specialist has diagnosed the patient's condition, but another person, who is not known to be a competent doctor, has recommended treatment, one may not rely on the latter's recommendation to desecrate Shabbos by preparing a medication that is not known to doctors.[10]

ספק פקוח נפש דוחה וכמו כן כשהספק מצד הרפואה ואף כשיש רק ספק בסכנה וגם ספק ברפואה מ״מ מותר דגדול כח הצלת נפש מישראל. עכ״ל.

והנה המעיין היטב בדברי העטרת חכמים יראה לנכון דפשט ספיקו של הפרמ״ג כפי שבארנו משו״ע הגר״ז, דהיינו (א) כשספק לנו אם החולה בסכנה, ספק נפשות להקל. (ב) כשהתרופה ידועה שמרפאה מחלה זו אך ספק אם תועיל לחולה זה, גם בזה נקטינן להקל. (ג) אך כשאין הרפואה ידועה כלל על פי רופא, ודאי דאין נותנים מספק כההיא דמהר״ם.

גם המהר״ם בן חביב זצ״ל בתוספת יום הכפורים דף פ״ג, האריך בדבר זה אך נראה מלשון מסקנתו כדברים הנזכרים לעיל וז״ל שם: ונשמע לי דכל רפואה טבעית שרגילין לעשות אע״פ שהיא ספק רפואה יכולים להאכילו לחולה אף שהוא דבר איסור או שצריכין לחלל שבת לעשות אותה רפואה — מחללים עליו השבת דספק נפשות להקל, עכ״ל. ונראה לי דכוונתו כמש״כ באופן ב׳ הנזכ״ל כשהרפואה ידועה דרגילין לעשות אותה למחלה זו אף שיש ספק אם יתרפא דישנם שמתרפאים מזה וישנם שלא — ודאי דנותנים ומחללים בכה״ג על הספק, דספק נפשות להקל. ודו״ק. (ולכאורה לא כך הבין בדבריו השדי חמד הנזכ״ל עיי״ש.)

וכתב לי מו״ר הגר״ז כהן שליט״א בנוסף לנזכר לעיל וז״ל: ונראה דאמנם הפוסקים דברו על ודאי תרופה למחלה זו ורק ספק לחולה זה נראה כנ״ל דה״ה ודאי תרופה לכמה מחלות כמו אנטיביאטיקה או קורטיזון וספק למחלה זו — גם פשוט דהוה ספק נפשות וחייבים להקל.

8 כן משמעות הרמ״א ביו״ד סי׳ קנ״ה סעיף ג׳ הנזכ״ל הערה 6 וע״ע בתהילה לדוד סי׳ שכ״ח שכתב וז״ל: וצריך לדקדק מאי היא הפי׳ שרפואה ידועה דלכאורה פרושו היא דידועה לרוב בני אדם שלחולה זו עושין רפואה זו, אבל אם אין ידועה לרוב בני אדם אף שמקצת ב״א אומרים שרפואה זו יפה לחולי זה לא מהני א״כ מומחה אומר כן עיי״ש באורך. ומסקנתו כך, דאם הספק הוא לב״א אם הרפואה מועילה או לא בזה אמרינן דלא מחללין מספק דחשיב אינה ידועה, אבל אם מומחה מסתפק — ספק לרופאים הוי ספק — ומחללים את השבת גם מספק. וראייתו מהר״ן הנ״ל דהתם ספק הוא לרופאים ובכ״ז מחללין, אבל בספק לסתם ב״א אין מחללין אף לחולה שיש בו סכנה ע״כ. עיי״ש.

9 דאם במקרים קודמים הועילה, וידוע כן עפ״י רופאים, מכלל ספק לרופאים לא יצאנו, ומחללים על כך את השבת.

10 ואף שבשו״ע סי׳ שכ״ח סעיף י׳ כתב די״א דכל אחד נאמן לומר על מחלה אם יש בה סכנה ומחללין שבת על פיו, יש לחלק בין קביעת סכנה בחולה שאכן רשאי לקבוע אף מי שאינו מוחזק כרופא (וכנזכר בדברינו לעיל פרק 8) לבין המלצה לשימוש בתרופה שאינה ידועה, שאין להסתמך

However, if a layman reports that he heard a doctor recommending a certain treatment, we may rely on his word even if the doctors present are not aware of it. Even unapproved medication may be administered if it is already prepared and may be brought to the patient when it does not involve Shabbos desecration, as long as the doctors are of the opinion that it will not cause the patient any harm.[11]

11. If a certain medication has not yet been proven effective in practice, but has been recommended by specialists, certain halachic authorities allow preparing it on Shabbos even if this involves Shabbos desecration.[12]

12. If a certain medication is to be prepared that includes two ingredients, and it isn't clear which one is the effective ingredient, can one desecrate Shabbos to prepare the medicine?

Halachic authorities have debated this question in depth. In practice, today such a situation is not applicable since medication cannot be administered if one does not know what it contains and its effects. There is a risk here than an unknown ingredient may be toxic to the patient and therefore disallowed on medical grounds, unless, of course, one is certain that the powder cannot cause any harm.[13]

אלא על רופא מוסמך בלבד, ואין מחללין את השבת על סמך המלצת מי שאינו מוחזק ברפואה. דכתב הטור יו״ד סי׳ של״ו לא יתעסק ברפואה אא״כ יהא בקי ויודע בחכמה ובמלאכה וכו׳ ואם לא נתעסק בה כלל הרי זה שופך דמים ובן גיהנם הוא בודאי עיי״ש באורך, ובפרט בחולה שיש בו סכנה אין להסתמך כלל על אדם שלא הוחזק כרופא ואין לו רשיון. אך אם ההמלצה היא רק על דברי מאכל ומשקה ואין צורך לחלל שבת בהכנתה אין זה בכלל רפואה ושרי, ואם לא יועיל לא יזיק.

11 על פי דברינו בהערה 10, דאם ההמלצה היא של אדם שאינו מומחה ברפואה אין מחללין על פיו את השבת, והיינו בדבר הצריך חילול, אך אם אין צריך חילול יש לשאול ברופאים דאם יזיק לחולה לא יתנו, ואם אינו מזיק, אפשר דשרי.

12 בנשמת אברהם ח״א סי׳ שכ״ח אות ח׳ כתב בשם השש״כ (לא מצאתי מקומו) ז״ל: והשש״כ מוסיף שגם מותר לרופא לערוך ניסויים לצורך הטיפול בחולה שיש בו סכנה וגם אם תועלתם של ניסיונות אלה מוטלים בספק לגבי חולה זה ואפילו כאשר ניסיונות אלה קשורים בחילול שבת באיסורי תורה. ע״כ.

13 באשל אברהם בגיליון השו״ע סי׳ שכ״ט אהא דאמרינן מי שנפלה עליו מפולת מפקחין אע״פ שיש כמה ספיקות, כתב ז״ל: ספיקות, וכן לעניין רפואה לחולה אע״ג דלא ידעינן בודאי שזהו הסם שיתרפא בה מדרך הטבע אלא עדיין הדבר תלוי בספק מחללין את השבת. דאף דלכאורה משמע מהרמב״ם דס״ל כרבנן דפליגי אר׳ מתיא בן חרש ואין מאכילין למי שנשכו כלב שוטה החצר כבד שלו לפי שהרפואה אינה בדוקה וכו׳ אבל נ״ד שהספק הוא מצד הסברה ודאי דנכלל בכלל ספק נפשות להקל. תשובת גינת ורדים סי׳ ב׳ (יין בשדי חמד הנ״ל שציון זה מוטעה וצר״ל תשובת קול בן לוי סי׳ ב׳) ואין להקשות מדברי הגהת מיימוני דאוסר לבעל נכפה לרפאות בשרץ באשר אין

Using *Segulos* and Amulets

13. Shabbos may be desecrated for a dangerously ill patient (*choleh sheyeish bo sakanah*) only in order to prepare medications. One may not transgress a Torah prohibition in order to prepare an amulet or other spiritual remedies.[14] One may, however, perform actions forbidden only by rabbinical law for this purpose, as long as the method has proven to be effective.[15]

    Therefore, one may not write an amulet on Shabbos or travel in order to bring an amulet to a sick person, even if the patient's life is in danger. But one may ask a non-Jew to deliver the amulet, or a Jew himself may ride a bicycle for this purpose.

14. An exception is the case of a woman who is giving birth and she requests a particular amulet. Since we are concerned that her emotional well-being will deteriorate to a dangerous degree if she does not receive the amulet, the Sages permit Shabbos desecration in this case, even if it means transgressing a Torah prohibition if necessary to maintain her mental stability.

הרפואה בדוקה וכו׳ משא״כ בנדון דידן דהרפואה בדוקה אלא דמספקינן בסם אם הוא אותו סם או לא מותר לכו״ע. ועיין תשובת רש״ל סימן תקפה והר״ן בפרק במה אשה, והרדב״ז סי׳ סו ותשובת הרשב״א סי׳ רפא. ע״כ לשון האשל אברהם. הביאו השדי חמד הנ״ל וכתב ע״ז וז״ל: ולפי מ״ש בסי׳ שכ״ח ס״ב נראה דאם הרפואה בדוקה רק שאין יודעין אם זה הוא הסם, הוי בכלל ספק פקוח נפש, ע״כ.

והרוצה לעמוד על כל דברי הענין הזה בספקות אלו יעיין בארוכה בשדי חמד הנ״ל שצלל במים אדירים בעומק וברוחב, ואכמ״ל יותר בזה.

אחר כל הדברים האלה נראה להעיר דבזמנינו אין כל אפשרות להתיר שימוש בסמי רפואה מספק, דהיינו כאשר יש לפנינו חומרים כימיים שונים בצורת אבקה לדוגמא ויש לנו ספק ממה מורכב החומר הזה שלפנינו יתכן שזה חומר שיוכל לרפא את החולה ממחלתו ויתכן שזה חומר מסוכן שיכול אף להחמיר את מחלתו — לא שייך בזה כלל ספק נפשות להקל, ואדרבא שב ואל תעשה עדיף, דחמירא סכנתא מאיסורא, אא״כ בידוע שהסם הנמצא בספק הוא בגדר אם לא יועיל לא יזיק אך בלאו הכי אין להתיר כלל. כנלע״ד.

14 דהנה הרמב״ם (בפרוש המשניות למסכת יומא פ״ח מ״ד) כתב דלהתרפאות בדברים שהם מרפאים בסגולתם אסור כי כוחם חלש. וכתב הרדב״ז דלדעת הרמב״ם רפואות הסגוליות אינם רפואות כלל, וההיתר לצאת בקמיע היינו רק באיסור דרבנן.

15 עיין בבאר היטב סי׳ שכ״ח ס״ק ג׳ מי שחלה בחולי הקדחת ועשו לו רפואות קמיעא א׳ של עשבים לתלות עליו ימים מספר, ובתשלום זמן מספר הימים ציוו לזרוק תוך הנהר מאחוריו והיה קמיע מומחה, ונשלם הזמן בשבת יכול לזורקה כיון דהנהר הוא כרמלית (שבות יעקב סי׳ נ׳ ע״ש) ע״כ. והיינו אסור דרבנן. וע״ע בשו״ת חתם סופר חיו״ד סי׳ שלי״ט דכ״כ דשרי לעבור אסור דרבנן לצורך רפואות סגוליות (יבואר בהרחבה לקמן הערה 18) וכן מבואר ברדב״ז הנ״ל.

15. Similarly, if a dangerously ill patient demands a particular amulet, even one that has not been proven effective, one should try to persuade him that the best "amulet" is the observance of Shabbos. But if this does not convince him, and there is a fear that as a result of his uneasiness his condition may worsen or he may panic, it is permitted to transgress a Torah prohibition — that is, to write the amulet or to travel to a place where it can be obtained — in order to bring it to the patient. This is permitted because his life may be endangered if we do not fulfill his request.[16] Of course, if a non-Jew is available to travel to procure the amulet, this is preferable.[17]

16. If the patient does not request such a remedy, one may not offer it to him. Only if the patient has requested it, and he is distressed if one does not obtain it for him, may one desecrate Shabbos to provide it.[18]

---

16 כ״ז נלמד מתוך דברי הרשב״א בתשובה ח״ד סימן רמ״ה וז״ל: יכול אדם לצאת בקמיע בשבת בין בצוארו בין בזרועו אחד חולה שיש בו סכנה ואחד חולה שאין בו סכנה כך שמעתי מפי הר׳ אהרון ז״ל: ועוד אמר שכותבין כל קמיע אפילו בשבת לחולה שיש בו סכנה או ליולדת היכא דאינהו תבעי ליתובי דעתייהו אע״פ שאין אנו יודעים אם הוא מומחה אם לאו. אבל אם אינם תובעים אלא שאמר חכם אחד יש לך קמיע א׳ שמועיל לאותו חולי אפשר שאין כותבין אותו בשבת מספק, אא״כ ידוע דאמחי קמיעא או אמחי גברא שרוצה לכתוב אותו קמיע. עכ״ל הרשב״א. יש להעיר שזה שלא כדעת הרמב״ם הנזכ״ל, דלדעת הרמב״ם אין כל היתר לעבור על איסור מדאורייתא כלל.

 וע״ע בביאור הלכה סי׳ שכ״ח סעיף י׳ ד״ה ורופא אחד, שגם בחולה שיש בו סכנה שייך טירוף דעת כדין יולדת, עיי״ש.

17 כן כתב בספר תורת היולדת.

18 והנה אף דמלשון הרשב״א הנזכ״ל בהערה 16 משמע דאי אתמחי גברא או אתמחי קמיעא שרי לכתוב אף אם אינם דורשים, לא כן שיטת אחרוני הפוסקים וכדלהלן.

כתב בברכי יוסף (או״ח ש״א ו׳) מעשה באיש אחד שמצא סגולה אחת בספר כתב יד מאדם גדול מהראשונים למי ששתה סם המות לכתוב לו ותיכף מקיא האדם וחוזר לבריאותו וכו׳ ויהי היום ליל שבת קודש אירע שנערה ישראלית שתתה סם המוות והתחילו לה דבקי מיתה ובאו אצל האיש הלז בליל שבת וקם וכתב הקמיעא לנערה ותיכף הקיאה ועמדה על בוריה, וביום השבת נודע בעיר כל אשר נעשה ולעזה עליו מדינה דחילל שבת וכו׳ והוא השיב דפקוח נפש דוחה שבת והיו מגמגמין בדבר, אי לזאת שאל האיש אם חטא בזה ואת״ל שחטא אי עבר אדאורייתא או אדרבנן. והשיב הגאון החיד״א זיע״א לאחר שדן בארוכה דאמנם לא שפיר למעבד הכי, והיינו משום דהוא דרך סגולה, אך לאחר מעשה כיון שכוונתו היתה להצילה ומש״ה לא שאל שהשואל ה״ז שופך דמים ונמצא שהצילה, לא עבר לא על אסורים מדאורייתא ולא אדרבנן, והיינו כיון שעשה רפואה סגולית. אך אם חילל עבורה בחילול רגיל אין כאן בית מיחוש אף שהביאה הצרה על עצמה, לית לן לזרוק אבן אחר הנופל. ע״כ. בתוך דבריו כתב בזה״ל: ואע״ג דאשכחן דהתירו לצאת בקמיעא מומחה וביצת החרגול וכיוצא שכל אלו סגולות, מ״מ לא התירו איסור תורה שכל אלו אין בהן אלא איסור דרבנן שאינו מוציא כדרך המוציאין וכו׳ עיי״ש. נמצא שמסקנתו דלכתחילה אין להתיר איסורי תורה לצורך רפואה סגולית, אלא רק באיסור דרבנן. ורק בשאר רפואות טבעיות שרי אף מלאכה מדאורייתא.

(The Rashba goes into detail regarding which types of amulets are permissible and which are not permissible even during the week.[19])

17. Regarding whether one may travel or send a telegram to a tzaddik requesting that he pray or bless the sick person, see chapter 13, "Choosing a Doctor and Seeking Medical Advice," paragraph 11.

עוד כתב החיד״א בשו״ת חיים שאל ח״ב סי׳ ל״א אות פ״א, ראיתי כתיבת יד ישן ״שרבינו פרץ ז״ל כתב בשבת שמות הקודש סגולה בדוקה ליושבת על המשבר״ ומריש הוה אמינא דאין לסמוך ע״ז (והביא מהרדב״ז שפקפק באמיתת כתב היד הנ״ל עיי״ש) אמנם זה מחלוקת קדום, דהרמב״ם סובר שאין עוברים על המצוות אלא ברפואה שהיא דרך הטבע לא בדבר שהוא דרך סגולה. וכתבו האחרונים דהרמב״ן והרשב״א פליגי על הרמב״ם דאפילו רפואה בדרך סגולה שרי לעבור על איסורי תורה, וכמו שכתבתי אני בעניי בספר הקטן ברכי יוסף א״ח סי׳ ש״א עיי״ש. ולפי״ז אפשר שרבינו פרץ ס״ל כסברת החולקים על הרמב״ם. ומיהו כבר כתבתי שם דצריך לעמוד ולברר דעת הרמב״ן והרשב״א בזה. עכ״ל.

וע״ע בברכי יוסף (יו״ד סי׳ ר״צ ס״ק ב׳) בעניין אחד שנכפה ואמרו המומחים לכתוב קמיע על קלף צבי ולא נמצא קלף צבי רק מספר תורה, צידד הרב שער אפרים סי׳ צ׳ לחתוך מהספר תורה ולגרור הכתב ולמחוק שמות. ודימה העניין לאחיתופל דהתיר למחוק שמות להצלה מק״ו מסוטה. והסיק שם דיש לחלק.

וע״ע בשו״ת חתם סופר חיו״ד סי׳ של״ט, שנשאל בכהן שיש לו חולי נכפה רח״ל מסוכן מאוד, ונמצא בספר שיתן ידו ליד עכו״ם מת, ויאמר לחש זה ״קח ממני החולי שאינו מזיק לך ולי אתה מטיב״ וכבר ניסה אחד רפואה זו ונתרפא ולכן שואל אם יכול הכהן לסמוך על זה וליטמא במגע עם מת עכו״ם והשיב דאם היה בבחינת אתמחי גברא וקמיעא ודאי שרי, אך השואל חושש שאין זה בדוק כ״כ. והשיבו באופן שהאיסור הוא רק מדרבנן שרי. עיי״ש העצה שכתב האיך יהיה האיסור רק מדרבנן. לעניינו משמע לכאורה דברפואה סגולית אם היא בדוקה ומומחית מותר לעבור נמי אדאורייתא, ואילו בספק מומחית שרי רק איסור דרבנן.

אולם בשדי חמד ח״ט מערכת יום הכיפורים סימן ג׳ אות כ״ד, כתב בשם גדולי האחרונים דלרפואה סגולית שרי רק איסור דרבנן, משא״כ איסור דאורייתא אין להתיר כלל. ודלא כשיטת הרשב״א, וגם לא כשיטת החתם סופר הנ״ל, דס״ל דאי אתמחי גברא ואתמחי קמיעא מותר לחלל שבת אף בדאורייתא. ועיין עוד בדברי המהר״ם בן חביב זצ״ל בתוספת יום הכפורים דף פ״ג שהאריך לבאר שיטת הרמב״ם והרשב״א ברפואות סגוליות. ואכמ״ל יותר.

19 בעיקר הדין אם אפשר להשתמש בקמיע עבור חולה ובאיזה קמיע שרי, כתב הרשב״א בתשובה חלק חמישי סי׳ קי״ט ובחלק שני סי׳ רפ״א ז״ל שאלת הקמיעים אם מותר לכתוב אותם ולהתרפאות בהם בין שיש בהם שמות בין שיש בהם פסוקים בלא שמות. תשובה. ודאי מותר להתרפאות בהן אפילו יש בהם שמות ובהדיא שנינו בפרק במה אשה יוצאה (דף ס״א) ולא בקמיע בזמן שאינו מן המומחה הא במומחה יוצאין בו בשבת לכתחילה וכ״ש בחול דמתרפאין בו... וכן נראה שהוא מותר לישא קמיעים שיש בהם פסוקים ודווקא להגן שלא יחלה אבל להתרפאות בהם מי שיש לו מכה או חולי לא, דגרסינן בשבועות פרק ידיעות הטומאה (דף טו:) שיר של פגעים וכו׳, ואקשינן והיכי עביד הכי והא אמר ריב״ל אסור להתרפאות בדברי תורה ומפרקינן להגן שאני ואלא כי אמר אסור דאיכא מכה עיי״ש באורך. וע״פ דבריו כתב השו״ע ביורה דעה סימן קע״ט סעיף י״ב ז״ל. מותר להתרפאות בקמיע אפילו יש בהם שמות, וכן מותר לישא קמיעים שיש בהם פסוקים ודווקא להגן שלא יחלה, אבל לא להתרפאות בהם מי שיש לו מכה או חולי, אבל לכתוב פסוקים בקמיעים אסור. ע״כ.

18. The rabbinical prohibition against healing on Shabbos ("grinding herbs") does not apply to the use of amulets on Shabbos.[20]

Handling Amulets and Other *Segulos*

19. A person who is sick, even if the illness is not life-threatening, may carry an amulet on Shabbos where there is no *eiruv*[21] providing he wears it like a piece of jewelry. He should not hold it in his hand while carrying it.

20. Similarly, one may wear a "health chain" or bracelet that relieves the pain of rheumatism while walking in an area where there is no *eiruv*.[22]

21. Some authorities permit wearing a mezuzah on a necklace for protection in a public domain on Shabbos.[23]

---

20 עיין בשו״ת באר משה ח״א סי׳ ל״ב דכל דבר שאין עושים אותו ע״י סממנים אין שייך בזה גזירת שחיקת סממנים, ועיין בזה בדברינו לעיל פרק ב׳ בביאור מה לא נכלל בגזירת שחיקת סממנים.

21 שו״ע סי׳ ש״א סעיף כ״ה.

22 נשמת אברהם ח״א עמוד ק״ע.

23 בשו״ת משפטי צדק סי׳ ל״ט דן בהיתר יציאה לרשות הרבים בשבת עם מזוזה בצווארו לשם הגנה, ומסיק להתיר. עיי״ש.

Chapter 17
Cooking

1. If a dangerously ill patient (*choleh sheyeish bo sakanah*) needs freshly cooked food, and there is no such food available, it is permissible to cook for him on Shabbos.[1] Some halachic authorities rule that there is no preference in asking a non-Jew to cook the food. Since cooking the food is permitted, it is actually preferable that a Jew prepare it.[2] Nevertheless, the Rema rules that if it does not involve undue delay, it is preferable to ask a non-Jew to cook the food.[3]

---

1 עפ״י המבואר ברמב״ן שעושים לו כל שרגילים לעשות לו בחול ממאכלים ורפואות, וממה שהתירו שחיטה בשבת לצורך החולה ודאי דשרי הבישול גופא.

2 שמלבד מאי דקיי״ל כל צרכי חולה שיש בו סכנה אין עושים ע״י נכרי אלא ע״י גדולי ישראל וחכמיהם וכנ״ל הכא חמיר טפי דבאפשר לבשל ע״י ישראל אין להתיר בשולי נכרים, וכן משמע בבית יוסף סו״ס שכ״ח בעניין בישול יין בשבת ע״י נכרי. וכן דעת הב״ח סי׳ שכ״ח ס״ק י״ד, שהישראלי יבשל היין ולא הא״י דמ״ש משוחטין. ובהגהות מרדכי שם כתב שימלא הישראלי ויבשל הא״י, הובא שם בב״י ובב״ח עיי״ש. אולם להשגת הדרכי משה שם נראה דשפיר שרי בישולי נכרים אף לחולה שיש בו סכנה עיי״ש. ועי״ע לקמן הערה 12 מש״כ בענין זה בהרחבה. וכתב לי הגרי״י זילברשטיין בזה״ל: יעוין באשל אברהם סי׳ ש״ל שכתב: יולדת בשבת קודש חלושה, שאלו אם לבשל המרק? והתרתי ע״י גוי...כי כנראה לא היה נוטה כ״כ לסכנה וכן גם להט״ז יש לעשות ע״י גוי יעו״ש. והוא יסוד גדול, שגם לדעת מרן המתיר לעשות ע״י ישראל אף שיש לפנינו גוי כמבואר בסימן שכ״ח סעיף י״ב, היינו דווקא בסכנה ודאית ולא בספק סכנה. ופשוט הוא.

3 כ״כ בדרכי משה ס״ס שכ״ח אות ט״ו ז״ל: אע״ג דמחללין שבת ולא מאכילין אותו נבלה יש לומר שאני נבלה שהיא גם כן איסור דאורייתא, אי נמי מטעם דלעיל שיקוץ החולה באכילתו, מנה שאין כן לגבי יין נסך וכו׳ דכל היכא דאפשר בגוי בלא שיהוי עושין הכל ע״י גוי וכו׳ עכ״ל.

2. Similarly, if the patient needs a hot drink, and there is no hot water available, one is permitted to boil water and place tea bags in the hot water for the patient on Shabbos.[4]

Cooking Methods

3. One may cook for a dangerously ill patient in any manner necessary, whether on a gas stove, an electric stove, or any kind of hot plate. Nevertheless, when time is not of the essence, the following criteria should be used in determining the preferable manner of cooking.

4. An electric heating appliance is preferred over a gas or kerosene stove.[5] The reason for this is that there are two actions being performed when using these fuel-based appliances: (1) creating a fire by striking a match and (2) igniting the gas with the lit match. When using an electrical appliance, however, only one action is being performed.

5. If there is an existing flame, such as a burning candle, one should ignite the gas oven with that fire rather than striking a match, since this avoids the additional action of lighting the match.[6] However, it is better to strike a match than to use an implement that creates an electric spark, since normally many sparks are created until the fire lights and thus involves more than one action, which is not the case regarding a match.[7]

---

4 עפ״י הגמ׳ (יומא פד ע״ב) מחמין לו חמין הן להשקותו והן להברותו. והובאה גמ׳ זו להלכה ברי״ף פרק שמונה שרצים. וע״ע בשער הציון סי׳ שכ״ח ס״ק י״א. ודע דאם אפשר להכין לו תה ע״י נתינת שקית תה בכלי שני או שלישי ודאי חייב להכין באופן זה ולא לבשל עלים בישול גמור.

5 כ״כ בשו״ת אור לציון ח״ב פל״ו שאלה ט״ז.

6 בבישול בשבת יש מספר איסורים וכדלהלן:

א) הולדת אש בהצתת גפרור.

ב) הבערת הגפרור עצמו.

ג) הבערת הגז.

ד) הבישול עצמו.

כשיש לפנינו נר דלוק ומדליקים דרכו את הגז חוסכים פעולה א׳ ו-ב׳, ובהדלקת הגז ע״י מצת לכאורה חוסכים פעולה ב׳, אולם יש ובמצת נעשות הרבה הצתות ואילו בגפרור ישנה הצתה אחת והבערה אחת. וע״ע בהערה 7 ולגבי עצם העדפה של מכשיר חשמלי על פני מכשירים אחרים — כ״כ בשו״ת אור לציון ח״ב פרק ל״ו שאלה ט״ז עיי״ש.

7 בספר מנוחת אהבה ח״א סימן כא סעיף מ״ז כתב, אם יש בבית מצית אלקטרוני — לא ידליק

6. In any case, it is forbidden to extinguish the flame or turn off the gas or electric stove when the cooking is finished.[8] It is also forbidden to add water to an empty electric kettle to prevent damage to the electric kettle. However, if one will need to boil more water for the patient later in the day, and he is afraid the gas supply will run out or the electric kettle will become unusable, it is permitted to turn them off.

7. Many electric kettles turn off automatically when the water starts boiling. Since this does not involve any act of extinguishing on the part of the user, this type of electric kettle is preferable for heating water on Shabbos. However, if this type of electric kettle has a light that goes on when the appliance is plugged in and another kettle that needs to be turned off manually does not have such a light, it may be better to use the one without the light. HaGaon Rav Y. Zilberstein argues, however, that since the user has no need for the light, it is considered a *melachah she'einah tzerichah l'gufah*; therefore, the electric kettle with the light is preferable over the kind that requires one to turn it off manually.[9]

גפרור לצורך הדלקת האש שבכיריים אלא ישתמש במצית. ובהערה 153 הוסיף שבהצתת מצית אלקטרוני אין איסור מבעיר רק איסור מוליד, ואילו בהצתת גפרור יש גם איסור מבעיר שכן הגפרור נשרף ע״י האש שנוצרה. ע״כ.

אולם בספר שמירת שבת כהלכתה פרק לב סעיף ע״ו הערה קצה, כתב וז״ל וכאשר מדליק כירי גז יעדיף להשתמש בגפרור לצורך הדלקתה שכן בשימוש במצית נוצרים ניצוצות מרובים, והרי הוא מעוניין בניצוצות האלה כדי שהם ידליקו את האש, ואילו בהצתת גפרור נוצרת רק להבה אחת. ע״כ. ועל פי מש״כ בהערה 6 מסתבר יותר שישתמש בגפרור ולא במצת אלא אם כן ברור לו שבמצית יצית הצתה אחת דאז יש להעדיף שימוש במצית וכנ״ל.

8 כיבוי הגז בשבת אין בו איסור תורה דמכבה, שכן אין נוצרים פחמים בכיבוי זה. כ״כ בספר מאורי האש דף פ״ח ע״א הובא בנשמת אברהם סי׳ רע״ח בשם הגרש״ז אוירבך שליט״א דכל דבר שאינו נעשה פם לא דמי למלאכת המשכן ולא חשיב כיבוי. עיי״ש. אך עכ״ז יש עדיין איסור מדרבנן בכיבוי אש או מנורה.

והעיר לי ע״ז מו״ר הגר״ז כהן שליט״א בזה״ל: יש להעיר לפי המבואר בביצה כ״כ שהמסתפק מן השמן חייב משום מכבה, והרי אין כאן פחם. ובלמא לדעת הרא״ש שם היינו מפני שהוא גורם את הכיבוי ויתכן שהמלאכה מחמת מה שבסוף יכבה ויהיה פחם, אבל לדעת התוס׳ שהכוונה מחמת ההשפעה של מיעוט האור באותו רגע א״כ היינו כיבוי האש ולא יצירת פחם. וכן מוכח משבת מ״ז ע״ב דבכיבוי ניצוצות איכא איסור כיבוי דאורייתא עיי״ש ברש״י ובתוד״ה מפני ומוכח שמדובר שם שאין ממשות אלא רק ניצוצות. עכ״ל. ובאמת שהאריך בכל זה מרן הגרש״ז אויערבאך זצ״ל בספרו מנחת שלמה סי׳ י״ב אות ג׳ עיי״ש.

9 וכתב ע״ז הגר״י זילברשטיין שליט״א בזה״ל: יתכן שעדיף להשתמש בקומקום החשמלי, מאחר ולא זקוק לנורה הנדלקת ועדיף מלאכה שאינה צריכה לגופה מכיבוי בהדיא, ובפרט להחזו״א יש בהוצאת החוט החשמלי חשש סותר.

Eating Food That Was Cooked on Shabbos

8. A healthy person may taste food that was cooked by a Jew on Shabbos for a dangerously ill patient in order to ascertain that it is fully cooked and tasty.[10] It is, however, forbidden for a healthy person, or even an ordinary bedridden patient (*choleh she'ein bo sakanah*), to partake of the food for his own sake. (As will be explained in chapter 25, "Food Cooked by a Non-Jew," only a non-Jew is permitted to cook food for the needs of an ordinary bedridden patient.) The reason for this prohibition is the concern that if we allow other people to enjoy the food cooked for a dangerously ill patient, greater quantities of food will be cooked in the first place to fill their needs, too.[11]

9. Once Shabbos is over, a healthy person may eat the leftover food that was prepared by a Jew on Shabbos for a dangerously ill patient. There is no need to wait the amount of time it would have taken to prepare the food after Shabbos.

10. After Shabbos, a healthy person may eat food cooked for a *choleh sheyeish bo sakanah* only if it was cooked by a Jew. But if a non-Jew cooked food for such a patient — whether on Shabbos or during the week — many authorities rule that a healthy person is forbidden to partake of the food because of the prohibition against eating food cooked by a non-Jew.[12]

---

10 מ״ב סי׳ שי״ח ס״ק י״א.

11 שו״ע סימן שי״ח סעיף ב׳.

12 דין זה נחלקו בו ראשונים ואחרונים, ונפרט בעזר השם בזה בהרחבה.

א) הרא״ה בבדק הבית (בית שלישי שער שביעי דף צ״ד ע״א) כתב וז״ל: אף אני אומר שהנכרי שבא לבשל לחולה והוא בשבת — בזמן האסור לנו לבשל — שלא אסרו משום בשולי נכרים כלל דלא שייך הכא משום חתנות, ולא עוד אלא שמותר לבריא במוצאי שבת וכו׳ עיי״ש. ומיירי הרא״ה בחולה שאין בו סכנה כדאמר התם חיה כל שלושים עושים לה ע״י ארמאי כדקיי״ל דכל צרכי חולה נעשים ע״י נכרים בשבת עיי״ש. ועוד דכתב ״והוא בשבת בזמן האסור לנו לבשל״ א״כ נראה דמיירי בחולה שאין בו סכנה.

ב) והנה הרמ״א ביו״ד סי׳ קי״ג סעיף ט״ז כתב וז״ל: עובד כוכבים שבא לבשל לחולה בשבת מותר למוצאי שבת אפילו לבריא ואין בו משום בשולי עובד כוכבים דכל כה״ג היכרא איכא. (ב״י בשם הר״ן שכ״כ בשם הרא״ה.)

ג) ובאמת שכבר הרשב״א ז״ל במשמרת הבית (שם על דברי בדק הבית) כתב וז״ל: בשבת עצמה התירו ולצורך חולה לא העמידו דבריהם אבל למוצאי שבת שאין לו בו צורך יאסר וכ״ש לבריא, וחלילה וחס שלא הותר אפילו לחולה עצמו אלא בעת צורך בלבד דהיינו בשבת הא למוצאי שבת חוזר לאיסורו, וכ״ש לבריא. עיי״ש.

Nevertheless, some maintain that in a case where a non-Jew cooked

---

ד) והנה הבית יוסף ביו״ד ס״ס קי״ג כתב וז״ל: ״והביא הר״ן כל זה בפרק אין מעמידין וז״ל בתשובה (תשובות הר״ן סימן ה׳ אות י״א) כתב הרא״ה גוי שבא לבשל לחולה בשבת מותר לבריא במוצאי שבת וליכא משום בישולי גויים ומשום חתנות דכל כי הא הכירא איכא. עוד התיר בגוי שבישל לעצמו בין בחול בין בשבת דברים המותרים אע״פ שהתבשיל אסור משום בישולי גויים אבל הכלי מותרת להשתמש בהם אחר הדחה דלגבי גיעולי הכלים לא מסתבר למימר דגזרו ואסרו בהא משום גיעולי גוים דבהא ליכא ודאי משום חתנות, אבל למעשה אני אוסר לפי שראיתי קצת מהגדולים שחלקו על הרא״ה ז״ל ובעל התרומה מכללם עכ״ל״.

ה) ובכוונת הר״ן במה שסיים אבל למעשה אני אוסר וכו׳ נחלקו גדולי האחרונים על מה נסובו דבריו, זאת משום שהר״ו הביא בדבריו שני דינים בשם הרא״ה. (א) דין תבשיל הגוי במוצאי שבת לבריא. (ב) דין הכלים אי שייך בהם גיעולי כלים. וסיים למעשה אני אוסר וכו׳ וכאן נשאלת השאלה האם חולק הר״ן על הרא״ה בשני הדינים או רק בדין גיעולי כלים.

ו) הבית יוסף ביו״ד סימן קכ״ג בסופו דן בענין דבש של הישמעאלים, ובהקשר לזה הביא את תשובת הר״ן הנזכרת וז״ל שם: ועל זה סמך הרא״ה בגוי שבישל לחולה בשבת שמותר לבריא במוצאי שבת דליכא בהא משום חתנות, ואף אני אומר שאפשר לדון להלכה שהדבש מותר שאין עליו תורת יין ומתחילת דריכתו לכך נתכוונו, אבל למעשה אני אוסר לפי שראיתי קצת גדולים חולקים על הרא״ה והרב בעל התרומה מכללם, לפיכך ראוי לנהוג איסור בדבש ופורץ גדר ישכנו נחש עכ״ל [הר״ן] עכ״ל הב״י. הרי שהבית יוסף פשט את כוונת הר״ן דפליג על הרא״ה גם בדין הראשון המתייחס בבישל הא״י בשבת שמותר לבריא במוצאי שבת, שלדעת הר״ן אסור לבריא במוצאי שבת וכנ״ל.

ז) הט״ז בסי׳ קי״ג ס״ק ט״ו הביא דברי הר״ן והרא״ה שהם מקור התירו של הרמ״א ואח״כ הביא דעת הרשב״א לאיסור ופסק כמותו לאיסור. וכן הט״ז בסי׳ קכ״ג ס״ק י״ח הביא את תשובת הר״ן כפי שהביאה הב״י הנ״ל באות ו׳ דמשמעות הר״ן דפליג על הרא״ה בדין בישל האינו יהודי בשבת לחולה דאסור לבריא במוצאי שבת וכנ״ל. ותמה שם על הרמ״א בסי׳ קי״ג שפסק כדברי הרא״ה, והסיק אילו ראה הרמ״א שהרשב״א פליג עליה ודאי היה ס״ל כוותיה.

ח) ברם, הש״ך בנקודות הכסף דרך אחרת לו בהבנת שיטת הר״ן המובאת בב״י. דהנה בסי׳ קי״ג עמש״כ הט״ז על דברי הרמ״א שאילו ראה את דברי הרשב״א לא היה סובר כרא״ה. כתב בנקודות הכסף וז״ל: ליתא, דאפשר אפילו ראו היו פוסקים כך דבשל סופרים הלך אחר המיקל, כ״ש בפת של עובד כוכבים דקיל טובא, ועוד שגם דעת הר״ן בתשובה כהרא״ה. ומש״כ בבית יוסף ס״ס קכ״ג טעות סופר הוא וכמ״ש לקמן ס״ס קכ״ג עיין שם עכ״ל. ובסי׳ קכ״ג כתב על דברי הט״ז שתמה על פסקו של הרמ״א וז״ל: לא קשיא מידי דטעות סופר הוא בהעתקה זו של תשובת הר״ן שבב״י, והמעיין בתשובת הר״ן עצמו יראה דאדרבה בדין של הרמ״א בבישל לחולה כ״ע מודו, וכמ״ש בש״ך ס״ק נ׳ע״ש עכ״ל. ואמנם בש״ך ס״ק נ׳ כתב דמה שכתב הר״ן שחולקים על הרא״ה זה על הדין השני שהביא הר״ן בשם הרא״ה בנוגע לכלים, עי״ש.

ט) אך גדולי הפוסקים דחו דברי הרמ״א שהתיר בשולי נכרים לחולה שאין בו סכנה במוצאי שבת. וראיתי במנחת יעקב על התורת חטאת כלל ע״ה אות כ״ט שפסק כדברי הרשב״א והביא שכן דעת הר״ן וכן משמעות המהרש״ל פ״ק דחולין ומהר״א שטיין בביאוריו לסמ״ג וכן האריך להוכיח בספר באר שבע דף לח ע״ב כדעת הרשב״א וכן פסק בעל שירי כנסת הגדולה באו״ח סי׳ שי״ח וכתב שגם דעת הב״י להחמיר כיון שהשמיט בספר הקצר דעת הרא״ה, ומי בעל דברים ייגש להתיר שאוסרים עמודי עולם עכ״ל. ובכף החיים שם אות צ״ו הביא עוד פוסקים דס״ל דלא כהרמ״א; כנסת הגדולה בהגהת ב״י אות ע״ט וכתב שכן דעת

food for a *choleh sheyeish bo sakanah*, the rabbinical prohibition against eating food cooked by a non-Jew was not imposed.[13] However, if the non-Jew cooked food for the needs of an ordinary bedridden patient

---

השו״ע שהשמיט בסי׳ זה סברת הרא״ה, פרי חדש אות כ״ו וכתב ודלא כהש״ך בנקודות הכסף ולקמן סו״ס קכ״ג, פרי תואר אות י״ט, מנחת יעקב על התורת חטאת כלל ע״ה אות כ״ט, לה״פ אות כ״ד, בית לחם יהודה אות כ״ב, ער״ה אות כ״ד, חכמת אדם כלל ס״ו אות י״ב. ע״כ. וכן משמעות ביאור הגר״א [ליקוט] ביו״ד סו״ס קכ״ג דלא כהרא״ה, וכ״מ הגר״א בסו״ס קי״ג ס״ק כ״ב דס״ל דלא כהרא״ה והרמ״א.

י) בספר ערוך השולחן ביו״ד קי״ג סעיף נ״ב כתב דלכתחילה כדעת הרשב״א עיי״ש אך לפלא בעיני שהבין דברי הר״ן כמסכים לדברי הרא״ה, והרי בפירוש אתמר שלא מסכים עמו שז״ל שם ״אבל למעשה אני אוסר לפי שראיתי קצת מהגדולים שחלקו על הרא״ה וכו׳ כמובא לעיל מהב״י״. וצריך לומר שהבין בעל הערוך השולחן כהבנת הש״ך בתשובת הר״ן הנ״ל.

יא) גם הרב ברכי יוסף או״ח סי׳ שי״ח אות ב׳ הביא דברי הרמ״א הנ״ל וכתב שבספר בית דוד ביו״ד סי׳ נ״א הביא הגהת מורם וכו׳ ונראה דתופס במושלם כמ״ש מורם דבשולי גויים לחולה בשבת מותר לבריא במוצאי שבת, וק״ק דהרי הרשב״א אוסר והר״ן מפקפק כמ״ש הרב שירי כנה״ג בסי׳ זה ושם ביו״ד וכתב דהלכה למעשה הורה הרב כנה״ג לאסור כסברת הרשב״א, וכתב שזה דעת מרן שהשמיט בשו״ע סברת הרא״ה עיי״ש. ומשמעות הברכי יוסף נוטה ג״כ לאסור לבריא במוצאי שבת. דעת המשנה ברורה יבואר להלן בהערה 13.

יב) והנה בשו״ת אור לציון ח״ב פרק לו שאלה ה׳ בהערות כתב וז״ל: בשו״ע סימן שכ״ח סעיף י״ט כתב, חולה שאין בו סכנה מותר בבישולי עכו״ם. וכתב שם במשנה ברורה ס״ק ס״ג שמ״מ הכלי צריך הכשר ע״ש. אך דעת מרן בב״י יו״ד סוף סימן קי״ג להתיר אף לבריא לאוכלו במוצאי שבת, ובוודאי שאין צריך הכשר, וכן כתב הרמ״א שם בסעיף ט״ז. ע״ש ואף המ״ב בסימן שי״ח ס״ק י״ג כתב להתיר אף לבריא באכילה, וצ״ע שסותר למש״כ בסימן שכ״ח, ומ״מ להלכה קיי״ל כדברי מרן, שהתיר אף באכילה, ובוודאי שאין צריך להכשיר את הכלי. ואעפ״י שכמה אחרונים החמירו בזה (ראה ט״ז ופר״ח ביו״ד שם וברכ״י וכנה״ג בסימן שי״ח) מנ״מ כיון שכן דעת מרן ואין כאן אלא חשש דרבנן, יש להורות להתיר כדברי מרן. ע״כ. אך נראה דגם מרן הגאון רב״צ אבא שאול שליט״א הבין כשיטת הש״ך בביאור דעת הר״ן. אך כאמור לעיל רב האחרונים לא ס״ל כדעת הש״ך בזה. ומה שכתב מרן שליט״א סתירה בדברי המ״ב אבאר בסמוך בהערה 13 בעזר החונן לאדם דעת דלא סתרי אהדדי.

13 בשו״ע סימן שי״ח סעיף ב׳ כתב ז״ל: המבשל לחולה אסור [בשבת] לבריא או לחולה שאין בו סכנה דחיישינן שמא ירבה בשבילו. הגה. ואפילו בישל ע״י עכו״ם אסור בשבת (תוס׳ פ״ק דגיטין ר״ן פ׳ אין מעמידין) ע״כ. וכתב בביאור הגר״א שם אמש״כ הרמ״א אסור בשבת — ״לאפוקי במוצאי שבת, ואין בו משום בשולי נכרים כיון דלא שכיחי אין בו משום חתנות ע״כ. והביא מדברי הגר״א אלו במשנה ברורה שם ס״ק י״ד. ובביאור דברי הגר״א אלו יש לומר ע״פ התוס׳ בפסחים (מו ע״ב ד״ה רבה) ז״ל ״ואם תאמר אי אמרינן הואיל א״כ בטלת כל מלאכת שבת הואיל וראוי לחולה שיש בו סכנה. וי״ל כיון דלא שכיח לא אמרינן הואיל״ ע״כ. וקיי״ל בכולא תלמודא מלתא דשכיחא גזרו בה רבנן ומילתא דלא שכיחא לא גזרו בה רבנן (עיין ביצה ב׳ ע״ב. י״ח ע״א. ערובין ס״ג ע״ב ועוד). והאי בשולי עכו״ם גזירה דרבנן היא משום חתנות, וממילא חולה שיש בו סכנה הואיל ולא שכיחא היא לא גזרו בו רבנן בשולי עכו״ם, ולכן בשבת אסור לישראל הבריא לאכול מבישולו (מדיני השבת) שמא ירבה בשבילו. אבל למוצאי שבת מותר מיד כיון דלצורך חולה שיש בו סכנה בישל הרי דבהתירא אתא קמן, ושרי אף לבריא. ולפי״ז דון מינא דהיינו דווקא בבישל הא״י לצורך חולה שיש בו סכנה — ומשום דלא שכיח. אבל אם בישל בשבת

(*choleh she'ein bo sakanah*), all agree that a healthy person may not eat the food.

11. A Jew may cook on Shabbos only the amount of food needed by the sick person on Shabbos itself. He may not cook food to be eaten after Shabbos. The only exception to this rule is if the patient will need the food at a specific time after Shabbos, and there will not be enough time to prepare it for him after the conclusion of Shabbos.

12. Utensils used by a Jew to cook food for a *choleh sheyeish bo sakanah* do not need to be kashered. But if a non-Jew cooked the food, some

---

לצורך חולה שאין בו סכנה דלא הוי מלתא דלא שכיח — אה״נ אסור במוצאי שבת — דבהא גזרו רבנן.

והנה בסימן שכ״ח סעיף י״ט כתב מרן בשו״ע ז״ל: חולה שאין בו סכנה מותר בבישולי א״י. ע״כ. וכתב שם המשנה ברורה ס״ק ס״ג וז״ל: ומה שנשאר למוצאי שבת אסור אפילו לחולה עצמו כיון שאפשר לבשל לו אז ע״י ישראל. ובשער הציון אות ל״ט כתב, אחרונים וכן מבואר ברשב״א. ע״כ. והוסיף שם בשער הציון אות מ״א ז״ל: דבלא״ה הרמ״א שם סתם כהרא״ה דאף לבריא מותר דאין ע״ז שם בישול א״י וכן דעת הנקה״כ שם, ונהי דלמעשה אין להקל וכמו שכתב בתו״ש בשם כמה אחרונים דס״ל כהט״ז, עכ״פ לענין הכלים יש לסמוך עלייהו עיי״ש.

ורבים מגדולי דורינו שליט״א תמהו על המשנה ברורה שסותר עצמו מיניה וביה דבסימן ש״ח כתב דלמוצ״ש מותר בשולי הא״י. ובסימן זה (שכ״ח) אוסר למוצש״ק אף לחולה. עיין לעיל בהערה י״ב שהבאנו תמיהא זו משו״ת אור לציון ח״ב, וכ״כ הגרע״י בלוית חן סי׳ פו. כמו״כ עיין בספר שמירת שבת כהלכתה מהדו״ק (הובא בנשמת אברהם ח״א עמ׳ קצ״ט) ז״ל: וראה בשש״כ שמנסה לתרץ את הסתירה בשם ספר תולדותיו של החפץ חיים מכתיבת יד בנו, דמרוב טרדות הזמן נאלץ הח״ח למסור חלק ממלאכת החיבור לבנו והוא חלק על אביו, אולם קשה לומר ההסבר הזה מכיון שגם הערוך השולחן מביא את שתי השיטות להלכה וצע״ג. עכ״ל הנשמת אברהם שם.

ובאמת דגם בערוך השולחן פוסק כן דבסימן ש״ח התיר למוצ״ש ובסימן שכ״ח אסר במוצ״ש עיי״ש. ולכאורה יקשה טובא שיטת הגר״א גופא דביו״ד משמע דס״ל דלא כהרמ״א בשם הרא״ה שהתיר בשולי נכרים שבישל לחולה בשבת וז״ל הגר״א שם ע״ד הרמ״א: כ״כ הרא״ה וכשיטתו דכל שלא שייך חתנות מותר. אבל הרשב״א חלק עליו ועט״ז ופר״ח. עכ״ל. משמע דלא ס״ל כהרמ״א בשם הרא״ה. וא״כ איך כתב באו״ח סי׳ ש״ח דשרי בישולי נכרים שבישל לחולה שיש בו סכנה. וגם לא ציין להרמ״א בשם הרא״ה ביו״ד. וצ״ע לכאורה.

אך האמת יורה דרכו דלפי ההקדמה שהקדמנו יבואר הדבר בס״ד. דיש לחלק טובא בין אם הא״י בישל בשבת עבור חולה שיש בו סכנה — דכיון דחולה שיש בו סכנה לא שכיח לא גזרו בו רבנן בשולי עכו״ם משום חתנות, ורק בשבת אסור לבריא מדיני שבת שמא ירבה בשבילו אבל למוצא שבת מותר מיד. משא״כ אם בישל הא״י בשבת עבור חולה שאין בו סכנה שזה ודאי שכיח וגזרו רבנן, אך בשבת התירו לחולה שאין בו סכנה דא״א ע״י ישראל אבל למוצאי שבת אסור בין לבריא ואפילו לחולה דבבישול זה ודאי איכא גזירה דבישולי נכרים. וא״כ מה שכתב מרן בשו״ע סי׳ ש״ח אירי בבשול לחולה שיש בו סכנה, ומש״כ בסי׳ שכ״ח איירי בחולה שאין בו סכנה. ובזה נתיישבו דברי המשנה ברורה ושני פסקיו עומדים וקיימים על פי שיטת הגר״א וכמש״כ.

authorities maintain that the utensil should be kashered,[14] while others disagree.[15] In practice, one may act leniently if he waits twenty-four hours before using the utensil.[16]

Shechitah on Shabbos

13. One is permitted to ritually slaughter an animal for a *choleh sheyeish bo sakanah* if fresh meat is necessary for his health and well-being.[17]

14. Kosher slaughtering of an animal on Shabbos is preferable to feeding fresh non-kosher meat to a dangerously ill patient. However, if the patient needs the meat immediately and non-kosher meat is readily available, while it will take some time to slaughter a kosher animal and prepare fresh kosher meat for him, he may be fed the non-kosher meat.[18]

15. If a large chicken and a small chicken are both readily available, and

---

ובאמת יש לציין שכל מה שכתבנו בזה הוא לשיטת הגר״א והמ״ב דמתירים בבישול ע״י א״י לצורך חולה שיש בו סכנה וכאמור משום שחולה שיש בו סכנה לא שכיח. אך לעולם דעת הט״ז ודעימיה שהבאנו בהערה 12 ס״ל דלא שנא ובין אם בישל הא״י לחולה שיש בו סכנה ובין לחולה שאין בו סכנה — אסור במוצאי שבת משום בישולי עכו״ם. עיין בכל זה בכף החיים סי׳ שי״ח אות ל״א ובסי׳ שכ״ח אות קכ״א ושם ציין כל הפוסקים בשיטת הט״ז הנזכר ואכמ״ל יותר.

14 נחלקו בזה הרשב״א והרא״ש הובא בטור יו״ד סי׳ קי״ג. דהרשב״א ס״ל שכלים שבשלו בהם גויים דברים שיש בהם משום בישולי גויים אסורין. והרא״ש ס״ל שאין צריך לחוש לזה כלל שלא החמירו בבישולי גויים לאסור פליטתו. וכתב הב״י שם דהעיקר אך מ״מ יש להקל בו יותר מבשאר איסורין דאילו כלי חרס שנשתמש באחד מן האיסורים רותח אין לו תקנה אלא שבירה או חזרת כבשונות, אבל כלי חרס האסור משום בשולי גויים מגעילו שלש פעמים ודיו מפני שאין לאיסור זה עיקר בדאורייתא. ע״כ הב״י. וכ״פ בשו״ע שם סעיף ט״ז.

יש להעיר: שכל האמור הוא רק כשבליעת הכלים היא משום בשולי נכרים, אך כמובן שהתבשיל עצמו כשר למהדרין ולא חלילה נבלות או טרפות של הנכרי — דבזה לא הותר ולא שנא משאר איסורים, וברור.

15 שיטת הרא״ש הנזכר בהערה 14, וכן היא שיטת הרא״ה ודעימיה הנזכר בהערה 12 וכן הביא בכף החיים יו״ד סי׳ קי״ג אות צ״ט דהער״ה כתב דאין צריך הכשר דיש לסמוך בזה על הרא״ה עיי״ש. וכן העלה בשו״ת אור לציון ח״ב פרק ל״ו שאלה ה.

16 הכרעת האחרונים הובא בכף החיים הנ״ל דלכתחילה יש להכשיר ולאחר מעל״ע יש להקל עיי״ש. וע״ע בכף החיים או״ח סי׳ שי״ח אות ל״ב מסקנתו שם וז״ל: ונראה לענין דינא כיון שרבו הדעות בזה דלכתחילה יש להחמיר להכשירם, ובדיעבד אם בישל בהם בלתי הכשר אפילו תוך מעל״ע התבשיל מותר, והמיקל שלא להגעילם כלל ולהשתמש בהם אחר מעל״ע לא הפסיד. עכ״ל.

17 שו״ע סי׳ שכ״ח סעיף י״ד.

18 שו״ע שם.

either chicken will suffice for the patient's needs, it is preferable to slaughter the smaller chicken.[19]

16. One should not fulfill the mitzvah of covering the blood of slaughtered fowl with dirt on Shabbos. Rather, he should wait until Shabbos ends, and then, if the blood can still be seen, it should be covered.[20]

17. The meat may be salted on Shabbos in order to feed the patient kosher meat and prevent him from transgressing the prohibition of eating blood,[21] unless there is no time to do so. This is because we are afraid the patient will become disgusted with having to eat non-kashered meat, and this may result in a deterioration of his condition.[22]

18. If a doctor prescribes lean or unsalted meat as necessary for the patient's recovery, a lean fowl may be slaughtered or cooked without salting it. If possible, however, the chicken should be roasted over an open fire. If the unsalted chicken was cooked in a pot, the utensils used to cook it must be kashered.

19. If the patient is a minor, it is better to feed him non-kosher meat rather than perform the *melachah* of *shechitah* on his behalf. But if even non-kosher meat is not available, a Jew is permitted to slaughter an animal for the minor. A non-Jew should not be asked to slaughter the animal.[23]

---

19 עיין בשו״ת רב פעלים חאו״ח ח״א סי׳ כ״א שדן בזה בארוכה, ומסקנתו דלכתחילה אם נמצאו לפניו שנים אחד גדול ואחד קטן וסגי לחולה בקטן — ישחט הקטן. כמו״כ מי שמגיש לשוחט ויש לו בביתו קטן וגדול יביא הקטן לשוחט. אלא דאין צריך לחזר אחר קטן. עי״ש באורך.

20 שו״ע יו״ד סי׳ כ״ח סעיף ט״ז, והוסיף שם דיש מי שאומר שאם היה לו אפר מוכן לכסות בו צואה יש לכסות בו הדם אפילו בשבת. וע״ע בבאר היטב שם בשם הש״ך דהאידנא ביו״ט יש ליתן בכלי מעט עפר ויקבל לתוכה הדם עד הלילה. ה״ה נמי בשוחט לחולה בשבת יוכל לקבל הדם בכלי עם עפר ולכסותו במוצאי שבת.

21 יש לדון אם מותר למלוח במקום שאין החולה יכול להרגיש בזה שאינו מוכשר, דלפי הטעם של שמא ימאס — אסור למלוח משום שאינו יודע. אלא עדיין יש לדון להתיר למלוח אעפ״כ, מאחר שאם יכשירו איכא איסור דרבנן אחד על כל החתיכה מאחר שא״א להכשיר חלק בלי להכשיר את הכל, משא״כ באכילה איכא איסורא בכל משהו מהדם המבושל. ועוד יש לדון דשמא אסור מדרבנן גם משום דמיחזי כמעבד (עיין במ״ב סי שכ״א ס״ק כ״א).

22 שש״כ בשם מהר״ם שיק סימן קל״ח ודעת תורה סימן שכ״ח סעיף ד׳.

23 כ״כ המ״ב בסי׳ שכ״ח ס״ק ל״ט. וכ״כ בקצות השולחן סי׳ קל״ה סעיף ו׳. וע״ע בחזון איש או״ח סי׳ נ״ט אות ב׳. וסיים והלכך לאו שפיר עבדי השוחטין שמביאין אותן לשחוט לקטן ואינם שוחטים, שעי״ז מתאחר הדבר עד שמבקשים אחר נכרי, וזה נגד מה שאמרו השואל וכו׳.

Chapter 18

Turning Lights On and Off

1. One may turn off a light on Shabbos to help a dangerously ill patient (*choleh sheyeish bo sakanah*) sleep.[1] Similarly, if the patient awakens and needs light, a light may be turned on for him.[2]

2. If, instead of turning off the light, it can be removed from the room or covered (like a lamp), or if the patient can be moved to a darker room without causing him unnecessary inconvenience, this is preferable to turning off the light.[3]

3. Similarly, if a light can be brought in from another room, this is preferable to turning on an additional light for the patient; moving *muktzeh*, a rabbinical prohibition, is preferable to turning on the light, which constitutes the Torah prohibition of lighting a fire.[4]

4. If there are two wax candles of different sizes, and the smaller one will

---

1 שו״ע סימן רע״ח.

2 מ״ב שם ס״ק ב׳ והוסיף שם ובכל זה אם א״י מזומן לפניו ואפשר לעשות על ידו בלי איחור יעשה על ידו (סימן שכ״ח סי״ב בהג״ה).

3 ביאור הלכה שם ד״ה מותר. ועין בדעת תורה סי׳ רע״ח ד״ה שיש בו סכנה וז״ל: עי׳ תו״ש בשם פרשת דרכים דאם אפשר להוציא הנר ע״י עכו״ם לא יכבנה אף בחולה שיש בו סכנה, עיי״ש.

4 ראה בספר תורת היולדת פ״ה סעיף ב׳ ובהערה ה׳ ובשש״כ פל״ב סעיף ס״ה.

be sufficient for the patient's needs, the smaller one should be lit, not the larger one.[5]

5. It is better to turn on an electric light rather than kindle a candle. The reason for this is that when lighting a candle one must first strike a match and then transfer the flame from the match to the candle, whereas only one prohibited action is involved in turning on an electric light.[6]

6. Various types of electric lights work in different ways. These differences affect the number and severity of prohibitions involved in their use. The various methods are described in the *Talmudic Encyclopedia* ("Electricity Addendum," p. 715). Its conclusions are as follows:

   "There are many different types of electric lights besides the standard incandescent bulb, which contains a heating element that lights up due to an electric current. One of these is a fluorescent lamp in which an electric current flowing through a gas causes it to luminesce. This lamp has no heating element other than a wire that ignites in the starter at the moment the light is turned on. This spark lasts only a few seconds. Occasionally the electrodes that conduct the electricity to the gas also glow. A neon light has no wires that glow, nor do the electrodes ever glow.

   "Another type of lamp is a digital light (known as a 'light emitting diode' or 'LED'), which consists of diodes that give out light. In this case, the light comes from a cold source and does not involve the use of fire at all."

7. A neon light is preferable to a regular light. If an incandescent bulb is screwed into the lamp, it may be better to change the bulb to a neon bulb before turning on the lamp. This requires further investigation.

8. A fluorescent lamp is preferable to an incandescent bulb.[7]

9. If an incandescent light is being used, and there is no need to use a

---

5 שש״כ שם סעיף ס״ח.

6 תורת היולדת שם סעיף ד׳. וכ״כ בשו״ת באר משה ח״ו קונטרס אלקטרי סימן ל״ב.

7 כמבואר לעיל שאין הפלואורסצנט חשיב לאש כלל. ורק הסטרטר נדלק לזמן קצר.

100-watt bulb, it is better to use a 60- or 40-watt bulb, depending on the patient's need. The smaller the wattage, the less Shabbos desecration involved in lighting a fire and burning metal.[8]

10. If there are two switches, one that turns on one light and one that turns on a number of lights, and the patient needs only one light on, one should flip the switch that lights one light.[9]

11. The *Toras HaYoledes* rules that where there is no great urgency, and a timer can be reset to turn on the lights earlier than the time for which they were set before Shabbos, this is preferable to actually turning on a light. This is because moving a Shabbos clock back involves only an act of *gramah*. This should be done even if the Shabbos clock controls a number of lights.

12. Turning off an electric light involves the transgression of a lesser prohibition than extinguishing a burning candle.[10] Turning off a fluorescent lamp is less severe than turning off an incandescent bulb.[11]

---

8 תורת היולדת שם. וששי״כ שם סעיף ס״ז.

9 ששי״כ שם. ועי״ש עוד מש״כ דאם צריך להדליק את המפסיק הראשי ואם ידליקנו ידלקו נורות רבים. עדיף קודם לכבות המתגים של כל הבית, ורק אח״כ להדליק את המפסק הראשי. אך כתב לי ע״ז מו״ר הגר״ז כהן שליט״א דצ״ע טובא דמנ״ל להתיר אפילו איסור דרבנן אחד כדי למנוע ספק איסור ריבוי בשיעורין. וגם בששי״כ בהערה בשם הגרש״ז אויערבאך זצ״ל שצ״ע בזה ויותר נראה לא לעבור על איסור דרבנן. עכ״ל.

10 משום שבנר או בפתילה הכיבוי גורם להיווצרות פחמים ובכך איסור הכיבוי הוי כעין שהיה במשכן, משא״כ בכיבוי נורת חשמל לא נוצרים פחמים.

11 כיבוי נורת להט יש בה חום ודמוי אש ודמי לכיבוי ממש משא״כ בכיבוי נורת פלואורסצנט או נורת ניאון או נורות דיגיטליות (LED) אין בהם אש כלל כנ״ל. וע״ע בדברינו לקמן פרק 21 סעיפים 11–8 ובהערות שם.

Chapter 19

General Assistance for a Choleh Sheyeish Bo Sakanah

In this chapter we will discuss various activities done for the general welfare of a dangerously ill patient. These activities include

a. cleaning the patient's room,

b. changing the patient's bed linen,

c. preventing bedsores,

d. heating or cooling the patient's room, and

e. bathing or washing the patient.

Cleaning the Patient's Room

1. One of the great benefits we can provide for the patient is to keep his room clean and orderly. Our Sages elaborate on how these activities are integral to the great mitzvah of *bikur cholim* (visiting the sick), the performance of which has no limits. They report (*Nedarim* 40a) that one of Rabbi Akiva's students had fallen ill, and none of the Sages came to visit him. When Rabbi Akiva visited his student, he swept and washed the floor for him. After he recovered, the student called Rabbi Akiva "Rebbe who brought me back to life." Rabbi Akiva then went out and expounded, "Anyone who does not visit the sick is considered to have shed blood."

2. Even if the patient's room had been swept and washed before Shabbos, it usually gets dirty (with excrement, vomit, blood) during the course of the day. Waiting until after Shabbos to clean the room again will cause the patient great aggravation. We must do everything within our power to maintain the patient's peace of mind, and a clean, orderly environment goes a long way in creating a pleasant atmosphere, which is conducive to his swift recovery.

3. Therefore, one is permitted to sweep the room[1] and even wash the floors with plain water.[2] The water should be collected with a squeegee mop (such as those used in Israel, called a "*sponja* stick") into a pail or drain. After the water has been cleared away, one may drag a dry rag over the floor and soak up any remaining moisture. If a non-Jew is available, one may ask him to wash the floor in the normal manner.

Changing the Patient's Bed Linen

4. It is very uncomfortable for a sick person to lie in bed for long periods of time. One should make him as comfortable as possible. One way to do this is to frequently change his sheets and his hospital gown.

Preventing Bedsores

5. If the patient is bedridden for an extended period, he must be treated to prevent bedsores. This may involve rubbing an ointment into his skin. It is best to apply the ointment just before Shabbos and then right after Shabbos.[3] If it has to be applied on Shabbos, this should be done either with the hand or with a nonabsorbent synthetic material and the ointment should preferably be in liquid form.

In general, one should try to avoid desecrating Shabbos even for a

---

1 דאף בעלמא שרי לטאטא האידנא דרוב הבתים מרוצפים, אך אף בלא זה שרי לצורך חולה (שו״ע סי׳ של״ז סעיף ב׳).

2 ואף שבשו״ע שם אוסר להדיח הרצפה גזירה משום קרקע שאינה מרוצפת, וגם דאין כל כך צורך בהדחה כמו כיבוד במטאטא — מ״מ לצורך החולה יש צורך גדול להדיח את חדרו הן מפני הזוהמה הן מפני האוורור הנצרך לו, ובעיקר כדי להשרות אוירה נעימה לחולה ולהחיותו בזה כמאמר רבי עקיבא לעיל. אך עדיין יש להיזהר שלא יעשה כדרכו בחול ע״י שרית סמרטוט רצפה במים וסחיטתו דכל מה שאפשר לשנות משנין, אלא ידיח במים בלבד ויגרפם וכו׳ כמבואר.

3 דין השימוש במשחה בשבת יבואר לקמן בפרק 26 סעיפים 34–25.

choleh sheyeish bo sakanah by doing as much as possible before Shabbos to avoid doing it on Shabbos (as long as this won't cause a worsening of the condition). If this was not done, or if there is still a need to apply the ointment on Shabbos, it is permissible to do so for a *choleh sheyeish bo sakanah*.[4] (See chapter 47, "Other Apparatus Used by Doctors and Patients," paragraph 11, where the use of an air mattress to prevent bedsores is discussed.)

Heating and Cooling the Room

6. It is permissible to heat a room that is being used by a *choleh sheyeish bo sakanah*,[5] because the cold is considered dangerous for him.[6] If possible, the heater or air conditioner should be turned on with a *shinui*.[7] No attempt should be made to keep the patient warm by covering him with an additional sheet or blanket; this may disturb his rest, and the weight of the extra blanket may cause him discomfort.

---

4 נשמת אברהם ח״א סימן שכ״ח אות ס״א בשם השש״כ פ״מ סעיף ה׳.

5 בגמ׳ שבת קכ״ט ע״א, אמר רב יהודה אמר שמואל עושין מדורה לחיה בשבת, סבור מינה לחיה אין לחולה לא, בימות הגשמים אין בימות החמה לא, אתמר אמר רב חייא בר אבין אמר שמואל הקיז דם ונצטנן עושין לו מדורה אפילו בתקופת תמוז. ופרש״י הקיז דם, וכ״ש חולה. וכן פסקו הרי״ף והרא״ש דלא שנא חיה ל״ש חולה, ל״ש בימות הגשמים ל״ש בימות החמה. עיי״ש. וכן פסק הטור באו״ח סי׳ ש״ל עיי״ש.

אבל הרמב״ם פוסק (פ״ב מהלכות שבת הלכה י״ד) שעושין מדורה לחיה, אבל אין עושין מדורה לחולה להתחמם בה. ועיי״ש במגיד משנה דביאר שיטת הרמב״ם בטוב טעם. ועיין בב״י (סי׳ ש״ל) שהביא שיטות הראשונים הנזכ״ל, ונראה שמצדד כדעת הרמב״ם, אך בשו״ע לא הזכיר דין מדורה לחולה לא בסימן שכ״ח ולא בסימן ש״ל, אלא בסימן שכ״ח הזכיר דין מדורה למקיז דם ובסימן ש״ל הזכיר דין מדורה ליולדת. בכף החיים (סי׳ ש״ל אות לו) הביא שיטת הב״ח שהכריע את העניין בדרך זו. דבשו״ע השמיט דין חולה דמספקא ליה אם הגון להחמיר כהרמב״ם, ונראה דבחולה שאין בו סכנה פשיטא דיש להתיר אמירה לעכו״ם לעשות לו מדורה אפילו בימות החמה אם צריך למדורה כגון שנצטנן. אבל בחולה שיש בו סכנה אין לישראל לעשות לו מדורה אם אפשר ע״י עכו״ם, ואם אי אפשר ע״י עכו״ם ורופא אומר שצריך למדורה, כדאי הם רש״י והרי״ף והרא״ש והטור לסמוך עליהם להקל בספק נפשות עכ״ד (הב״ח) וכ״כ שיורי כנסת הגדולה בהגהת ב״י אות ד׳, א״ר אות ט׳. עכ״ל הכף החיים שם.

6 מ״ב שם ס״ק ס״ב.

7 וכתב הגרי״י זילברשטיין שליט״א יש לעשות זאת בשינוי לדעת הרמ״א בסי׳ שכ״ח סעיף י״ב, ומסתבר דגם לדעת מרן שלא סובר שם שחייבים לשנות (כי אם ביולדת כמבואר בסימן ש״ל) היינו דווקא בודאי סכנה אבל לא בספק, והרי קשה לקבוע מהי מידת קור שיסתכן בה ולכן מסתבר שלכו״ע צריך לשנות, וכמבואר בא״א סי׳ ש״ל דיש לבשל ע״י נכרי (הובא לעיל פרק 17 הערה 12).

7. If a non-Jew is available, he should be asked to turn on the heater.

8. If the heater is turned on by a Jew, then the temperature or any necessary controls should be set first, and then the heater should be turned on. This will avoid the need to perform the additional prohibitive actions of adjusting the settings while the appliance is working.[8]

9. If it is very hot and the heat causes the patient discomfort, it is permissible for a Jew to turn on an air conditioner or fan if there is no non-Jew available to do it.[9]

10. If the weather has changed, and the heater now causes the patient discomfort, it is preferable to move the patient or the heater to another room rather than turning off the heater.[10] If this is not possible, one should ask a non-Jew to turn off the heater. If no non-Jew is available, a Jew is allowed to turn it off, with a *shinui* if possible.[11]

11. The same applies to air conditioning. If the vents can be directed away from the patient, this is better than turning it off. This is also true of a fan — it is better to direct the fan away from the patient. But if there is no alternative, one should ask a non-Jew to turn off the air conditioner or fan. If no non-Jew is available, a Jew may do so, with a *shinui* if possible.[12]

Bathing and Washing the Patient

12. It is very important for the patient's welfare that he be bathed and washed frequently. This gives him a sense of well-being besides being important medically. It is thus a great mitzvah to bathe him even on Shabbos.[13] However, even in our case of a dangerously ill patient (*choleh*

---

8 שמירת שבת כהלכתה פל״ב סעיף פ״ד.

9 שם סעיף פ״ו.

10 עפ״י המבואר לעיל פ״ח גבי נר, ועפ״י הביאור הלכה סימן רע״ח ד״ה מותר, דה״ה הכא גבי תנור וכיו״ב.

11 ששי״כ שם.

12 ששי״כ שם ועי״ע בשו״ת אגרות משה ח״ג סי׳ מ״ב בסו״ד.

13 עפ״י דברי הגמ׳ ביומא פ״ג מחמין לו חמין בין להשקותו ובין להברותו ופסקו הפוסקים כדברי הגמ׳ ועי״ע בשו״ע סי׳ שכ״ח סעיף ד׳ שעושים לו כל שרגילים בחול ממאכלים ורפואות, ואף לשיטת המ״ב בבא״ה שם דכל דבר שאין סכנה במניעת הדבר אע״פ שצריך לו אין עושין אותו

sheyeish bo sakanah), for whom it is permissible to desecrate Shabbos, we can minimize the number of prohibitions involved by considering the following:

a. The source of the hot water
b. The type of soap used
c. The type of sponge used
d. The way the patient is dried

The Source of the Hot Water

13. The least problematic method is to use water heated by solar energy. There is never any question of a Torah prohibition using water heated by the sun.[14]

14. If there is no solar heater, one may turn on an electric water boiler to heat up water for the patient in spite of the fact that the hot-water tank contains much more water than he will need.[15] Heating up a hot-water tank using electricity is preferable to heating water on a gas stove (see also chapters 17 and 18).

15. If possible, one should set up a timer before Shabbos so that the electric water heater will go on and off by itself. If this is not possible, it may be connected to a timer even on Shabbos itself.[16]

16. If lukewarm water is needed, it is better to heat up a large amount of water to the desired temperature rather than boiling a small amount

---

בשבת אלא ע״י א״י וכו׳, מ״מ כתב שם בשער הציון (ס״ק יא) דאילו לצורך הרבה אפילו לדעת המחמירין שרי כההיא דתניא ביומא פ״ג מחמין לו חמין בין להשקותו ובין להברותו. ע״כ.

14 עיין באחרונים שדנו בענין שימוש במים שהוחמו ע״י דוד שמש בשבת. עיין בשו״ת ציץ אליעזר ח״ז סימן מ״ד, וח״ח סי׳ י״ד, דס״ל דהוי כמים שהוחמו בחמה ולא כתולדת חמה. וע״ע בשו״ת יביע אומר ח״ד סימן ל״ד שהאריך בזה דהוי מלאכה שא״צ לגופה, ואינו מתכוון וגרמא באיסור דרבנן ועוד. וע״ע בשו״ת אור לציון ח״ב פרק ל׳ שאלה ב׳. וע״ע בשו״ת מנחת יצחק ח״ד סימן מ״ד שדעתו להחמיר בזה. אך לכו״ע לצורך רחיצת החולה ודאי שרי ועדיף טפי מכל מים חמים שהוחמו באופנים אחרים.

15 עיין שש״כ פרק ל״ב סעיף פ״ב.

16 דפעולת השעון שבת יחשב לגרמא, וכמה דאפשר למעט בחילול שבת במלאכה מדאורייתא ממעטינן. אופן השימוש בשעון שבת בשבת — עיין לקמן פרק 44 סעיפים 1–3.

of water and then adding cold water to it.[17] "Lukewarm" means here water that is at a temperature lower than the temperature of *yad soledes* (less than 45° C, or 113° F).

17. Some authorities note that it is better that a non-Jew or a minor or even the patient himself turn the faucet[18] rather than a Jewish attendant.[19]

The Type of Soap

18. It is best to use liquid soap, since all authorities agree that it is permissible to use this type of soap on Shabbos.[20] If only bar soap is available, it may be used. One should not be stringent in this matter; bathing the patient without using soap is purposeless.

19. Similarly, if the patient is perspiring and suffers discomfort as a result, one may wash his hair with shampoo. If the patient is capable of shampooing his hair himself, this is preferable.

20. If, for medical reasons, it is necessary to apply creams or ointments, it is preferable to use liquid creams or lotions whenever possible. But if these are not available, any cream or ointment may be used if it is medically necessary. Creams that are rubbed and absorbed into the skin are halachically preferable to those that are smoothed onto the surface of the skin.[21]

---

17 שש״כ שם סעיף פ״א.

18 בתורת היולדת כתב כן בפרק ל״ד סעיף ו׳.

19 שם בהערה י״א ביאר טעמו דעדיף שהיולדת תפתח את הברז ולא האחות, שליולדת חשיב הפתיחה כפסיק רישא דלא איכפת ליה, משא״כ האחות ניחא לה שיכנסו מים קרים, כדי שיהיה תמיד מים ליולדות אחרות. ועיי״ש שהביא עוד טעם דבכל חילול הנעשה לחולה, אם החולה עצמו יכול לעשות החילול — עדיף שיעשה החולה ולא אחר. עיי״ש טעמיו במקורותיו. ואכמ״ל יותר.

20 דהנה במשנה ברורה סי׳ שכ״ו ס״ק ל׳ ס״ל לאסור רחיצה בסבון מוצק בשבת, וע״ע בשו״ת אור לציון ח״ב פרק ל״ה שאלה ה׳ שהורה דמותר לרחוץ בסבון נוזלי, אבל אין לרחוץ בסבון מוצק. וכ״כ בתורת היולדת פרק ל״ד הערה כ׳. אך לעומתם עיין בשו״ת יביע אומר ח״ד סימן כ״ז. ובספרו לוית חן סעיף פ״ב להתיר שימוש בסבון בשבת, וסיים שם ז״ל: ועכ״פ לרופא שמטפל בחולים וכיוצא בו בודאי יש להקל בזה עיי״ש. והיינו אם אין אפשרות לחטא את ידיו בחומר נוזלי.

21 עיין בשו״ת מנחת יצחק ח״ז סימן כ׳ דדעתו דאם נספגת המשחה בגוף — יש להקל. ורק אם המריחה היא על העור חמיר טפי עיי״ש. כמובן שאם יש צורך רפואי למרוח משחה אף שאינה נספגת — כיון שמדובר בחולה שיש בו סכנה — ודאי שרי אם אין אפשרות אחרת. וכ״כ בספר מנוחת אהבה ח״ב.

The Type of Sponge

21. It is better to wash the patient with a sponge made from synthetic material in order to minimize the prohibition of squeezing out a liquid.[22] If there are no synthetic sponges available, one may use a wash towel.[23]

Drying the Patient

22. One should avoid squeezing out water from the patient's hair,[24] but one may place a towel on his head so that it will absorb the water.[25] If one is concerned that by not drying the hair quickly the patient will become chilled, he may dry his hair in the normal way.[26]

23. It should be noted that, for reasons of modesty, it is of the utmost importance that in any Jewish hospital or medical center, women should bathe women and men should bathe men (see chapter 13, "Choosing a Doctor and Seeking Medical Advice," paragraph 3).

---

22 תורת היולדת שם.

23 דכל כמה דאפשר למעט באיסור שבת ממעטין אף שמדובר בחולה שיש בו סכנה. אך בכ״ז אם א״א לעשות באופן הקל — ויש לו צורך בזה — מותר אף באיסור סחיטה.

24 תורת היולדת שם. ועיין במ״ב סי׳ שכ״ו ס״ק כ״א.

25 תורת היולדת שם.

26 דיכול לבוא מזה לידי פיקוח נפש ובפרט כשמצב גופו חלש — נתון להשפעות חיצוניות בנקל — צריך שמירה יותר.

Part 3

Choleh She'ein Bo Sakanah

Chapter 20

The Definition of Choleh She'ein Bo Sakanah

1. A person whose illness causes him to be bedridden but is not life-threatening is classified as a *choleh she'ein bo sakanah*, an ordinary bedridden patient.[1]

2. Also, someone who experiences weakness and pain that affects his entire body is classified as a *choleh she'ein bo sakanah*, even if he is not bedridden as a result of his condition.[2]

3. A person who may become bedridden if he is not treated or does not take medication is classified as a *choleh she'ein bo sakanah*, even though he is presently functioning normally.[3] For example, a person who must take medication to treat migraine headaches is considered a *choleh*

---

1 שו״ע סי׳ שכ״ח סעיף י״ז.

2 רמ״א שם, והוסיף בערוך השולחן סעיף י״ט דמי שיש לו חום שכרגיל אין יוצאים מפתח הבית מחמת מחלה זו אפילו שלא נפל למשכב חשיב כחולה שאין בו סכנה.

3 עיין נשמת אברהם ח״ד עמ׳ להי׳ בשם הגרש״ז אויערבאך שליט״א. וע״ע באגרות משה חאו״ח ח״ג סי׳ צ״א שדן בעניין מעין זה גבי חולה שאין בו סכנה שאם לא יטופל בתרופות ביום הכיפורים יחמיר מצבו לחולי של סכנה. ואף שבנידון דידן מדובר שאינו כרגע אפילו בגדר חולי שאין בו סכנה שהרי חש בכאבים בעלמא, ורק אם לא יטופל בתרופות יחמיר מצבו ויפול למשכב, מ״מ מתוך דבריו שם בתשובה משמע דגם זה חשיב בכלל המצב שעומד לקרות אם לא יטופל ושרי כבר עכשיו ליטול תרופות לטיפול מונע. וע״ע בנשמת אברהם ח״א סי׳ שכ״ח אות ג׳ ז״ל: וכתב לי הגרש״ז אויערבאך שליט״א נלע״ד אדם שעלול בקל להצטנן ולקבל דלקת ראות או מחלה אחרת אשר לאחר שיחלה בה יהיה מותר ברפואה, למה לנו להמתין עד שיחלה אם אפשר למנוע, ולכן מותר ודאי להשתמש בוויטמינים אם הצורך לקבל את זה כל יום גם בשבת עכ״ל עיי״ש. ואמנם גם הוראה זו לא בדיוק כנידון שלנו אך דוק מינה כדברינו. וק״ל.

she'ein bo sakanah, since his condition might worsen to the point where he will be bedridden as a result of his affliction.[4]

4. A woman who has given birth is classified as a *choleh she'ein bo sakanah* from the seventh day after giving birth until the thirtieth day.[5,6]

5. A child's needs are considered to have the same halachic status as those of a *choleh she'ein bo sakanah*.[7] Opinions differ regarding the maximum age of the child with regard to this ruling.[8]

---

4 הובאה דוגמא זו בנשמת אברהם ח״ד הנ״ל בשם הגרש״ז אויערבאך שליט״א.

5 שו״ע סי׳ ש״ל סעיף ג׳.

6 לעיל פרק 1 סעיף 19 נתבאר דין יולדת בקצרה, אולם כלל דיני יולדת לא נתבאר במסגרת ספרנו.

7 שו״ע סי׳ שכ״ח סעיף י״ז בהגה. והנה בספר תהילה לדוד סי׳ שכ״ח אות כ״ד אהא דכתב הרמ״א דסתם צרכי קטן כחולה שאין בו סכנה דמי וכו׳ כתב וז״ל: בסי׳ ש״ח ס״ק מ״ז כתבתי דנראה דדווקא צרכי אכילתו, אבל לא שאר צרכיו, ובסימן ש״ט ס״ק ב׳ וכן בסי׳ שכ״ו ס״ק ו׳ הבאתי ראיות לזה עכ״ל. אולם בשו״ת מנחת יצחק ח״ד סי׳ קכ״ד העיר על דברי התל״ד בזה ודעתו דאין חילוק בין צרכי אכילה או שאר צרכים והכל נקרא בכלל צרכי קטן, ועיי״ש דסמך דעתו על הא דכתב הגר״א במקור הדין דצרכי קטן נעשים בשבת, מהגמרא בשבת (קמ״א) בדין תינוק שיש לו געגועים על אביו עיי״ש, והתם לא מיירי במידי דאכילה, וחשיב כחולה שאין בו סכנה. ע״כ.

8 והנה עד איזה גיל יש לדון קטן כחולה שאין בו סכנה — נחלקו גדולי הפוסקים בדורנו (הובאו חלקם בנשמת אברהם ח״א סי׳ שכ״ח אות נ״ד, ובספר ליקוטי הלכות עמ׳ קע״ז ונבררם בקיצור). תחילה הביאו שיטת החזון איש סימן נ״ט אות ג׳ ואות ד׳ דס״ל דקטן לעניין זה הוא בן שתיים או בן שלוש שנים. וסיים בנשמת אברהם שכך היא שיטת הגאון רש״ז אויערבאך שליט״א. אך לענ״ד החזון איש לא כתב כן, שהמעיין שם בחזו״א יראה דבאות ג׳ דן בעניין סתם תינוק מסוכן הוא אצל חלב כמבואר במסכת יבמות (קי״ד ע״א) ועל זה כתב החזו״א משם התוס׳ בשבת דתינוק לעניין זה הוא כבן שתיים או שלוש שנים. ובאות ד׳ כתב החזו״א שם את דברי הרמ״א שצרכי קטן נעשין בשבת ע״י אינו יהודי, ולא ביאר באיזה גיל מיירי לעניין זה. ובאמת מקור דין הרמ״א בתלמוד כתב הגר״א שם להגמרא בשבת (קמ״א) בתינוק שיש לו געגועים על אביו, והתם קיי״ל דהוא עד כבן שש וכבן שבע. עכ״פ החזון איש לא גילה דעתו בעניין זה דקטן שעושים לו כל צרכיו ע״י אינו יהודי עד איזה גיל מדובר ורק על הסוגיא דתנוק מסוכן אצל חלב איירי דהוא כבן שתים או שלוש וכנ״ל וצ״ע.

בשו״ת ציץ אליעזר ח״ח סי׳ ט״ו פי״ב אות ז׳ שיטתו דקטן לעניין זה כבן שש שנים או שבע שנים, ודבריו תואמים לציון הגר״א על שיטת הרמ״א כנזכר לעיל.

בשו״ת מנחת יצחק ח״ט סי׳ ל״ה דן עד כמה שנים נקרא קטן לעניין דהוי כחולה שאין בו סכנה והסיק דעד גיל תשע שנים חשיב קטן לענין זה. וראייתו מדברי האו״ה הארוך כלל נ״ט אות כ״ח ז״ל שם: ואמרינן במסכת יום הכיפורים כל מידי דאית ליה רבותא לינוקא לא גזור ביה רבנן והלכך יכול לומר לכנעני לעשות לתינוק אש ושאר כל צרכיו אפילו בשבת, וכן אם אין לתינוק מה יאכל יכול לומר לכנעני שיבשל לו פאפ״א בשבת ע״כ. ומוכיח המנחת יצחק דכיון שדימה דין יום הכיפורים לשבת לעניין קטן ושם מיירי בקטן עד גיל תשע שנים דאין לחנכו בתענית וכיו״ב ה״ה לקטן לעניין שבת שעושין לו כל צרכיו ע״י אינו יהודי עד גיל תשע. וכ״כ במנחת יצחק ח״א סי׳ ע״ה.

וכמו״כ כתב בשמירת שבת כהלכתה פרק ל״ז סעיף ב׳ דילד עד גיל תשע או עשר — לפי מצב התפתחותו חלש הוא בגופו וזקוק לטיפול מיוחד ולכן התירו חז״ל לעשות בשבילו כל מה

Chapter 21

Forbidden Actions on Behalf of a Choleh She'ein Bo Sakanah

The halachic status of an ordinary bedridden patient, a *choleh she'ein bo sakanah*, is completely different from that of a *choleh sheyeish bo sakanah*, a person with a life-threatening illness. Many Shabbos transgressions that are permitted in the case of the latter are not permitted for the former.

Everything discussed in this chapter refers to a person who is clearly categorized as a *choleh she'ein bo sakanah*, as defined in the previous chapter. However, if there is the slightest concern that the patient's life may be in danger, he is treated as a *choleh sheyeish bo sakanah*. Moreover, if the patient or those around him think that the patient may be in danger, he is treated as a *choleh sheyeish bo sakanah*, even without a doctor's diagnosis.

General Principles

1. A Jew may not transgress any Torah prohibition for the needs of a *choleh she'ein bo sakanah*.[1]

שהתירו לעשות בשביל חולה שאין בו סכנה אם יש צורך בזה. בשו״ת אור לציון ח״ב פרק ל״ו שאלה ד׳ כתב וז״ל עד איזה גיל יש לקטן דין חולה שאין בו סכנה? תשובה, קטן עד שלוש עשרה שנה נחשב לחולה שאין בו סכנה, ומותר לעשות בשבילו כל מה שמותר לעשות לחולה שאין בו סכנה. עיי״ש.

1 שו״ע סי׳ שכ״ח סעיף י״ז.

2. A non-Jew may be asked to perform any action, even if it involves a Torah prohibition, for the needs of a *choleh she'ein bo sakanah*.

3. A Jew may transgress any rabbinical prohibition for the needs of a *choleh she'ein bo sakanah* if he does so with a *shinui*, that is, in an unconventional manner. (As to whether a Jew may transgress a Torah prohibition in an unconventional manner, see chapter 4, "*Melachah* Forbidden Only by Rabbinic Law," paragraph 3.)

4. The rule that a Jew many not transgress a Torah law on behalf of a *choleh she'ein bo sakanah* applies also to the patient's doctor, nurse, and close relatives, as well as the patient himself.

Writing

5. Therefore, a Jew may not record the details or test results of a *choleh she'ein bo sakanah*, nor may he write up a prescription for him.[2] However, he may instruct a non-Jew to do so.

6. When necessary, and there is no non-Jew available, a Jew may record the required information in an unconventional manner, for example, by writing with his left hand[3] or by holding the pen so that it points up and flipping over his hand to write.

7. Although the number of letters written should be kept to a minimum, it is better to write more letters in a foreign language than fewer letters in Hebrew.[4]

---

2 מה שכתב בכף החיים סי׳ שכ״ח אות קי״ד בענין חולה שאין בו סכנה מותר ליתן לרופא דיו וקולמוס ונייר לכתוב רצפט לחולה שאין בו סכנה כשא״א ע״י עכו״ם, כלכלת שבת ע״כ. אין כוונתו שמותר לישראל לכתוב רצפט בשבת, אלא התם מיירי ברופא נכרי, והנדון הוא האם מותר להגיש לו את הדיו והקולמוס אם אין נכרי אחר לבקשו על זה והאיסור שם הוא מצד טלטול מוקצה ע״י הישראלי לצורך חולה שאין בו סכנה. ולכן סיים בכף החיים שם ז״ל מיהו אם אפשר יעשה בשינוי. ע״כ. והיינו הטלטול.

3 שכתיבה בשינוי הוי איסור דרבנן, כ״כ במשנה ברורה סי׳ ש״מ ס״ק כ״ב, ז״ל: הכותב בשמאל או לאחר ידו [דהיינו בגב ידו שאוחז הקולמוס באצבעותיו והפך ידו וכתב], ברגלו בפיו במרפקו [באצילי ידיו] פטור מפני שאין דרך כתיבה בכך. ומ״מ איסורא יש אפילו ברגלו וכה״ג, ע״כ. א״כ הכא בחולה שאין בו סכנה ואין אפשרות ע״י גוי, בשעת הדחק אפשר להקל אף ע״י ישראל בשינוי. וכ״כ בנשמת אברהם ח״ד עמ׳ ל״ה בשם החיי אדם כלל ט׳ סעיף ב׳, והמ״ב בסי׳ ש״מ דכתיבה ביד שמאל חשיבה כשינוי ואינו חייב משום כותב. וע״ע במש״כ לעיל פרק 4 הערה 1 בארוכה.

4 הרמ״א בסי׳ ש״ו סעיף י״א כתב גבי הדין שמותר לקנות בית בארץ ישראל מן האינו יהודי

Lighting and Extinguishing a Candle

8. A Jew may not light a candle nor turn on an electric, fluorescent, or neon light for a *choleh she'ein bo sakanah*.[5]

9. When necessary, a burning candle may be moved from one room to another so that the patient will have light. Similarly, if the light disturbs the patient, a Jew may remove it from the room. If possible, this should be done with a *shinui*, in an unconventional manner,[6] being very careful not to extinguish the candle while moving it.

10. It is questionable whether a Jew may extinguish a light for a *choleh she'ein bo sakanah*.[7]

בשבת וחותם ומעלה בערכאות, כתב בהגה בכתב שלהם דאינו אסור אלא מדרבנן, ומשום ישוב ארץ ישראל לא גזרו. ע״כ. והנה אמנם במשנה ברורה שם ס״ק מ״ז ובביאור הלכה ד״ה בכתב שלהם האריך והרחיב לבאר שמקור דברי הרמ״א שהוא האור זרוע — דעת יחד הוא ואין לפסוק כן, עיי״ש באורך. מ״מ עיין במ״ש בשו״ת יביע אומר ח״ג חאו״ח סימן כ״ג שדחה כל ראיותיו והוכחותיו של הביאור הלכה באריכות. אך בין למר ובין למר אם כבר בשעת הדחק צריך לכתוב בשבת — ודאי עדיף טפי לכתוב בכתב לועזי שבזה ודאי קל מכתב עברי. וכפי שהסיק בתורת היולדת פל״ד הערה י׳. ועיי״ש עוד במש״כ בהערה ל״ז דאם ע״י הכתיבה בלועזית מוסיף אותיות שעדיף לכתוב בכתב עברי — זה נכון אם נפסוק כהכרעת המשנה ברורה שכתב לועזי אינו מדרבנן, אך אם נפסוק כדעת הרמ״א וכפי שהכריע ביביע אומר הנ״ל — בכל מקרה עדיף כתב לועזי על כתב עברי, וכמובן שאם כותב בשינוי בכתב לועזי כגון ביד שמאל הרי זה כשבות שלא כדרכו, ויש להקל בזה טפי.

5 כנ״ל דכל מלאכה האסורה מן התורה אסור לישראל לעשותה לצורך חולה שאין בו סכנה עפ״י דברי השו״ע בסי׳ שכ״ח סעיף י״ז.

6 שטלטול הנר הוי איסור מוקצה שאיסורו מדרבנן, ושרי היכי שמשנה קצת.

7 בשו״ע סי׳ רע״ה כתב דמותר לכבות הנר בשביל שישן החולה שיש בו סכנה. וכתב שם במשנה ברורה ס״ק ג׳ ז״ל: אבל בשביל חולה שאין בו סכנה אסור לכבות לכו״ע ואפילו לפוסקים דס״ל דאין על הכיבוי חיוב חטאת משום דהוי מלאכה שאין צריך לגופה [שהרי אין צריך לתכלית המלאכה כי א״צ לכיבוי בשביל עצמו אלא שהוא מכבה בשביל איזה עניין כגון כדי שישן החולה וכו׳] אפילו הכי אסור מדברי סופרים עכת״ד. וכתב בדעת תורה שם ד״ה שיש בו סכנה ז״ל עיין שו״ת גור אריה יהודה חאו״ח סי׳ ק״צ שפסק דגם לצורך חולה שאין בו סכנה מותר לכבות הנר ע״י שינוי, כיון דהוי רק איסור דרבנן, ושכן פסק בספר עצי שטים, והוא חוכך קצת בזה עיי״ש. ועמג״א סי׳ ש״ז ס״ק ז׳ שהאריך שם וכתב שאין לדמות דבר לדבר בענייני השבותים וכו׳ וסיים דבמקום הפסד גדול יש להתיר שבות ע״י עכו״ם אפילו כדרכו וע״י ישראל שלא כדרכו עיי״ש. ובביאור הלכה סוד״ה בשביל שישן כתב ז״ל: מיהו אפילו בחולה שאין בו סכנה אם הרופא אומר שע״י מניעת השינה יתגבר עליו החולי יותר, ואפשר שיבוא ע״י זה לידי סכנה — גם זה שרי, והשו״ע קמ״ל שבחולה מסוכן גם בסתמא שרי ע״כ. בדין כיבוי מנורת ליבון בנשמת אברהם ח״א עמ׳ קי״ח הביא דברי הגרש״ז אויערבאך שליט״א בספרו מאורי אש ז״ל: כל דבר שאינו נעשה פחם לא דמי למלאכת המשכן ולא חשיב כיבוי וכו׳ ומיהו בנ״ד כבר נתבאר שבמנורות ליבון שלנו אין בהם כי אם חוט מלובן בלי כל תוספת של שלהבת ומזה בא האור המבוקש, וא״כ נראה ודאי דחשיב רק כגחלת של מתכת ולא אסור לכבותו אלא מדרבנן עכ״ל.

11. Reducing the intensity of a flame is included in the Torah prohibition of extinguishing and may not be done for a *choleh she'ein bo sakanah*.[8] However, one may be lenient regarding an electric light that has a dimmer — if necessary, one is permitted to change the intensity of this type of light for the needs of a *choleh she'ein bo sakanah*.[9]

Traveling by Car or Using an Elevator

12. A Jew may not drive a *choleh she'ein bo sakanah* to a doctor, drive the doctor to the patient, or drive to a pharmacy to obtain medication or for any other medical need of a *choleh she'ein bo sakanah*.[10] However, he may ask a non-Jew to perform any of these tasks.[11] Nevertheless, if there is even the slightest possibility of danger to life, a Jew may drive the patient to the doctor or the doctor to the patient. This is permitted even if it turns out that the patient's life was not in danger.

13. Similarly, an ordinary bedridden patient (*choleh she'ein bo sakanah*) may not use an elevator, even if he lacks the strength to climb the stairs.[12] Even

---

8 ביאור הלכה שם סוד״ה החולה עיי״ש.

9 בשו״ת מנחת שלמה למרן הגרש״ז אויערבאך זצ״ל סימן י״ב בסופו כתב בזה״ל: ונדון זה נוגע למעשה במנורות חשמל מסוג זה אשר החוט שבתוך הנורה דולק ומאיר במקצת כל הזמן והוא ממש אש גם לאחר שכבר כבה, ואפילו הכי יכולים גם ללחוץ על כפתור ולהגביר בכך את הזרם והחוט שבתוך הנורה מתחמם יותר עד שהוא מלבין ומפיץ אור חזק. ויש להסתפק אם חייב משום מבעיר (וזהו שמוסיף להתרכך ולהתבשל יותר, נראה דהו״ל כתבשיל שנתבשל כל צרכו, דתו לא שייך בו בישול) וכן אם הוא מחליש אותו ומחזירו לקדמותו אם נחשב בכך כמכבה גחלת של מתכת, ויתכן שאף אם ננקוט כדעת החזו״א שסגירת מעגל חשיב בונה ופתיחתו כסותר, מ״מ בנד״ד שהוא רק מוסיף זרם או ממעט זרם אפשר דאינו חשיב לא בונה ולא סותר. ויש להדגיש דאף שאם החוט שבתוך המנורה לוהט יותר הוא נראה לעיניים יותר עבה וכאילו גם הגדיל לעשות שלהבת, מ״מ אין זה אלא מראית עין בלבד, כי לאמיתו של דבר אי אפשר כלל שתהיה שלהבת בתוך הנורה. וגם לא אסור משום מוליד אש, כיון שאין זה דבר חדש אלא שהגדיל והוסיף על מה שכבר יש מקודם והו״ל כאולודי ריחא דשפיר שרי למלול או להוסיף גם בשמים אחרים אם הם מאותו המין שכבר היה קודם, והי״ה נמי בנד״ד אם נאמר דאינו קרוי מבעיר, אפשר שה״ה נמי דליכא גם מוליד אפילו מדרבנן. עכ״ל המנחת שלמה. וא״כ לדידן לצורך חולה שאין בו סכנה ודאי יש להקל להגביר או להנמיך את עוצמת האור במפסק מיוחד זה כמו שביארנו.

10 וכנ״ל שמלאכות האסורות מן התורה אסור לישראל לעשותם בשבת עבור חולה שאין בו סכנה.

11 שכל צורכי החולה שאין בו סכנה נעשים ע״י א״י, שו״ע סי׳ שכ״ח סעיף י״ז.

12 שנסיעה במעלית יש בה כמה מלאכות מדאורייתא, בהזמנתה ובהפעלתה ועוד, מיהו אם מצטרף לרופא בתפקיד הנוסע במעלית או מצטרף לחולה שיש בו סכנה — מותר להצטרף אליו ובלבד שלא ילחץ על שום כפתור ושלא יצטרכו ללחוץ עבורו על הקומה הרצויה לו שאין זה בכלל

one who is, God forbid, handicapped and confined to a wheelchair may not use an elevator on Shabbos unless it is operated by a non-Jew.

14. A *choleh she'ein bo sakanah* may, however, use what is called a "Shabbos elevator."[13] A Shabbos elevator stops at each floor automatically, and there is no need to press any buttons. It is questionable, however, whether a healthy person may accompany the patient in such an elevator on Shabbos.[14]

15. An escalator has the same halachic status as a Shabbos elevator and may be used by a *choleh she'ein bo sakanah*. Visitors and other healthy people should refrain from using an escalator on Shabbos.

Automatic Doors

16. Hospitals and all other medical facilities should disable electric-eye-operated automatic doors on Shabbos. The use of these doors on Shabbos involves many Torah prohibitions, and there is generally no medical or security need for having them operate on Shabbos.

17. If an automatic door has not been disabled, and the electric eye is functioning on Shabbos, a *choleh she'ein bo sakanah* may not enter or exit through that door. It goes without saying that a healthy person, even one who comes to visit a dangerously ill patient (*choleh sheyeish bo sakanah*), may not go through these doors on Shabbos.[15]

ההיתר עבורם אלא יורד בקומה שהרופא או החולה שבסכנה ירדו. וכאמור אם מצטרף לנכרי מותר לומר לנכרי באיזה קומה צריך והנכרי ילחץ עבורו. כמו״כ יש להיזהר במעלית שיש עין אלקטרונית במזוזת הכניסה למעלית שעם כניסת אדם נשבר קרן אור ונכבית או נדלקת נורה, גם בזה חשיב בכלל איסורי שבת, אף דהוי מלאכה שאינו צריך לגופה עכ״פ מדרבנן ודאי אסור. ועל כן יש להצטרף עם הנכרי ביחד, וקשה לצמצם בזה. ונראה שבשעת הדחק יש להקל משום זה. יש להדגיש דהיינו דווקא לחולה עצמו שאין בו סכנה אבל למלוויו אין להתיר לכתחילה אלא כשהמדובר בחולה תינוק שיש צורך ללוותו גם במעלית, או המלווה חולה במטה באופן שיש היתר לחולה המסוים הזה לעלות במעלית, אזי גם למלווה מותר להצטרף כדי לשאתו וכיו״ב. וע״ע בשו״ת באר משה ח״ז סי׳ ק״ז.

13 עיין בשו״ת יביע אומר ח״ה סי׳ כ״ז במילואים שבסוף הספר.

14 עיין בשו״ת אור לציון ח״ב פרק מ״ז סעיף ל״ו וז״ל: אין להתיר להשתמש במעלית שבת המצויות כיום אלא לזקן או לחולה בלבד.

15 עיין בתורת היולדת פרק כ״ד, וע״ע בנשמת אברהם ח״ד עמ׳ י״ט מש״כ בשם הגרש״ז אויערבאך שליט״א.

18. If the patient must enter the medical facility through an automatic door, he may ask a non-Jew to get the door to open. The patient should enter after him quickly, immediately moving away from the door so that he will not cause it to close. He may also walk through the door together with a doctor or nurse who are on their way to treat a patient in a life-endangering situation (*choleh sheyeish bo sakanah*).[16]

19. Some automatic doors operate mechanically by air pressure. One may enter through these doors as long as the air compressor operates on a timer that activates it every few minutes regardless of the level of air pressure in the system.[17]

Electrical Appliances and Medical Instruments

20. A Jew may not activate any electrical appliance, such as a humidifier, for a *choleh she'ein bo sakanah*, even if it serves a medical purpose.[18] These appliances should be either turned on before Shabbos or set to go on with a timer. The timer can be set to go on and off every half-hour or so as needed (for more details, see chapter 44, "Operating Medical Equipment on Shabbos").

21. Similarly, one may not turn on or off an air conditioner or heater on Shabbos for a *choleh she'ein bo sakanah*.

22. A Jew may not take an X-ray[19] or perform any laboratory work that involves Shabbos desecration for a patient who does not suffer a life-threatening illness. But these may be done by a non-Jew (see chapter 23, "*Melachah* Done by a Non-Jew for a *Choleh She'ein Bo Sakanah*").

23. A Jew may not set a cast on Shabbos. However, this may be done if there is a possibility of danger if the cast is not applied on Shabbos.[20]

---

16 כמבואר שם בתורת היולדת ובנשמת אברהם.

17 ועי״ע בספר הלכה ורפואה ח״א מאמרו של הרב לוי יצחק הלפרין בעמ׳ שס״א שהאריך והרחיב בעניין דלתות אוטומטיות עיי״ש.

18 אופן הפעלת מכשירי אדים ואנהלציה וכיו״ב והחילוק בין המכשירים השונים עיין לקמן במערכת מכשירים וטיפולים רפואיים בשבת פרק 46, סעיפים 6–4, וסעיפים 37–31.

19 שו״ת באר משה ח״ז סי׳ נ׳. דע״י נכרי מותר אך ע״י ישראל אסור, ורק אם נפגע מתאונה במכונית או במקום סכנה שרי ע״י ישראל.

In most cases, a temporary sling will suffice until after Shabbos, and therefore a cast should not be applied.

24. One may not use a telephone to call a doctor or medical emergency service for a *choleh she'ein bo sakanah*[21] where there is no danger to his life. However, if there is the slightest doubt as to the patient's status, one is obligated to contact a doctor or emergency service for consultation. (Of course, if it is clear that time is not of the essence, and professional advice can be obtained without desecrating Shabbos, such as by walking to the doctor's house or to the medical center, this is preferable. See chapter 9, "Levels of Urgency," regarding what is permitted in emergencies for a person in a life-endangering situation.)

25. A Jew may not cook for a *choleh she'ein bo sakanah*.[22] The patient may not even be given food that was cooked on Shabbos for a person in a life-endangering situation (*choleh sheyeish bo sakanah*). (See chapter 17, "Cooking," for the laws regarding cooking for a person in a life-endangering situation; see also chapter 25, "Food Cooked by a Non-Jew for a *Choleh She'ein Bo Sakanah*.")

---

20 שיציקת הגבס מלאכה היא מדאורייתא משום לש ובונה ועוד, ואם אין דחיפות לכך ידחה לאחר השבת , עם כל זה ע״י נכרי מותר גם בשבת כדלקמן בפרק 23 ובפרק 37 סעיף 17.

21 עיין בשו״ת יביע אומר ח״א חאו״ח סי׳ כ׳. אך אם הא״י מתקשר בטלפון לרופא א״י מותר לישראל לשוחח עם הרופא ולספר לו ממצבו של החולה, שעצם השיחה לצורךהחולה אין לאסור.

22 עיין בשו״ע סי׳ שי״ח סעיף ב׳.

Chapter 22

Permitted Actions on Behalf of a Choleh She'ein Bo Sakanah

The Sages do not permit a Jew to transgress any Torah prohibitions for the needs of a *choleh she'ein bo sakanah*. But in certain cases, they permit a Jew to violate rabbinical prohibitions. Rabbinical prohibitions that relate to a *choleh she'ein bo sakanah* can be divided into five main categories:

1. *Melachos done in a manner forbidden only by rabbinic law.* This refers to actions that are considered one of the thirty-nine *melachos* but are performed in manner that is forbidden only by rabbinic law. Included in this category are Torah prohibitions performed with a *shinui*, through *gramah*, by two people, and *she'einah tzerichah l'gufah* (when the *melachah* is not done for its normal purpose).[1] This leniency should not be employed for a *choleh she'ein bo sakanah* except in extreme situations.

2. *Rabbinic prohibitions that do not involve any action by a Jew.* An example of this would be asking a non-Jew to perform an act that the Torah prohibits, but which the Sages permit for the needs of a *choleh she'ein bo sakanah*.[2] For example, the Talmud records that the Sage Ameimar permitted asking a non-Jew to apply ointment to treat an eye ailment.[3]

---

1 עיין במש״כ בכל זה לעיל פרק 4 בהרחבה.

2 בגמ׳ שבת קכ״ט. ופרטי דין אמירה לנכרי נתבאר ברמב״ם פ״ו מהלכות שבת. ובשו״ע סי׳ ש״ז.

3 בגמ׳ ביצה כב. אמימר שרי למכחל עינא מנכרי בשבת.

3. *Rabbinical prohibitions that involve an action.* This refers to rabbinical injunctions that do not involve any specific *melachah*. Examples include handling *muktzeh*,[4] healing ("grinding herbs"),[5, 6] bathing, measuring and weighing,[7] and squeezing fruit juices (other than grapes and olives; squeezing these is prohibited by Torah law).[8]

   The Sages permit transgressing a rabbinical prohibition for the needs of a *choleh she'ein bo sakanah* provided it is done with a *shinui*;[9] it is forbidden to do such an action in the normal manner.[10] However, where one of the patient's limbs is in danger (*sakanas eiver*),[11] even where there is clearly no danger to life, one may transgress a rabbinical prohibition even in the normal manner.

4. *Food that is muktzeh*. Halachic authorities disagree as to whether a *choleh she'ein bo sakanah* is permitted to eat food that is *muktzeh* (for example, a fruit that was picked or fell off a tree on Shabbos). According to some, this is to be regarded as a forbidden food, which may not be given to a *choleh she'ein bo sakanah*.[12]

---

4 נתבאר דין זה בהרחבה ברמב״ם בפכ״ד מהלכות שבת בסופו.

5 שם פרק ב׳, ופרק כ״א. ובשו״ע סי׳ שכ״ח.

6 נתבאר בשו״ע סי׳ שכ״ו.

7 עיין בשו״ע סי׳ ש״ו סעיף ז׳, ובמ״ב שם ס״ק ל״ה ול״ו.

8 כמבואר בשו״ע סי׳ ש״כ סעיף א׳ ונבאר דין זה לקמן פרק 24 הערה 10.

9 שו״ע סי׳ שכ״ח סעיף י״ז בשיטה שלישית שהיא שיטת הרמב״ן בתורת האדם שער המיחוש, עיי״ש באורך בעניין זה.

10 בגמ׳ שבת קל״ד. הובא ברמב״ן שם, ונפסק להלכה בשו״ע סי׳ של״א וע״ש במג״א ס״ק ו׳.

11 רמב״ן שם, הובא להלכה בשו״ע סי׳ שכ״ח סעיף י״ז. ודין סכנת איבר יבואר לקמן פרק 28.

12 כתב הרמ״א בסימן שכ״ח סעיף י״ז וז״ל: מותר לומר לעכו״ם לעשות תבשיל לקטן שאין לו מה לאכול דסתם צרכי קטן כחולה שאין בו סכנה דמי (רבינו ירוחם נתיב י״ב חלק ט׳ ורמב״ן ורשב״א) ע״כ. וכתב המגן אברהם ס״ק ט״ו ז״ל: לעשות תבשיל, ומותר להאכילו מוקצה בידיים אם אי אפשר בענין אחר (או״ה) עכ״ל. ומקורו כפי שציין מהאיסור והיתר הארוך כלל נ״ט אות כ״ט, וז״ל האו״ה: ואם אין התינוק רוצה לאכול כי אם ע״י אימו, השיב השר מקוצי שמותר לאם להאכילו אפילו בתבשיל חלב שחלבו ובשלו כנעני בשבת דהוי חולי שיש בו סכנה בשבת שאין רוצה לאכול ע״י אחר עכ״ל, ונראה מאחר שאין במאכלו אלא משום מוקצה ה״ה אפילו לחולה שאין בו סכנה, ולרווחא דמילתא נקט לה. עכ״ל האו״ה. והנה בספר ישועות יעקב כתב בסי׳ ש״ט בפשיטות דמוכח מהמג״א להתיר אכילת מוקצה כגון פירות הנושרין בשבת לצורך חולה שאין בו סכנה, דקטן נמי הוי כחולה שאין בו סכנה (הובאו דבריו בכף החיים סי׳ שכ״ח אות קי״ד) ונמשכו אחר הישועות יעקב בספר שביתת השבת (מלאכת דש אות פ״ג) להתיר מוקצה לחולה שאין בו סכנה עיי״ש. וכן מוכח באגלי טל במלאכת טוחן עיי״ש.

ובאמת שהגאון רע״א בתשובותיו סימן ה׳ הסתפק בדבר זה אי שרי ליתן לחולה שאין בו סכנה מוקצה דפירות הנושרים או לא? ופירש ספיקו האם מוקצה דפירות הנושרים חשיבי כשאר

5. *Foods forbidden to be eaten by rabbinic law.* An example of this is the meat of a fowl that has been cooked with milk[13] or wine that has been touched by a non-Jew.[14] A *choleh she'ein bo sakanah* may not eat such foods.[15]

Actions Permitted by the Sages to Be Performed for a *Choleh She'ein Bo Sakanah*

6. As stated above, the Sages permitted one to perform actions that do

---

איסורי אכילה דרבנן דקיי״ל (ברמ״א בי״ד סי׳ קנ״ה) דאסור לחולה שאין בו סכנה, או דלמא מוקצה דפירות הנושרין אינו אסור מצד עצמו אלא יומא קגרים, וממילא שרי לצורך חולה שאין בו סכנה. והאריך הרבה בראיות לכאן ולכאן ופלפל בענין גונח יונק חלב אי הוי מוקצה החלב ושרי לצורך חולה שאין בו סכנה עיי״ש באורך אך לא הכריע בתשובתו שם. והנה בפתחי תשובה (ביו״ד סי׳ קנ״ה אות ה׳) הביא דברי הגרעק״א הנ״ל ופי׳ כוונתו שהכריע להיתר, ובשו״ת לחם שלמה או״ח נ״ו הבין דמסקנת הגרעק״א לאסור. והמעיין יראה כנ״ל שלא הכריע הדבר. ורבים מן האחרונים התחבטו בדבר זה והאריכו מאוד בצדדי ספק זה. החיי אדם (כלל ס״ט סעיף ט״ז) ובנשמת אדם שם האריך מאוד בענין ומסקנתו לאסור מוקצה לחולה שאין בו סכנה על פי דברי הרא״ה בבדק הבית (בית שלישי שער ז׳ דף פ״ט ע״א), ועוד הוכיח בראיות ברורות ויצוקות לאסור אכילת מוקצה דפירות הנושרים לחולה שאין בו סכנה. ולא דמי לקטן שאין לו מה יאכל כ״א מוקצה דשרי עיי״ש באורך. בכף החיים הביא דברי הישועות יעקוב הנ״ל באות קי״ד אך בסוף דבריו באות קכ״ג הביא דברי החיי אדם ומסתבר דס״ל כוותיה לאסור. גם בספר קצות השולחן (סי׳ קל״ד ס״ק ז׳) האריך כיד ה׳ הטובה עליו בכל עניינים אלו ומסקנתו לאסור.

ועיין בספר לוית חן להגר״ע יוסף שליט״א דהקשה על הישועות יעקב הנ״ל דהא דשרי השו״ע לחולה שאין בו סכנה איסורי דרבנן היינו דווקא בשינוי כדעה שלישית שהביא השו״ע בסעיף י״ז ולזה הסכימו כל הפוסקים פה אחד, ואי״כ היאך שרי אכילת מוקצה דהוי שבות דרבנן בלא שינוי. וע״ע שם שהאריך והרחיב לבאר דלא כהישועות יעקב ומסקנתו לאסור אכילת מוקצה לחולה שאין בו סכנה. ורק לקטן שאין לו מה יאכל שרי מוקצה וכמ״ש האו״ה.

ודע דאין להוכיח כלל מדשרי טלטול מוקצה לצורך חולה שאין בו סכנה שיהיה מותר גם אכילת מוקצה דיש מקום גדול לחלק ביניהם, עיין בתוס׳ ביצה דף ב׳ ע״א ד״ה ביצה, דאף אם נתיר לטלטל מוקצה מ״מ באכילה יש לאסור, עיי״ש. ממילא אף אם נתיר לטלטל נר לצורך חולה או שאר מוקצה, ודאי דאין ללמוד מזה על אכילת מוקצה דחמירא טפי. ולענין דינא לא מלאני לבי להכניס ראשי בין ההרים הגבוהים ולעמוד במקום גדולים, והבוחר יבחר.

13 בעניין ההמתנה בין בשר לחלב, אין להחמיר לחולה להמתין שש שעות כפי המנהג, לא מבעיא אחרי אכילת בשר עוף אלא אפילו אחר אכילת בשר בקר. וע״ע בשו״ת באר משה ח״ד סי׳ כ״ד.

14 סתם יינן למרן השו״ע ביו״ד סי׳ קכ״ג סעיף ב׳ אסור לעשות מרחץ מסתם יין לחולה שאין בו סכנה. והרמ״א בסימן קנ״ה סעיף ג׳ כתב דבזמן הזה מותר לעשות ממנו מרחץ אע״פ שהוא כדרך הנאתן, ובלבד שלא יאכל וישתה האיסור. וכ״כ בתשובות הרשב״א המיוחסות סי׳ קכ״ז דאסור מרחץ בסתם יינן. וע״ע במשנה למלך פ״ה מהלכות יסודי התורה ה״ו. וראה עוד בב״י יו״ד סימן קל״ד בשם הרשב״א שקרא תגר על אותם רופאים שנותנים לחולי קדחת חומץ שבא מסתם יינם, וסיים בתיבות אלו, ״וח״ו לא נעשה כן במקומנו ולא בכל מקומות ישראל ששמענו שמען, וכל העושה כן למה יבדל מהקהל הגולה, ישקע הדבר ולא יאמר״ עכ״ל.

15 בשו״ע שם כתב בסעיף ג׳ בשאר איסורים מתרפאים במקום סכנה אפילו דרך הנאתן, ושלא במקום סכנה כדרך הנאתן אסור שלא כדרך הנאתן מותר חוץ מכלאי הכרם ובשר בחלב

not involve a Torah prohibition for the needs of an ordinary bedridden patient (*choleh she'ein bo sakanah*). For example:

a. A non-Jew may be asked to perform any action, even those prohibited by Torah law.[16] (For details, see chapter 23, "*Melachah* Done by a Non-Jew for a *Choleh She'ein Bo Sakanah*.")

b. A Jew may perform actions forbidden by rabbinic law if he employs a *shinui*.[17] (For details, see chapter 24, "*Melachah* Done by a Jew for a *Choleh She'ein Bo Sakanah*.")

c. An ordinary bedridden patient may eat food cooked by a non-Jew.[18] (For details, see chapter 25, "Food Cooked by a Non-Jew for a *Choleh She'ein Bo Sakanah*.")

d. The decree against healing on Shabbos ("grinding herbs") does not apply to a *choleh she'ein bo sakanah*. He is therefore permitted to take any necessary medication.[19] (For details, see chapter 26, "Medication for a *Choleh She'ein Bo Sakanah*.")

e. The decree against bathing in hot water[20] does not apply to a *choleh she'ein bo sakanah*. (For details, see chapter 27, "Bathing and Applying Oils.")

שאסורין אפילו שלא כדרך הנאתן אלא במקום סכנה. ועי״ע במשנה ברורה סי׳ שכ״ח ס״ק ס״ג. כמו״כ, עיין בשו״ת הגרעק״א סי׳ נ״ה שכתב במפורש דלא שרינן איסורי אכילה מדרבנן לצורך חולה שאין בו סכנה.

16 שו״ע סי׳ שכ״ח סעיף י״ז.

17 שו״ע שם.

18 שו״ע שם סעיף י״ט.

19 עיין בבית יוסף סי׳ שכ״ח גבי אוכלים ומשקים שהם מאכל בריאים וכו׳ דכתב שם וז״ל: אבל אם היה חולה שאין בו סכנה, הרי אמרו שצרכיו נעשים ע״י א״י, ומשמע דאוכל הוא אוכלים המרפאים אותו לא חיישינן שמא ישחק סמנים, כיון שלא התירו לעשות מעשה הרפואה ע״י ישראל ואפילו ע״י החולה עצמו, עיי״ש. ואמנם הב״ח חולק על דברי הב״י, אך הרמ״א בסי׳ שכ״ח סעיף ל״ז ס״ל כהב״י בזה. ועי״ע במ״ב שם ס״ק קכ״א דכן הלכה, ועיי״ש שדן אם צריך שינוי בנטילת תרופות, דכיון דמה שהתירו לחולה שאב״ס איסורי דרבנן ע״י ישראל היינו דווקא בשינוי. עי״ש דלא צריך שינוי. והאריך בזה שם בביאור הלכה עיי״ש.

20 עיין בביאור הלכה בריש סימן שכ״ו בשם הגרע״א דמצטער אע״פ שאינו חולי כל הגוף י״ל דמותר לרחוץ. וכן הובאו דברי הגרע״א בכף החיים שם אות ד׳. ועי״ע בכף החיים סימן שכ״ח אות רנ״ג. ופשוט שהיינו דווקא במים שהוחמו מערב שבת וכדלקמן.

Chapter 23

Melachah Done by a Non-Jew for a Choleh She'ein Bo Sakanah

1. A Jew is permitted to ask a non-Jew to perform any action for the needs of a *choleh she'ein bo sakanah*.[1] These include
   a. turning on and off a light or kindling and extinguishing a candle,
   b. operating medical appliances such as a humidifier,
   c. turning on and off a heater or air conditioner,[2]
   d. driving to a doctor or hospital or to acquire medication,
   e. operating an elevator, and
   f. cooking for Shabbos.[3]

2. Similarly, Jewish hospital staff may ask a non-Jew to carry out the following activities on behalf of an ordinary bedridden patient:
   a. Open a file, print labels, and record the results of laboratory tests, blood tests, blood pressure, pulse, and the like

---

1 שו״ע סימן שכ״ח סעיף י״ז.

2 עיין עוד לעיל פרק 19 הערה 5 בעניין זה באורך.

3 פרטי דין בישולי עכו״ם לחולה שאין בו סכנה יתבארו לקמן בפרק 25.

b. Operate various medical instruments, such as an otoscope, ophthalmoscope, ECG machine, or X-ray machine, even where there is no danger to life but there is a medical need to obtain the test results — and even where there is a possible danger to life, it is still preferable to ask a non-Jew to operate the machinery if possible[4]

c. Perform various laboratory tests[5]

d. Set a cast

e. Insert an IV

f. Draw blood (see note 5)

g. Grind medicinal herbs and prepare medication (see note 5)

h. Cut and apply bandages

3. It should be noted that a non-Jew may be asked to perform a *melachah* for a *choleh she'ein bo sakanah* only if it is needed on Shabbos itself. But one may not ask a non-Jew to prepare on Shabbos something that will be needed only after Shabbos and there will be enough time after Shabbos to prepare it. For example, one may not ask a non-Jew to carry out a test on Shabbos if the results will not be needed until Sunday morning.[6] This rule also applies to preparing medication that will not be taken until after Shabbos; it may not be prepared on Shabbos even by a non-Jew.[7]

---

4 כגון חולה שהגיע עם כאבים בחזה או עם קשיי נשימה, ויש חשש כלשהוא על בעיה קרדיאלית, מותר לעשות בדיקת א.ק.ג. לוודא שהכל תקין, אך ודאי שיש להעדיף הפעלת המכשיר ע״י נכרי היכי דאפשר. ועיין לקמן במערכת מכשירים וטיפולים רפואיים בשבת — אופן הרכבת האלקטרודות והפעלת המכשיר.

5 עיין עוד לקמן סעיף 3.

6 יש להעיר שבבתי חולים המאיישים עובדים נכריים במעבדה למשל, דאין היתר לבצע בדיקות שאינם דחופות לצורך השבת כגון בדיקות שונות לסגירת תיק חולה וכיו״ב, שאין דחיפות לעשותה בשבת.

7 בשו״ת רב פעלים ח״א סימן כ״ז נשאל בחולה שאין בו סכנה שהוכן לו תרופה מע״ש לצורך השבת וצריך לה לכמה ימים ונפסדה התרופה. אי שרי לומר לרופא נכרי להכין התרופה בשבת לצורך ימי החול, ובאופן שאחר השבת הרופא הנזכר לא ימצא, ואינה יכולה להיעשות ע״י רופא אחר. והשיב. לעניין הלכה במלאכה מדאורייתא שהוא מבשל הסמנים אסור לעשות בשביל צורך יום אחר דלא התירו לעשות שבות רחוקה ע״י נכרי. ועוד דאיכא תרתי איסורי מלאכה והכנה. מיהו אם הרופא אינו עושה מלאכה מדאורייתא אלא דרבנן דהו״ל שבות דשבות יש להתיר אפילו בשבות רחוקה והמחמיר תע״ב. ע״כ.

4. It is reasonable to assume that the permission granted to ask a non-Jew to perform a *melachah* on behalf of a *choleh she'ein bo sakanah* is limited to activities that relate to the treatment of the patient's illness. But one may not ask a non-Jew to perform a *melachah* that is unrelated to the patient's medical treatment. For example, one may not ask a non-Jew to drive a car to bring the patient something to read or study, nor may he ask him to turn on a light so he can read. (However, some authorities differ concerning this.[8])

---

8 שוב מצאתי בשו״ת ציץ אליעזר ח״ב סימן מ״ב שדן אי שרי אמירה לנכרי להדליק החשמל בשבת — לצורך חולה שאין בו סכנה שאינו יכול להירדם — כדי שילמוד בספר, והעלה להתיר משום דהוי דבר מצווה וגם כקצת חולי, ומ״מ סיים שם דמן המובחר שיעשה זאת בדרך רמיזה כגון שיאמר לנכרי ״אינני יכול לישון ושוכב בשיעמום״ וכו׳, עיי״ש.

Chapter 24

Melachah Done by a Jew for a Choleh She'ein Bo Sakanah

1. Halachic authorities differ as to which activities a Jew may perform for an ordinary bedridden patient (*choleh she'ein bo sakanah*). The conclusion of the *Shulchan Aruch*[1] is that a Jew may perform only activities forbidden by rabbinical law and those only if done with a *shinui*.

2. The following are examples of actions a Jew, including the patient himself, may perform on Shabbos:

    a. Administer an insulin injection to a diabetic[2]

    b. Administer an intramuscular injection (IM) or subcutaneous injection (SQ) (intravenous injections are not allowed[3] if it involves inserting the IV, but if the IV was inserted before Shabbos, called a "saline lock" or a "ventflow," injection into such a device has the least halachic objection on Shabbos)

---

1 שו״ע או״ח סימן שכ״ח סעיף י״ז.

2 עיין נשמת אברהם ח״ד סי׳ שט״ז אות א׳, ועי״ע בשו״ת ציץ אליעזר ח״ח סימן ט״ו פי״ד אות ט׳. ועי״ע בילקוט יוסף שבת ד׳ עמוד קפ״ג.

3 דבזריקה תוך ורידית איכא חשש איסור מדאורייתא — עיין בשמירת שבת כהלכתה פרק ל״ב סעיף נ״ח, והטעם דכיון שצריכים להוציא מעט דם לפני ההזרקה כדי לוודא שהמחט אמנם נמצאת בתוך הוריד, וחייב בזה משום דישה. אולם בשו״ת ציץ אליעזר מיקל בזה לחושבו כאיסור דרבנן, עיין בציץ אליעזר ח״ח סי׳ ט״ו פי״ד, ובח״ט סי׳ י״ז פ״ב, ובח״י סי׳ כ״ה פ״ח, ובחי״ג סימן מ״ה.

c. Administer an enema to a person with digestion problems[4]
d. Adjust the volume of a hearing aid[5, 6] — but one may not turn it on
e. Test a urine sample with a urine dipstick or other substances that do not require the liquid to be heated first — one may not use a chemical that causes the urine to boil[7]
f. Add water to a cold water vaporizer that does not heat the water[8]
g. Bathe the patient in hot water that was heated before Shabbos[9]
h. Squeeze fruits to extract their juice, with the exception of grapes and olives[10]
i. Move *muktzeh*, such as a burning candle, medication, or medical instruments, with a *shinui*[11]

---

4 עיין במגן אברהם סימן שכ״ח ס״ק נ״ה, ובמ״ב ס״ק ק״נ, ובכפה״ח אות ער״א. ועי״ע בקצות השולחן סימן קל״ח סעיף ז׳ ובבדי השולחן ס״ק י״ד. ובשו״ת באר משה ח״א סי׳ ל״ג אות י״א. ובשו״ת ציץ אליעזר ח״ח סי׳ ט״ו פרק ט״ו אות כ׳, וכתב שם דמ״מ אם אפשר לפתוח הבני מעיים ע״י תרופה עדיף מחוקן. ובאופן הרכבת המכשיר והשימוש בו עיין לקמן פרק 41 סעיף 27 ולקמן במערכת מכשירים וטיפולים רפואיים בשבת פרק 46 סעיפים 28–25.

5 עיין בשו״ת אגרות משה או״ח ח״ד סימן פ״ה. ובשו״ת באר משה ח״א סי׳ י״ז אות ו׳. ובשו״ת מנחת יצחק ח״א סימן ל״ז וחלק ה׳ סימן ב׳ וג׳. ובשו״ת יביע אומר ח״א סימן י״ט אות י״ט.

6 בשו״ת באר משה ח״ו בקונטרס עלעקטרי סימן ט״ו הביא דעת הגרש״ז אויערבאך שליט״א וכ״כ בשמירת שבת כהלכתה פל״ד סעיף כח בשם הגרש״ז אויערבאך שליט״א להתיר בזה. נתבאר גם לקמן בדברינו פרק 47 בדין מכשירי עזר לרופא ולחולה. אולם בילקוט יוסף שבת ה׳ עמ׳ ר״כ החמיר בזה.

7 עיין בשו״ת באר משה ח״ח סימן כ״ד. ועי״ע בשו״ת ציץ אליעזר ח״י סי׳ כ״ה פרק א׳ אות ד׳. ועי״ע לקמן בפרק 48 בענין בדיקות מעבדה שונים.

8 עיין שו״ת באר משה ח״ו סימן נ״א. אופן השימוש במכשיר והגבלות שונות בעצם השימוש עיין לקמן במערכת מכשירים וטיפולים רפואיים בשבת פרק מ״ה.

9 עיין ביאור הלכה בריש סימן שכ״ו בשם הגרעק״א, וכתבתיו לעיל פרק 22 הערה 20.

10 סחיטת פירות למעט זיתים וענבים איסורם מדרבנן כמבואר בשו״ע סי׳ ש״כ סעיף א׳ ולצורך חולה שאין בו סכנה יש להתיר לישראל איסורים מדרבנן ע״י שינוי ולכן מותר לסחוט פירות למשקין שלהם ע״י שינוי כגון שיסחט ביד ולא במסחטה ידנית וכיו״ב. (ואין להקשות מכף החיים סימן ש״כ אות י׳ שכתב ז״ל: הגה לרפואה לבד אין לחוש, משמע אם סוחטין אותו למשקה אע״ג שהוא רוצה אותו לרפואה אסור לסחוט ע״כ. דהתם לא מיירי בחולה שאין בו סכנה עיי״ש. ודו״ק.) אולם הרא״ש בתשובה כלל כ״ב סעיף ג׳ העלה לאסור סחיטת רימונים אפילו לצורך חולה שאין בו סכנה. עיי״ש.

11 כמבואר במ״ב סי׳ שכ״ח ס״ק׳ נ״ח, ועיין בשמירת שבת כהלכתה פל״ג סעיף ו׳ בהיתר טלטול מנורת חשמל לצורך החולה.

j. Give a massage or physiotherapy.[12] One should use a liquid as a lubricant for this purpose and not a cream. The use of electric machines to assist in massages or physiotherapy is not permitted. When there is a great need, one may connect the machine to a timer before Shabbos, but this may be done only for the patient and not for a healthy person.

3. Where there is a great need to perform an action forbidden by Torah law for a *choleh she'ein bo sakanah* and no non-Jew is available, some authorities permit a Jew to do it with a *shinui*.

4. A *choleh she'ein bo sakanah* should not go to a nonobservant Jewish doctor if he knows the doctor will desecrate Shabbos in a situation where there is no danger to life.[13] However, if the patient's condition is not clearly known, and there is a chance that his condition will worsen and endanger his life, the patient is permitted to see a nonobservant doctor.

---

12 דכל אלו בכלל גזירת שחיקת סממנים (כמבואר לעיל פרק 2) דשרו לחולה שאין בו סכנה. אך יש להיזהר לעשות המסז׳ בחומר נוזלי וכמבואר.

13 עיין בשו״ת ציץ אליעזר ח״ח סי׳ ט״ו פרק י״ג שדן בזה ומסקנתו שיש להימנע מביקור אצל רופא שאינו שומר תורה ומצוות בשבת עבור חולה שאין בו סכנה, אלא יש להעדיף ולבחור ללכת דווקא אצל רופא המשמר שבתו. וכ״כ ביסודי ישורון סוף מערכת חולה שאין בו סכנה עיי״ש. וע״ע בספר רב ברכות להגאון רבינו יוסף חיים זיע״א מערכת הלמד סעיף ג׳ בענין לפני עיור לא תתן מכשול.

Chapter 25

Food Cooked by a Non-Jew for a Choleh She'ein Bo Sakanah

1. The *Shulchan Aruch*[1] permits a *choleh she'ein bo sakanah*, an ordinary bedridden patient, to eat food that was cooked by a non-Jew. The patient may even eat completely kosher food that was cooked by a non-Jew (that is, even food which is not forbidden by rabbinical law), which a Jew may not ordinarily eat.[2]

2. Therefore, a sick person who is lacking appropriate food for his needs and requires warm food for his recuperation — even if there is no danger to life — may ask a non-Jew to cook for him on Shabbos. Similarly, if he needs a cup of hot tea or warm milk, he may ask a non-Jew to boil water for him.

3. A healthy person may not eat from the patient's leftover food or hot water if it was cooked on Shabbos. This is forbidden for two reasons: the prohibition against deriving benefit from a *melachah* done by a non-Jew on Shabbos on behalf of a Jew, and the general prohibition against eating food that was cooked by a non-Jew. Therefore, even in cases when the prohibition against eating food cooked by a non-Jew does not

---

1 סימן שכ״ח סעיף י״ט.

2 דאין היתר ליתן לחולה שאין בו סכנה מאכל איסור, אפילו אם איסורו מדרבנן כמבואר בשו״ע יו״ד סימן קנ״ה סעיף ג׳ ורק שלא כדרך הנאתו התירו איסורים מדרבנן כמבואר שם. ועי״ע במשנה ברורה סי׳ שכ״ח ס״ק ס״ג.

apply, such as boiled water and the like, it is still forbidden to drink the water because it was prepared on Shabbos for the needs of a Jew.[3]

Eating the Leftovers after Shabbos

4. Once Shabbos is over, neither the sick person nor a healthy person may eat food that was prepared by a non-Jew on Shabbos. Since a Jew can now prepare food for the sick person without Shabbos desecration, the patient is no longer permitted to eat the food prepared by the non-Jew.[4] But if the sick person needs the food immediately after Shabbos and there is no time for a Jew to prepare fresh food, he may eat the leftover food that was prepared by the non-Jew on Shabbos.[5] Opinions differ regarding the question of whether it makes a difference if the food was cooked in a Jew's house or that of the non-Jew.[6]

Utensils in Which Food Was Cooked

5. Utensils in which kosher food was cooked by a non-Jew may be used by others without kashering them first. Some authorities do require that the utensils be kashered before use,[7] and one who is stringent in this matter is commendable.[8]

---

3 פשוט, דלא הותר לבריא להנות ממעשה שבת ומבישולי עכו״ם.

4 מ״ב שם, ובכף החיים אות קכ״א. ועיין עוד בארוכה בכל עניין זה מש״כ לעיל פרק 17 סעיף 9 וסעיף 10 ובהערות שם. וגם החילוק בין בישל האינו יהודי לצורך חולה שאין בו סכנה, או בישל לצורך חולה שיש בו סכנה עיי״ש באורך.

5 כן מתבאר מדברי כף החיים הנ״ל.

6 בעיקר הדין אם אפשר לאכול מבשולי עכו״ם ללא השאלה של מעשה שבת, רבו הפוסקים המתירים זאת אם מבשל העכו״ם בבית הישראל או בבית חולים, עיין בלוית חן סימן מ״ב בסופו, ונשמת אברהם ח״א עמ׳ קצ״ט שיש פוסקים המחלקים בין בישולי עכו״ם הנעשים במקום העכו״ם לבין אם שכרו הישראל כגון בבית חולים יהודי או בביתו של הישראל — שיש להקל לאכול מהנשאר למוצאי שבת.

7 נחלקו בזה הראשונים הובאו בב״י יו״ד סימן קי״ג. הבאתי מקצת דינים אלו לעיל פרק 17 סעיף 12.

8 במשנה ברורה שם כתב ז״ל: והכלים של בישולי א״י צריכים הכשר, ואפילו כלי חרס כיון דעיקר איסורו אינו אלא מדרבנן דיו אם מגעילו ב״פ. ובדיעבד אם בישל בו בלי הגעלה ויש רוב בתבשיל מותר. ויש מקילין דאין צריכין הכשר כלל, והסומך עליהם לענין כלים שבשלו בהן לחולה בשבת לא הפסיד. ובכף החיים ביו״ד סי׳ קי״ג אות צ״ט העלה דאין צריך להכשיר, וכ״כ בשו״ת אור לציון ח״ב פל״ו שאלה ה׳. ומ״מ עיין בכף החיים או״ח סי׳ שי״ח אות ל״ב דכתב ז״ל: ונראה לענין דינא כיון שרבו הדעות בזה, דלכתחילה יש להחמיר ולהכשיר ובדיעבד אם בישל בהם בלתי הכשר אפילו תוך מעת לעת התבשיל מותר, והמיקל שלא להגעילם כלל ולהשתמש בהם אחר מעל״ע לא הפסיד עכ״ל.

Chapter 26

Medication for a Choleh She'ein Bo Sakanah

1. The Sages permit a *choleh she'ein bo sakanah* to take medication on Shabbos.[1] There are, however, a number of halachic guidelines regarding the preparation of the medication, the method of taking it, and the necessity of taking it. (See chapters 31 and 32, where specific types of medications for various ailments are discussed.)

Preparing Medicine

2. Nowadays most medication comes prepared, and there is almost never a need to prepare medication from raw materials. But there are some medications whose preparation involves Shabbos desecration. For example, mixing a powder with a liquid to create an ointment involves the

---

1 עיין ב״י סי׳ שכ״ח גבי אוכלים ומשקים לרפואה, וברמ״א בשו״ע שם סעיף ל״ז, וע״ע במ״ב שם ס״ק קכ״א, ובכף החיים אות רכ״ב שהביא דעות הפוסקים להתיר ודלא כשיטת הב״ח והט״ז שרצו לפקפק בהיתר זה, עיי״ש. וכן מפורש להיתר בשו״ע הגר״ז סימן שכ״ח סעיף י״ט בסופו. עיי״ש. וע״ע בקצות השולחן סי׳ קל״ד בבדי השולחן אות ז׳ האריך בכל זה והסתפק אם בזמננו שמא ישתנה הדין (ויותר ליתן תרופות אף לשאינם בגדר חולה שאין בו סכנה) כיון שאין אנו שוחקין סמנים והתרופות מוכנות בבית מרקחת, והאריך בזה ומסקנתו שהתקנה לא זזה ממקומה וההיתר לתרופות הוא אכן רק לחולה שאין בו סכנה.

melachah of *lash* (kneading),[2] as does preparing a tooth filling. Setting a filling involves the *melachah* of *boneh* (building).[3] Preparing and setting a cast involves both *lash* and *boneh*.

Similarly, crushing herbs to prepare an herbal medicine or cooking them to prepare a syrup involves the *melachos* of *bishul* (cooking), *tochein* (grinding), and *lash*. It is forbidden for a Jew to make these preparations for a *choleh she'ein bo sakanah*; a non-Jew must be asked to do it.

3. Crushing a pill into a powder is permissible on Shabbos for the needs of a *choleh she'ein bo sakanah*, since this does not involve the prohibition against grinding — there is no prohibition against grinding something that has already been ground.[4] Nevertheless, one should refrain from using a utensil that is designated for crushing.[5]

4. One may mix a powder with a liquid to make a syrup, as long as the patient needs the medication on Shabbos. This is because the *melachah* of *lash* is limited to a case where two objects are combined to form a solid; it does not apply if the mixture results in a liquid.[6]

5. One may measure or weigh medications for a sick person, since this is considered weighing and measuring for the purpose of a mitzvah, which is permitted on Shabbos.[7] But one may only use a mechanical scale, not a digital one that works on electricity.

---

2 דנתינת נוזל לאבקה שהיא בר גיבול דהיינו שהפרודות של האבקה עם מגעם בנוזל מתאחדים ליציקה אחת בצורת משחה — הרי זה כמבואר בשו״ע סי׳ שכ״א סעיף י״ד ובמ״ב שם ס״ק נ׳ בדין לישה מדאורייתא בדבר שהוא בר גיבול, עיי״ש.

3 כנ״ל דשייך בזה דין לישה, ועוד דע״י שמתקשה בצורה מסוימת יש בזה איסור של מלאכת בונה.

4 עיין בשו״ע סי׳ שכ״א סעיף י״ב בהגה. וכ״כ הפרמ״ג בעניין כתישת חתיכות סוכר, הובא במ״ב שם ס״ק ל׳.

5 עיין במ״ב שם ס״ק מ״ה, ובביאור הלכה ד״ה לפורר לחם.

6 דכל איסור לישה היינו דווקא בדבר שהוא בר גיבול, ואפילו באינו בר גיבול דאסור מדרבנן היינו דוקא בבלילה עבה אבל בהפיכת אבקה לנוזל, שרי אפילו לכתחילה כמבואר בשו״ע סי׳ שכ״א הנ״ל וכל זה במשקה ממש (כמו סירופ) אבל אם נעשה סמיך כמו דייסה או ג׳ילי יש לעשות דווקא בשינוי כמבואר שם, אך משום שאין זה מצוי לא הרחבנו בזה.

7 עיין בשו״ע סי׳ ש״ו סעיף ז׳. ותמהני על מקצת מחברים שכתבו להחמיר שלא לשקול ולמדוד מאכלים הניתנים לתינוקות בכפית מידה או בבקבוק תינוק, באומרם שזה חשיב לאיסור שבת אלא יעשו על פי אומד בלבד, ולכאורה דברים אלו אינם, מחמת שני סיבות א׳ ברוב המקרים יש צורך רפואי לדייק במינונן של המרכיבים השונים. ב׳ תינוק יש לו דין חולה שאין בו סכנה, ולצורך חולה שאין בו סכנה שרי מדידה ושקילה, ומשום כך אין להחמיר מה שלא גזרו רבותינו.

Administering Medication

6. There are various ways to administer medication:
   a. Orally (PO), such as tablets, capsules, and syrups
   b. Intravenous (IV), such as transfusions, injections, infusions, or parenteral nutrition (TPN)
   c. Intramuscular (IM) or subcutaneous (SQ), which includes various injections and vaccinations
   d. Rectal (PR) or vaginal (PV), such as suppositories and enemas
   e. Externally, such as ointments, liquid solutions, eyedrops, and ear drops

Oral Medication

7. A *choleh she'ein bo sakanah* may take any oral medication he needs to treat his condition according to the directions of his doctor.[8]

8. Some authorities do not permit such a patient to take medication for minor aches and pains that are not related to the sickness that is making him bedridden.[9]

9. Where possible, one should prepare medication before Shabbos, removing it from its sealed packaging in order to refrain from tearing the wrapping on Shabbos.[10] If it is necessary to tear open the package of medication on Shabbos, it should not be opened by tearing along the perforation. Care should also be taken not to tear any letters, even those written in languages other than Hebrew.[11]

10. As noted above, one may crush a pill into a powder since the *melachah* of *tochein* does not apply to a substance that has previously been ground. But one may not use a utensil specifically designated for grinding. Similarly, one may dissolve pills in water, making a liquid mixture in

---

8 כנ״ל הערה 1.

9 אגרות משה חאו״ח ח״ג סי׳ נ״ג.

10 דכמה שאפשר למעט באיסורי שבת אפילו מדרבנן יש למעט. ובודאי שאם לא פתח מער״ש שמותר לקרוע בשבת להוציא הכדור, וכמבואר בשו״ע סי׳ שי״ד סעיף ו׳.

11 מ״ב סי׳ ש״מ ס״ק מ״א.

order to drink it. For example, one may dissolve a calcium pill, vitamin C pill, or baking soda for a *choleh she'ein bo sakanah*.[12]

11. Certain antibiotics come in powdered form, and water is added to the powder to form a syrup. One may prepare this syrup on Shabbos.[13]

Intramuscular and Subcutaneous Medication

12. It is permitted to administer an intramuscular (IM) or subcutaneous (SQ) injection to a *choleh she'ein bo sakanah*.[14] It is therefore permissible for a diabetic to inject insulin before meals on Shabbos.[15]

13. If there is no urgent need to administer intramuscular vaccinations on Shabbos — for example, those given to the general population — they should not be administered on Shabbos.[16] However, in the case of a contagious viral disease, in a situation where inoculation is not possible on a weekday, or if the delay might increase the risk of contracting the disease, it is permitted to administer these vaccinations on Shabbos.[17]

    Similarly, a tetanus shot may be administered to someone who suffered an injury on Shabbos and the doctor recommends the vaccination to prevent infection. But if the doctor says the vaccination can be postponed until after Shabbos, it should not be done on Shabbos.[18]

14. Even in situations where vaccinations are permitted, it is preferable to take an oral vaccine if available, as long as the oral vaccine is both equally effective and equally safe. (For more details regarding giving

---

12 ואמנם שלבריא יש לאסור המסת כדורים בשבת — וכדכתבו האחרונים, עיין בדעת תורה סימן שכ״ח סעיף ל״ז, ובקצות השולחן סי׳ קל״ח בבדי השולחן ס״ק ל״א לענין אבקת סודה לשתייה עיי״ש. מ״מ לצורך חולה שאין בו סכנה מותר.

13 עיין בנשמת אברהם ח״א עמ׳ ר״א וז״ל: תרופות כמו סוגי אנטיביוטיקה שבאים בצורת אבקה ומוסיפים מים עד צוואר הבקבוק לפני השימוש, מותר להכינם בתוספת מים בשבת עבור ילד או חולה שאין בו סכנה ואין בו משום לש (חזו״א או״ח סימן נ״ח ס״ק ט׳) וגם לא משום הכנה משבת לחול, כי זקוק הוא לכל כמות המים כעת כדי שידע ריכוז התרופה בנפח מסוים של הנוזל, וגם מכיון שהוא נותן את כל המים לתוך הבקבוק בבת אחת. ע״כ.

14 שש״כ פרק ל״ג סעיף ז׳.

15 שו״ת ציץ אליעזר ח״ח סי׳ ט״ו פי״ד אות ט׳.

16 דכל שאינם מצורכי החולה אין ליתן בשבת.

17 שש״כ פרק ל״ב סעיף ס״א וס״ב.

18 שש״כ פרק ל״ה סעיף מ׳. ובנשמת אברהם ח״א סי׳ שכ״ח אות כ״א.

injections on Shabbos, see chapter 46, "Equipment Used in Treatments and Procedures.")

Intravenous Injections or Infusions

15. Since some authorities rule that an intravenous injection involves the *melachah* of *dash* (because one draws blood to ensure the proper insertion of the needle into the vein), a Torah prohibition, one should refrain from administering these injections to a *choleh she'ein bo sakanah*.[19] Therefore, if there is no urgent medical need, a Jew should not insert an IV in a *choleh she'ein bo sakanah*. He may, however, ask a non-Jew to do so. If there is a concern that the patient will become dehydrated, or if the IV is given to prevent complications that could lead to a worsening of his condition and endanger his life, a Jew may insert the IV.
16. If a person was hooked to an IV before Shabbos, it is permissible to add medication to the IV bag, as long as it is not necessary to insert a new needle into the vein.[20] It is also permissible to measure the amount of medication that needs to be added.
17. An infusion pump (a machine that controls the drip rate of the IV and counts the number of drops that go through the tube) should not be used for a *choleh she'ein bo sakanah*.[21] It may be used for a *choleh sheyeish bo sakanah*, such as when giving medication to treat low blood pressure.

Total Parenteral Nutrition (TPN)

18. A patient who is being fed intravenously, such as one suffering from ulcers or burns of the digestive tract, a post-surgical patient, or a patient with a small bowel obstruction, is regarded as being dangerously ill

---

19 עש״כ בשם הגרש״ז אויערבאך שליט״א פרק ל״ב סעיף נ״ח ובהערה קנ״א, עיי״ש באורך. אולם בשו״ת ציץ אליעזר בכמה מקומות; בחי״ט סי׳ י״ז פרק ב׳ אות ל״ו. ובח״י סימן כ״ה פרק א׳. ובחי״ג סי׳ מ״ה האריך והרחיב לבאר דעתו דאף בזריקה לתוך הוריד אין בזה איסור תורה, ואם יש צורך מותר להזריק גם בווריד, אך מ״מ גם מסקנתו דאם אפשר בדרך אחרת ראוי לנהוג כן.

20 דזה ודאי עדיף ניקוב שקית העירוי במקום המיועד לכך, מאשר זריקה לתוך הוריד.

21 כ״כ בהלכות והליכות בית החולים לניאדו, פרק ה׳ סעיף ד׳ עיי״ש. וראה עוד לקמן במערכת מכשירים וטיפולים רפואיים בשבת פרק 46 מש״כ בעניין משאבות אינפוזיה.

(*choleh sheyeish bo sakanah*), and it is permissible to insert an IV to feed him on Shabbos.[22]

Rectal or Vaginal Medication

19. A rectal suppository to activate the bowels, lower fever, or for any other medical need may be used by a *choleh she'ein bo sakanah*.[23]

20. One should take care not to apply a cream, petroleum jelly, or surgical lubricant to the patient to make it easier to insert the suppository. But it is permitted to dip the suppository in the cream or place the cream on the patient without smearing it and then inserting the suppository.[24]

21. If the patient is suffering from constipation, it is permissible to administer an enema in order to induce a bowel movement. As noted above (paragraph 20), a cream may be placed on the enema tube, but it may not be smeared on it.[25]

22. When necessary, laxatives or other medication may be added to the enema for a *choleh she'ein bo sakanah*.[26]

23. For further details concerning the use of enemas, see chapter 46, "Equipment Used in Treatments and Procedures."

24. Vaginal medication may be administered on Shabbos where there is a medical need to do so. A rabbinical authority should be consulted

---

22 פשוט, ומסתמא ברוב המקרים מדובר בחולה שיש בו סכנה.

23 עיין שש״כ פל״ג הערה מ״ט דלא דמי למש״כ בשו״ע סי׳ שכ״ח סעיף מ״ט דיש חשש להסרת נימין. ובשו״ת ציץ אליעזר ח״ח סימן ט״ו פרק ט״ו אות כ׳ כתב דאם ניתן ליתן את אותה תרופה דרך הפה יש להעדיפה על פני פתילה, משום דגם בפתילה וגם בחוקן יש בעיות שונות אם בהשרת נימין או בהרכבת הסט בחוקן, ולכתחילה יש להימנע אם כי מעיקר הדין שרי. והמליץ על מה שכתב בקצות השולחן סי׳ קל״ח בבדי השולחן ס״ק י״ג דעדיף שאחר יניח הפתילה ולא החולה עצמו. וע״ע בדברי הציץ אליעזר בח״ט סי׳ י״ז פרק ב׳ דין כ״ה.

24 כדלהלן בביאור דין השימוש במשחות.

25 מגן אברהם סי׳ שכ״ח ס״ק נ״ה, וכ״כ במ״ב ס״ק ק״נ ובכף החיים אות ער״א ושאר אחרונים. וע״ע לקמן פרק 46 בעניין עשיית חוקן בשבת.

26 דכיון שהוא חולה שאין בו סכנה אפשר גם בסמנים המרפאים. עיין בכף החיים אות ער״א, והוסיף שם דהיינו לחולה שאין בו סכנה, אבל לבריא הסובל מכאבי בטן (שלא נפל למשכב) ומכשיר החוקן מוכן ולא צריך להרכיבו, ורוצה לפתוח הנקבים ע״י החוקן, במקום צער יש להקל. עיי״ש. וכ״כ בשו״ת באר משה ח״א סימן ל״ג אות י״א.

to determine whether there are any other halachic considerations involved.[27]

External Medication

25. There are many different types of medication that are administered externally. They can be divided into five categories:

    a. All-purpose creams or ointments

    b. Antiseptic and medicated solutions

    c. Powders

    d. Drops

    e. Medicated patches (TTS)

    (See chapter 38, "Wounds and Dressings," for the laws on using bandages, band-aids, and cotton. For the laws on using appliances such as a vaporizer, see chapter 46, "Equipment Used in Treatments and Procedures.")

Creams and Ointments

26. Ointments and creams are used for one of the following functions:

    a. To smooth a surface to prevent friction; for example, when using a rectal thermometer, petroleum jelly is used to ease insertion of the thermometer. Petroleum jelly is also used when inserting an enema or suppository.

    b. To avoid dryness or for some other medical purpose and the cream is totally absorbed into the skin.

    c. To form a protective coating over a wound or infection.

    d. To cleanse, such as toothpaste. In this case, the cream acts as a vehicle for the cleansing agent, which is the primary active ingredient. The cream is used only to enable convenient and efficient use of the product.

---

27 שו״ת באר משה שם אות ט׳. וע״ע בשו״ת באר משה ח״ב סי׳ ל׳ שדן אם מותר להניח משחה באותו מקום כדי לאפשר קיום מצוות עונה כשאין אפשרות בלא זה, עי״ש שהתיר הנחה בלא מריחה.

e. To administer medicine through the skin, such as nitroglycerin ointment.

27. From a halachic standpoint, there are a number of prohibitions to consider in the use of creams and ointments on Shabbos:

    a. Any medicated cream involves the rabbinic injunction against healing on Shabbos ("grinding herbs").[28] This injunction is waived for the needs of a *choleh she'ein bo sakanah*.[29] The use of medicated creams is forbidden for someone with a minor illness (*choleh b'miktzas*) or someone experiencing a minor pain or discomfort (*michush*).[30]

    b. Smoothing a cream or ointment on any part of the body involves the *melachah* of *memarei'ach* (smoothing), a Torah prohibition.[31] This is prohibited even for the needs of a *choleh she'ein bo sakanah*.

    c. Transforming a solid substance into a liquid by rubbing it with one's hands involves the rabbinic prohibition of *molid* (the creation of a new substance. This is similar to crushing snow, ice, or hail to make a liquid[32] or melting tallow to place on a wound.[33]

28. One may use a cream to facilitate the insertion of a rectal thermometer or an enema as long as one does not smear the cream on the thermometer or enema tube itself. Rather, he should dip the object into the cream, apply the cream to the instrument with a tongue depressor, or squeeze the cream onto the object.[34] There is no concern that this will involve the rabbinical prohibition against grinding herbs (see chapter 2, "The

---

28 ככל תרופה שיש חשש לשחיקת סמנים וכדין סיכה שאינה מותרת אלא בשמן שהבריאים סכין בה, אבל כל סיכה ומשיחה אחרת נכללת בכלל גזירת שחיקת סממנים כמבואר בשו״ע סי׳ שכ״ז סעיף א׳ ובמ״ב ס״ק א׳ עיי״ש.

29 כנ״ל בתחילת הפרק סעיף 1.

30 כדין סיכה בשאר שמנים המבואר בסי׳ שכ״ז הנזכ״ל.

31 עיין במגן אברהם סי׳ שט״ז ס״ק כ״ד, והסכמת כל הפוסקים, עיין דעת תורה שכ״ח כ״ו, קצות השולחן סי׳ קל״ו סעיף י״א. ציץ אליעזר ח״ז סי׳ ל׳. מנחת יצחק ח״ז סי׳ כ׳. יביע אומר ח״ד סי׳ כ״ז וסי׳ כ״ח. באר משה ח״א סי׳ ל״ו אות ד׳ וח״ב סי׳ כ״ט אות ג׳. שש״כ פל״ג סעיף י״ג. ועי״ע בכף החיים.

32 שו״ע סי׳ ש״כ סעיף ט׳.

33 שו״ע סי׳ שכ״ח סכ״ב. ובסי׳ שכ״ו ס״י בהגה, ועיי״ש במ״ב ס״ק ל׳.

34 עיין שש״כ פרק מ׳ סעיף ב׳ בעניין הטבלת מדחום במשחה.

Ordinance against Preparing Medicine"), since there is no medical need for the application of the cream. Thus, this method is permissible even if the person is not in the category of a *choleh she'ein bo sakanah*.

29. Applying a cream or ointment on the skin so that it will become absorbed does involve the rabbinic injunction against healing ("grinding herbs").[35] This is because in this case the cream is applied for therapeutic purposes. Thus it is only permitted for the needs of a *choleh she'ein bo sakanah*. Since the cream becomes absorbed in the skin and is not smoothed over the surface of the skin, the *melachah* of *memarei'ach* (smoothing) is not involved. But it may be done only if there is a medical need for absorption of the medication into the skin.[36]

30. If there is no medical need, it is forbidden to use skin creams — for example, to prevent dryness, to keep the skin fresh, or as makeup — even if the cream is completely absorbed.[37]

31. Spreading a cream on a wound to form a protective coating where it does not become absorbed in the skin involves the Torah prohibition of *memarei'ach* and is thus forbidden even for the needs of a *choleh she'ein bo sakanah*.[38] If necessary, a non-Jew may be asked to do it.

    If the *choleh she'ein bo sakanah* has a great need for the ointment, or if the ointment is needed for an infant, the following methods may be used:

    a. The cream may be squeezed from the tube onto the wound, or an applicator may be used to place the cream over the affected area.

---

35 כן מבואר מהמג״א סי׳ שט״ז ס״ק כ״ד והובא במ״ב שם ס״ק מ״ט. וכן היא הסכמת גדולי האחרונים, עיין דעת תורה סימן שכ״ח סעיף כ״ו, ובסימן שי״ד סעיף י״א. וע״ע בשו״ת מנחת יצחק ח״ז סימן כ׳. וכן דעת הגאון רש״ז אויערבאך שליט״א הובא בשש״כ פל״ג הערה נ״ח. ושכן הוא במנחת שבת סימן צ״ב ס״ק ל׳. וע״ע בשו״ת ציץ אליעזר ח״ז סי׳ ל׳, וח״ח סימן ט״ו פרק י״ד.

36 שו״ת מנחת יצחק ח״ז סימן כ׳ שאל״כ יש חשש גדול שלא יעשה כן ויכנס לחשש איסור ממחק מדאורייתא.

37 דאין זה כדין סיכת שמן לבריאים המבואר בסי׳ שכ״ז. יתר על כך כתב הרמ״א שם בסעיף ב׳ דאפילו שמן במקום שאין סכין אלא לרפואה אסור, ובפרט שאין זה כשמן, אלא משחה הנבלעת בגוף שיש אוסרים אף בחולה, אנו אין לנו להתיר לבריא אף שיש לו יובש בשפתיים או בגב היד וכיו״ב — אין להתיר כלל.

38 כמבואר לעיל סעיף 27 ובהערה 31.

Then a gauze bandage may be placed over the wound, even if the resultant pressure will spread the cream over the area.[39]

b. The cream may be placed on gauze, which may then be placed over the affected area without smoothing it onto the skin. If possible, it is preferable to place the cream on the gauze before Shabbos and store it in a clean place until it is needed.[40]

c. A woman who has cracks or sores from nursing and fears infection may place oil, cream, or ointment on a nursing pad and then place the pad on the sores.[41] But she may not smear the cream over the affected area. If the cream must become absorbed into the skin in order to be effective, she may massage the area so that the cream will become absorbed.[42]

32. It should be noted that one may apply a cream in the manner described above only if there is a medical need or if it is done to relieve itching or irritation. But if it is done to draw out pus or blood from a wound, a Torah prohibition is involved, and it is forbidden to do so for a *choleh she'ein bo sakanah*.[43]

33. Halachic authorities disagree as to whether one may use toothpaste on Shabbos. Since there are many conflicting views, it is best to refrain from using toothpaste, particularly since there are many alternatives, such as mouthwash and liquid toothpaste.[44] (See also chapter 34, "Dental Diseases and Hygiene," paragraphs 1–4.)

---

39 מסקנת האחרונים ולמדים זה מהחזון איש או״ח סי׳ נ״ב ס״ק ט״ז. עיין בשש״כ פל״ג סעיף י״ד ובהערה ס״ב. וע״ע בשו״ת ציץ אליעזר ח״ח סימן ט״ו פרק י״ד אות ה׳.

40 שש״כ שם.

41 עיין שו״ת באר משה ח״ג סי׳ קפ״ה אות ד׳.

42 על פי דברי הפוסקים המבוארים לעיל בהערה 35.

43 מגן אברהם סי׳ שכ״ח ס״ק ל״ג, שאסור להניח צו״ק זלא״ב (משחה שחורה) על המכה שאין בה נקב. והיינו מפני שמושך הליחה מהמכה ואסור משום מפרק. ועיין בשו״ת ציץ אליעזר ח״ח סימן ט״ו פרק י״ד אות ה׳, שהביא דברי המג״א הנ״ל ושכ״כ בשו״ע הגר״ז סעיף ל״ד, ושכן כתב להדיא בהגהות מיימון פכ״א מהלכות שבת ועוד שלא יתן ע״ג מכה דבר המושך ליחה ודם דהוי מפרק. והביא גם מספר קצות השולחן סי׳ קל״ו בבדי השולחן ס״ק י״ג, דכיון דישנו בזה משום מפרק דאיסורו מן התורה — אסור אפילו ע״י נכרי אא״כ חלה בכל גופו. וכ״כ במשנה ברורה סי׳ שכ״ח ס״ק קמ״ז ז״ל: ויש שסוברים (מג״א בשם הגהת מיימוני) דה״ה אם מניח על המכה דבר המושך ליחה ודם כגון צו״ק זלא״ב וכיו״ב ג״כ הוי מלאכה מדאורייתא כיון שנתכוון לזה ועכ״פ איסור בודאי יש. ע״כ.

44 בשו״ת ציץ אליעזר ח״ז סי׳ ל׳ אוסר שימוש במשחת שיניים. וכ״כ בשו״ת אגרות משה או״ח

34. One may inhale Vicks VapoRub in order to breathe easier. This is certainly permitted for a *choleh she'ein bo sakanah*, but it is even permitted for a person who suffers from a slight head cold.[45] Rubbing Vicks on the body, however, is subject to the restrictions outlined above.

Antiseptic and Medicated Solutions

35. It is permissible to apply antiseptic solutions on an external wound or cut to prevent infection. This is permitted not only for an ordinary bedridden patient, but even for a someone with a superficial wound that doesn't involve any illness.[46]

36. However, a solution that contains antibiotics or some other therapeutic agent may be used only by an ordinary bedridden patient, whether the solution is meant to be absorbed into the skin or whether it is applied to the affected area without being absorbed.[47]

37. When applying antiseptic or antibiotic solutions, one should not dip a cloth or cotton into the solution. Rather, one of the following methods should be used:[48]
    a. Pour some of the liquid directly onto the wound, then wipe it with precut cotton or tissue paper.[49]
    b. Use an eye dropper to draw some of the liquid from the bottle and apply it to the wound (see note 49).

ח״א סי׳ קי״ב. אולם בשו״ת יביע אומר ח״ד סכ״ז וסכ״ח האריך להוכיח דשרי דכיון שנמסה המשחה ורוחצה תיכף אין זה בכלל ממרח כלל עיי״ש בטעמו ונימוקו. וכ״כ בקצות השולחן סי׳ קל״ח בבדי השולחן ס״ק ל״א. ועיי״ש דכל זה לגבי המשחה עצמה אבל לגבי השימוש במברשת אסר משום עובדין דחול.

45 שו״ת באר משה ח״ו סי׳ מ״א. ואולם בקצות השולחן הנ״ל רוצה לפקפק בהיתר הרחת הויקס לשאר אדם שאינו חולה — מפני שהיא מבטלת את הנזילה והויא רפואה לפי שעה. וע״ע בכף החיים מש״כ בזה.

46 שו״ת באר משה ח״ו סימן ל״ח.

47 שיש בזה הגזירה דשחיקת סממנים ושרי רק בחולה שאין בו סכנה אבל בסתם מכה אסור וכמבואר בשו״ע (סימן שכ״ח סעיף כ״ט) דמי שניגפה ידו מניח יין על גבי מכתו שזה עוצר את הדם, אבל לא יניח חומץ משום שזה גם מרפא, ואם האדם מעונג שגם יין מרפא אותו כמו חומץ — גם יין אסור.

48 דעובר על איסור סחיטה שנסחט הנוזל מהגזה או מהצמר-גפן.

49 סש״כ פל״ג סעיף י׳ וי״ג.

c. Dip an applicator or brush with synthetic bristles into the solution and apply it to the wound.

38. It is permissible to disinfect one's hands with alcohol before and after treating a patient. One should pour the alcohol onto the hands and rub them together. This procedure should be followed by a *mohel*, doctor, nurse, or anyone who is treating an ill person.

Powders

39. The use of medicated powders also comes under the rabbinic injunction against healing ("grinding herbs"). But nonmedicated talcum powder, which does not contain any active ingredients, may be used, even by a healthy person, in order to prevent perspiration.[50]

40. Similarly, powders that are used to contract the blood vessels (vasoconstrictors), such as Dermatol, which is used at a bris milah to staunch bleeding, do not come into the category of healing and may be used on Shabbos even for a person who is not considered a *choleh she'ein bo sakanah*. These powders may be applied, for example, to superficial wounds and abrasions to stop the bleeding.

41. Any medicated powder that contains active ingredients, for example, powders used to heal burns, may be used only by a *choleh she'ein bo sakanah*. This is also true of powders that, in addition to staunching the flow of blood, also promote the healing of the wound.

42. It is permissible to inhale snuff, even if the person's intention is to relieve a runny nose. Since it is normal for healthy people to inhale snuff, it is permissible even with the intention of improving one's condition.[51]

43. Powder may be used to disinfect bathwater only for a *choleh she'ein bo sakanah*.[52]

---

50 דפעולת אבקת הטלק אינה פעולה רפואית אלא היא חומר לספיגת לחות, ואמנם אם יש בה חומר פעיל — אסור להשתמש בה משום גזירת שחיקת סממנים, ורק לחולה שאין בו סכנה או לקטן שדינו כחולה שאין בו סכנה מותר להשתמש בטלק זה.

51 עיין משנה ברורה שכ״ח ס״ק קכ״ז. וכן בכף החיים שם כתב דשרי להריח באוריגאנ״ו מפני הנזילה דריחא לאו מילתא. וע״ע לעיל בסעיף ל״ד בענין הרחת הויקס.

52 דמוכחא מילתא דעביד לרפואה.

44. It is permissible to use spider webs to stop bleeding.[53] (Modern medicine does not use this form of therapy.)

Drops

45. A person who suffers from an eye ailment that requires bed rest is classified as a *choleh she'ein bo sakanah* and is allowed to use eyedrops.[54]

46. Similarly, one who suffers from a respiratory ailment, chills, or a bad cough to the point that he is bedridden may use nose drops or any other medication to relieve his symptoms.[55] It is also permissible to prepare a saline solution to be administered as nasal drops. Similarly, ear drops may be used by a person who is bedridden as a result of an earache.

47. If the patient is a minor, drops may be administered at the onset of any slight ear or eye inflammation, in accordance with the doctor's instructions, even if the child is not bedridden.[56]

48. One may rinse his eyes with water or saliva[57] upon awakening in the morning to remove sticky secretions from the eyelids, but he should not apply any medication or tea.

---

53 שו״ע סי׳ שכ״ח סעיף מ״ח.

54 פשוט, ככל דין חולה שאין בו סכנה. ופרטי דין מחלות עיניים עיין לקמן במערכת מחלות ותופעות מצויות חלק מחלות עיניים, פרק 35.

55 שו״ת מנחת יצחק ח״ח סי׳ ה׳. והיינו בסתם חולי שנפל למשכב, אבל אם יש לו דלקת ראות הרי דינו כמכה של חלל, דחשיב כחולה שיש בו סכנה. או מצב של קוצר נשימה — הרי הוא כחולה שיש בו סכנה ומחללין עליו את השבת לכל צרכיו כגון להפעיל עבורו מכשיר אנהלציה וכיו״ב.

56 משום דכל צורכי קטן כחולה שאין בו סכנה חשיבי. ועיין לעיל פרק כ׳ סעיף ה׳ והערה ח׳ עד איזה גיל נחשב קטן לענין סיווגו כחולה שאין בו סכנה.

57 עיין בכפה״ח סימן שכ״ח אות קל״א. ועי״ע לקמן פרק 35 בענין רפואת עיניים בשבת.

Chapter 27
Bathing and Applying Oils

Bathing

1. A *choleh she'ein bo sakanah* may bathe in water that was heated before Shabbos[1] or in water that was heated by solar energy[2] in order to strengthen him and improve his health. Similarly, it is permitted to clean or bathe a baby with hot water that was heated with solar energy.

---

1 דלא גזרו בחולה גזירת מרחצאות כמש״כ הביאור הלכה בסי׳ שכ״ו בשם הגרעק״א עיי״ש. ומקורו מהגהות הגרעק״א על השו״ע בסימן ש״ז סעיף ה׳ עיי״ש.

2 דמים שהוחמו בשבת ע״י דוד שמש, רבו הפוסקים שהתירו, ואף הפוסקים שאסרו שימוש במים אלו בשבת — משום איסור דרבנן נגעו בה, שיש להתירה לצורך חולה שאין בו סכנה או לצורך קטן. ולהלן נבאר חלק מדעות האחרונים בזה בקצרה.

א) בשו״ת ציץ אליעזר ח״ז סי׳ י״ט התיר להדיא שימוש בדוד שמש, וחיילי דיליה משום דהוי כמים שהוחמו בחמה עצמה דשרי לכתחילה. ע״כ ואי משום גזירת מרחצאות — בחולה שאין בו סכנה שרי גזירת מרחצאות כדלעיל הערה 1.

ב) בשו״ת אור לציון ח״ב סי׳ ל׳ שאלה ב׳ הביא שהשימוש בדוד שמש בשבת שרי דמה שהמים מתחממים בשמש מאליהם הוי חמי חמה דשרי לכתחילה, אלא דע״י פתיחת הברז בבית נכנסים תיכף ומיד מים קרים לדוד ומתחממים מהמים החמים שבדוד? על כך אומר האור לציון דהוי תרי דרבנן דשרי, דפתיחת הברז בבית הוי גרמא לכניסת המים בדוד וחימום המים הקרים מהמים שבדוד הוי תולדת חמה, ממילא תרי דרבנן שרי. ע״ש שם בביאור העניין באורך.

ג) בשו״ת יביע אומר ח״ד סי׳ ל״ד האריך והרחיב מאוד בדין השימוש במי דוד שמש בשבת, ואמנם שלדעתו חימום המים ע״י השמש לא חשיבה כחמי חמה אלא כתולדת חמה, מ״מ שרי משום דהוי גרמא במלאכה שאינה צריכה לגופה ואינו מתכוין דשרי. (עיין בשו״ת מנחת

2. Water that was heated even before Shabbos in an electric boiler should not be used to bathe a child or even to wash parts of one's body, even if the electricity has been turned off and will not be activated when the hot-water faucet is turned on.[3]

3. A *choleh she'ein bo sakanah* may perform actions that cause perspiration, such as taking pills,[4] placing his hands and feet in hot water,[5] and entering a sauna[6] (that is not operated by Jews).[7]

Applying Oils

4. One may apply oil and any other liquid to the body of a *choleh she'ein bo sakanah*, whether for massage, physiotherapy, warmth, or to relax the

---

יצחק ח״ד סי׳ מ״ד שביאר שיטת היביע אומר ושיטת הציץ אליעזר בטוב טעם עיי״ש.) עכ״פ לענין חולה ודאי דיש להתיר בשופי.

ד) גם בשו״ת מנחת יצחק ח״ד סי׳ מ״ד דן בזה באורך, ואמנם מסקנתו לאסור שימוש במים שהוחמו ע״י דוד שמש בשבת אפילו לרחיצת ידיים או כלים, וסברתו לאסור משום דהוי תולדת חמה ואין זה כמלאכה שאינה צריכה לגופה אלא מעוניין בכך שיכנסו מים אחרים לדוד, ועוד ס״ל לאסור משום דהוי הטמנה בשבת. עכ״פ אפילו לשיטתיה — לצורך חולה ודאי יש להקל באיסור דרבנן אפילו לצורך רחיצת כל גופו וכמו שביארנו.

3 דרחיצה במים שהוחמו בשבת ע״י האור אסור ואפילו לרחיצת ידיו ורגליו יש לאסור. וע״ע בשו״ת יביע אומר ח״ד סי׳ ל״ה מה שהאריך והרחיב בעניין זה. וכשעדיין הדוד מחובר לרשת החשמל אסור כלל לפתוח את הברז בדירה דכל פתיחה בבית מפעילה גוף חימום ע״י כניסת מים קרים לדוד. ורק לצורך חולה שיש בו סכנה יש להתיר רחיצה במים אלו בשעת הדחק. אבל לצורך חולה שאין בו סכנה אין להתיר גם כאשר נותק מבעוד יום החיבור לרשת החשמל, ורק הוחמו מים אלו מערב שבת ע״י החשמל, שהרי כאשר נכנסים מים קרים ומתחממים הוי תולדת האור ואסור מדאורייתא. ולצורך חולה שאין בו סכנה גם בשעת הדחק אין להתיר, אלא אם כן המים פושרים.

4 דגבי חולה שאין בו סכנה לא אמרינן הגזירה משום שחיקת סממנים, ורק במיחושים בעלמא כתב בשו״ע בסי׳ שכ״ח סעיף מ״ב שאין מתעמלין וכו׳ כדי להזיע, וטעם האיסור כיון שניתן להגיע למטרת הזיעה ג״כ ע״י תרופות לכן אסור כל דרך הביאה לידי זיעה — גזירה משום שחיקת סמנים. וכמבואר שם במשנה ברורה ס״ק קי״ל.

5 אחרונים בשם שו״ת לב חיים ח״ג סי׳ צ״ז. ועיין בכפה״ח סי׳ שכ״ח אות ר״ן.

6 כנ״ל בהערה 4 דכל איסור כניסה למרחץ — כדי להזיע כמבואר בשו״ע סי׳ שכ״ו סעיף י״ב — היינו דווקא לבריא, אבל לחולה שאין בו סכנה שרי.

7 דאין היתר להנות ממעשה שבת שנעשה ע״י יהודיים אפילו לצורך חולה שאין בו סכנה. ואם נעשה ע״י יהודי לצורך חולה שיש בו סכנה ובא חולה זה שאין בו סכנה ורוצה להנות אף הוא מפעולה זו צ״ע, אך מסתבר דשרי דאינו דומה לבישול בסי׳ שי״ח סעיף ב׳ דאסור לחולה שאין בו סכנה לאכול ממה שהכינו עבור חולה שיש בו סכנה, דהתם יש החשש שמא ירבה בשבילו משא״כ הכא לא שייך גזירה זו ועכ״ז צ״ע.

abdomen.[8] (See chapter 26, "Medication for a *Choleh She'ein Bo Sakanah,*" regarding the prohibition against using creams and ointments.)

5. Similarly, one may apply oil to the body of an infant for any purpose.[9]

6. See chapter 31, "*Michush* — Minor Aches and Pains," regarding the use of oils for one who suffers from minor aches and pains (*michush*) and is not in the category of an ordinary bedridden patient (*choleh she'ein bo sakanah*).

---

8 ומה שנאמר בשו"ע סי' שכ"ז החושש במותניו לא יסוך שמן וחומץ וכו', איירי במחושים בעלמא, אבל לחולה שאין בו סכנה שרי.

9 שו"ת באר משה ח"א סי' ל"ו אות ד'.

Chapter 28

Sakanas Eiver — Danger to a Limb

A category that is less serious than that of a dangerously ill patient (*choleh sheyeish bo sakanah*), but more serious than that defined as an ordinary bedridden patient (*choleh she'ein bo sakanah*), is that of danger to a limb (*sakanas eiver*).[1] This applies to one whose condition may result in the loss of a limb or organ or its function.

In practice, anything that may be done for a *choleh she'ein bo sakanah* may certainly be done for someone in the category of danger to a limb. In addition, though a Jew may transgress a rabbinical prohibition on behalf of a *choleh she'ein bo sakanah*, he may do so only with a *shinui*.[2] But no *shinui* is required when danger to a limb exists. This is called "*shevus k'darko*," meaning that a rabbinical prohibition may be performed in the normal manner.[3] This is the basic difference between a *choleh she'ein bo sakanah* and *sakanas eiver*.

---

1 עיין ברמב״ן בספר תורת האדם שער המיחוש (הובא בחידושיו על הש״ס בסוף סדר מועד על מסכת ביצה דף כב׳ בסוגיית עין שמרדה). וע״ע בר״ן בשבת פרק שמונה שרצים בהגהתו על הרי״ף, ובחידושיו למסכת ע״ז דף כ״ח. וכן הוא בריטב״א בחידושיו עמ״ס שבת קכ״ח. וכ״כ הב״י בהקדמתו לסימן שכ״ח עיי״ש ועוד.

2 כך היא הדעה השלישית המוזכרת בשו״ע סי׳ שכ״ח סעיף י״ז ומקורה בדברי הרמב״ן הנ״ל. וכ״כ הריטב״א הנ״ל והיא הסכמת כל הפוסקים.

3 עפ״י הרמב״ן שם.

The Definition of *Sakanas Eiver*

1. A person who was injured and is in danger of losing a limb, an organ, or the use of a limb,[4] either totally or partially,[5] if he is not treated immediately is classified as a patient whose limb is in danger (*sakanas eiver*).

2. It should be emphasized that we are dealing with a situation where there is definitely no danger to life; only the injured limb is in danger. However, today doctors concur that when a patient is injured and faces the loss of a limb or of the use of it, the danger of infection that could lead to a life-threatening situation must be addressed. If there is even the slightest chance of the injury leading to danger to life, the person is classified as a *choleh sheyeish bo sakanah*.[6] If only the limb is in danger, the person is regarded as *sakanas eiver* even if he feels fine and is not bedridden.

---

4 בגמ׳ במסכת עבודה זרה כ״ח מובא דין עין שמרדה שמותר לחלל עליה את השבת לרפאותה משום דשורייני דעינא בליבא תליא (שגידי העיניים קשורים ללב). ומביאה הגמ׳ מעשה בשפחתו של מר שמואל שמרדה עינה בשבת וצווחה וליכא דמשגח בה פקע עינא ומתה, נפק מר שמואל ודרש ״עין שמרדה מותר לכוחלה בשבת״. עיי״ש. ומבארים הראשונים, הר״ן בפרק שמונה שרצים, והרמב״ן הנ״ל, שדווקא היכא ששייך חשש סכנה. וז״ל הר״ן ומהא שמעינן דמשום סכנת אבר אין מחללים את השבת אלא אם כן יש בדבר סכנת מיתה דטעמא דשורייני דעינא בליבא תליא הא לאו הכי דמשום סכנת עוורון בלחוד אין מחללין את השבת. ושמעינן נמי מהא דכל היכא דאיכא סכנת אבר אע״פ שאין מתירין בו מלאכות של תורה, מלאכות של סופרים מתירים בו אפילו ע״י ישראל שהרי אפילו היכא דשחיק סממנין מאתמול, שבות של דבריהם יש בו גזירה משום שחיקת סממנים ואפילו הכי שרי ליה ע״י ישראל, והיינו נמי דאמרינן לקמן בסוף פרק חבית [קמח]. הלכה מחזירין את השבר וכיון שאנו מתירין שבות ע״י ישראל כ״ש אמירה לנכרי במלאכה גמורה שיותר הוא חמור שבות ע״י ישראל ממלאכה גמורה ע״י נכרי. וכו׳ עיי״ש וכן היא מסקנת הרמב״ן בתורת האדם הנזכ״ל.

5 כן מצאתי שחידש בקצות השולחן סי׳ קל״ח בבדי השולחן סוף ס״ק י״ח והביאו נמי בשש״כ פל״ג סעיף א׳ ס״ק ה׳ עיי״ש.

6 והנה דעת הרופאים כהיום, דגם בסכנת אבר פעמים שאנו מתייחסים אליו כאל סכנת נפשות, משום שבמקרה של זיהום באחד מחלקי הגוף, אם מגיע הזהום לכלי דם וכדומה עלול לפגוע באיברים פנימיים ולהוות סכנה לכל הגוף, ולכן יש לחקור כל מקרה לגופו לשאול ברופאים אם אין השלכות שליליות מחולי זה, ועכ״פ לוודא שאין זה אפילו בגדר ספק, שהרי ספק פקוח נפש נמי חשבינן ליה כחולה שיש בו סכנה, אלא אם כן יאמרו הרופאים שאמנם יש בזה חשש סכנה אך הוא ממתין ואינו דוחק לחלל עליו את השבת. דהא אפילו בידוע שיש בו סכנה אם הוא חולי ממתין אין מחללין עליו את השבת וכנ״ל פרק 9 סעיף 10.

Examples

3. If a person has a dislocated bone, the possibility exists that if the bone is not relocated, he will lose hand or leg function. It is therefore permitted to relocate it on Shabbos.[7] (It should be noted that not all relocations require *melachah*.)
4. A person with a broken bone that will not heal properly and will result in limited function of the limb is considered *sakanas eiver*.[8]
5. A woman who suffers from gynecological problems that could result in infertility if she does not take medication for it is regarded as *sakanas eiver*.[9] Of course, this applies only if the treatment is urgent and cannot wait until after Shabbos.[10]

---

7 שו״ע סי׳ שכ״ח סעיף מ״ז. ״עצם שיצא ממקומו מחזירין אותו״. ומקור הדבר בגמ׳ שבת קמ״ז. והביאוה כל הראשונים להלכה כדוגמא לסכנת איבר דשרי בשבת, ומתוכם הר״ן הנזכ״ל, הרמב״ן והריטב״א הנזכ״ל, הרי״ף והרא״ש על הדף, כמו״כ הרמב״ם בפירוש המשניות בסוף פרק חבית כתב וז״ל: ואמרם אין מחזירים את השבר אינה הלכה והפסק מחזירין את השבר עכ״ל. וכן כתב הרמב״ם בהיד החזקה במפורש בפ״ב מהל״ש ה״י. ועיין במשנה ברורה בסימן שכ״ח ס״ק קמ״ה על מה שכתב בשו״ע עצם שיצא ממקומו מחזירין אותו כתב וז״ל: ״המגן אברהם חולק ע״ז וס״ל דדווקא עצם הנשבר מותר להחזירו כדאיתא בגמ׳, אבל עצם הנשמט ממקומו אסור להחזירו דאפילו לשפשף הרבה בצונן אסרו כדאיתא בסעיף ל׳ וכ״ש חזרה והעתיקוהו כמה אחרונים, ומ״מ ע״י א״י נראה שאין להחמיר. ובספר שולחן עצי שיטים חולק על המגן אברהם וכתב דכל שיצא ממקומו לגמרי שקורין אוי״ש גילענקי״ט חשיב סכנת איבר כמו נשבר אם לא יחזירנו מיד ושרי להחזיר ע״י ישראל וכבסעיף ״יז״ עכ״ל, והאי דלעיל סעיף ל׳ איירי לדעתו בשלא נשמט לגמרי ממקומו. ונראה דגם לדעת המגן אברהם אם הרופא אומר שנפרק בחזקה ויוכל לבוא לידי סכנת איבר שמותר למשוך ולהחזירו למקומו כדרך שעושה בחול״. עכ״ל המשנה ברורה.

8 כנ״ל גבי עצם שיצאה ממקומה ובהא אפילו המגן אברהם שמחמיר בפריקה מודה בשבירה דיש חשש סכנת איבר ושרי לקבעה.

9 עיין בנשמת אברהם ח״ד עמ׳ לחי שכ״כ בשם הגרי״י נויבירט שליט״א.

10 ועיין לקמן פרק 32 סעיפים 2–3 דתרופות שנוטלת כדי שתכנס להריון או בהיתר מפוסק מובהק למניעת הריון שרי ליטלם בשבת.

שאלה: ישנם נשים שעבר עליהם שנים שלא נתעברו ועוברות טיפולים ומעקב רצוף עם בדיקות שונות לידע את זמן הביוץ, ובבא העת מקבלות זריקות מסוימות לקליטת ההיריון, וטפול זה כרוך מלבד הזריקות בעוד בדיקות מעבדה ובדיקות אולטרא סאונד ועוד שהם כרוכים רובם ככולם בחילולי שבת, האם מותר לעבור טיפולים אלו בשבת או ביו״ט כדי לזכות זוג בישראל בפרי בטן?

תשובה: נראה דיש לחלק שאלה זו לשניים: (א) התחלת הטיפול כאשר האשה עדיין ריקנית ולא נקלטה כלל. (ב) אחר שנקלטה בהריון בעזה״י ויש צורך במעקב לחזק את רחמה ולהסיר כל מכשול בהריון. באופן הראשון כאשר עדיין לא נקלטה ונמצאת במעקב על תהליך זמן הביוץ וכדו׳ אין היתר לעשות מלאכות הכרוכות בחילול שבת מן התורה כגון בדיקת אולטרא סאונד, זריקות תוך ורידיות (IV) הפרדה והשבחת זרע ושאר טיפולים ובדיקות הכרוכים במלאכות

6. An infant who is suffering from testicular torsion, which causes a blockage in the blood vessels leading to the testes and can result in loss of the testicle and infertility if not treated immediately, is classified as a patient whose limb is in danger. Since this may lead to gangrene of the teste, there is some question as to whether this is an actual case of *pikuach nefesh*, danger to life. Intestinal torsion (known to physicians as "volvulus"), which can lead to strangulation of the intestines and gangrene and severe stomach cramps, is considered an internal injury, and the patient is treated like a *choleh sheyeish bo sakanah*. Prompt treatment in such situations can prevent the need for surgery.

7. Sometimes an infected tooth can be saved through treatment or antibiotics but will have to be extracted if left untreated. This, too, is considered *sakanas eiver*.[11] Therefore, the patient may be treated by a non-Jew, or even by a Jew if only rabbinical prohibitions will need to be violated.[12]

8. In addition, injury to any limb or any other part of the body that will cause it to lose or limit its function if treatment will not be supplied promptly is categorized as *sakanas eiver*. An example would be a supracondylar fracture of the elbow or knee dislocation.

9. It should be noted, however, that extreme caution must be exercised upon detecting any sign of necrosis. This may be indicative of a blood clot or some other blockage of the blood vessels and should be treated as a real danger to life.

שבת, אמנם בדיקות שאינם כרוכים בחילול שבת כגון מדידת חום או תרופות שונות, כמו״כ זריקות תוך שרירי (IM) וכיו״ב שאינם אסורים אלא מדרבנן — נראה דיש להקל. באופן השני כאשר נקלטה האשה בהריון ויש צורך בטיפולים דחופים שאינם סובלים דיחוי אחר השבת ועלול לסכן את ההריון אפילו בספק — מותר לעשות פעולות אלו גם בשבת, כנלע״ד.

11 דשן חשובה לאיבר, דהרי עבד יוצא בשן ועין וחשיבי בכלל איברים שאינם חוזרים. ועיין בשו״ת שבט הלוי ח״ח סי׳ צ״ב אות א׳ שדן בגדר שן אי חשיב בר והעלה דלא חשיב אבר, שהרי לא חשיב ברמ״ח אברים במשנה דאהלות ועוד עיי״ש. אולם אחר המחילה אין דבריו מוכרחים לכאורה לענ״ד. דהתם קחשיב רק אברים שיש בהם עצם ולא קחשיב שאר איברים דאף לב כבד וכליות לא קחשיב התם, ולענין שבת ודאי חשיבי אבר. ועוד יש להאריך בענין זה אך אכמ״ל.

12 יתר דיני רפואת שיניים בשבת יתבאר בהרחבה לקמן פרק 34.

Due to its complex halachic content, this chapter is presented in its original Hebrew.

Chapter 29

בירור שיטות הפוסקים בדין חולה במקצת

Halachic Opinions Regarding Choleh B'Miktzas

להלן יבואר מקור הדין של חולה במקצת המבואר בראשונים, ובתוך הדברים נברר בס״ד שיטות הראשונים בסווגי החולאים השנים, עם תוספת נופך בסיעתא דשמיא, שקלא וטריא בדברי גדולי אחרוני הפוסקים בענין זה.

בירור שיטות הראשונים במקור דין ״חולה במקצת״

א. בראשונים הובאו ארבעה סוגי חולים באופן כללי ואלו הם:

א) חולה שיש בו סכנת חיים.
ב) חולה שאין בו סכנת חיים אך יש לו סכנת אבר.
ג) חולה שאין בו לא סכנת חיים ואף לא סכנת אבר.
ד) מיחושים בעלמא ומתחזק והולך כבריא.

כך הובא בראשונים; הרא״ש (ע״ז כ״ז ע״ב), הר״ן (שבת פרק שמונה שרצים). הרמב״ן בתורת האדם שער המיחוש (הובא בחידושיו ס״ס מועד על הגמ׳ ביצה דף כב:). הריטב״א (שבת קכח:). וכן כתב הב״י בהקדמת סימן שכ״ח. אולם ממשמעות הרמב״ם והשו״ע והמגיד משנה מבואר שיש עוד סוג חולה המסווג בין חולה שאין בו סכנה לבין חולה עם מיחושים וכאבים בעלמא, ומוגדר כ״חולה במקצת״, וגם דינו שונה משאר חולים, שמותר לעשות עבורו שבות ע״י נכרי, והיינו שבות דשבות. ועתה נבאר מקור הדברים בעזר ה׳ יתברך.

ב. הרמב"ם פ"ו מהלכות שבת הלכה ט' כתב וז"ל: "דבר שאינו מלאכה ואין אסור לעשותו בשבת אלא משום שבות מותר לישראל לומר לנכרי לעשותו בשבת והוא שיהיה שם מקצת חולי או יהיה צריך לדבר צורך הרבה או מפני מצוה. (הלכה י') כיצד אומר ישראל לנכרי בשבת לעלות באילן או לשוט על פני המים כדי להביא לו שופר או סכין למילה או מביא לו מחצר לחצר שאין ערוב ביניהם מים חמין להרחיץ בהם קטן ומצטער וכן כל כיוצא בזה" עכ"ל. (העתק ממהדורות שבתי פרנקל)

וכתב הראב"ד שם ז"ל: והוא שיהיה שם מקצת חולי. א"א אם היה מקצת חולי הוא עצמו עושה שהרי גונח יונק חלב בשבת (כתובות ס.) וכן אמרו הלכה מחזירין את השבר (שבת קמח). וכן אמרו במקום הפסד כגון צנור שעלו בו קשקשין ממעכן ברגלו (כתובות ס.) עכ"ל. (העתק ממהדורת שבתי פרנקל).

המגיד משנה כתב שם וז"ל: "ובהשגות א"א אם היה מקצת חולי הוא עצמו עושה שהרי גונח יונק חלב בשבת. וכן אמרו הלכה מחזירין את השבר וכן אמרו במקום הפסד כגון צנור שעלו בו קשקשין ממעכן ברגלו ע"כ. כל אלו יתבארו בדברי רבינו (גונח בפכ"א הי"ד, והחזרת השבר בפ"ב ה"י, צנור שעלו בו קשקשים לא מצאתי להלכה ברמב"ם. מ.ח.) ואמנם כוונתו בכאן שאין כאן חולי כולל כל הגוף ולא סכנת אבר אלא קצת צער וזהו שכתב "מקצת חולי" או "מצטער" , ועוד שזה מה שעושה הוא כדרכו".

והנה מבואר מהמגיד משנה שישנה הגדרת חולי שאינה בגדר חולה שאין בו סכנה אלא דרגא אחת פחות מחולה שאין בו סכנה, ועל סוג זה כתב הרמב"ם שמותר הישראל לומר לנכרי לעשות לו בשבת דבר האסור משום שבות.

ואין לומר שמה שכתב המ"מ מקצת חולי הינו מיחושים בעלמא ומתחזק והולך כבריא, שהרי בפרק ב' מהלכות שבת הלכה י' כתב הרמב"ם וז"ל: חולה שאין בו סכנה עושין לו כל צרכיו ע"י נכרי וכו'. וכתב המגיד משנה שם וז"ל: ופירוש דווקא בדבר שיש בו ממנו חולי לכל גופו של אדם כגון חיה ל' יום וכגון לכחול העין בסוף אוכלא שהוא נופל למשכב או מצטער וחולה ממנו, אבל חושש והוא מתחזק והולך כבריא אין מתירין לו אפילו שבות דדבריהם ואפילו ע"י גוי, ולא עוד אלא דברים שאין בהם מלאכה ולא כלום בעולם גזרו משום שחיקת סמנים ע"כ כתב הרשב"א ז"ל בשם הרמב"ן ז"ל ודברים ברורים הם יתבארו בדברי רבינו פרק כ"א (הלכה כ' והלכה ל"א). ע"כ.

הדרן לדוכתין דמשמע מהמ"מ בדעת הרמב"ם לחלק בין מיחושים שמתחזק והולך כבריא שאין עושין צרכיו ע"י נכרי כלל לבין חולה במקצת שעושין לו שבות שהיא מדרבנן ע"י נכרי. ובאמת תמהני על פרוש קדמון ממצרים שביאר שם בפרק ו' הלכה י' בדברי הרמב"ם "ואם היה שם מקצת חולי" כלומר חולי שאין בו סכנה וכבר נתבאר בפרק ב' שעושין כל צרכיו ע"י גוי עכ"ל, א"כ תימה לי דלדבריו מה משמיענו הרמב"ם שאומרים לגוי לעשות שבות דרבנן, הא התם שרי אפילו מלאכה מדאורייתא, וצע"ג. אלא ודאי כוונת הרמב"ם כמו שכתב המגיד משנה וכמבואר לעיל.

ג. בשולחן ערוך סי' ש"ז סעיף ה' הביא פסקו של הרמב"ם בפ"ו הנ"ל להלכה, וז"ל: דבר שאינו מלאכה ואינו אסור לעשות בשבת אלא משום שבות מותר לישראל לומר לא"י לעשותו בשבת והוא שיהיה שם מקצת חולי וכו' עיי"ש. וע"ע במ"ב ס"ק כ"א, ובכף החיים אות מ' ודו"ק.

ד. והנה המגן אברהם שם ס״ק ז׳ כתב וז״ל: ״מקצת חולי, דאלו בחולה ממש הכולל כל הגוף או שיש בו סכנת אבר אפילו ישראל עושה שבות לחד מ״ד כמ״ש סי׳ שכ״ח ס״ז, ושבות שלא כדרכה אפילו במצטער שרי כמ״ש שם סל״ג. ודע שאין מדמין דבר לדבר בעניני השבותים ואין לך בם להתיר אלא מה שאמרו חכמים, דלגבי מילה לא התירו שבות כמ״ש סי׳ של״א ס״ו, וגבי לוקח בית בא״י מותר כמ״ש סי׳ ש״ו ס״א, עכ״ד המ״מ פ״ו. ומשמע מדבריו שהיה גורס ברמב״ם מקצת חולי או מצטער (פי׳ צער קצת) [מ״מ] וכ״כ הטור בשמו, ול״ג או יהיה צורך הרבה, אבל מדברי הראבד משמע דגרס ליה שכתב וז״ל א״א אם היה מקצת חולה הוא עצמו עושה וכו׳ וכן אמרו במקום הפסד כגון צנור כמ״ש סי׳ של״ו ס״ט. (עכ״ל המגן אברהם השייך לענינינו)

ה. ויש לעיין טובא בדברי המגן אברהם הנ״ל הן בהבנת השו״ע והן בהבנת המגיד משנה, ונברר הדברים בעזר ה׳ יתברך.

מש״כ המגן אברהם בתחילת דבריו ז״ל: ״ושבות שלא כדרכה אפילו במצטער שרי כמ״ש שם סל״ג״, כוונת המג״א על מש״כ בשו״ע סימן שכ״ח סעיף ל״ג וז״ל: ״גונח מותר לינק חלב מהבהמה דבמקום צער לא גזרו רבנן״ ע״כ. ומשמע מדברי המג״א ממש״כ ושבות שלא כדרכה ״אפילו״ במצטער שרי דהיינו ״גונח״, דחשיב גונח רק כמצטער ואינו בכלל חולה שאין בו סכנה.

וקשה לי טובא אמאי חילק המג״א דין גונח משאר דין חולה שאין בו סכנה שהביא בראש דבריו שכתב דאלו חולה ממש הכולל כל הגוף או שיש סכנת אבר אפילו ישראל עושה שבות לחד מ״ד וכו׳ הרי גם גונח בכלל זה ואמאי כתב ״ושבות שלא כדרכה אפילו במצטער שרי והיינו גונח, דמשמע שגונח הוא בדרוג פחות מחולה שאין בו סכנה. דלכאורה משמע בראשונים שהבינו דין גונח שהוא בכלל חולה שאין בו סכנה , דכ״כ התוס׳ בכתובות ס ע״א ד״ה גונח וז״ל: לאו בשיש בו סכנה איירי דא״כ מאי אריא משום דהוי מפרק כלאחר יד וכו׳ והכא בצער של חולי שהוא קרוב לסכנה וכו׳ עיי״ש.

וכ״כ בהגהות אשר״י שם דגונח הוי חולה שאין בו סכנה, וכן הרי״ף בפרק חבית טורח לדחות מי שרצה לפרש שגונח הוי כמקום סכנה והוכיח בראיות שאין בו סכנה, וכן הר״ן שם איירי דהוי חולי שאין בו סכנה וכמו שהקשה שם אמאי לא אמרינן שיעשה ע״י נכרי דכל דבר שאין בו סכנה אומר לנכרי ועושה עיי״ש. וכ״כ הרמב״ם פכ״א הלכה י״ד דגונח הוי חולה שאין בו סכנה עיי״ש.

וא״כ תימה מה ראה המגן אברהם להוציא דין גונח מכלל חולי שאין בו סכנה ולהגדירו בפני עצמו כדין חדש ״מצטער״. ועיין עוד ברמב״ן בספר תורת האדם בהא דכתב דחולה שאין בו סכנה עושין לו צרכיו ע״י נכרי או ע״י ישראל בשינוי, מקורו מהא דגונח יונק דהוי חולה שאין בו סכנה וקשרי ליה מלאכה בשינוי, עיי״ש. ועי״ע בביאור הגר״א סימן שכ״ח סעיף י״ז בביאורו סברה שלישית, וביאר מקור דין חולה שאין בו סכנה שעושין לו צרכיו הישראל ע״י שינוי, מדין גונח עיי״ש.

ו. ועוד יש לעיין בדברי המגן אברהם הנ״ל בהבנת המגיד משנה בפ״ו (המובא לעיל אות ב׳) דכתב המג״א ״ומשמע מדבריו שהיה גורס בהרמב״ם מקצת חולי או מצטער״ ולא גרס ברמב״ם ״או יהיה צריך לדבר צורך הרבה״, ומדברי הראב״ד משמע שגרס כפי המובא ברמב״ם שלפנינו.

ובעניותי ובקוצר בינתי לא הבינותי מה הכריח את המגן אברהם לבאר כן בדברי

המגיד משנה, דהרי המ״מ לכאורה לא שינה שום נוסח מלשון הרמב״ם שלפנינו, וכלל לא ציטט את לשון הרמב״ם, אלא בא לתרץ את קושיות הראב״ד על דברי הרמב״ם, דהיינו שהראב״ד ס״ל שיש רק סוג אחד שנקרא ״חולה שאין בו סכנה״ דשרי הוא עצמו לעשות שבות דרבנן ולא רק ע״י נכרי. דהרי גונח יונק והרי מחזירין את השבר וכו׳ וא״כ מדוע הרמב״ם כותב בקצת חולי עושה רק הנכרי ורק איסורי שבות ? וע״ז כותב המ״מ ומיישב שהרמב״ם בא להשמיענו דין נוסף מחוץ לדין חולה שאין סכנה, — שיש חולי שאינו בגדר חולה שאין בו סכנה וגם אינו בגדר מיחושים וכאבים בעלמא אלא גדר חדש של ״מקצת חולי״ וזהו מה שכתב הרמב״ם ״מקצת חולי״ או ״מצטער״. ע״כ. ואין כוונת המ״מ לשנות את גירסת הרמב״ם חלילה אלא מבאר שלשונות אלו נקט הרמב״ם בהלכות אלו דבהלכה ט׳ נקט לשון ״מקצת חולי״, ובהלכה י׳ כשהביא דוגמאות לדין החדש נקט הרמב״ם לשון ״מצטער״ וגדר אחד להם. (ולשון הרמב״ם הובא לעיל אות ב׳) וא״כ קשה לי מה ראה המגן אברהם להבין בדברי המגיד משנה שמשנה את גירסת הרמב״ם מכפי המבואר לפנינו. וצ״ע.

בירור שיטות הראשונים בדין חולה שאין בו סכנה, סכנת אבר והמסתעף

ז. הרמב״ם פ״ב מהלכות שבת הלכה י׳ גבי דין חולה שאין בו סכנה כתב וז״ל : ״חולה שאין בו סכנה עושין לו כל צרכיו ע״י נכרי. כיצד אומרין לנכרי לעשות לו והוא עושה לבשל לו ולאפות ולהביא רפואה מרשות לרשות וכיוצא באלו. וכן כוחל את עיניו מן הנכרי בשבת אע״פ שאין שם סכנה. ואם היו צריכים לדברים שאין בהם מלאכה עושין אותם אפילו ישראל. לפיכך מעלין אזנים בשבת. ומעלין אנקלי ומחזירין את השבר וכן כיוצא בזה מותר״. ע״כ

ובדברי הרמב״ם הללו נחלקו הפוסקים ולענ״ד שלש שיטות בדבר ; שיטת הטור (להלן אות ט), שיטת המגיד משנה (בשיטת המ״מ נחלקו הב״י והמג״א וכדלהלן אות י׳ ואות י״ב), שיטת הב״י (להלן אות י״א). והנה קודם שנבאר שיטות הפוסקים בביאור דברי הרמב״ם נקדים בענין זה את ספיקו של הרא״ש שהסתפק במסכת עבודה זרה פרק ב׳ ס״י בסוגיא של עין שמרדה שמותר לכוחלה בשבת.

ח. הרא״ש בע״ז פ״ב ס״י אחר שהביא דין הגמרא בענין עין שמרדה להלכה כתב שם וז״ל :

שמעינן מהכא דמה שהוא סכנת אבר אין מחללין עליו את השבת באיסור דאורייתא אבל באיסור דרבנן מחללין, דאפילו כי שחיקי סמנין מאתמול נמי איכא איסורא דרבנן, דכל רפואה אסורה משום שחיקת סממנים, והכא נמי כל צורכי חולה נעשין ע״י עובד כוכבים בשבת ולא שני לן בין שבות דאית ביה מעשה לשבות דלית ביה מעשה, או שמא איכא לפלוגי בין חסרון אבר לחולה שאין בו סכנה, כדאמר (ערובין דף קב :) אין מחזירין רטיה במדינה, או שמא חזרת רטיה למכה ליכא חולה אלא חשש בעלמא ולהכי לא שרינן ביה שבות שאית ביה מעשה וצ״ע.

A. שיטת הטור בדעת הרמב״ם

ט. הטור בסי׳ שכ״ח (סעיף י״ז) הביא ספיקו הנ״ל של הרא״ש וז״ל : אבל בחולי שאין בו

סכנת אבר נסתפק א״א הרא״ש ז״ל אם מותר לחלל עליו בשבות דאית ביה מעשה דשמא לא התירו אלא אמירה לא״י אבל לא שבות דאית ביה מעשה אלא בסכנת אבר. ע״כ. ובהמשך דבריו הביא דברי הרמב״ם הנ״ל וס״ל דהרמב״ם פשט ספיקו של הרא״ש לקולא, וז״ל שם: ״אבל הרמב״ם ז״ל כתב חולה שאין בו סכנה עושין כל צרכיו ע״י א״י ואם היו צריכים לדברים שאין בהם מלאכה עושין אותם אפילו ע״י ישראל, לפיכך מעלין אזניים ומעלין אנקלי בשבת ומחזירין את השבר וכל כיוצא בזה.״ עכ״ל הטור. ואם כן שיטת הטור (על פי הב״י, ועין לקמן דהפרישה הבין אחרת בדעת הטור) שהרמב״ם התיר לעשות לחולה שאין בו סכנה צרכים שאין בהם מלאכה ע״י ישראל אע״פ שכל רפואה אסורה משום שבות, — לפיכך מותר לישראל לעשות כל שבות דרבנן אפילו כדרכו.

ב. שיטת המגיד משנה בדעת הרמב״ם

י. המגיד משנה בפ״ב ה״י כתב לבאר דברי הרמב״ם הנ״ל וז״ל: ״וכבר נתבאר בדברי רבינו שכל שבות מותר בחולי שאין בו סכנה כיון שהוא חולי כולל כל הגוף, בין שבות דאמירה לא״י בין שבות הנעשה ע״י ישראל. אבל באבר אחד כיון שאין בו סכנה לא הותר לישראל אפילו שבות גמור, וזהו שלא התירו לכחול אלא מן הא״י אע״פ שאין בכוחל אלא משום שבות. אבל מלאכה גמורה בישראל לא הותרה אפילו בסכנת אבר אחד אלא בסכנת נפשות״.

וכתב הב״י ז״ל: ומתוך דבריו נראה שנתיישב ספק זה דהא דשרינן שבות הנעשה ע״י ישראל אף ע״פ שאין בו סכנה היינו דווקא בחולי הכולל כל הגוף, והא דלא שרינן למיכחל אלא מן א״י אע״פ שיש בו סכנת אבר, משום שאינו חולי הכולל כל הגוף, ולפי זה צריך לומר דהעלאת אזנים ואנקלי והחזרת שבר הם חולאים כוללים כל הגוף שאם לא כן לא היו מתירים לעשותם ע״י ישראל. עכ״ל. ועי״ש שהקשה עליו מה שהקשה. עכ״פ משמעות המגיד משנה בשיטת הרמב״ם בסכום דרק חולי הכולל כל הגוף מותר לישראל שבות אפילו ללא שינוי ואילו בסכנת אבר שאינו סכנת הגוף לא שרי שבות ע״י ישראל.

ג. שיטת הב״י בדעת הרמב״ם

יא. הב״י לאחר שדחה את הבנת הטור בדברי הרמב״ם ואת הבנת המ״מ כתב שם וז״ל: ״ולפיכך נראה לי דבכלל חולה שאין בו סכנה הוי בין שהוא חולי הכולל כל הגוף בין שאינו כולל, בין שיש בו סכנת אבר בין שאין בו, בכל גונא לא התירו שבות הנעשה ע״י ישראל, מיהו הני מילי בשבות שיש בו עיקר מלאכה שהוא נסמך לה כגון כוחל שאסור מפני שהוא ככותב, או לעשות שום רפואה בסם דאיכא למיחש משום שחיקת סמנים, אבל שבות שאין עיקר מלאכה שהוא נסמך עליה מותר אפילו ע״י ישראל. עכ״ל. וע״ע שם שהאריך בזה. והביא הב״י דעה זו בשו״ע בדעה הרביעית בסעיף י״ז שם.

יב. המגן אברהם בסי׳ שכ״ח אות י״ב בהא דכתב השו״ע סעיף י״ז ז״ל: ולחלל עליו הישראל באיסור דרבנן בידיים יש מתירים אפילו אין בו סכנת אבר. כתב המג״א שם וז״ל: משמע דכ״ש כשיש בו סכנת אבר דמותר אפילו אינו חולה שכולל כל הגוף, וזו דעת המגיד משנה מה שסיים ״אבל באבר אחד כיון שאין בו סכנה אסור, וזה

שלא התירו לכחול אלא מן העכו״ס״ עכ״ל, פי׳ שאין באבר סכנה, דלא כהב״י, וכ״כ המ״מ אח״כ ״אבל מלאכה גמורה בישראל לא הותרה אפילו בסכנת אבר״ ע״כ. ומשמע דשבות מותר בסכנת אבר, ואם אין בו סכנת אבר מותר ע״י עכו״ם והיינו עובדא דאמימר, וכמ״ש סימן ש״ז ס״ה שבות דשבות שרי במקצת חולי, ומיחוש בעלמא אפילו ע״י עכו״ם אסור וכמ״ש ס״א ועמ״ש סי׳ תצ״ו. עכ״ל המגן אברהם שם.

יג. והמעיין היטב בדברי המגן אברהם בשיטת המ״מ יראה מסקנת דבריו כך:

א) דחולה בכל גופו ואין בו סכנת אבר — מותר שבות ע״י ישראל.

ב) חולה באבר אחד ויש בו סכנת אבר — גם כן מותר שבות ע״י ישראל.

ג) חולה באבר אחד ואין בו סכנת אבר — אסור אפילו שבות ע״י ישראל, ורק ע״י עכו״ם מותר, והיינו שכוחל מן העכו״ם, וזהו שכתב בשו״ע ש״ז ס״ה דשבות דשבות שרי במקצת חולי ע״י עכו״ם, ואמימר שהתיר לכחול בשבת מן העכו״ם וכו׳, איירי באינו חולה בכל גופו אלא באבר אחד ואין בו סכנת אבר.

ד) מלאכה ע״י ישראל אפילו בסכנת אבר אסור.

ולהלן אות (טו) נדון ונברר בס״ד במסקנות אלו.

יד. גם הפרישה (סי׳ שכ״ח אות ה׳ ואות ו׳) האריך בהבנת שיטת הרמב״ם על פי הבנת הטור, ועל פי הבנת המ״מ כפי ביאור המגן אברהם הנ״ל, ואצטט כאן את עיקר מסקנת דבריו בקצרה, וז״ל: (באות ו׳) ״לכן אני אומר דודאי רבינו ס״ל פי׳ הרמב״ם כמ״ש בראשונה, דברישא איירי בחושש בכל גופו דווקא, ועליו כתב בסיפא דעושה גם ע״י ישראל צרכים שאין בהם מלאכה. ומציעתא דאיירי בחושש רק באבר אחד דהיינו העין וגם אין בו סכנה, משום הכי שרי דוקא ע״י א״י ואפילו מלאכה דאורייתא כדדייק לישנא דוכן, ולא ע״י ישראל כלל אפילו צרכים שאין בהם מלאכה דאורייתא, ומש״כ בסיפא שנעשין ע״י ישראל צרכין שאין בהם מלאכה לא קאי אלא ארישא אחושש בכל גופו, ומשום הכי לא מייתי רבינו אלא רישא וסיפא דדברי הרמב״ם״. עכ״ל הפרישה בביאור דעת הטור. ובהמשך דבריו כתב ז״ל: ״וגם המ״מ ס״ל כרבינו דמ״ש הרמב״ם בסיפא דנעשה ע״י ישראל ארישא אחששת כל הגוף קאי דווקא. ואמציעתא כתב המ״מ דהטעם דהרמב״ם כיון שאין בו סכנה לא הותר לישראל אפילו בשבות, וא״כ לא התיר לכחול אלא ע״י א״י. ונ״ל פשוט דמ״ש המ״מ כיון שאין בו סכנה ר״ל אפילו סכנת אבר העין אין בו, וזהו שמסיק המ״מ וכתב ז״ל אבל מלאכה גמורה בישראל לא הותרה אפילו בסכנת אבר אחד וקאי אטעם שכתב לפני זה דמש״ה אסור ע״י ישראל משום דאין בו סכנת אבר דמשמע דמכח הא אי הוה בו סכנת אבר מותר אפילו ע״י ישראל מלאכה דרבנן דומיא דכחילה, ומש״ה מסיק אבל מלאכה גמורה אסור אפילו בסכנת אבר. וזהו הפירוש פשוט בעיני ותמה אני על הרב ב״י דפי׳ לדברי המ״מ דמ״ש כיון שאין בו סכנה דר״ל סכנת כל הגוף ויש בו סכנת אבר וכו׳. עכ״ל הפרישה.

ומבואר בדברי הפרישה כפי שביאר לעיל המג״א דהרמב״ם איירי בכחילת עין כחולי באבר אחד ולא נפל למשכב ואין בו אפילו סכנת אבר, ולכן שרי רק ע״י א״י, והיינו שביאר סוגיא דאמימר דאיירי נמי בקצת חולי וכדפירשתי בשיטת המגן אברהם.

טו. ובאמת יש לתמוה טובא האיך שייך להעמיד הגמ׳ בביצה כ״ב בסוגיא דאמימר דאיירי ב״מקצת חולי״ ולא בגדר חולה שאין בו סכנה, ושרי ביה רק שבות דשבות כמבואר ברמב״ם פ״ו הלכה ט׳ (הנזכ״ל אות ב׳) ובשו״ע סי׳ ש״ז סעיף ט׳ (הנזכ״ל אות ג׳). הרי הגמ׳ שם איירי במפורש בחולה שאין בו סכנה, וכמאמר רב אשי שם לאמימר מאי דעתיך דא״ר עולא בריה דרב עלאי צורכי חולה עושין ע״י נכרי בשבת, ואמר רב המנונא כל דבר שאין בו סכנה אומר לנכרי ועושה וכו׳ ורב המנונא ורב עולא איירו בחולה שאין בו סכנה, וכך סיימה הגמ׳ שם דאיירי בסוף אוכלא והיינו חולי שאין בו סכנה. וביותר תימה איך המג״א מבאר כן בשיטת המגיד משנה, הרי המ״מ עצמו בריש דבריו כתב ז״ל: ״דווקא בדבר שיש בו ממנו חולי לכל גופו של אדם כגון חיה ל׳ יום וכגון לכחול את העין בסוף אוכלא שהוא נופל למשכב או מצטער וחולה ממנו אבל מתחזק והולך כבריא אין מתירין לו אפילו שבות דדבריהם ואפילו ע״י נכרי וכו׳ עיי״ש. הרי שהמ״מ גופא מבאר סוגיא דאמימר בחולה בכל גופו ונופל למשכב, והיינו חולי שאין בו סכנה, ודלא כפי׳ המג״א בדבריו, וצע״ג.

טז. ואמנם גם כפי שפירש הב״י בדברי המ״מ צ״ע, וכפי שהוכיחו הפרישה והמג״א מהמשך לשון המגיד משנה שכתב ז״ל: ״אבל מלאכה גמורה בישראל לא הותרה אפילו בסכנת אבר אחד אלא בסכנת נפשות״ וא״כ משמע שמש״כ לעיל מיניה ״אבל באבר אחד כיון שאין בו סכנה לא הותר לישראל אפילו שבות גמור״, לכאורה בהאי לישנא איירי שאין בו סכנה לאותו אבר, ולא כפי׳ הב״י דאיירי שאין בו סכנה היינו סכנת חיים. ומצווה ליישב. [ונראה לומר בקצת דוחק ליישב דברי הב״י בדעת המ״מ באופן זה בס״ד, דהנה בהגדרת חולה שאין בו סכנה בעינן שחולה בכל גופו או נפל למשכב, ובסכנת אבר לכאורה לא בעינן לא נפל למשכב ולא חולה בכל גופו, וא״כ יש לכאורה אופנים שונים של חולי בדרגות שונות וכדלהלן; א. יתכן מצב שחולה בכל גופו וגם בנוסף יש בו סכנת אבר, ובזה יש מקום לומר דחמיר טפי מסתם חולה שאין בו סכנה כלל לכאורה, ב. כמו״כ יש חולה שנפל למשכב אך אין בו סכנה כלל, ג. יש חולה שאינו נופל למשכב ואינו חולה בכל גופו אלא נמצא בסכנת אבר אחד. וא״כ יש לבאר את שיטת המ״מ בביאור דעת הרמב״ם עפ״י הב״י באופן זה. בתחילת דבריו דיבר על שבות דרבנן, ואמר חולי שאין בו סכנה כיון שכולל כל הגוף עושין לו כל שבות דרבנן אפילו ע״י ישראל, אבל אם אינו חולה בכל גופו ולא נופל למשכב אלא חולה באבר אחד שיש בו סכנת אבר, אין עושין לו שבות ע״י ישראל אלא ע״י עכו״ם [וכהבנת הב״י במ״מ] ואח״כ דן המ״מ על מלאכה גמורה, ואמר דבמלאכה גמורה ע״י ישראל לא מיבעיא חולי בכל גופו ואין בו סכנה שאין עושין לו מלאכה ע״י ישראל, אלא אפילו חולה בכל גופו ונופל למשכב ויש לו גם סכנת אבר, הו״א דשרי ליה מלאכה ע״י ישראל, קמ״ל ומלאכה גמורה בישראל לא הותרה אפילו בסכנת אבר אלא בסכנת נפשות. ולעולם סוגיא דאמימר באמת איירי בחולה שלא נפל למשכב אבל אית ביה סכנת אבר אחד, וס״ל להמ״מ דכל שלא נפל למשכב אין עושין לו צרכיו אלא ע״י עכו״ם, ולעולם ע״י עכו״ם שרי אפילו מלאכה דאורייתא כשאר חולה שאין בו סכנה, ורק ע״י ישראל יש לחלק בין חולה שאין בו סכנה לסכנת אבר כמבואר. ודו״ק.]

יז. ומה שהקשו האחרונים בהבנת הב״י בדעת המ״מ, דלכאורה מכל השיטות שהביא השו״ע משמע שסכנת אבר קיל טפי משאר חולה שאין בו סכנה וא״כ מה הסברה לומר שהמ״מ העמיד סברתו כנגד כל שיטות הראשונים בדבר עקרוני כזה, דבחולה

שאין בו סכנה שרי שבות ע״י ישראל ובחולה בסכנת אבר לא שרי. י״ל דעל פי מש״כ לא קשיא מידי, דמה שכתב המ״מ דבסכנת אבר לא שרי שבות ע״י ישראל איירי בסכנת אבר גרידתא וללא כל חולי בשאר גופו ולא נופל למשכב, ובזה איירי דאין עושין צרכיו אלא ע״י עכו״ם, אבל אה״נ חולה בכל גופו וגם אית ביה סכנת אבר, לית מאן דפליג דאף המ״מ ס״ל דשרי שבות ע״י ישראל, וכפי שביארו כל הראשונים.

יח. בשו״ע סי׳ תצ״ו סעיף ב׳ כתב מרן וז״ל: אין חילוק בין ראשון לשני אלא לענין מת וכן לכחול את העין, (הגה, או שאר חולי שאין בו סכנה) אע״פ שאסור בראשון אלא ע״י עכו״ם אם אין בו סכנה, בשני מותר אפילו ע״י ישראל ע״כ. וכתב שם המג״א ס״ק ג׳ לכחול את העין, אע״פ שאינו חולי הכולל כל הגוף עסי׳ שכ״ח סי״ז דבחולי הכולל כל הגוף אפילו בשבת שרי לעשות שבות, לכן השמיט הרב״י ״או שאר חולי״ וכו׳ והרמ״א בא להורות דאפילו להאוסרים בשבת מתירין ביו״ט. ע״כ.

יט. והנה הב״י שם בסי׳ תצ״ו (שהוא מקור דברי הרמ״א) הביא את דברי הר״ן וז״ל: וכתב הר״ן ומינה שמעינן דכל צורכי חולה שאין בו סכנה עושין ביו״ט שני של גלויות, מיהו איכא למימר דהני מילי כגון מיכחל עינא דמלאכה גופא שבות היא אבל להתיר אבות מלאכות אין לו, וכתב הרב המגיד בפ״א מהלכות יו״ט (הכ״ד) שזה דעת הרמב״ן בתורת האדם שאין מתירין מלאכות גמורות ע״י ישראל אבל כל שבות מתירין לו ע״כ.

גם הט״ז בס״ק א׳ כ״כ וז״ל: ולכחול העין, כתב הר״ן מטעם דמלאכה גופא היא שבות, אבל שאר אבות מלאכות לא, וא״כ מה שכתב הרמ״א ע״ז או שאר חולי שאין בו סכנה הוא נמי במידי דאין בו רק שבות וכ״ה מסקנת הר״ן, עכ״ל.

ולפי״ז צר״ל דאין הכרח דאיירי הכא בכוחל משום דחשיב כקצת חולי, (וא״כ המג״א מוכיח לשיטתו דסוגיא דאמימר ודין כוחל היינו במקצת חולי) אלא עדיין י״ל דכוחל איירי בחולה שאין בו סכנה, ואכתי הא קיי״ל בשבת דאסור לכחול ע״י ישראל אלא ע״י עכו״ם (לשיטת הר״ן) או ע״י ישראל בשינוי (לשיטת הרמב״ן) דקיי״ל כמותו, וקמ״ל דביו״ט שני שרי כל איסורי דרבנן אפילו ע״י ישראל להדיא. ואמנם עיין במ״ב שם ס״ק ה׳ שכתב ז״ל: דמיירי שחש בעינו קצת וכל גופו בריא ואינו מרגיש מיחוש בגופו מחמת העין דבכגון זה בשבת ויו״ט אסור לעשות שום רפואה ע״י עצמו אפילו בשינוי וכמו שנתבאר לעיל שכ״ח סי״ז ובמ״ב ס״ק נ״ב, והכא ביו״ט שני שרי לכתחילה ואפילו בלא שינוי, עכ״ל. וצ״ע אמאי נדחק לבאר כן דמיירי באינו חולה, הרי הרמ״א עצמו כותב דאיירי בחולה שאין בו סכנה ובפשטות דכוונתו דנפל למשכב כדין כל חולה שאין בו סכנה, ואמאי דחק דמיירי בבריא, וצ״ע.

בירור שיטות גדולי הפוסקים האחרונים בסווגי החולאים השונים

כ. בשו״ע הגר״ז בביאורו את סיוגי החולאים השונים חילק דין חולה שאין בן סכנה לחמשה חלקים כדלהלן:

א) נפל למשכב או מצטער כל כך עד שנחלש כל גופו.
ב) סכנת אבר
ג) לא נחלש כל גופו אלא שיש לו צער גדול.
ד) מקצת חולי ואין לו צער גדול.

ה) מי שיש לו מיחוש בעלמא.

ונעתיק בזה את לשונו בסימן שכ״ח סעיפים י״ט כ׳ השייך לענינינו.

דין חולה שאין בו סכנה וסכנת אבר

חולה שנפל מחמת חוליו למשכב ואין בו סכנה או שיש לו מיחוש שמצטער כ״כ עד שנחלש ממנו כל גופו שאז אע״פ שהולך כנפל למשכב הוא דומה, הרי צרכיו נעשין ע״י נכרי אפילו במלאכות גמורות של תורה כגון לאפות לו או לבשל לו אם צריך לכך וכו׳.

אבל אין מחללין עליו שבת ע״י ישראל באיסור של תורה אפילו יש בו סכנת אבר כל שאין בו סכנת נפש. ולחלל עליו ישראל באיסורי דברי סופרים בידיים כגון לעשות לו כל רפואה שהיא אסורה משום גזירת שחיקת סמנים אע״פ שאין בה בעצמה שום סרך מלאכה בעשייתה אפילו מד״ס או אפילו יש גם בה בעצמה איסור מד״ס בעשייתה מותר לעשותה לו בלא שום שינוי מדרך החול אם יש בו סכנת אבר אע״פ שלא נפל למשכב וגם לא חלה ממנו כל גופו, אבל אם אין בו סכנת אבר אלא שנפל למשכב או שמצטער כ׳ עד שחלה ממנו כל גופו איחן עושין לו דבר האסור מדברי סופרים ע״י ישראל אלא בשינוי מדרך החול.

וע״י שינוי מותר לעשות אפילו מלאכה גמורה כגון הגונח (שמותר לינק בפיו) כמו שיתבאר שכיון שמשנה בעשייתה אינה אסורה אלא מדברי סופרים.

דין מצטער, מקצת חולי ומיחושים בעלמא

ואם לא נפל למשכב וגם אינו מצטער כ״כ עד שנחלש כל גופו (אבל עכ״פ יש לו צער גדול) מותר לעשות לו ע״י ישראל כל שבות הנעשה בשינוי אפילו היא מלאכה, אבל אסור לו לאכול מאכלים הניכרים שהם לרפואה וכ״ש שאר שבותים שלא בשינוי אע״פ שאין בהם סרך מלאכה, וכן לעשות מלאכה גמורה ע״י נכרי שזהו שבות גמור שלא בשינוי.

ואם אין לו צער גדול ולא חולי הכולל כל הגוף אלא מקצת חולי, — אזי מותר לו לעשות כל שבות מד״ס ע״י נכרי אפילו שלא בשינוי כמ״ש בסי׳ ש״ז, אבל לא ע״י ישראל אפילו בשינוי, ולכן מותר לו לעשות רפואה מבחוץ ע״י נכרי שיניחנה שם עליו כיון שהוא אינו עושה מעשה בזה, ואף שמסייע לו קצת אין בכך כלום כמו שנתבאר למעלה. (אבל אסור לאכול מאכלים הניכרים שהם לרפואה ע״ד שיתבאר.)

אבל אם אין לו אפילו מקצת חולי אלא מיחוש בעלמא אסור לעשות לו אפילו ע״י נכרי שום דבר הניכר שהוא לרפואה כמו שנתבאר למעלה. עכ״ל הגר״ז.

כא. ועיי״ש בגר״ז במקורותיו לדינים אלו שהם לכאורה נראים כחדושים שלא נזכרו חלוקים אלו במפורש בדברי הראשונים והפוסקים, והנה עמש״כ בדין מצטער שלא נחלש כל גופו ולא נפל למשכב, שמותר לו כל שבות ע״י ישראל בשינוי ואפילו במלאכה, ציין שם באות צ׳ ז״ל: עב״י, ועיין מג״א ס״ק מ״א, ועיין מ״ש לקמן סעיף מ״א. ע״כ. והנה במש״כ עב״י לא ידעתי למה ירמזון מיליו, ואפשר דכוונתו למש״כ הב״י סי׳ שכ״ח בדין חלב אשה שמקלחת לחולה, וז״ל הב״י בדין זה. כתב הרב בנימין מה שנוהגות שמקלחות מהחלב כדי שיאחוז הדד וינק מותר, אבל מה שנוהגות להתיז

מהחלב על נשיפת רוח רעה אסור, שאין בו סכנה, ״וצערא יתיראי״ נמי ליכא, עכ״ל. ובסוף סימן ש״ל הביא הב״י דברי המרדכי וז״ל: שאסור לאשה לחלוב מדדיה ביד בשבת להקל דלא שרי אלא ביניקת התינוק בלבד, מיהו יש מפרשים דוקא בכלי אסור דהוי מפרק והוי תולדה דדש, אבל בקרקע מותר לחלוב, עכ״ל. ומה שציין הגר״ז להמג״א ז״ל המג״א שם ס״ק מ״א, אהא דכתב הרמ״א אסור להתיז מחלבה על מי שנשף בו רוח רעה דלית ביה סכנה, וכתב המג״א: וצערא יתירה נמי ליכא שם הא לאו הכי שרי דמלאכה שאצ״ל הוא, עסי״ז וסי׳ רע״ח. גם מה שציין הגר״ז לעיין במ״ש בהמשך דבריו בסעיף מ״א כתב שם וז״ל: אבל אסור להתיז מחלבה על מי שנשף בו רוח רעה מפני שאין בו סכנה וגם לא צער גדול כדי שנתיר לו איסור מד״ס ע״י ישראל כמו שהתירו בגונח ודומיו. עססי״ שי״ל. ע״כ.

ובסי׳ ש״ל כתב וז״ל: וכן היא עצמה יכולה להוציא בידה חלב המצער אותה כיון שהחלב הזה הולך לאיבוד אין בו משום מפרק אלא מד״ס ומשום צערא לא גזרו. ע״כ.

הארכתי מעט בציון מקורותיו כדי להורות כוונתו המדויקת של הגר״ז.

כב. והנה בספר קצות השולחן סי׳ קל״ד הביא את מסקנות הגר״ז הנזכ״ל להלכה אלא שמשום מה שינה במקצת בדין ״מצטער״ ויש בזה משמעות גדולה, וז״ל שם סעיף ה׳ ואם לא נפל למשכב וגם לא נחלש כל גופו, אלא שיש לו עכ״פ צער גדול, התירו לו שבות דשבות דהיינו תרי דרבנן, לכן מותר לומר לנכרי לעשות לו כל מלאכה דרבנן אפילו בלא שינוי [ובבדי השולחן שם אות ח׳ הוסיף ״ז״ל אדמו״ר ז״ל בס״כ וכן [אסור] לעשות ״מלאכה גמורה״ ע״י נכרי שזהו שבות גמור שלא בשינוי״ עכ״ל, מוכח דאם הנכרי עושה מלאכה דרבנן דהוי תרי דרבנן לא בעינן שינוי] או מלאכה דאורייתא ע״י שינוי, וישראל מותר לעשות לו מלאכה דרבנן ע״י שינוי אבל אסור לו לאכול ולשתות סמי מרפא או מאכלים הניכרים שהם לרפואה שבזה עושה איסור דרבנן בלא שינוי [ובבדי השולחן שם אות ט׳ כתב ״שם סעיף כ״״] ע״כ.

כג. ותמהני שלא כך כתב הגר״ז שם, אלא דמותר לעשות ע״י ישראל כל שבות הנעשה בשינוי אפילו הוא ״מלאכה״. ובציוניו שם כתב לדין אשה שיש לה צער מרבוי החלב דשרי להקל מהחלב וכנ״ל, הרי להדיא פי׳ כוונתו למלאכה גמורה ע״י ישראל בשינוי דשרי למצטער ולאו דווקא היכא דאיכא שבות דשבות כלשון הקצות השולחן וצ״ע.

כד. עכ״פ ילפינו מדברי שו״ע הגר״ז לחלק בין סוגי החולים השונים דישנם עוד שני סוגי חולים המסווגים בין חולה שאין בו סכנה לחולה עם מחושים וכאבים בעלמא. האחד דין מצטער, והשני דין מקצת חולי. ודיניהם כמבואר דבמצטער שרינן שבות בשינוי ואפילו מלאכה בשינוי כדין הקלת חלב המבואר בשלהי סי׳ ש״ל וכנ״ל, דהתם לא מיירי בחולה שנפל למשכב וגם לא בחולי הכולל כל הגוף (ואף לא דווקא ביולדת תוך ל׳ יום) אלא במצטערת בלבד מחמת רבוי החלב וכיו״ב.

ובמקצת חולי פסק כמ״ש השו״ע בסי׳ ש״ז סעיף ה׳, והרמב״ם פ״ו מהל״ש ה״ט דשרינן בכה״ג שבות דשבות דהיינו אמירה לעכו״ם בדבר האסור מדרבנן ואפילו בלא שינוי, אבל ע״י ישראל אפילו בשינוי אסור.

כה. החיי אדם בהלכות שבת כלל ס״ט בנשמת אדם אות א׳ האריך טובא לבאר דברי הראשונים בסווגי החולאים ובדעות שהביא מרן המחבר בסי׳ שכ״ח סעיף י״ז בדין

חולה שאין בו סכנה, כמו״כ הזכיר שיטת המ״מ הנזכ״ל ודברי הפוסקים בביאור דבריו, כמו״כ הזכיר דברי המגן אברהם שחילק בין מקצת חולי לחולי גמור ושדין כוחל חשיב כמקצת חולי וכו׳, וכתב ע״ז בזה״ל: ״ודבריו צ״ע שמחלק עלינו השוין וכו׳ דמאן מפיס בין מיחוש למקצת חולי וכו׳ ואיך יהיה ניכר אם הוא מקצת חולי או חולי ממש, שהרי אפילו הולך ה״ז כנופל למשכב כמ״ש הרמ״א, ומ״ש המ״א דבמקצת חולי מותר ע״י נכרי דהוי שבות שבות לא הבנתי כלל דמאי ענין זה לשבות דשבות בסי׳ ש״ז דמתירין במקצת חולי היינו להביאו דרך כרמלית ושאר צרכיו שאסורים משום שבות, אבל רפואה שגזרו משום שחיקת סממנים מה יועיל שבות דשבות, והא דהתירו במקום צער דווקא בדבר שאינו שייך בו רפואה.

כו. ספר תהלה לדוד סי׳ שכ״ח אות כ׳ סיכם את שיטת המג״א בדעת המ״מ הנזכ״ל וז״ל: ונמצא עכשיו המדרגות לדעת המ״מ [בשיטת המג״א]:

א) מיחוש בעלמא — אסור שבות דשבות.
ב) קצת צער — מותר שבות דשבות.
ג) מצטער הרבה — מותר מלאכה ע״י שינוי ע״י ישראל והיינו דינא דגונח לדעתו.
ד) חולה כל גופו — מותר שבות כדרכו.

בהמשך דבריו, הביא את הסתיגויותיו של הנשמת אברהם הנזכ״ל מחלוקיו של המג״א, וסיים בזה״ל: ע״כ צריכין לחלק בין מיחוש למקצת חולי, ודברי המג״א ברורין דבמיחוש אף בדבר שאין שייך בו רפואה אסור שבות דשבות, ובמקצת חולי אף בדבר ששייך בו רפואה מותר, וכן דעת הח״מ והתו״ש והרב הגר״ז ז״ל. עכ״ל התהלה לדוד.

ובאמת שיש הרבה אריכות דברים לברר בדבריהם הקדושים של רבותינו ולברר מקחם של צדיקים אלו אך קצר המצע מהשתרע ואין ליבי רחב יותר להאריך עוד בענין זה. כמו״כ יש אריכות רבה לברר בדברי הראשונים בעניני השבותים השונים מה יותר קל ומה יותר חמור, וכבר הפליגו קמאי בענין זה באריכות, ואכמ״ל יותר.

כז. מסקנא דמילתא: היות ורבים מגדולי האחרונים הזכירו חילוק זה בין סווגי החולים וכמבואר הכי נקטינן, ואמנם שעל פי דרכו של המגן אברהם קשה מאוד לבאר הדברים וכפי שהארכנו לעיל, הן בביאורו דין ״גונח״ (לעיל אות ה׳) והן בביאורו דין כחילת העין וביאור סוגיא דאמימר (לעיל אותיות י״ב-ט״ו) אך עכ״פ נראה לבאר הענין כפי שביארו בשו״ע הגר״ז וכמבורר לעיל, ופרטי הדינים יבוארו להלן בביאור דין חולה במקצת ומצטער. ואני תפילה לה׳ יתברך שיצילנו מן השגיאות והטעויות ויראנו מתורתו נפלאות אמן.

Chapter 30

Choleh B'Miktzas — *A Slightly Ill Person*

1. A *choleh b'miktzas,* a slightly ill person, is someone who suffers from a minor ailment or injury to a limb. This applies to someone who has a condition that affects one of his limbs[1] or who has suffered an injury to a part of the body, but there is no danger to the limb. He does experience pain as a result of the ailment or injury, but not to the extent that he is bedridden.

2. Examples of a slightly ill person include someone who has a foot wound or irritation that causes pain, like eczema[2] or a fungal infection. (If the wound is open and has become infected, and certainly if the patient has a fever and signs of erysipelas or cellulitis and the like, he is categorized as a *choleh she'ein bo sakanah*.)

3. One who suffered an injury or abrasion as a result of a fall and needs medication or the wound to be dressed to prevent infection is regarded as a *choleh b'miktzas*.

---

1 דאלו חלה בכל גופו, הוי כחולה שנפל למשכב ואין בו סכנה.

2 דצריך למרוח משחה או תמיסה על רגליו, וכן צריך לרחוץ רגליו במים, ולעיתים אף לחבוש מקומות מסויימים בגופו, הן למניעת חכוך, והן לשמירה מפני זיהומים שונים וכיו״ב. והנה אותו אדם מתנהג כאחד האדם בחייו הפרטיים וממשיך בעסקיו ואינו מוגדר כחולה כלל, אלא שיש לו קצת צער. וכן בדוגמאות הבאים.

4. One who suffers from light or first-degree burns that can be treated with medication is regarded as a *choleh b'miktzas*. If the burns are serious (third degree) and have penetrated the skin or sensitive parts of the body where internal organs may be affected, the patient is considered as being dangerously ill (*choleh sheyeish bo sakanah*). Someone who has suffered moderate or second-degree burns is regarded as a *choleh she'ein bo sakanah*.

5. One who experiences swelling that resulted from a fall (sprain) or some other injury (not including being struck with a metal implement) is considered a *choleh b'miktzas* unless he is bedridden as a result of the injury.

6. A baby with a rash (usually in the diaper area) is not regarded as a *choleh b'miktzas*, but rather as a *choleh she'ein bo sakanah* since he is a minor. Therefore, infant rashes may be treated on Shabbos but only with liquid medication, not with creams (see chapter 26, "Medication for a *Choleh She'ein Bo Sakanah*").

The Laws Applicable to a *Choleh B'Miktzas*

7. A *choleh b'miktzas* may not take medication or other foods that are consumed only for medicinal purposes.[3]

8. A non-Jew may not be asked to perform an action that involves a Torah prohibition for a *choleh b'miktzas*.[4]

9. A non-Jew may, however, be asked to perform an action that involves a rabbinical prohibition for a *choleh b'miktzas*.[5] Thus, a non-Jew may be asked to perform external treatments that do not involve the patient taking medication. For example, the non-Jew may prepare a bandage and place it on the wound, and he may change a bandage — assuming all these actions do not involve Torah prohibitions (such as opening the package without tearing across any letters).[6]

---

3 שאינו מוגדר כחולה שאין בו סכנה, ואסור בתרופות (שו״ע הגר״ז סי׳ שכ״ח סעיף כ׳).

4 שו״ע סימן ש״ז סעיף ס״ה.

5 שו״ע שם.

6 שו״ע הגר״ז סי׳ שכ״ח סעיף כ׳ . וכתב בספר אסור והיתר הארוך כלל נ״ט סעיף כ״ב וז״ל: לכן אם חתך באצבעו או נפל חבורה בראשו או במקום אחר בשבת והוא מוציא דם — מותר לומר

10. Actions that are not done for the purpose of healing may be done for a *choleh b'miktzas*. For example, the affected organ may be washed with water[7] as long as no therapeutic substance is added to it. The patient may also bathe in hot water that was heated before Shabbos even though he is not in the category of a *choleh she'ein bo sakanah*.[8] Similarly, one may place a protective bandage over the wound to prevent friction or infection, as long as the bandage is not cut on Shabbos and tape is not used.[9]

Relieving Pain

11. A nursing woman who is engorged and suffers pain as a result, even if she is not bedridden, may express milk by hand or with a manual pump, as long as the milk is rendered inedible. For example, if she is expressing milk into a bottle, she should first place something in the bottle that will make the milk inedible, like soap. Alternatively, she may express the milk onto the ground or into the sink.[10]

12. It should be noted that if lumps develop as a result of engorgement, they must be promptly treated to prevent serious complications. Therefore all necessary treatment is permitted, such as washing the area with warm water or applying various substances and massaging the area.[11]

13. See chapter 26, "Medication for a *Choleh She'ein Bo Sakanah*," paragraph 31, regarding the use of oils or ointments to treat sore nipples.

לכנעני לסוכו ולקשור עליה רטייה מן אניצי פשתן ולובן ביצה או שאר משיחות של חבורות, ומותר ללחוש בשבת וגם למדוד החגורה שקורין פנימ״ין למי שחש בראשו בשבת, ע״כ. ובפשטות מיירי שלא נפל מחמת כן למשכב וגם אינו נחלש בכל גופו מחמת כן. ומ״מ התיר ע״י עכו״ם חבישות שונות ואפילו עם משחות. ודו״ק.

7 כאותה שמצינו במי שנשמטה פרק ידו או רגלו ממקומו לא ישפשפנה הרבה בצונן שזהו רפואתו אלא רוחץ כדרכו ואם נתרפא נתרפא (שו״ע סימן שכ״ח סעיף ל׳). וכמו שמצינו עוד שרוחצין במי גרר ובמי חמתן ובחמי טבריה וכו׳ שכן דרך לרחוץ בהם וליכא הוכחה דלרפואה קא עביד (שו״ע שם סעיף מ״ד) ודל מהאי הרי כל רחיצת אבר מותר כמבואר בסימן שכ״ו עיי״ש.

8 כמבואר לעיל פרק 27 הערה 1, ובפרק 22 הערה 20 דהגרע״א איירי אף במצטער שלא במקום חולי, עיי״ש.

9 ועיין בכל זה לקמן בפרק 38 בענין תחבושות וכו׳.

10 שו״ע סי׳ ש״ל סעיף ח׳, ועיי״ש במ״ב ס״ק ל״ב.

11 דכיון שאפשר לבוא לידי סכנה עי״ז דלפעמים יש צורך בניתוח כדי לנקז או לכרות את הגושים הללו, לכן יש להקל בזה.

Chapter 31

Michush — Minor Aches and Pains

The Definition of *Michush*

1. This chapter refers to a person who suffers from discomfort, aches, and pains in one of his limbs, including the stomach and head, but he is not bedridden and functions normally. He is forbidden to take any medication on Shabbos, even if administered by a non-Jew due to the rabbinical prohibition of grinding herbs, to prevent a person from grinding herbs for medicinal purposes.[1]

2. Examples of *michush* are a slight headache, heartburn, runny nose,[2] sore throat or light cough, minor toothache,[3] light stomachache,[4] dizzi-

---

1 שו״ע סי׳ שכ״ח סעיף א׳.

2 והיינו הבאה מחמת הצטננות קלה. שאלה: נזלת הבאה בעקבות תקופת הפריחה ושינויי העונות, דישנם אנשים אלרגיים לתקופות אלו, והמנהג ליטול כדור אחד ליום כדי למנוע נזלת והתעטשויות וכיו״ב, אך האדם מתפקד בכל עיסוקיו בחיי היום יום כאחד האדם. האם מותר ליטול כדורים אלו בשבת? תשובה: אין ליטול כדורים אלו בשבת, ויוכל ליטול כדור אחד קודם השבת ואחד לאחר השבת. (וכשחל יו״ט לפני או אחרי השבת, אם מצטער הרבה יש להקל שייטול ביו״ט.) ועיין בדעת תורה סי׳ שכ״ח סעיף ל״ז בסופו מש״כ בעניין רפואה ביו״ט.

3 פרטי הדינים במחלות שיניים עיין לקמן במערכת מחלות ותופעות מצויות פרק 34 בעניין מחלות שיניים.

4 כאבי בטן וכמו״כ שלשולים הבאים כתוצאה מאכילה ושתייה בלתי מבוקרת, המנהג בדרך כלל להימנע מאכילה ושתייה במשך יום שלם כדי שמערכת העיכול תחזור לתפקודה הרצוי. ואמנם יש גם טפול תרופתי הגורם למניעת ושכוך הכאבים ועצירת השלשולים, אך אין ליטול תרופות

ness, minor rash, cut, or scratch.[5]

Even if the ailment bothers the person and he would normally take a pain reliever or some other medication to relieve the symptoms, as long as he is not experiencing extreme pain and there is no fever, vomiting, or severe diarrhea and he can still function normally, he is regarded as one who suffers from discomfort.

The Laws of *Michush*

3. One who suffers from discomfort may not take any medication on Shabbos to relieve it, whether it is administered by a Jew or by a non-Jew and even if the action involves only a rabbinical prohibition. Therefore, he may not take any painkillers, use eye, ear, or nose drops, or take baking soda to relieve heartburn. He may not apply cognac or whiskey to his gums to relieve a toothache[6] or take medicated cough drops or lozenges.

4. Similarly, one may not eat or drink any food that is not normally consumed by healthy people and is used only for relieving minor aches and pains.[7]

אלו בשבת. הערה: אין הדברים אמורים במקרה של תינוקות או קטנים שדינם שונה. כאבי בטן שמקורם בלתי ידוע ויש חשש למחלה פנימית או ספק סכנה — כגון כאבים חזקים בתחתית הבטן בצד ימין — מגלה בדרך כלל על חשש להתקף התוספתן (אפנדיציט) כמו״כ שאר כאבים כאשר ידוע שאין זה מחמת קלקול קיבה שגרתי, אלא סימפטומים של מחלה פנימית — הרי זה בגדר ספק פקוח נפש, ויש להתייעץ על כך עם רופא ומותר לחלל שבת עבור זה. מחלות מערכת העיכול נתבאר לקמן פרק 41 בהרחבה.

5 שריטה או חתך קל, אמנם הוי כמחושים וכאבים בעלמא, אך מ״מ מותר לו ליתן תכשיר אנטי ספטי לעצירת הדם ולחיטוי המקום, כמבואר בשו״ע סי׳ שכ״ח סעיף כ״ט מי שנגפה ידו או רגלו צומתה ביין כדי להעמיד הדם. ובעניין הנחת אגד מדבק וכיו״ב עיין מש״כ לקמן פרק 38 הערה 14.

6 בשו״ע סי׳ שכ״ח סעיף ל״ב כתב ז״ל: החושש בשיניו לא יגמע בהם חומץ ויפלוט אבל מגמע ובולע או מטבל בו כדרכו ע״כ. וע״ש במ״ב ס״ק ק״ב לא יגמע בהם חומץ וה״ה יין שרף ג״כ דינו כמו חומץ, אך במקום צער גדול אפשר לסמוך ביי״ש דמותר לשהותו בפיו. וע״ע לקמן במערכת מחלות ותופעות מצויות פרק מחלות שיניים פרק 34 מה שנכתוב בזה.

7 הר״ן בפרק שמונה שרצים כתב בשם הרמב״ן בתורת האדם דאפילו דברים שאמנם אינם מאכל בריאים אך נאכל גם לבריאים ומותרים הבריאים לאוכלם בשבת — אם ניכר שיש לאדם מחושים וכאבים אסור לו לאכול מאכלים אלו משום שניכר שאוכלם לרפואה עיי״ש.

Leniencies

5. The Sages permit a number of palliative activities on Shabbos for a person who suffers from a minor ailment to alleviate his symptoms:
    a. He may soak a gauze pad in a solution on Friday and rinse his eyes with it on Shabbos.[8]
    b. He may prepare a solution of baking soda on Friday and use it on Shabbos to relieve heartburn.[9] This is permitted because it is not apparent to others that the solution is being taken for medicinal purposes — the preparation was done before Shabbos, and people who see him drinking this solution cannot tell that he is taking medication because it looks like water.
    c. A person is permitted to inhale smelling tobacco or Vicks VapoRub to relieve congestion.[10]

---

8 שו״ע סי׳ שכ״ח סעיף כ״א.

9 בספר קצות השולחן בסוף סימן קל״ח כתב על כמה מחושים ומחלות, וזה לשונו השייך לעניינינו. ״כתב המנחת שבת דחולה גרעבצין ישתה סודה בשינוי, דהיינו שיקח הסודה לפיו וישתה עליו מים, ונראה דחולה גרעבצין היינו מי שיש לו מיחוש ששורף וקודח בלבו אחר אכילתו מחמת ריבוי החמצן בקיבה. והנה השינוי שכתב המנחת שבת אינו שינוי דהרבה פעמים עושים כן בחול ליקח הסודה לפה ולשתות עליו מים, אבל ידוע שאין הסודה רפואה לעצם החולי, אלא שמשקיט הכאב לפי שעה, ומ״מ לא דמי להא דשפין השיניים בסם לריח הפה, דהתם ריח הפה אינו בכלל חולי, אבל כאן זהו מיחוש גמור, ע״כ יש לעשות בשינוי, ונראה שלשים הסודה לפיו גרוע יותר דהא עי״ז ניכרת הרפואה, אבל אם יש לו מי סודה מוכן מערב שבת, מותר לשתות, דלדידיה איכא היכרא שהכינו מערב שבת, ולאחרים אינו ניכר ששותה רפואה, כיון שהוא שותה מים מוכנים יאמרו דמים הוא שותה, וכמו מי ששרה קילורין מע״ש דמותר לתת ע״ג עינו בשבת, אבל צריך שיהא נימס הסודה היטב שלא יהיה ניכר במים, ואם לא הכין מערב שבת יעשה שינוי שיתן הסודה לתוך כוס טיי, וישתה לגימות לגימות״. עכ״ל. וע״ע בילקוט יוסף שבת ד׳ עמ׳ קס״ד שחילק בין שתית מי סודה דשרי בכל עניין דהרי הוא משקה לבריאים, לבין אבקת סודה לשתייה דאסורה, משום שהיא אינה משקה בריאים, ופשוט. ונראה על פי מה שנבאר להלן מדברי האגרות משה זצ״ל דאם הכין מי סודה מערב שבת שפיר אפשר לשתותו בשבת ודמי ממש לשורה אדם קילורין מערב שבת ורוחץ בהם את עיניו בשבת. עיין בהערה 11.

10 כתב בספר קצות השולחן חלק ז׳ עמ׳ ק״ג ז״ל: כתב המשנה ברורה (ס״ק קכ״ז) בשם האחרונים דמותר לשאוף טבק בנחיריו בין שעושה כן לפי שעלול במיחוש הראש ובין להפיג השכרות דכיון ששואפים הטבק משום תענוג לא מוכחא מילתא דעביד לרפואה, ובהלק״ט כתב היתר זה לשאוף טבק לבטל הנזילות, ועי׳ שע״ת בשם מים רבים, ובס׳ כף החיים הביא מספר פדה את אברהם דמותר להריח באוריגאנ״ו מפני הנזילה דריחא לאו מילתא היא, אמנם ממש״כ הפוסקים הנ״ל היתר לטבק משום דגם בריאים שואפים אותו, מוכרח דריחא מילתא להא מילתא. ולכן יל״ע אם מותר להריח במשחה שקורין ״ויקס״ למי שיש לו נזילה והספק הוא דאם הויקס מרפא ממש את הנזילה פשיטא דאסור, דנזילה היא חולי שבאה מהצטננות אבל לפי הניסיון אין הויקס מרפא

d. One may crush a tablet and mix it with water and sugar before Shabbos and then take it on Shabbos. This is similar to preparing an eyewash solution, which is permissible since it was prepared before Shabbos.[11] Nevertheless, one may not mix drops or dissolve or crush pills in water on Shabbos itself.[12]

אלא ריחו החזק פותח צינורות הנשימה שנסתמו מפני הנזילה, והאדם מרגיש הקלה בשעת ההרחה, וגם מפסיק לשעה קלה את נזילת הליחה ואח״כ חוזרת כמו שהיתה. ואם נחליט דאין זו רפואה יש לדמותו להא דשפין את השיניים בסם משום ריח הפה, לפי שאינו מרפא את הריח אלא מעבירו לפי שעה, וכמ״ש האגלי טל (מ״ט סכ״א). ויש לחלק ביניהם קצת, דסם לשיניים אינו מבטל את ריח הפה כלל אלא שמתוך ריח החזק של הסם אין מורגש ריח הפה, אבל משחת הויקס היא מבטלת את הנזילה והוא רפואה לפי שעה, ע״כ א״א להתיר הרחת הויקס. עכ״ל. אולם גדולי האחרונים פליגי עליה וס״ל להתיר להריח ה״ויקס״ בשבת עיין בשו״ת באר משה ח״ו סי׳ מ״א, וכן בשו״ת ציץ אליעזר ח״ח סי׳ ט״ו פרק ט״ו אות כ״א — דחה דברי קצוה״ש וס״ל להתיר הרחת הויקס בשבת עיי״ש. וע״ע בספר לוית חן סי׳ צ״א. וכפי שמשמע מפשטות דברי הכף החיים הנזכר בסי׳ שכ״ח אות רי״ד לענין הרחת באוריגאנו. עיי״ש.

11 עיין שו״ת באר משה ח״א סי׳ ל״ג שכתב דיש שהתירו נטילת אספירין בשבת משום דחשיב כמאכל בריאים, אך הוא דעתו לאסור נטילת אספירין להדיא, והתיר רק אם מכינו מערב שבת. וטעמו ונימוקו מהא דשרי לשרות קילורין מערב שבת ולהניחן בשבת כנזכ״ל, ה״ה הכא שמכין מער״ש ע״י שכותש הכדור ומערבו עם מאכל או משקה הוי שינוי לדידיה ושרי. והנה בילקוט יוסף שבת ד׳ עמ׳ קמ״א כתב דיש מצדדים להקל בכדורים שהם רק למניעת ולשכוך כאבים — שאינם תרופה. אך אין נראה לענ״ד לחלק בזה ומידי מאכל בריאים ודאי לא הוי, ואסור אם לא נפל למשכב. כמו״כ בשו״ת אגרות משה או״ח ח״ב סי׳ פ״ו נראה דפליג עליה, דביאר דין שורה אדם קילורין וכו׳ בעניין אחר ואצטט בזה את לשונו השייך לענייננו. ״ויותר מסתבר בהיתר שריית קילורין מער״ש שכיון שהוא הדרך לשרות בשעת הנחת הקילור על העין, הוי זה ששרה בערב שבת כהתחלת הנחה על העין שלדידיה נחשב כהניח על העין כבר מערב שבת מצד שהצריכו לעשות התחלת ההנחה ע״י השריה שעושין בשעת ההנחה. ויש למילף מזה רק למיני רפואה שצריך ליקחם ע״י שיערבם באיזה מאכל ואיזה משקה והדרך שהוא בעצמו נותן לתוך המאכל והמשקה בשעה שצריך ליקח הרפואה, שיהיה מותר ליתן להמאכל והמשקה בע״ש, וליקח בשבת, אם לאחרים לא יהיה ניכר שהוא רפואה שיאמרו שהוא רק מאכל והוא רק משקה, דזה דמי ממש להא דשורה קילורין מע״ש״. וסיים שם בזה הלשון. ״דגם בשריית קילורין פשוט שלקנות קילורין שרויין וחולה לא יצטרך לעשות כלום אלא הנחה על העין לבד — יהיה אסור דהוא כרפואה שלא חסר כלום לחולה לעשות שאסור. ורק ברפואות שהחולה צריך לעשות בשעת לקיחת הרפואה כקילורין שצריך לשרות, וכן הרפואות שצריך החולה ליתנם למאכל ולמשקה בשעת לקיחת הרפואה — מותר כשעושה זה מע״ש מטעמים דלעיל. ידידו משה פיינשטיין.

וע״ע בשו״ת מנחת יצחק ח״ו סימן כ״ח שדן בהיתר זה וכתב בזה״ל הנה המצאה זו, לערב דבר רפואה במאכל בריאים, מקורה בשיטה מקובצת, הובא בהגהות מהרש״ם לספר אורחות חיים (סי׳ שכ״ח אות כ״ז) אבל לפי מה שמחלק שם המהרש״ם, אין היתר עיי״ש. אך ראיתי בספר שערים המצוינים בהלכה (סי׳ צ״א אות ב׳) שהביא משו״ת משפטי צדקה הספרדי להתיר עיי״ש, וביותר י״ל כן אם מערב מעש״ק, דשייך בזה היכרא שכתב בספר קצה״ש, ובמקום שמצטערים הרבה יש על מי לסמוך בכה״ג עכ״ל. עיי״ש.

12 עיין דעת תורה סי׳ שכ״ח סעיף ל״ז סד״ה וכל, וז״ל: אם מערב מאכל במאכל ואין דרך בריאים בכך [כלומר דאין דרך בריאים לאכול או לשתות בתערובת זו] אפילו הכי שרי, כיון שגוף המאכל

e. If a person started taking a medication before Shabbos, and discontinuing the medication on Shabbos would undermine the medicine's effect, he may continue taking the medicine on Shabbos.[13]

f. Therapy that does not involve taking pills, such as for treating a sprain or physical therapy, is permitted on Shabbos as long as the person does not exert so much effort that it causes him to sweat.[14]

g. Applying liquid ointment or gargling in the manner of a healthy person is also allowed for relief of minor aches and pains.

Applying Ointments and Gargling

6. One who suffers from muscle pains may apply a liquid ointment or any other liquid substance[15] to relieve his pain, but only if the following two conditions are fulfilled:

   a. The action must be performed in the same manner as healthy people who do not suffer from that condition.[16]

הוא של בריאים, מיהו י״ל דהיינו דווקא אם כל מאכל לבדו מאכל בריאים [כהא דשתיתא ויין שמערבים בהם מים הרבה] אלא שאין דרך בריאים לערבבם יחד, משא״כ אם מאכל א׳ אינו מאכל בריאים אסור [אע״פ שהעיקר מאכל בריאים הוא] ובפרט אם הוא הרוב, ונפק״מ לענין שתית מים המיוחדים לרפואה מעורב בחלב וכדומה שאסור. והגיה שם נכדו הגאון רבי שלום מרדכי הכהן שבדרון שליט״א בשולי הגיליון בזה״ל ונפק״מ לעניין מי סעלצער מעורב בחלב. עיי״ש מה שביאר באורך. כמו״כ בשו״ת באר משה ח״א סימן ל״ג הנ״ל כתב דכל התירו היינו דווקא אם מכין הכדור מער״ש אבל בשבת עצמה לערבו עם מאכל או משקה לא שרי עיי״ש. וע״ע בשו״ת מנחת יצחק ח״ג סימן ל״ה פרק ב׳ שכתב אודות אלו שהתירו אספירין בשבת מטעם דהוי כמאכל בריאים, וסתר דבריהם וס״ל דאסור ליטול אספירין על מחושים ורק במקום צער גדול שרי, עיי״ש. וע״ע במש״כ לעיל בסוף הערה 11 משמיה דהמנחת יצחק אודות שחיקת ותערובת הכדור במאכל מערב שבת.

13 עיין בספר יוסף אומץ להרב החיד״א סי׳ מ׳, שהוכיח כן מדברי הרמב״ם פרק כא לעניין חלתית דאף שאינו מאכל בריאים אם כבר השתמש בה קודם השבת שרי אף בשבת, והטעם שאם יפסוק בשבת יחלה. גם בדעת תורה סי׳ שכ״ח סעיף ל״ז הביא בדבריו את דעת המהרש״ק בספר החיים שצידד להקל בהתחיל לשתות איזה ימים קודם שבת שאין צריך להפסיק בשבת ומדמה דין זה לרטייה, עיי״ש שחולק עליו וס״ל דרק היכא שמסתכן דינא הכי ומבואר דבדליכא סכנה גם בכה״ג [שהתחיל קודם השבת] אסור. וכן מורה בשו״ת באר משה ח״א סי׳ ל״ג אות ז׳ לאיסור.

14 עיין לעיל פרק 2 הערה 9 מש״כ בזה באריכות.

15 שו״ע סי׳ שכ״ז סעיף א׳.

16 עיי״ש בשו״ע סעיף ב׳ סכין וממשמשין להנאתו ע״י שינוי דהיינו שסך וממשמש ביחד ובמ״ב שם ס״ק ו׳ ע״י שינוי מכפי הרגיל לעשות בחול שאין דרכו אז לסוך ולמשמש ביחד.

b. The type of liquid ointment used must not be one designated for medicinal purposes.[17]

Since today most healthy people do not apply ointments on their bodies, in practice it is forbidden for one who suffers from muscle pains to do so.[18]

7. Since it is unusual for healthy people to gargle cognac and spit it out, a person who suffers from a toothache may not do so either. But he may leave the cognac in his mouth and then swallow it.[19] One who brushes his teeth with mouthwash (toothpaste may not be used on Shabbos) may gargle and spit it out, since healthy people normally gargle and spit out mouthwash and because mouthwash is normally used by healthy people.[20]

Lubricants

8. It is normal to apply olive oil or baby oil to a healthy baby's skin. Therefore, one may apply a liquid oil to relieve pain. However, this is permissible only if the action is performed with a slight change from the usual manner.[21] This can be done, for example, by placing the lubricant on the part of the body that is hurting and massaging in the oil gently without exerting pressure. However, since healthy people do not apply oil mixed with vinegar to their bodies, it is forbidden for someone

---

17 כמ״ש השו״ע אבל לא בשמן ורד משום דמוכחא מילתא דלרפואה קא עביד, ובמ״ב שם שדמיו יקרים ואין אדם סך אותו אלא לרפואה וכל מילי דרפואה אסור. ואפילו ע״י א״י אסור אם הוא מתחזק והולך כבריא.

18 וכתב הב״י שם וז״ל: ונ״ל דכיון דבזמן הזה אין אנו רגילים לסוך בשום שמן כשאנו בריאים אסור לסוך שום שמן ע״ג המכה בשבת דודאי מוכחא מילתא דלרפואה עביד. עכ״ל. והוסיף הב״ח שם בשם שלטי הגבורים וז״ל, ומכאן אזהרה למי שיש לו חטטין בראשו שסכין אותו בשמן ואסור בשבת עיי״ש.

19 שו״ע סי׳ שכ״ח סעיף ל״ב ז״ל: החושש בשיניו לא יגמע בהם חומץ ויפלוט אבל מגמע ובולע או מטבל בו כדרכו. ובמ״ב שם ס״ק ק״ב כתב ז״ל וה״ה יין שרף ג״כ דינו כמו חומץ, אך במקום צער גדול אפשר לסמוך ביי״ש דמותר לשהותו בפיו ולבלוע אח״כ [ח״א] עוד כתב דה״ה דאסור ליתן על השן נעגעליך או שפירטוס וסובין חמין דכ״ז מוכח שהוא לרפואה, אם לא דכאיב ליה טובא שמצטער כל גופו.

20 דאין הגרגור עצמו איסור, רק משום דמיחזי כרפואה. אך המצחצח שיניו במי פה שכן הוא דרך כל הבריאים ליכא חשש מידי.

21 שו״ע סי׳ שכ״ז סעיף ב׳ וכדלעיל הערה 15.

who suffers from discomfort to do so. This is also true of aromatic or other expensive oils that are used only for medicinal purposes. For this reason, one may not rub alcohol or alcoholic drinks on the abdomen to relieve a stomachache, since this is not normally done by healthy people.[22]

Itching

9. People who suffer from an itchy foot ailment, such as athlete's foot, usually soak their feet in water[23] many times during the day and then apply a liquid that contains alcohol and other substances that cure infections. Since this is not something healthy people do, it is forbidden to do so on Shabbos.[24] It is certainly forbidden to apply any cream to the skin.[25] Nevertheless, one may apply talcum powder on one's feet or place the powder in one's shoes, since this is something that healthy people do to absorb moisture and prevent perspiration.[26]

10. If a child has a stomachache, olive oil or baby oil to relieve the pain may be applied.[27] It is also permitted to apply cognac or some other substance for any of the child's needs, since children have the halachic status of a *choleh she'ein bo sakanah*.[28]

---

22 שו״ע שם סעיף א׳.

23 דין רחיצת הרגלים במים חמים שהוחמו מער״ש שרי שכ״כ בשו״ע סי׳ שכ״ו סעיף א׳ ״אבל מותר לרחוץ פניו ידיו ורגליו״. ואם הוחמו בשבת אף לרחוץ בהם פניו ידיו ורגליו אסור (כף החיים שכ״ו אות ה׳) ומה שמותר לרחוץ הרגלים בשבת גם אם מתכוין לרפואה, היינו דווקא כשאין עושה כן כדי להזיע דאילו רחיצת רגליו להזיע אינו מותר אלא לחולה שאין בו סכנה כמבואר בסי׳ שכ״ח בכף החיים אות ר״ן.

24 דאין דרך בריאים לסוך אלכוהול ושאר חומרים שסך בהם, ואי״כ כל שלא נפל למשכב ואינו בגדר חולה שאין בו סכנה אין היתר בתרופות כלל, ושייך בו גזירת שחיקת סממנים, ומיהו אם יש חשש שע״י שיניח הגירוי כמו שהוא יוכל להזדהם ולהגיע למחלה כמו ״שושנה״ או שאר מחלות זיהומיות המצויות ומתפתחות כתוצאה מפצעים פתוחים, יש להקל בזה.

25 דין שימוש במשחות מבואר לעיל פרק 26 סעיפים 34–28 עיי״ש.

26 שימוש באבקת טאלק בשבת מבואר לעיל פרק 26 סעיף 39 עיי״ש.

27 ולא דמי להנ״ל בסעיף 8 דקאי במבוגרים, אולם לתינוקות שרי סיכה בכל ענין כדין חולה שאין בו סכנה. ועיין לעיל פרק 20 הערה 8 עד איזה גיל מיקרי קטן לענין סיווגו כחולה שאין בו סכנה.

28 עיין בכף החיים סי׳ שכ״ז אות י״ג וז״ל: וכתב בא״א מהגה״ק דמותר לשפוך יי״ש לראש בשבת קודש מצד מיחוש משום שכבר נהוג לבריאים לשפוך לראש כדי לישן תיכף או כדי להמית כנימה שבשערות וכל הנעשה לבריאים אין חשש כמ״ש בשו״ע כאן ורק יש להיזהר על סחיטה.

Chapter 32
Medications and Vitamins

The use of various types of medication, both conventional and unconventional, has proliferated in our time. This makes it incumbent upon us to determine which of these medications are permitted on Shabbos.

The use of medications for a patient in a life-threatening situation (*choleh sheyeish bo sakanah*) was discussed in chapter 16, "Medication for a *Choleh Sheyeish Bo Sakanah*," and that for an ordinary bedridden patient (*choleh she'ein bo sakanah*) in chapter 26, "Medication for a *Choleh She'ein Bo Sakanah*." The present chapter is concerned with medications or other types of preparations that would be used by a person who does not fall into either of these categories. Some of these include:

- Vitamins
- Birth control pills
- Fertility pills
- Pills taken by brides to regulate their menstrual cycle
- Antibiotics taken before certain medical procedures, such as before a tooth extraction
- Pills that prevent allergic reactions or infection
- Sleeping pills
- Pills taken to improve sexual function
- Iron pills to treat anemia

- Vaccinations and pills taken to prevent contagious diseases
- Experimental pills taken by someone participating in a scientific experiment
- Pills taken daily to maintain one's state of well-being
- Pills taken to facilitate digestion

Medication for a Healthy Person: General Guidelines

It is clear from a halachic standpoint[1] that when a healthy person consumes food, it makes no difference in what manner the food was processed. Fruits, vegetables, and various herbs that are normally eaten by healthy people for nourishment purposes may be eaten raw, cooked, steamed, or dried. It also doesn't matter whether it was dehydrated, mixed with various chemical preservatives, or produced as a powder or as tablets or a liquid concentrate. Even when consumed for its medicinal properties, it is still considered a food for healthy people and thus allowed.

---

1 והנה טרם ניגש לביאור פרטי העניין נבאר את שיטות הפוסקים במקור הדין מהו מאכל בריאים ומה לא נחשב למאכל בריאים.

במסכת שבת דף קי"ט ע"ב נאמר במשנה, "אין אוכלין אזוביון בשבת לפי שאינו מאכל בריאים, אבל אוכל הוא את יועזר ושותה אבוב רועה, כל האוכלים אוכל אדם לרפואה וכל המשקים שותה חוץ ממי דקלים וכוס עקרין מפני שהן לירוקה אבל שותה הוא מי דקלים לצמאו וסך שמן עקרין שלא לרפואה" ע"כ. ושם בגמרא מובאים מינים שונים של צמחים וירקות והכלל העולה דמאכל שדרך בריאים לאוכלו מותר מכל וכל ואף אם מתכוון לרפואה, ואם אינו מאכל בריאים מותר לבריא לאוכלו להנאתו, ולחושש במחושים שונים ולוקחו לרפואה אסור גזירה משום שחיקת סממנים.

הרמב"ם פכ"א מהלכות שבת הלכה כ-כ"ב. כתב וז"ל: לפיכך אסור לבריא להתרפאות בשבת גזירה שמא ישחוק הסממנין כיצד לא יאכל דברים שאינן מאכל בריאים כגון אזוביון ופואה ולא דברים המשלשלין כגון לענה וכיו"ב וכן לא ישתה דברים שאין דרך הבריאים לשתותן כגון מים שבשלו בהן סממנים ועשבים. אוכל אדם אוכלין ומשקין שדרך הבריאים לאוכלן ולשתותן כגון הכוסברא והכשות והאזוב אף על פי שהן מרפאין ואוכלן כדי להתרפאות בהם מותר הואיל והם מאכל בריאים. שתה חלתית מקודם השבת והרי הוא שותה והולך מותר לשתותו בשבת אפילו במקומות שלא נהגו הבריאים לשתות החלתית, ושותין זיתום המצרי בכל מקום. עכ"ל הרמב"ם. והמגיד משנה שם ס"ק כ"א כתב וז"ל: כל הדינים האלו הן בבריא שאינו נופל למשכב ולא חולה כמו שהזכרנו בפרק שני עיי"ש.

הרא"ש בשבת פי"ד סימן ח' כתב ז"ל: כל האוכלים אוכל אדם לרפואה וכל המשקים שותה הוא לרפואה חוץ ממי דקלים וכוס של עקרין מפני שהם לרפואה אבל שותה הוא מי דקלים לצמאו וסך שמן של עקרים שלא לרפואה. והרב קרבן נתנאל שם אות כ' כתב ז"ל: אבל שותה הוא מי דקלים לצמאו אבל לרפואה עם היות שהוא בריא אסור לאכול לרפואה כיון שאינו מאכל בריא וכ"כ המגן אברהם באריכות סימן שכ"ח ס"ק מ"ג ע"ש, עכ"ל.

ואמנם כ"כ במגן אברהם שם וז"ל: אבל אם אין לו שום מיחוש מותר [מג] מיחוש מותר,

However, when the ingredients of a tablet aren't edible and are not normally consumed by healthy people, such as substances derived from medicinal herbs or chemicals, it is considered medicine. Even eating these herbs in their natural form is included in the injunction against grinding herbs and not allowed on Shabbos.

We will now evaluate the various reasons and needs for consuming different foods and medications and clarify their halachic status.

1. *Vitamins*. Halachic authorities[2] allow a healthy person to take vitamins on Shabbos to keep him strong, particularly if he ordinarily takes them during the week. However, a person who feels weak or is in pain may

---

בטור כתוב ושותה אותו לרעבו לצמאו מותר, משמע דאם עושה לרפואה אסור, אף ע״פ שהוא בריא, וכ״מ בסמ״ד דהא הרוחץ בים בריא הוא, וכ״מ בירושלמי דף י״ד ע״ג גבי מי משרא ועוד דקאמר בגמ׳ אע״פ שיש לו חטטין בראשו וכו׳ ע״ש. וכן משמע ספכ״ב דשבת דאמרינן אסור לעמוד בקרקע דיומסית שמעמלת ומרפא, וכ״מ בברכות ד׳ ל״ח, דפריך ורפואה בשבת מי שרי, ולא משני דמיירי באדם בריא אלא ע״כ אפילו באדם בריא אסור. וכ״כ ט״א ד״ז ע״ב. וכ״כ הרמב״ם ומ״מ בהדיא פכ״א עיי״ש דין ז׳, וכ״מ בתוס׳ דף י״ח ע״ב בד״ה ומתרפאת עמ״ש סכ״א וכ״מ בגמרא דף ק״ח רבין הוה אזיל בתריה דר״י א״ל מהו למימשי מהנהו מיא וכו׳ משמע דבריא היה, ועמש״כ סמ״ב וע״ש בתוס׳. עכ״ל המג״א.

אולם בבית יוסף כתב בזה״ל: ומשמע דכל שאינו חולה כלל מותר לו לאכול ולשתות אוכלים ומשקים שאינם מאכל בריאים דכיון שאינו חולה ליכא למיגזר מידי, הלכך אפילו אינו לא רעב ולא צמא מותר לאוכלן ולשתותן, והא דנקיט [הטור] לרעבו ולצמאו לאו דווקא אלא אורחא דמילתא נקט, עכ״ל הב״י.

והנה מסוגיית הגמ׳ שם מבואר להדיא דאם אוכל צמחים ועשבים שדרך בני אדם בריאים לאוכלן, או שותה משקים שדרך בנ״א בריאים לשתותם — לא משום סגולתם הרפואית אלא מפני טעמם הטוב מרכיבים תזונתיים עשירים, מראה וריח טוב וכיו״ב ממאכלים ומשקים. אכל מאכלים עשבים צמחים או משקים שאין דרך הבריאים לאוכלם או לשתותן, כמו״כ אם הדרך לאוכלם רק למטרה רפואית — אסור לאכול או לשתות מאכל או משקה זה בשבת.

ויש להוסיף עוד בזה בהבנת הדבר, כאשר הבריא אוכל צמח או עשב העומד לאכילה, אין זה משנה כלל אם אוכלו כמו שהוא חי, כבוש או מבושל או טחון ומעורב עם עוד מיני מאכלים בתוספת חומרי מאכל טעם וריח וחומצות שונות. וגם צורתן אינה משנה אם אוכלו בצורת קציצה או עוגייה, כסוכריה או כגלולה. ומעולם לא נאסר על אדם לאכול קציצות בשבת — גזירה שמא יטחן את הצמח בשבת ויעשהו קציצה.

כמו״כ — מאידך — כאשר אסרו חכמים לאכול צמחי מרפא, אין זה משנה כלל צורת האכילה, שאפילו אם אוכל את הצמח כמו שהוא חי, ואפילו דרך אכילתו כך כמו שהוא חי — אסור לאוכלו בשבת והיינו משום גזירת שחיקת סממנים שמא יטחן צמח זה או צמח אחר ויעשה סממנים ויכין תרופה.

2 עיין בשו״ת אגרות משה או״ח ח״ג סי׳ נ״ד. ובשו״ת ציץ אליעזר ח״ד סי׳ נ׳. וכ״כ בשו״ת באר משה ח״א סי׳ ל״ג אות א׳ והוסיף שם דויטמינים הרגילים לבריאים מותר, ושאינם לבריאים — אסור. ובשו״ת אור לציון ח״ב פרק ל״ו אות י׳. ובאז נדברו ח״ו סי׳ ע״ב. וכ״כ בילקוט יוסף שבת ד׳ עמ׳ קמה עיי״ש.

not take vitamins to make him stronger. He may, however, eat large quantities of fruit to increase his vitamin C intake, since any food that is normally eaten by healthy people may be consumed for medicinal purposes on Shabbos.

2. *Contraceptive pills*. A woman who may not become pregnant for health or psychological reasons, or a woman who has been through a difficult pregnancy and childbirth and becoming pregnant immediately afterward may put her life into physical or emotional danger, must discuss her situation with a competent medical professional and then with her personal *rav*. If the situation warrants that she be permitted to take birth control pills,[3] she may take these pills on Shabbos.[4]

3. *Fertility pills*. A woman who has been instructed by her doctor to take a series of pills that will facilitate conception may take them on Shabbos.[5]

4. *Pills to regulate the menstrual cycle*. In order to avoid the situation of a *chuppas niddah*, where a bride is a *niddah* at her wedding, many brides are advised to take pills that regulate their menstrual cycle. These pills may be taken on Shabbos. It should be noted that before taking these pills the bride should discuss her personal situation with her marriage instructor. She should also discuss the matter with her doctor, since many of these pills may have an adverse effect on fertility.[6]

Prophylactic Medication

5. *Medication taken before a medical procedure*. Patients who are scheduled for surgery may be advised to take a series of antibiotics for a few days before undergoing the medical procedure, such as a tonsillectomy or

---

3 עיין באגרות משה אבן העזר ח״ד סי׳ ע״ד אות ב׳.

4 עיין שו״ת באר משה ח״א סי׳ ל״ג אות ח׳ ובח״ו סימן ל״ט. וע״ע בשו״ת אז נדברו ח״ג סימן י״ב. ובשו״ת ציץ אליעזר ח״א סי׳ ל״ז כתב בשם שו״ת מהר״ם בריסק סי׳ כ״ד דשרי ליתן כדורים באותו מקום קודם תשמיש כדי למנוע קליטת הריון, עיי״ש דטעמו דהסמים אינם מרפאים שום מחלה ורק עושין פעולה למנוע קליטה דשרי. וע״ע בנשמת אברהם ח״א עמ׳ קנ״ט.

5 שו״ת באר משה ח״א סימן ל״ג אות ח׳. ובח״ו סי׳ ל״ט. ובטעם הדבר כתב שאין כאן שום מחלה, ולא מצינו איסור בדבר.

6 עיין בשו״ת אגרות משה אבן העזר ח״ב סימן י״ז וז״ל: ועתה נשמע שהפילן (גלולות) הם דבר שמזיק לאשה במחלות אחרות ולכן אין ליקח פילן מצד חשש סכנה לדבר אחר.

dental surgery. Assuming the person is healthy and is only taking the antibiotics to prevent possible infection from the treatment, it seems that if it is possible to schedule the treatment so that he can avoid taking the antibiotics on Shabbos, this is preferable. However, if this is not possible, since the person is healthy and the medication is taken for protection against possible infection, it may be taken on Shabbos.

6. *Preventive medicine*. Certain people suffer from various ailments at certain times of the year, such as hay fever or other allergies. This could result in a cough, rash, or other allergic reactions. Doctors recommend taking a certain medication in order to forestall the onset of the allergic reaction. Since the person does not presently suffer from any ailment, there is no reason to take the medication on Shabbos.[7]

7. *Sleeping pills*. Halachic authorities disagree as to whether or not a person who was advised by his doctor to take a pill to help him sleep may take these pills on Shabbos. Some authorities do not consider insomnia an illness (and hence do not regard sleeping pills as medicine); whereas others maintain that "healing" one's nervous tension is no different from other forms of healing that are forbidden on Shabbos.[8] They also

---

7 עיין שו״ת ציץ אליעזר ח״א סי׳ ל״ז דתרופה שהיא ניתנת לאדם שכרגע בריא ורק לוקח תרופה למנוע היווצרות מחלה או כאבים דשרי, דכל האסור הוא רק במי שכבר יש לו מחושים, ונטל תרופה לעצור הכאבים עיי״ש וזה שלא כדעת המג״א שהובא במבוא לפרק זה אלא כהב״י דשרי תרופות לאדם בריא. עיי״ש. ובנידון דידן נלע״ד שאם עדיין לא בא לכלל אלרגיה אין זה בוער לקחת כדור בשבת, ואם ייקח אחר השבת לא ישנה דבר, לכן אין ליטול כדורים אלו בשבת אא״כ קיבל חלילה התקפה חריפה שכידוע אפשר להגיע לידי נפילה למשכב — שרי ליטול תרופות אלו.

8 כתב בספר קצות השולחן סי׳ קלח בבדי השולחן אות ל״א. ז״ל: מי שאינו יכול לישון אא״כ לוקח סם מיישן כגון כדורי ״סליקט״ וכיוצא נראה דמותר גם בשבת, דאין זה רפואה לחולי, שהעדר שינה אינה חולי והסם אינו מרפא אלא משכר שמביא שינה, ודמי למי שנשתכר שמותר לסוך רגליו בשמן ומלח להפיג שכרותו. שכ׳ הט״ז שאינו רפואה, ה״ה דמותר לקחת סם להביא השינה (ובמקום צערא יש לסמוך על הט״ז אע״פ דלטעם המג״א אסור) וכו׳. ומסיים שם וז״ל: אבל כדורי שינה אין להם פעולה אחרת לרפואה והעדר שינה הוא צער גדול ושובר כל הגוף, וכיון דלא שייך בזה גזירת שחיקת סמנים דאין זה רפואה יש להתיר. גם בספר שמירת שבת כהלכתה פל״ג סעיף ט״ז צעד בעקבותיו וכתב בזה״ל: מי שמצטער הרבה מחוסר שינה מותר לו לקחת כדורי שינה ע״כ ומסתמך על קצות השולחן הנ״ל ועל פסק מרן הגרש״ז אויערבאך שליט״א. וכ״כ בשו״ת באר משה ח״ו סי׳ ל״ט. וכ״כ בילקוט יוסף שבת ד׳ סימן שכ״ח סעיף נ״ג עיי״ש. אולם בשו״ת מנחת יצחק ח״ג סי׳ כ״א נראה שפליג עלייהו וס״ל לאסור, ואף שבנידון דידיה קאי על כדורים למניעת שינה, נראה מלשונו שם דלא מפליג בינייהו. כמו״כ בשו״ת ציץ אליעזר ח״ח סי׳ ט״ו פרק ט״ו מחמיר בזה , והניף ידו בשנית בח״ט סי׳ י״ז פרק ב׳. וכן בשו״ת אז נדברו

disagree as to whether a person who wishes to study Torah on Friday night may take pills to help him stay awake.[9]

8. *Pills to improve sexual function*. Men can sometimes have difficulty functioning sexually. To improve this condition, they take medication such as Sidenifil. These medications may be taken on Shabbos in order to fulfill the mitzvah of cohabitation.[10]

9. *Iron pills to treat anemia*. There is no question that a child with anemia may take medication on Shabbos for this condition. This is because all the needs of a child are considered to have the halachic status of a *choleh she'ein bo sakanah*. The question arises as to whether adults, such as pregnant women or others suffering from iron deficiency, may take medication on Shabbos. If omitting one day will adversely affect the efficacy of the treatment and the medication, it may be taken on Shabbos. But if one can skip taking the medication on Shabbos without any adverse effects, it should not be taken.

10. *Vaccinations against contagious diseases*. Since there is no immediate urgency in administering the series of vaccinations given to children, these should not be administered on Shabbos. However, if there is an outbreak of a contagious disease, such as polio or tuberculosis, Heaven forbid, which may spread and affect the general population, these vaccinations may be administered on Shabbos. Ideally, the vaccination should be oral. If this is impossible, intramuscular injection is the next best choice. Only if neither of these methods are feasible may an intravenous vaccination be administered on Shabbos. Rabies vaccine or antibodies often must be given immediately.

ח״א סימן לו, ובחי״ד סימן י׳ אות ב׳ עיי״ש. ובאמת שלא מצינו טעם מספיק להיתר זה דמה לי אם מרפא בסמי רפואה שונים ומה לי אם מרפה את העצבים וגורם לשינה, גם בזה פשוט דשייך גזירת שחיקת סמנים, ואפשר דאם היה ברור לבעל הקצות השולחן שמרכיבי הכדורי שינה הרי הם חומרים רפואיים שמרפאים ממש וכפי שהעיד הציץ אליעזר שם — היה חוזר בו מהתירו דלא דמי כלל לשמן ומלח לשכרות, כן נראה לי פשוט. אך מ״מ אם מצטער הרבה, ויש חשש לבטול עונג שבת, אם ניתן הדבר לשוחקו ולערבו עם מאכל מערב שבת ולאוכלו קודם השינה — בשעת הדחק יש להתיר בזה בצרוף דעת המתירים הנ״ל ליטול כדורים בשבת באופן זה.

9 בשו״ת באר משה הנ״ל התיר וכ״כ בילקוט יוסף הנ״ל. אולם בשו״ת מנחת יצחק הנ״ל ובשו״ת ציץ אליעזר הנ״ל דעתם לאסור.

10 עיין שו״ת מנחת יצחק ח״א סי׳ ק״ח, ועיין שו״ת באר משה ח״א סי׳ ל״ג אות ט׳. ובשו״ת ציץ אליעזר ח״ח סימן ט״ו פרק ט״ו אות י״ד עיי״ש.

11. Similarly, if someone suffers an injury with the possibility of infection, it is permissible to administer a tetanus shot on Shabbos.[11] We discussed above (see chapter 9, "Levels of Urgency") that a vaccine can be deferred until after Shabbos for a patient that has received the original series, but a person who must receive tetanus antibodies can receive the injection on Shabbos. In addition, if a member of the family has contracted hepatitis and the doctor advises that the rest of the family receive gamma globulin shots immediately, they may be administered on Shabbos.

12. *Experimental drugs*. Experimental drugs given to a group of people as part of an experiment to test their reaction to certain drugs should not be taken on Shabbos where there is no specific need for the person to take the medication.

13. *Daily medication*. If a person functions normally but was advised by his physician to take medication on a daily basis to maintain his health, he may take this medication on Shabbos; for example, someone with a heart condition whose doctor has prescribed a daily regimen of medication or diabetes patients who must take insulin before a meal.

14. *Medication to assist digestion*. Any medication taken for the treatment of gastrointestinal disorders or for the prevention of such disorders may be taken on Shabbos.

15. For example, a person suffering from achalasia, a condition in which the muscles in the lower end of the esophagus and the sphincter at the opening to the stomach fail to relax after swallowing food, may take medication to relax the esophageal muscles on Shabbos prior to meals.

16. A person who suffers from hemorrhoids and was advised by his physician to drink paraffin oil before meals in order to facilitate bowel movements may do so on Shabbos.[12]

---

11 עיין לעיל פרק 9 סעיף 16, דעת רופא דאם הדבר קרוב למוצאי שבת ולא יגיע שום ריעותא לחולה אם ימתינו בהזרקת החיסון — יש לדחותו למוצאי שבת.

12 עיין בזה בשו״ת ציץ אליעזר ח״א סי׳ ל״ז עיי״ש.

The following is a summary of the types of actions that are permissible and prohibited on Shabbos with regard to illness and medicine. Numbers in parentheses indicate the chapter and paragraph where details of these laws are discussed.

Action done on Shabbos	*Choleh sheyeish bo sakanah* (life-threatening illness)	*Sakanas eiver* (danger to a limb)
Torah prohibition transgressed by a Jew	Permitted (1:16)	Forbidden (ch. 28)
Rabbinical prohibition transgressed by a Jew	Permitted (4:2)	Permitted (ch. 28)
Torah prohibition transgressed by a non-Jew	Permitted (3:2)	Permitted (ch. 28)
Rabbinical prohibition transgressed by a non-Jew	Permitted (3:2)	Permitted (ch. 28)
Taking medication	Permitted (16:1)	Permitted (ch. 28)
Eating or drinking food only for medical purposes	Permitted (ch. 32)	Permitted (ch. 28)
Asking a non-Jew	Permitted (3:2)	Permitted (ch. 28)
Eating food cooked by a non-Jew	Permitted (17:1)	Permitted (ch. 28)
Eating non-kosher meat when there is no kosher meat available	Forbidden; in emergency, permitted (17:14)	Forbidden (ch. 28)

Choleh she'ein bo sakanah (standard bedridden patient)	*Choleh b'miktzas* (minor illness)	*Michush* (slight pain or discomfort)	Healthy person
Forbidden (21:1)	Forbidden (30:8)	Forbidden (31:3)	Forbidden (31:1)
Forbidden; if done with a *shinui*, permitted (24:1)	Forbidden (1:21)	Forbidden (31:3)	Forbidden (31:1)
Permitted (23:1–2)	Forbidden (30:8)	Forbidden (31:3)	Forbidden (31:1)
Permitted (23:1–2)	Permitted (30:9)	Forbidden (31:3)	Forbidden (31:1)
Permitted (26:1)	Forbidden (30:7)	Forbidden (31:3)	Forbidden (2:1–2)
Permitted (ch. 32)	Forbidden (30:7)	Forbidden (1:22, 31:4)	Permitted (1:22)
Permitted (23:1–2)	Rabbinical prohibition permitted (3:5, 30:9)	Forbidden (3:6, 31:2)	Forbidden (3:1, 3:6)
Permitted (25:1)	Forbidden (ch. 25)	Forbidden (1:22, 31:4)	Forbidden (25:3)
Forbidden (22:4–5, 25:1)	Forbidden (25:1)	Forbidden (1:22, 31:4)	Forbidden (25:1)

Part 4

Common Illnesses

Part

Common Illnesses

Chapter 33

Fever, Hypothermia, and Measuring Temperature

Almost everyone experiences abnormal temperature, for different reasons and in varying degrees. A change in body temperature may indicate a life-threatening illness or may be fleeting and benign. Fever may aid the body to overcome an infection, but it may also cause dehydration, heart failure, delirium, or convulsions.

Our Sages decreed (*Avodah Zarah* 28a) that abnormal temperature is dangerous and that Shabbos may be desecrated for its evaluation and treatment. The *Shulchan Aruch* (*Orach Chaim* 328:7) states: "One may desecrate Shabbos for every wound...and for anyone who has a high fever or fever with chills..." (see also *Mishnah Berurah* and commentaries of *Acharonim* there).

In this chapter, we will clarify:

a. General causes of change in body temperature

b. What temperature level constitutes danger

c. The permissible way to measure temperature on Shabbos

Causes of Abnormal Temperature

Changes in body temperature are generally caused by one or more of the following:

a. Infection or inflammation in any part of the body
b. External or environmental factors, such as dehydration, food poisoning, poisonous gas, animal bites, or insect bites or stings
c. Heat-induced illness, such as heatstroke
d. Cold-induced illness (hypothermia)
e. Unknown causes in infants less than three months old
f. Other causes, such as tumors, drug reactions, neurological disorders, metabolic disorders, or endocrine (thyroid) disorders

Infectious or Inflammatory Diseases

1. Infections caused by various bacteria or viruses may be destructive, life-threatening, or harmless. Even though an infection is not life-threatening, it may require treatment.
2. The immune system is comprised of white blood cells and antibodies capable of fighting infectious invaders of the body. Sometimes the immune system alone can eradicate the invader, but sometimes it requires external help, such as antibiotics or incision and drainage.
3. In determining treatment, the location of the bacteria is essential, for two reasons:
   a. If the bacterial infection is in the brain or another sensitive organ, it is life-threatening and requires immediate treatment.
   b. The type of antibiotic and its administration (intravenous, oral, or injection) depends on the location of the bacterial infection, the symptoms, and the offending organism.
4. When the body is invaded by bacteria, its temperature rises or lowers (usually proportionally to the danger) along with other symptoms that assist in identifying the location of the bacterial infection. Therefore, any information on the patient's condition is important in determining the severity of his condition.
5. The following are symptoms that indicate the severity of the patient's condition:

a. Fever accompanied only by vomiting may be indicative of a life-threatening illness (possibly meningitis) and requires emergency medical treatment.

b. Fever accompanied by vomiting and diarrhea is less worrisome. This depends on the patient's appearance. If the patient looks sick, immediate treatment is required. If he looks healthy, there is no concern of immediate danger.

c. Some fevers that are not associated with any symptoms may resolve without treatment. However, a fever of unknown etiology that continues for more than twenty-four hours and, in particular, if accompanied by signs of dehydration, requires medical attention.

d. Fever of known etiology (such as an ear infection, pneumonia, bronchitis, hepatitis, urinary tract infection, erysipelas) that is already being treated by a doctor, may be of lesser concern. The medications prescribed for these illnesses may be taken on Shabbos.

Fever Caused by External Factors

6. Body temperature changes caused by environmental factors may be dangerous. The following are some external causes of fever:

   a. *Dehydration*. Dehydration caused by lack of fluid intake combined with heavy perspiration, especially on hot days, and accompanied by vomiting and diarrhea may cause the temperature to rise. If this occurs, the patient requires emergency medical treatment.

   b. *Food poisoning*. Food poisoning may have many causes, from radioactive irradiation to insecticides on fruit and vegetables that were not properly washed.

   c. *Environmental hazards*. Poisonous gases, thick smoke from fire, being closeted in a sealed room, sleeping in a heated room without ventilation, biological or chemical warfare, and similar agents and conditions cause the body temperature to rise. This is indicative of a life-threatening situation.

   d. *Bites and stings*. Bites and stings of animals or insects may be poisonous. This may cause the temperature to rise and may be life-threatening (see chapter 36, "Bites and Stings").

Heat-Induced Illness

7. Heat-induced illness, such as sunstroke, is caused by excessive sun exposure without sufficient fluid intake. This is life-threatening and requires emergency treatment. Treatment includes immediate cooling (with fans and ice packs) and prolonged intravenous administration of fluids. Blood tests for fluids and electrolytes (salts) should also be carried out. All this may be done on Shabbos. (For more details on sunstroke and sunburn, see chapter 39, "Skin Diseases," paragraphs 16–18.)

Cold-Induced Illness (Hypothermia)

8. Hypothermia occurs mainly in infants or the elderly and mostly in the winter months. In adults, consultation with a doctor is warranted when temperature is lower than 35° C (95° F). In babies, a temperature less than 36° C (96.8° F) is suspicious and requires a doctor. Symptoms may include changes in the person's mental state, cardiac arrhythmias, respiratory insufficiency, or signs of infection. Treatment may include various cardiac and respiratory support, rewarming, and medication. Depending on the degree of the cold injury and symptoms, the condition may be life-threatening and require desecration of Shabbos for treatment.

Fever in Infants

9. Infants at the delicate age of one to two months are not capable of reacting properly to infectious agents. Thus, when there is a temperature rise to even 37.8° C (100° F), the infant should be examined immediately by a doctor to determine the treatment that may be needed. Lethargy and decreased feeding are particularly worrisome.

10. Babies older than two months may also require urgent medical attention for an even mild temperature rise. This depends on the baby's appearance. If the baby is lethargic and appears sick, one should immediately obtain medical treatment even on Shabbos.

11. Infants older than three months with a mild fever (lower than 38° C or 100.4° F) are most likely not critically ill. Still, a doctor should make that determination.

12. Some children are more vulnerable to temperature changes, such as children with neurological disorders, metabolic disorders, or chronic disorders. These children may be in a life-threatening situation when the temperature deviates from normal. One should react to any temperature change in such children as if it were life-threatening.

13. Fever caused by immunization (vaccines) can be treated by bathing, applying cold compresses, and administering medication to lower the temperature. If the temperature does not lower, other complications of the vaccination may be a factor. A doctor should be consulted to determine the severity of the situation and prescribe the necessary treatment.

14. If the infant is prone to febrile seizures upon a slight rise in temperature (37.5° C or 99.5° F), medications to lower the temperature should be administered immediately to prevent seizures. A doctor should be consulted right away to determine the cause of the fever.

Temperature that Warrants Shabbos Desecration

15. As stated before, the *Shulchan Aruch* rules that Shabbos may be desecrated for a person with a high fever or fever with chills. However, it does not provide a clear definition of what constitutes a high fever.[1]

16. In Eretz Yisrael and Europe, the temperature is measured in centigrade, or Celsius (° C), whereas in the United States and some other countries, the temperature is measured in Fahrenheit (° F). Some rabbinical authorities wrote their halachic decisions using degrees centigrade, whereas others used degrees Fahrenheit. To simplify, for those who want to read the sources, below is a table that converts centigrade to Fahrenheit.

---

1 והנה במשנה ברורה סי׳ שכ״ח ס״ק י״ט כתב וז״ל: חום ביותר, הוא הנקרא ״טיפוס״ וכדומה. ובס״ק כ׳ כתב ז״ל: עם סימור, מלשון תסמר שערת בשרי והוא הנקרא שוידעריי״ן בלשון אשכנז, שבה הקרירות והחמימות בפעם אחת לאפוקי קדחת המצוי שבא מתחילה הקרירות ואח״כ החמימות אין זה בכלל חולה שיש בו סכנה [אחרונים] ומ״מ ע״י א״י מותר לחלל שבת. ע״כ אך עדיין לא נתברר שיעור החם.

°C	35	35.5	36.1	36.6	37.2	37.7	38.3	38.8	39.4	40	40.5	41.1	41.6
°F	95	96	97	98	99	100	101	102	103	104	105	106	107

17. It is important to note that in most cases fever is not dangerous, except if it is very high. If it is high, medication may be taken to lower it, as in the case of the *choleh she'ein bo sakanah*. Only if the temperature is high, the patient feels very ill, and the reason for the fever is unknown should one act as if the person's life is in danger.

    An infant or an elderly person with an elevated temperature is treated as being dangerously ill (*choleh sheyeish bo sakanah*), even if the temperature is not very high, if the reason for the fever is not clear.[2]

18. Therefore, one who has a fever, even if it is not very high, is regarded as a *choleh she'ein bo sakanah*, an ordinary bedridden patient, and he is permitted to take medication to lower the temperature.[3,4] However, this state does not warrant Shabbos desecration. (See note 4 regarding the temperature at which one is permitted to take medications on Shabbos; similarly, Rabbi Moshe Feinstein, *zt"l*, in his *Igros Moshe*, summarizes the different laws and circumstances that justify the desecration of Shabbos for a fever.[5])

---

2 כן כתב בספר נשמת אברהם ח״א עמ׳ קפ״ב.

3 עיין שו״ת ציץ אליעזר חי״ד אות ו׳ עיי״ש.

4 בספר קצות השולחן סי׳ קל״ח בבדי השולחן עמוד צ״ט כתב וז״ל: מי שיש לו חום גבוה קצת כגון 38 קוים במדחום [שקורין גראד] (צלסיוס) שזה נחשב כבר לחום יתר על המידה, נראה שמותר לקחת סמים להוריד החום אע״פ שאין בו סכנה אבל הוא בכלל חולה כל הגוף שהרי החום ממלא כל איברי האדם, ומותר לשתות רפואות, ואם יש לו חום גדול ורוצה להורידו ע״י קומפרס של מים עם חומץ שנותנים על הראש ומחליפים בכל איזה דקים (נתבאר לעיל איך לנהוג שלא לבוא לאיסור מדאורייתא). עכ״ל.

5 בספר אגרות משה או״ח ח״א סי׳ קכ״ט כתב תשובה מפורטת בענין זה ונצטט את דבריו השייך לענייננו ככתבם וכלשונם. בענין שיעור קדחת חום ביותר להיתר חלול שבת.... הנה אין בזה דבר ברור, אבל אין צריך שיהיה ברור שהוא בסכנה דעל ספק נמי מחללין וכל שהאדם חושש לזה שמא הוא חום ביותר מחללין ורק מה שתופס שהוא רק מעט חום בברור אין מחללין. וסתם בני אדם חוששין כשהוא קרוב למדת 102 שהוא חום ביותר ולכן על מידה זו מחללין ואין רשאין להחמיר. ואם אחד חושש גם בקרוב ל-101 ורוצה שיחללו עליו נמי מחללין דלא גרע ממכה שאינה של חלל שאם החולה אומר שצריך לחלול שמחללין. ובתינוק שאין שייך זה אם רואין שמצטער ביותר וכדומה לזה מה שניכר שהוא חולה אף שהחום הוא קטן רק יותר מ-100 מחללין. סוף דבר אם רק לא ברור להו להחשיב שהוא מעט חום מחללין. עוד נראה לענ״ד ברור, שאם החום הוא בא ממחלה שבריאה או ממחלת שאר איברים פנימיים הוא מכה של חלל ומחללין אף אם הוא רק חום קטן. וכל הנדון בקדחת הוא בצינון בעלמא שלא בא מאיבר מיוחד

19. In summary, the conditions that justify Shabbos desecration can be categorized as follows:
    a. Fever in babies
    b. A temperature over 38° C (100.4° F) in adults that originates from infection or internal illness
    c. A temperature over 38.5° C (101.3° F) that stems from a common cold (the person is considered a *choleh she'ein bo sakanah* and may take medication)
    d. Temperature below 36° C (96.8° F) in the elderly or an infant, when hypothermia is suspected
    e. Immunodeficient people in whom disease, infection, or any small illness can cause the temperature to rise to 40° C (104° F)

Using a Thermometer on Shabbos

20. In any situation where abnormal temperature is suspected, it is required and permitted to measure the temperature with a thermometer that may be used on Shabbos.[6] There is no halachic basis whatsoever for not measuring the temperature.[7] One should not try to sense the temperature by placing a hand on the patient's forehead or by checking the pulse.[8]

21. Several kinds of thermometers are available on the market:

רק שזה גופיה שנצטנן הביא עליו חום או שבא החום ממחלה באיבר שמבחוץ כגון מידו ורגלו צריך שיהיה חום ביותר והשיעור הוא כדביארתי, וכן הוא כשמרגיש הצינון בחוטם ואף אם הוא מהצוואר אף שהוא של חלל, כיון שהוא צינון המצוי אם הוא חום מעט אין מחללין וכדבארתי השיעור. משה פיינשטיין.

6 עיין בשו״ת מנחת יצחק ח״ג סי׳ קמ״ב. ועי״ע בשו״ת אור לציון ח״ב פרק ל״ו תשובה י״ג. ובשו״ת אגרות משה ח״א סי׳ קכ״ח. ובשו״ת ציץ אליעזר ח״ג סי׳ י׳.

7 והמחמיר בזה הרי הוא מיקל בפקוח נפש ורעתו גדולה ואין זו אלא חסידות שטות, ומועל בפיקדון שהפקיד בידינו בורא עולם ועתיד ליתן את הדין על כך, ועיין במש״כ החסיד רבינו יונה בספרו איסור והיתר הארוך כלל ס׳ אות ח׳.

8 משום שעל פי הניסיון גם כאשר לא ניכר כלל חום ע״י מגע היד, לאחר מדידה במדחום יש הפתעות, וגם כאשר ניכר ונרגש מעט חום — לאחר מדידה במדחום יש הפתעות (עי״ע בהערה הקודמת). וכך מקובלנו מפי קודש הגאון הצדיק רבי שמריהו גריינמאן זצוק״ל — שלא להסתמך כלל על מדידת החום ע״י כף היד או הדופק.

a. A mercury thermometer
b. A battery-powered digital thermometer (with or without a beep)
c. A plastic strip which has a color-coded scale (such as from blue to red), where the level of the temperature causes the strip to change color

22. In general, it is recommended to use a mercury thermometer[9] and to avoid using the plastic-strip thermometer.[10] The digital thermometer should not be used[11] on Shabbos, unless a life-threatening situation is suspected and there is no other thermometer available.

23. The thermometer may be sterilized in alcohol or another antiseptic before use, whether the goal is to facilitate lowering the mercury or to sterilize the thermometer.[12]

24. A rectal thermometer may be dipped in oil or petroleum jelly or other lubricant in order to facilitate insertion. However, one should be careful not to smear the ointment on the thermometer, but to dip it in the ointment.[13]

25. Similarly, it is permitted to lower the mercury before use. However, if it is possible, without difficulty, to prepare the thermometer before Shabbos, it is appropriate to be stringent and prepare it before Shabbos.[14] After use, the mercury should not be lowered to prepare

---

9 עיין בשו״ת מנחת יצחק ח״ג סי׳ קמ״ב, ששאלו הרב השואל אם חשיב חימום הכספית כמלאכת מבשל, עיי״ש. וע״ע בזה בשש״כ פרק מ׳ הערה ג׳. ובילקוט יוסף שבת ד׳ עמוד קכ״ב.

10 בדין מדחום העשוי מסרט פלסטי שלפי מידת החום מאירים בו אותיות שונות או מספרים — נחלקו בזה גדולי הפוסקים בדורות האחרונים, הללו מתירים והללו אוסרים, וע״כ יש להימנע משימוש בסרט זה בשבת, מה גם שאינו מקובל אפילו בימות החול להשתמש בזה והדרך להשתמש בחול או במדחום כספית או במדחום דיגיטלי ובשבת ברור שאסור להשתמש בדיגיטלי כמבואר. הפוסקים שדברו בזה; עיין בשו״ת מנחת יצחק ח״ז סי׳ כ״ב. שו״ת באר משה ח״ו סימן ע״ז. שו״ת ציץ אליעזר ח״יד סי׳ ל׳ וסי׳ ל״א. שו״ת יחווה דעת ח״ד סימן כ״ט. עיי״ש.

11 פשוט, וכ״כ בילקוט יוסף שבת ד׳ עמוד קכ״ד .

12 עיין בשמירת שבת כהלכתה פרק מ׳ סעיף ב׳, ובשו״ת ציץ אליעזר חלק ח׳ סי׳ ט״ו פ״יד אות י״א.

13 שש״כ שם.

14 בספר שו״ת שבט הלוי ח״א סי׳ ס״א, ובשו״ת להורות נתן חלק ה׳ סי׳ י״ט דנו בעניין הורדת הכספית ואסרוהו בשבת דהוי כמכה בפטיש, ועצתם להכין המדחום מע״ש ולחילופין להניחו

the thermometer for the next usage.[15]

Lowering Temperature

26. Medications to lower the temperature may be given to infants in any situation and to adults with a temperature over 38° C (100.4° F). Similarly, it is permitted to soak both feet in alcohol or wash any part of the body with alcohol in order to lower temperature. (However, sponging with alcohol is permitted only if no squeezing will be involved. One should rub the body with the alcohol and afterward dry it with a cloth, but not with a sponge.) Using alcohol is discouraged, however, since toxic absorption can occur, especially in children.

27. Similarly, it is permitted to place a bottle of ice[16] on the soles of the feet or the forehead or to make an ice bath, according to a doctor's instructions and with medical supervision.

במים קרים שירד ויתכווץ מאליו, עיי״ש. אולם רבים מגדולי האחרונים לא ס״ל כוותייהו והתירוהו, עיין בשו״ת ציץ אליעזר ח״א סי׳ ל״א ובח״ב סי׳ מ״ד אות ב׳. וע״ע בשו״ת אז נדברו ח״א סי׳ ס״ב, ובח״ד סי׳ ל״ה. וע״ע בשש״כ פרק מ׳ סעיף ב׳ ושם בהערה ז׳ שכן דעת הגרש״ז אויערבאך שליט״א להיתרה. וכ״כ בילקוט יוסף שבת ד׳ עמוד קכ״ג.

15 דזה אינו לצורך החולה כלל ויש לחוש להכנה ובפרט יש לחוש בזה לפוסקים דס״ל דהוי כמכה בפטיש. ופשוט שבמסגרת בית החולים וכיו״ב אין צורך להתחשב במגבלה זו כיון שבכל עת וזמן נזקקים למדחום לצורך החולים.

16 עיין שו״ת באר משה ח״א סי׳ ל״ז אות י״ז.

Chapter 34

Dental Diseases and Hygiene

When it comes to dental diseases, a distinction must be made between which treatments are prohibited on Shabbos, which are permitted on Shabbos, and when immediate treatment is obligatory.

This chapter will discuss the following topics:

a. Dental hygiene for healthy teeth

b. Dentures and orthodontia

c. Cavities that cause minor pain (toothache)

d. Cavities that cause a person to be bedridden from extreme pain

e. Gingivitis, trauma, and fractures

f. Scurvy

Dental Hygiene

1. It is permitted to brush one's teeth on Shabbos with a toothbrush and mouthwash if there is no possibility of bleeding when brushing.[1]

---

1 ואין בשימוש במי פה חשש איסור רפואה וגזירה משום שחיקת סממנים. עיין בספר קצות השולחן חז׳ עמוד צט׳, ובילקוט יוסף שבת ד׳ עמ׳ ע״ג, ואף אם המי פה מכילים חומרים רפואיים המועילים לשיניים כפלאוריד וכיו״ב, אין בזה איסור רפואה. דכל שהוא דרך בריאים וניקיון הגוף מותר, דהרי כל אדם בריא רוחץ את שיניו כדי שלא יזדהמו ויבא לידי חולי, וגזירת שחיקת סמנים נאמרה רק במקום שאין דרך בריאים לעשותה, וע״ע בזה בשו״ת ציץ אלעזר חי״ד סי׳ נ׳.

However, if it is possible that toothbrushing will cause bleeding, then it is prohibited.[2] One may, however, rinse one's mouth with mouthwash and rub one's teeth with a finger.

2. Since using a toothbrush may cause bleeding, there are some who are stringent not to use a brush at all on Shabbos. Even someone who is stringent, however, may rinse his mouth with mouthwash and then rub his teeth with his finger. One who is stringent in this matter is commendable.

3. Toothpaste should not be used on Shabbos, whether "brushing" with a finger or with a toothbrush.[3] Some are lenient and permit liquid toothpaste.

4. After using the toothbrush (according to the aforementioned lenient opinion), one should not rinse it off if it will not be used again on Shabbos, since this constitutes preparing it on Shabbos for the next day.[4]

5. Toothpicks may be used to clean between the teeth,[5] provided that this does not cause bleeding. The toothpicks should be ready for use on Shabbos.[6] It is prohibited to break off wood slivers from a board, to

---

2 הסכמת כל הפוסקים דאם ע״י צחצוח השיניים במברשת יש חשש ליציאת דם מהחניכיים יש לאסור בזה, עיין בשו״ת אור לציון ח״ב פרק ל״ה שאלה ו׳, ובשו״ת יביע אומר ח״ד סי׳ כ״ט אות יז׳.

3 כן כתבו האחרונים בדבר תשובותיהם כדלהלן: באגרות משה ח״א סימן קי״ב אוסר שימוש במשחת שיניים ומתיר עם מברשת ובתנאי שלא ילחלחנה במים קודם השימוש מחשש סחיטה בשיער, ואחר הניקוי לא ירחץ המברשת משום שאין לו צורך שוב היום ואין לרחוץ בשביל מחר. ע״כ. גם בשו״ת ציץ אליעזר ח״ז סימן ל׳ אוסר השימוש במשחה לצורך צחצוח שיניים. גם בשו״ת מנחת יצחק ח״ג סימן מ״ח וסימן נ׳ אוסר שמוש במשחת שיניים משום איסור ממרח. עיי״ש. גם בשו״ת אור לציון ח״ב פרק ל״ה שאלה ו׳ אסר השמוש במשחת השיניים מאיסור ממרח. עיי״ש. ואולם בקצות השולחן ח״ז עמ׳ צ״ט התיר להשתמש עם משחת שיניים ויעץ שיקח המשחה ביד וישפשף בה השיניים ואין בזה משום ממרח. עיי״ש. וכמו״כ בשו״ת יביע אומר ח״ד סימנים כז׳-ל׳ האריך להתיר בזה, ועכ״פ אף הוא הסיק למסקנא שמהיות טוב אם אפשר להשתמש במי פה ודאי שיש להעדיף את זה. עיי״ש. וע״ע בילקוט יוסף שבת ד׳ עמוד ע״ה. עיי״ש.

4 כ״כ באגרות משה הנ״ל, וכן הוא מסקנת הפוסקים.

5 דכל שאסרו בגמ׳ היינו לתקן קיסם דהוי תקון כלי ואסור, אך אם מיועד ומוכן לכך אין איסור מתקן. ועיין במ״ב סי׳ שכ״ב סיק י״ד. ולעניין אי שרי לחצוץ שיניו בגפרור, נראה דשתיים רעות יש בזה, א׳ שהגפרית שבה מזהמת את הפה ומביאה מחלות זיהומיות לאדם. ב׳ דאין אפשרות לחצוץ עם הגפרור עצמו אא״כ שוברו ומפצלו ויש בזה חשש תקון כלי, מלבד מה דאיכא בזה איסור מוקצה.

6 מ״ב, שם.

peel a match, or to make a toothpick from any other wooden implement on Shabbos.[7]

6. It is prohibited to chew natural or artificial chewing gum that has ingredients or medicines for dental health purposes, since this is regarded as taking medicine on Shabbos.[8] Chewing gum to eliminate bad breath is permitted since this is not regarded as medicinal. (Similarly, it is permitted to drink syrup or swallow raw eggs in order to enhance one's voice.[9])

Orthodontia and Dentures

7. All actions associated with making false teeth (dentures), such as measuring, preparing, and fitting them, whether for individual teeth or a group of teeth on one palate, is prohibited on Shabbos. There is no urgency in making dentures on Shabbos.

8. Similarly, preparing a crown or orthodontia as a preparation for bridges and anything similar is prohibited on Shabbos. It is, however, permitted to insert false teeth that have already been prepared and fitted.

9. It is prohibited to apply adhesive powder to dentures in order to keep them in place.[10]

10. A plate, bridge, crown, or anything that is not permanent and is removed at times, such as before sleep, may be removed or replaced in the mouth on Shabbos.

11. Cleaning dentures is permitted even with a toothbrush and mouthwash.[11]

---

7 עיין בשו״ע סי׳ שכ״ב סעיף ד׳, דרק קיסם שהוא מאכל בהמה שרי ליטלו ואפילו לפצלו כדי לחצוץ בו שיניים דכיוון דמאכל בהמה הוא ל״ש ביה מתקן כלי אבל קיסם ועץ שאינו מאכל בהמה אפילו ליטלו כמו שהוא כדי לחצוץ בו שיניו אסור.

8 שו״ע סימן שכ״ח סעיף ל״ו.

9 שו״ע שם סעיף ל״ח.

10 שש״כ פרק י״ד הלכה ל״ח, ושם בהערה צ״ט כתב דהיינו משום איסור לישה שהאבקה מתערבת ברוק ונדבקת לחיך. עי״ש. אולם בילקוט יוסף שבת ד׳ עמוד קכ״ו כתב ז״ל וכן מותר להשתמש באבקה שמניחים על השיניים תותבות כדי להדקם במקומם, ואין לחוש לאיסור שחיקת סממנים. עכ״ל. אך לא דן בזה אי שייך ביה לישה או לא. עיי״ש.

11 כיוון שהוא לצורך היום ואין כל חשש דימום וכיו״ב אך עם משחה עדיין דינו כדין משחה לשינים רגילות.

Similarly, on an *erev Pesach* which falls on Shabbos, one is permitted to soak the dentures in water in order to soften food particles and clean them so that one may eat with them on Shabbos afternoon.[12]

Opinions on Treating Toothache on Shabbos

12. Our Sages stated (*Avodah Zarah* 27b) that Shabbos may be desecrated to treat any internal wound. Briefly, "wound" refers to an injury, fracture, or inflammation. "Internal" refers to any body cavity, which according to the Gemara and *poskim*, includes the mouth cavity and all other internal parts of the body, down to the thoracic and abdominal cavities, as explained earlier in chapter 7, "The Definition of *Choleh Sheyeish Bo Sakanah*" (see paragraph 7 there for details). Thus, dental diseases can be considered "internal wounds."

13. According to the *Shulchan Aruch* (328:3), one may desecrate Shabbos to treat any internal injury or infection — including the teeth. However, minor aches and pains are not called "injuries." Nevertheless, according to the *Beis Yosef,* a person with a toothache may ask a non-Jew to extract it.

    The *Shulchan Aruch* (328:32) also says that a person with a toothache should not gargle with vinegar and then spit it out. He should drink the vinegar and actually swallow it or use it as a dressing and eat it in the normal manner.

14. As explained above, Shabbos may not be desecrated to treat minor ailments or pains, such as cavities that do not affect the entire body (that is, one can still function normally) or that don't cause inflammation, swelling, or similar symptoms (see paragraphs 20–25 below regarding treatment of cavities).

    However, if one is in extreme pain, it has to be determined whether one is considered a *choleh she'ein bo sakanah*, a standard bedridden

---

12 אך אם מנקה אותו לשבת לצורך אכילת הלילה, איסור הכנה יש כאן ואסור, אלא ישתמש בהם בשבת. והעולם נהגו לשרות במים השיניים תותבות מערב שבת למשך 24 שעות והיינו קודם השבת ובזה ליכא חשש, אך עם כל זה אם מצחצחים ומברישים בשבת לצורך הלילה לאו שפיר דמי אא״כ משתמש בהם גם בשבת.

patient, or if the ailment is in the category of an internal injury and one could therefore be considered a *choleh sheyeish bo sakanah*, a dangerously ill patient.

We will now discuss a situation where there is extreme pain and whether this places the person in the category of *choleh she'ein bo sakanah* or if it is considered an internal injury and therefore life-threatening.

15. Commenting on the opinion of the *Shulchan Aruch* that tooth ailments are regarded as "internal injuries," the *Mishnah Berurah* writes (328:8): "This refers to a case where [the tooth] causes such great pain that the entire body is affected, even though the patient is not bedridden." (This comes to exclude the case of an ordinary toothache.)

    In a footnote (*Sha'ar HaTziyun* 328:3), the *Mishnah Berurah* writes: "The Gemara says, 'Only a mild [toothache] is not considered an internal injury. But if it causes extreme pain, then it is [considered an internal injury.' This implies that extreme pain alone is sufficient, and we do not require a physical injury to the teeth [to label the person *choleh sheyeish bo sakanah*]."

    It is evident from the words of the *Mishnah Berurah* that a person with a very painful toothache is to be regarded as a *choleh sheyeish bo sakanah*, a person with a life-threatening illness.

16. However, the implication of the *Mishnah Berurah*'s comments elsewhere (on *Shulchan Aruch* 328:32) is that he holds (citing *Chayei Adam*) that a person with a very painful toothache is to be regarded only as a *choleh she'ein bo sakanah*. This appears to leave the matter unresolved.

17. The Kaf HaChaim writes (beginning of chapter 11): "Every 'internal wound' of the teeth…can be categorized as a 'wound' only if the pain is severe, but one may not desecrate Shabbos for an ordinary toothache. Nevertheless, if it affects the entire body [so that he cannot function normally], the Rabbis permit desecration of Shabbos by a non-Jew to treat it. However, a wound in the teeth is regarded as an internal wound, and thus, in general, even a Jew may desecrate Shabbos to treat it, even if it means violating a Torah prohibition."

    Similarly, in chapter 17, the Kaf HaChaim writes: "But aches are not called wounds, and one cannot desecrate Shabbos for them, even if one is in a lot of pain. If it distresses the person to the point that he is bedridden and can't function normally, a non-Jew may treat it, even if it means performing a *melachah*, work that is prohibited by the Torah on Shabbos. If the pain does not distress him so much, then only a rabbinical prohibition may be transgressed for him by a non-Jew."

18. The *She'eilos U'Teshuvos Shevet Levi* (70:2) differentiates between different teeth ailments:

    "In general, according to my humble opinion, there are several levels of severity [of teeth ailments]:

    a. "If the toothache is caused by a cavity, but there is no inflammation, nerve injury, or swelling around the tooth, the treatment consists of filling the cavity. The law regarding filling cavities is as stated later in [*Shulchan Aruch* 328 in] paragraph 32: one may not desecrate Shabbos for it, and only the actions mentioned there are permitted [that is, he may not treat his tooth by gargling vinegar — see paragraph 13 above].
    b. "If there is facial swelling or a lot of pus around the tooth, in the gums, it appears that one is permitted to desecrate Shabbos to treat it, unless a doctor says it is unnecessary.
    c. "If the nerve is affected and especially if it is exposed and painful, causing extreme pain, then it appears from the *poskim* that it is considered an internal wound and one may desecrate Shabbos to treat it.

    "Nevertheless, since we do not have an explicit statement by Chazal that Shabbos desecration is permitted in these situations, we rely on a doctor to decide whether treatment can be delayed."

19. These principles will serve as the basis for the subsequent presentation of the following laws:

- Cavities and toothaches (see paragraphs 20–25 below)
- Extreme pain that affects the entire body so that one cannot function normally, which puts the person in the category of *choleh she'ein bo sakanah*, an ordinary bedridden patient (see paragraphs 26–36 below)

- Inflammation, fractures, and injuries to the teeth, which are classified as internal wounds, and the patient thus acquires the status of *choleh sheyeish bo sakanah*, a dangerously ill person (see paragraphs 37–44 below)

Cavities

20. If a person has a toothache that causes minor pain, but otherwise he feels healthy and can function normally, the toothache cannot be treated on Shabbos. The cavity is classified as *michush*, a minor ache.[13]

21. Therefore, it is prohibited to take analgesics for pain relief. It is also prohibited to apply powder or other remedies to the tooth to relieve the pain, since this gives the appearance of medical treatment, which is prohibited for a minor ailment on Shabbos.[14]

22. One may drink and swallow an alcoholic beverage or vinegar in the ordinary manner and, while drinking, pass the liquid with his tongue over the affected tooth. One must swallow the drink; it is prohibited to spit it out or to gargle in the usual manner, since then it will appear as if he is taking medicine.[15]

23. Taking medication, giving sedative injections, and filling cavities or extracting teeth involve *melachah* that is prohibited by Torah law.[16] Therefore, these actions are prohibited for treating a toothache that is considered *michush*, a minor ache, even when done by a non-Jew.

24. Children age 6 and above begin losing their baby teeth. If a baby tooth is loose, it is prohibited to extract the tooth in the normal manner, since this would cause bleeding.

25. If the child is suffering greatly, then it is permitted to extract the tooth with a *shinui*, in an unusual manner.[17]

---

13 הגדרה זו עונה על הנאמר בשו״ע סי׳ שכ״ח סעיף ל״ב החושש בשיניו לא יגמע בהם חומץ ויפלוט אבל מגמע ובולע או מטבל בו כדרכו.

14 כמבואר בשו״ע הנ״ל דאסור לו לעשות כל דבר שנראה לרפואה.

15 ע״פ המבואר בשו״ע הנ״ל.

16 משנה ברורה בסי׳ שכ״ח ס״ק ק׳.

17 עיין בשו״ת שבט הלוי ח״ה סימן ל״ט אות ד׳. ומסתבר שבהוצאת שן המתנדנדת לילד לא

Being Bedridden Due to a Toothache

26. A person who has a cavity that causes him to suffer to the point that he is bedridden is regarded as a *choleh she'ein bo sakanah*, an ordinary bedridden patient.[18] If, however, the tooth or gums are infected, it is considered an internal wound (see paragraphs 37–44 below).

27. In this case, it is permitted to take pills and other medication to reduce the pain.[19] Similarly, it is also permitted to apply medicated powder to the tooth. It is also permitted to gargle with whiskey or vinegar and spit it out.[20]

28. However, one should avoid spreading ointment on the teeth or gums, even if one is bedridden, since this involves transgressing a Torah prohibition, which is not permitted for a *choleh she'ein bo sakanah*.[21]

29. A *choleh she'ein bo sakanah* is permitted to take medicine, as stated above (paragraph 27). Similarly, his other needs may be attended to as long as this requires transgressing only rabbinical decrees. However, transgression of Torah prohibitions is not permitted for such a person. Therefore, it is important to know which actions involve transgressing a Torah prohibition on Shabbos and may not be carried out for a *choleh she'ein bo sakanah* and which are prohibited only by a rabbinic decree.

30. Below is a brief list of the types of dental treatment prohibited on Shabbos because they involve Torah prohibitions:[22]

בהכרח יצא דם, וגם אם יצא מעט דם הוי מלאכה שאינה צריכה לגופה. ולא דמי לעקירת שן האמורה להלן סעיף ל״ג ושם בהערה כ״ג שביארנו דהוי מלאכה הצריכה לגופה, דכאן לא עוקר שן מהמכתשית מחמת מחלה או דלקת דיש צורך בדימום כמבואר להלן, אלא תהליך טבעי דשן החולבת נופלת מאליה ותחתיה קיימת כבר השן הקבועה. ואין כאן חולי ולא מכה. ודו״ק.

18 נתבאר במבוא לכאבי שיניים לעיל סעיף 17 בשם כף החיים עי״ש.

19 עיין בכפה״ח סי׳ שכ״ח אות קפ״ח בשם הט״ז ס״ק כ״ד.

20 מדשרי ליה תרופות וליכא גזירת שחיקת סממנים, וממילא שרי מגמע ופולט אף דמיחזי כרפואה, וכ״ה במ״ב סי׳ שכ״ח ס״ק ק״ב בשם ח״א.

21 בדין השימוש במשחות לרפואת חולה שאין בו סכנה עיין לעיל פרק 25 סעיף 31 וע״ש באורך.

22 פרוט סוגי הטפולים וסווגם המובאים בסעיפים 30 ו31 הועתקו ממאמר רפואי בספר רפואה והלכה ח״א עמוד קכ״ד.

a. Tooth extractions
b. Drilling the tooth and bone
c. Making an incision
d. X-rays
e. Abscess drainage by instruments and vacuum
f. Initiation of root canal work
g. Preparation of filling material, which requires *lash*, kneading
h. Making permanent fillings or fillings intended to remain for a long period of time (in essence, affixing the filling so that it will be permanently attached)
i. Examinations with electrical lights
j. Mandibular injections — this may at times involve transgression of a Torah prohibition, for example, when aspirating to check that it has not entered the blood vessels

31. The following actions involve transgressing only rabbinical prohibitions:

a. Taking medicine, both for healing and sedation
b. Hot or cold compresses, provided that they do not involve squeezing
c. Local anesthetic injections (subcutaneous)
d. Manual abscess drainage
e. Moving *muktzeh* items (such as dental instruments)
f. Applying temporary fillings
g. Cutting cotton or sponges

32. Therefore, a Jewish doctor may not make a permanent filling for a patient who is classified as a *choleh she'ein bo sakanah*, since this involves transgressing the Torah prohibitions of *lash*, kneading, and *boneh*, building. The same applies to any action that involves a Torah prohibition.

33. Similarly, a Jewish doctor may not extract the tooth[23] of a *choleh she'ein bo sakanah*, nor may the patient do it himself. (In the case of an infected tooth which the doctor advises should be extracted, see paragraph 40 below and note 31.)

34. A *choleh she'ein bo sakanah* is permitted to ask a non-Jewish doctor to prepare medication for him, even if this involves grinding or kneading or other prohibited actions.[24]

35. Still, even if a non-Jewish doctor is available, if the treatment can be postponed until after Shabbos by taking pain relievers, the dental procedure should be postponed. However, if the procedure must be carried out on Shabbos, the non-Jew may perform any necessary treatment, including filling a cavity, which involves transgression of Torah prohibitions.

---

23 המגן אברהם סי׳ שכ״ח ס״ק דהוצאת שן מלאכה דאורייתא דהא חובל לרפואה חייב. ע״כ. ועיין בביאור הלכה ד״ה ומצטער דכל ההיתר לעקור שן ע״י נכרי היינו דווקא בחולה כל גופו אבל במצטער לחודיה לא שרי ע״י נכרי. ובשו״ע הגרי״ז ס״ל דאף במצטער בדלא חלה כל גופו שרי לעקור ע״י א״י. משמע דס״ל דעקירת שן אינה אסורה מהתורה. ובהמשך דבריו כתב הבאור הלכה ז״ל: ולענ״ד ג״כ יש לעיין במה שכתב המ״א דהוצאת שן הוא מלאכה דאורייתא דהיא חובל לרפואה, ורצונו לומר דבזה חייב אפילו למ״ד מקלקל בחבורה פטור דזה מתקן הוא, הא הוא אינו מכוון רק להוציא השן והדם ממילא קאתי ואף דהוי פ״ר הא הוי עכ״פ פ״ר דלא אכפת ליה ואין איסורו אלא מדרבנן. והנה למ״ד מקלקל בחבורה חייב, חייב גם בזה כמש״כ הגר״א בסימן שנ״א ס״ו אבל למ״ד פטור אמאי חייב בזה, ואף דע״י ישראל בודאי יש להיזהר בזה עכ״פ ע״י א״י אפשר דיש להקל אף באינו חולה כל גופו. עכ״ל. גם בספר תהלה לדוד תמה על פסקו של המ״א דחשיב הוצאת שן למלאכה מדאורייתא ומשום כך הצריך דווקא בחולה כל גופו והוצאת שן ע״י א״י, דלכאורה המג״א ס״ל כהמ״מ דאמירה לעכו״ם בדרבנן שרי אף במצטער ולכאורה הוצאת הדם הוי מלאכה שאינה צריכה לגופא ואסורה מדרבנן (עיין באורך בדברינו בביאור שיטת המגן אברהם והמגיד משנה בדין ״מצטער״ לעיל פרק 28) ומסכם התהל״ד דפשט דברי המג״א בכאן משמע דס״ל דהוי מלאכה הצריכה לגופה. ובאמת אחר העיון מסתבר דהוצאת שן וכתוצאה מכך הוצאת הדם שהיא בגדר ״חובל לרפואה״ — אכן הוי מלאכה הצריכה לגופה. דהנה בספר הלכה ורפואה ח״א עמוד קכ״ג נכתב מאמר רפואי על עקירת שן ובין השאר נאמר שם בזה״ל: הוצאת שן (עקירה) באה להוציא את השן הפגועה לאחר שלא ניתן לרפאותה, והדימום עם עקירת השן היא תוצאה ישירה של העקירה, אולם אנו מפיקים תועלת ריפוי מן הדמום, שמקום העקירה במקרה של דימום נוח לריפוי ולקרישת הדם ומונע מכאבים מיותרים, וגם מונע הסתבכויות מיותרות. במידה ואין דימום לאחר העקירה (מכנית) והמכתשית יבשה, יש צורך לגרום שיבא דימום במכתשית ע״י חתכים מסביב למכתשית בריקמת החניכיים ומזרימים דם לתוך המכתשית. במקרה שאין דימום לאחר העקירה ואין נוקטים גורמים לדימום, לא השגנו את המטרה לשחרר את המטופל מכאבים אלא נגרום לו הסתבכויות וכאבים חזקים, שעצם המכתש החשוף ללא קריש דם שיכסה ויגן עליו מביא כאבים חזקים ביותר. עכ״ל המאמר הנ״ל. ומבואר שהדימום הינו מלאכה הצריכה לגופה, וא״כ דברי המג״א מבוארים היטב.

24 ככל דין חולה שאין בו סכנה שאומר לנכרי ועושה לו כל צרכיו כמבואר בשו״ע סי׳ שכ״ח סעיף י״ז.

36. Similarly, a non-Jewish doctor may extract a painful tooth,[25] even if the patient participates in the treatment (by opening his mouth, tilting his head). Such participation is insignificant.[26]

Infection of the Teeth and Gums

Above (paragraphs 20–25) we explained the laws regarding minor aches and pains caused by cavities. These laws apply only in a case where the teeth and gums are not infected and treatment can wait until after Shabbos.

We also explained the laws pertaining to a person with such extreme pain that he cannot function normally and is bedridden — this person is classified as a *choleh she'ein bo sakanah*. In this case, the pain can usually be controlled by means of a local sedative, which allows postponing further treatment until after Shabbos. Nevertheless, any type of treatment done by a non-Jewish doctor is permitted, since any needs of a *choleh she'ein bo sakanah* may be provided by a non-Jew on Shabbos, even if this involves a Torah prohibition.

In this section, we will discuss the status of a person whose teeth or gums have become infected or who has a tooth exposed prior to a root canal in which infection is suspected. In these circumstances, the condition is considered an internal wound. This classifies the patient as a *choleh sheyeish bo sakanah*, someone with a life-threatening illness, who may be treated even by a Jewish doctor.[27]

37. First aid: In the case of infections in the teeth, one may initiate treatment with antibiotics or any other prescribed medications.

38. A doctor's opinion or the sick person's feelings are sufficient basis for

---

25 כ״כ הב״י סי׳ שכ״ח וז״ל: כתוב באורחות חיים החושש בשינו ומצטער עליו להוציאו אומר לאינו יהודי להוציאו, וטעמו משום דכל דבר שאין בו סכנה אומר לא״י ועושה כמו שיתבאר. עכ״ל. ובדרכי משה שם כתב ״וכ״כ באו״ה״. ואמנם כ״כ באו״ה כלל נ״ט סעיף כ״ד ז״ל: וכן התיר מהר״ז ז״ל לתלוש שן ע״י עכו״ם בשבת והיינו מטעמא דלעיל דחולי שאין בו סכנה אומר לכנעני ועושה וכו׳. עכ״ל. והביא דין זה הרמ״א בשו״ע סימן שכ״ח ס״ג עיי״ש.

26 שיטת הב״ח והט״ז דהוי מסייע ואסור, אך רבו דעות החולקים על הנחה זו וס״ל דמסייע אין בו ממש. עיין בש״ך בנקודות הכסף יו״ד סי׳ קצ״ה, וע״ע במ״ב סי׳ שכ״ח ס״ק י״א ובשעה״צ שם ס״ק ט׳.

27 כמבואר בשו״ע סי׳ שכ״ח סעיף ג׳ שהשיניים בכלל ״מכה של חלל״. והגדרת מכה של חלל היינו אם יש חבלה או דלקת (בועה) וכיו״ב. כמבואר לעיל במבוא לכאבי שיניים עיי״ש.

deciding whether first aid treatment will suffice to reduce the pain and to postpone further treatment until after Shabbos or if immediate definitive treatment is necessary and essential. If immediate treatment is necessary, then it is permitted to do all actions needed to eradicate the infection.[28]

39. According to the principle of Chazal, "Begin with that which is minor" (that is, try to minimize doing forbidden activities as much as possible by doing lesser transgressions first),[29] one may explore alternative possibilities to using electric instruments as much as the circumstances allow. Whatever can be done manually, by nonelectric instruments, is preferable. This depends on the doctor's opinion, the availability of alternatives, and the patient's condition. A non-Jew is not subject to limitations concerning the use of electric instruments.

40. Therefore, when there is a need, even a Jewish doctor[30] is permitted to treat the patient and do everything that is necessary. This includes surgery, X-rays, fillings, and extractions.[31]

---

28 עיין לעיל במבוא לכאבי שיניים בסעיף 15 מש״כ בשם שו״ת שבט הלוי ח״ט.

29 כלל זה נאמר אמנם ביום הכפורים כאשר מאכילים חולה בסכנה או מעוברת שהריחה ומסתכנת או במי שאחזו בולמוס. אך גם בהלכות שבת הורו חז״ל בכל מה שניתן לצמצם בחילולי שבת מצמצמים, כמבואר גם בשו״ע סי׳ שכ״ח סעיף ט״ז לענין אמדוהו לשתי גרוגרות וכו׳ עיי״ש.

30 דהנכרי עושה לצורך הנוחיות שלו בהפעלת המכשירים, ואף שעושה כן לצורך הישראל שרי, ואפילו אם הנכרי עושה זאת לצורך חולה שאין בו סכנה שרי אף במלאכה דאורייתא כמבואר בשו״ע סי׳ שכ״ח סעיף י״ז. והכא שעושה לצורך חולי שיש בו סכנה ודאי שרי.

31 בענין עקירת שן לצורך חולה שיש בו סכנה נאמר ברמ״א סימן שכ״ח סעיף ג׳ ז״ל: מיהו מי שחושש בשיניו ומצטער עליו להוציאו אומר לא״י להוציאו (ב״י בשם א״ח ואו״ה הארוך).

א) הנה בדברי הרמ״א נחלקו הפוסקים אם מש״כ שעקירה מותרת ע״י א״י, היינו משום דאיירי בחולה שאין בו סכנה, והכלל הוא דכל חולה שאין בו סכנה אומר לא״י ועושה. ולעולם אם נמצא לפנינו חולה שמוגדר כחולה במכה של חלל דשרי מלאכה ע״י ישראל, וממילא שרי עקירה נמי ע״י ישראל. או דלמא דאף במכה של חלל נהי דשרי שאר מלאכות לצורך רפואה ע״י ישראל, אבל ״עקירה״ שרי רק ע״י אינו יהודי.

ב) ובפרי מגדים אשל אברהם ס״ק ג׳ מבאר דהיינו בחושש בשינו וחשיב כחולה שאין בו סכנה שלכן מותרת מלאכת עקירה (שהיא מלאכה מדאורייתא כדמבאר המג״א סק״ג) ע״י א״י. ומשמע מדבריו דבכאיב ליה טובא או היכא דחשיב כמכה של חלל שרי העקירה אף ע״י ישראל. גם בשו״ע הגר״ז כתב שבחושש ומצטער שרי עקירה ע״י אינו יהודי ומשמע דבמכה של חלל שרי אף ע״י ישראל.

41. Similarly, when absolutely necessary, one is permitted to travel on Shabbos to the doctor or to travel to obtain medication that is urgently needed for the treatment of the tooth. One may do whatever is permitted for a sick person whose life is in danger (*choleh sheyeish bo sakanah*).

ג) ובאמת שמקור דברי הרמ״א הם בב״י סי׳ שכ״ח וז״ל: כתוב באורחות חיים החושש בשינו ומצטער עליו להוציאו אומר לאינו יהודי להוציאו, וטעמו משום דכל דבר שאין בו סכנה אומר לא״י ועושה כמו שיתבאר. עכ״ל.

ד) אולם במשנה ברורה סי׳ שכ״ח ס״ק י׳ משמע דס״ל דאיירי הרמ״א אף בחולי שיש בו סכנה ובכ״ז לא שרי עקירה אלא ע״י א״י, וז״ל שם: ואף דמתחלה מבואר דחולי השיניים מקרי של חלל מ״מ אינו מותר ההוצאה ע״י ישראל דהוצאת השן אינה רפואה ידועה [א״ר] ואדרבה לפעמים יש חשש סכנתא עי״ז והא דמתיר השו״ע מקודם לחלל עליהם השבת היינו לרפאות המחלה ע״י סמים שלא יהיה צריך להוציאן. עכ״ל. ודבריו צ״ע דהא מקור דברי הרמ״א לא איירי אלא בחולה שאין בו סכנה ומשו״ה קאמר אומר לא״י ועושה, וכמבואר לעיל.

ה) ובשער הציון ס״ק ו׳ כתב לדחות דברי הפמ״ג הנ״ל וז״ל: וראיתי בפמ״ג שדחק עצמו לומר דמיירי דלא כאיב ליה טובא דאל״ה אמאי אינו מותר ע״י ישראל. ולא ראה דברי האו״ה שכתב בהדיא דהוא חולי שיש בו סכנה הך דההוצאה אינה רפואה דאדרבא סכנתא היא. עכ״ל.

ו) והמעיין בדברי האסור והיתר הארוך כלל נ״ט סעיף כ״ד יראה דהאו״ה איירי בחולה שאין בו סכנה. דז״ל שם: וכן התיר מהר״ז ז״ל לתלוש שן ע״י עכו״ם בשבת והיינו מטעמא דלעיל דחולי שאין בו סכנה אומר לכנעני ועושה דכה״ג במקום צער לא גזרו אבל מחמת סכנה ליכא למימר דאדרבא תלישת שן הוי סכנה כדאיתא לעיל. עכ״ל וכוונתו למש״כ שם בסעיף י״ב וז״ל: וכאב השיניים יש בו סכנה שהרי יש שיניים שתלוי בהם בת העין ושורייני דעינא בליבא תליא עכ״ל. שוב מצאתי בכף החיים סי׳ שכ״ח אות ט״ו שהביא דברי האו״ה הנ״ל והוסיף ע״ז וז״ל: והכי איתא בפסחים קי״ג ע״א אמר ליה רב לחייא בריה לא תעקר ככא. ופי׳ הר״ח כלומר אם יכאב לך אל תעקרהו שמא תכחש עיניך. יעו״ש.

ז) וצריך לומר דאה״נ ס״ל לרבינו יונה דפעולת העקירה היא דבר מסוכן, אך לא אמר דמשום הכי שרי העקירה רק ע״י א״י, ואדרבא שם בסעיף כ״א משמע דשרי לחלל עליה את השבת אם מסוכנת ליפול ובסתם איירי בישראל, וז״ל שם: וכן מתיר בסמ״ק לכואב לו שיניו לגמוע חומץ אפילו לרפואה אבל לא לחזור ולהפליטו שנראה לכל שעושה לרפואה, וצר״ל שהיינו שכואבין לו קצת ואינם מסוכנים ליפול דאם לא כן אף לרפאותה ולחלל עליה מותר כדאיתא לעיל. עכ״ל.

ח) בשו״ת שבט הלוי ח״ט סי׳ ע׳ אות ו׳ דחה דברי המ״ב ופרך ראיותיו מהב״י והאו״ה הנזכ״ל וס״ל דאיירו בחולה שאין בו סכנה. ואולם בחולה שיש בו סכנה ודאי דשרי עקירת השן אף ע״י ישראל. וסיים דבריו שם בזה״ל: ובלא״ה בזמן הזה קשה להחמיר במקום סכנה מטעם האו״ה דגם הוצאת השן סכנתא היא דאנו רואים שאם נעשית בזהירות כחק הרפואה היא רפואה בדוקה רובו ככולו כנזכר לעיל ומקרים לא טובים שייכים גם בשאר רפואות ולא גרע הוצאת השן מהם במקום שאיכא היתר פקוח נפש. עכ״ל.

ט) כמו״כ בספר נשמת אברהם כתב דהאידנא הוצאת השן היא רפואה ידועה ומותרת אף ע״י רופא ישראל, כשהלה קובע שזה הכרחי משום סכנת נפשות, ובשם הגאון רבי שלמה זלמן אויערבאך שליט״א כתב שם ז״ל: חושבני דבזמנינו מותר אפילו אם זה רק ספק הצלה, כיון דבזמנינו אין שום סכנה בעקירת שן.

Scurvy

42. Scurvy[32] is mentioned in the Gemara[33] and defined in halachah as a life-endangering illness. The Gemara relates that Rabbi Yochanan was sick with scurvy, and he permitted the preparation of medication to treat his illness on Shabbos, even though this involved transgressing a Torah prohibition.

43. One symptom of the illness is that placing an object in one's mouth causes bleeding from between the teeth. The illness begins with the teeth and ends with gastrointestinal bleeding.[34] Treatment is urgent because the patient's life is in danger.

44. Scurvy differs from other diseases in that (if a person is definitely diagnosed with this illness) even if a doctor or the sick person says that Shabbos should not be desecrated to treat him, their opinion is disregarded. Shabbos should be desecrated for treating this disease, since Chazal defined it as a life-threatening illness.

---

32 מחלת הצפידנא המוכרת כיום לרופאים, מוגדרת ברפואה בענין אחר לגמרי, והוא הגדרה לחולי בחוסר ויטמין סי.

33 מסכת עבודה זרה דף כ״ח ע״א.

34 ונגרמים דמומים מפושטים בכל הגוף ובחללין (הערת רופא, דר׳ מ. שרם).

Chapter 35
Diseases of the Eye

The *Shulchan Aruch* (328:9) says: "If one is concerned because both eyes or one eye are hurting, or the pain causes tears to come to one's eyes, or they are bleeding, or there is a discharge or signs of an eye disease [see *Avodah Zarah* 28b], one may desecrate Shabbos to treat it."

1. If an eye disease goes untreated, it is likely to become more severe and even endanger one's life. There are three categories of eye disease:
    a. Eye diseases that are life-threatening or may be life-threatening (*yeish bo sakanah*)
    b. Eye diseases that are not life-threatening but the person still cannot function normally (*ein bo sakanah*)
    c. Minor ailments of the eye

    These categories will be explained below, as well as symptoms and severity of various eye diseases and a description of treatments that are permitted on Shabbos.[1]

Eye Diseases that Are Life-Threatening

2. Life-threatening eye diseases include:

---

1 המונחים הרפואים שבפרק זה לקוחים ברובם מספר רפואה והלכה ח״א, ממאמרו של ד״ר יוחנן ידוואב עמ׳ ר״א ר״ב. וחלק מההלכות ממאמרו של הגאון ר׳ משה הרשלר זצ״ל ״תרופות ורפואות בשבת״ עמ׳ ק״ו–ק״ט.

a. Acute purulent infection of the conjunctiva and the eyelids

b. Acute lacrimation (tearing) caused by infection, irritation, or foreign bodies

c. Acute infection of the cornea

d. Acute loss of vision, even in one eye caused by

i. acute infection of the cornea or inner eye;

ii. partial inflammation of the choroids, retina, or vitreous humor;

iii. acute attack of increased intraocular pressure (glaucoma);

iv. acute hemorrhage outside the eye in the adventitia or within the eyeball, such as within the retina in the area of the macula, within the vitreous, or within the anterior chamber of the eye;

v. retinal detachment;

vi. acute infection of the ophthalmic nerve, in any one of its divisions; or

vii. occlusion of the artery or vein of the retina or the choroids

e. Injury to the eye of any type, by an external factor, such as a dull or sharp object, ultraviolet light, or chemical or similar agents

f. Increased intraocular pressure of any type

g. Rheumatic diseases that cause papillary inflammation, whose symptoms include redness of the eye, pain, and visual loss; as a result of the injury to the pupil, one develops glaucoma or intraocular pressure, cataract, opacification of the eye, and even blindness

3. In any situation where there are signs of eye disease or where a person feels that perhaps a serious eye illness is developing, the person is regarded as being in danger of his life. Therefore, even Torah prohibitions may be transgressed for all his needs, whether to make a telephone call or to travel to a doctor or a hospital or to perform any necessary tests or examinations. Any treatment — X-rays, dressings, and such — may be performed as well, as in any life-threatening situation.

4. Note that there is no difference whether the disease is in one eye or both eyes.

Non-Life-Threatening Eye Disease

5. The second category of eye disease is defined in the Gemara as "the end of *uchla*" (see *Avodah Zarah* 28b). This is referring to the last stage of the illness when it is no longer life-threatening or carries a risk of blindness. Nevertheless, the patient is still very ill. This stage may include frequent conjunctivitis, whose symptoms are discharge of tears or pus and irritation and red conjunctiva in the corners of the eye. These infections generally heal well with the appropriate treatments and sometimes even without treatment.

6. Therefore, if there is mild inflammation of the eyes, even with a discharge, but there is no infection, then the person is regarded as being a *choleh she'ein bo sakanah*, an ordinary bedridden patient. The same is true if the illness has already healed except that the eye is still slightly inflamed and red or if medication is needed to strengthen the vision. Similarly, a person with extreme eye pain that causes him to be bedridden or prevents him from functioning normally is regarded as a *choleh she'ein bo sakanah*. A Jew may not transgress Torah prohibitions for the patient. However, a non-Jew is permitted to do anything the patient needs, as for any *choleh she'ein bo sakanah*.

7. It is permitted to administer eyedrops or an ointment to the eye of a *choleh she'ein bo sakanah*. One should be careful not to smear the ointment, but only to place it on the eye. After administering the medication, the eye may be dressed as needed.

8. It is permitted to wash the eye, even with medication, such as boron solution (boric acid) or oxidizing solution. In ancient times, eyes were washed with wine or saliva. Any similar liquid is permitted.

9. In certain circumstances, some use tea essence (extract) or tea extract from chamomile leaves to make a hot compress to place on the eye. Tea essence may not be prepared on Shabbos for this purpose because of the prohibition of *bishul*, cooking. However, if the tea was prepared and placed on gauze before Shabbos, it is permitted to use the compress. The gauze may be placed close to a hot utensil in order to warm it

slightly before putting it on the eye. A non-Jew may prepare tea for this purpose even on Shabbos.

10. When washing the eyes with boric acid or other medications using cotton, care must be taken not to violate the prohibition of *sechitah*, squeezing, pressing, or wringing. Similarly, the cotton should be precut before Shabbos.

11. When placing a dressing, care should be taken not to spread the ointment on Shabbos, as mentioned earlier. However, the ointment may be placed from the tube directly on the eye or on the dressing.

12. Other laws applicable to a *choleh she'ein bo sakanah* are enumerated in part 3, "*Choleh She'ein Bo Sakanah*."

Minor Eye Ailments

13. Mild eye pain can be treated without medication. It needs only washing and local cleansing. This category includes:
    a. Mild itching
    b. Dry eyes
    c. A small amount of mucous discharge
    d. Mild derangement of the refraction of the eyes (astigmatism) which does not involve sudden loss of visual acuity
    e. Mild redness of the eyes
    f. Mild impairment in the action of the eye muscles, such as weakness in focusing, but without the sudden onset of double vision

14. Concerning these and similar circumstances, the *Shulchan Aruch* (328:20) states: "One may not place wine in the eye. It may be placed on the eyelids provided that one does not open and close them. Saliva may not be placed even on the eyelids, since it is evident that this is done for healing."

    The *Shulchan Aruch* states (328:21) further: "A person may soak [a dressing in] a salve for the eye on Friday [before Shabbos] and place it on the eye on Shabbos, since this has the appearance of washing [the eye rather than medicating it]. [However, this is permitted] only if he does not close and open [the eyes]. [This is not included in] the prohibition of 'grinding herbs' [for medicine], since the dressing was soaked on Friday."

15. Therefore, if a person suffers from a mild irritation of the eye, he should not be given any medical treatment. No drops should be administered, and no dressing should be placed on the eye. However, one can place drops in the eyes and place a dressing on Friday, before Shabbos, and the dressing can remain there the whole Shabbos.

16. Similarly, one may wash one's face with hot water or with water in which boron crystals or other medications have been dissolved, as long as they are not recognizable in the water. These medications, however, must be prepared and dissolved in the water on Friday. This is permitted because it merely looks like one is washing the eyes with plain water.

17. However, one may not wash with water to which a colored antiseptic had been added, since this is recognizable as a medical treatment. Eyelids that stick together in the morning may be washed to open them, since this is not a medicinal treatment. However, it is prohibited to wash the eyes with tea essence or similar agents, even if it was prepared on Friday before Shabbos, since this has the appearance of a medicinal treatment.

18. A person who started treatment by putting eyedrops in his eyes during the week is permitted to continue the treatment on Shabbos.

Aids for Impaired Vision

In this section we will explain the laws pertaining to various aids for treating vision impairment, such as contact lenses and glasses.

Glasses

19. A nearsighted person (myopia) who wears glasses to correct his vision, whether the glasses are used for seeing in the distance or for reading only, may wear them on Shabbos. This is not included in the prohibi-

tion against preparing medicine ("grinding herbs").

20. It is even permitted for one to go into a public domain on Shabbos with glasses, but only when actually worn. However, if the eyeglasses are for reading only, they may not be worn on Shabbos in the public domain, because then they are regarded as being carried.

21. Eyeglasses that became dismantled may not be reassembled on Shabbos. Furthermore, the parts may not be handled because of the prohibition of *muktzeh*.[2]

Contact Lenses

22. Contact lenses may be placed in the eyes on Shabbos. Similarly, one may wash the eyes with a saline solution before putting in the contact lenses; this is not regarded as violating the prohibition of preparing medications on Shabbos. Furthermore, it is permitted to use eyedrops on Shabbos to prevent dryness caused by wearing the lenses.

23. Similarly, rinsing and cleaning contact lenses on Shabbos with water or liquids made specially for this purpose is permitted.

Prosthetic Eyes

24. A prosthetic eye may be worn on Shabbos even when walking in the public domain.[3] This is because one is not prone to remove it.

25. Similarly, a person who is wearing a patch or dressing on his eye may go out with them on Shabbos into the public domain.[4]

---

2 עיין במש״כ בקצות השבת פרק ד׳ סעיף כ״ח ובהערה ס׳ שם.

3 שו״ת באר משה ח״א סי׳ כ״ז בשם שו״ת מהרש״ם ח״ב סי׳ ה׳.

4 שו״ת באר משה שם סי׳ י״ז.

Chapter 36
Bites and Stings

The *Shulchan Aruch* states (328:6): "A person bitten by a rabid dog or a venomous snake or insect, even if a doubt exists whether the sting or bite is deadly, is regarded as having been inflicted with an internal injury."

There are many animals and insects that are venomous. A bite or sting from a poisonous animal or insect can be life-threatening, causing the destruction of the circulatory system and resulting in immediate death, or the venom may cause only local burning and pain. This chapter discusses effects associated with snakebites, animal bites, and insect bites and stings, how one may protect oneself from them, and their treatment, particularly those that may be administered on Shabbos.

A Rabid Dog's Bite

1. A person bitten by a dog that may be afflicted with rabies is regarded as a *choleh sheyeish bo sakanah*, a dangerously ill person, even in cases of doubt.[1] It is permitted to trap the dog if necessary for the purpose of determining what illness the dog suffers.[2]

Snakebite

2. The bite of a poisonous snake, such as the black viper or albino viper in

---

1 כמבואר בשו״ע סימן שכ״ח סעיף ו׳ הנ״ל.

2 וע״ע בזה בנשמת אברהם ח״א עמוד קכא.

Israel or the rattlesnake or coral snake in the U.S., can result in extreme pain at the site of the bite, followed by swelling, elevated temperature, redness, and local tenderness. Recommended treatment is as follows:

a. The first step is absolute rest for the victim. Any running or panic only hastens the absorption of the venom.
b. It is recommended to capture the snake so that the antidote may be matched to the particular type of venom.
c. The site of the bite should be washed copiously with water and covered by sterile material. The victim should be brought to a hospital as quickly as possible.
d. Since there is a danger of shock, there may be difficulty in placing an intravenous catheter. Therefore, an intravenous line should be inserted as early as possible to enable the giving of fluids and medications. The intravenous catheter should, preferably, not be inserted in the site of the bite.

3. The hospital personnel will check vital signs such as blood pressure and pulse, monitor for signs of shock, and inspect the site of the bite. The Poison Control Center may be contacted for consultation on the appropriate antidote.

4. Any snakebite is treated as potentially life-threatening, and Shabbos should be desecrated to treat the victim even if one is not positive that the person's life is in danger.[3] Thus, it is permitted to capture the snake and to bring it to the hospital on Shabbos, even carrying it through a

---

3 שו״ע שם. והעיר לי בזה הגרי״י זילברשטיין שליט״א בזה״ל: כאשר יש ספק אם הנחש ארסי, מהראוי לעשות את חילול השבת ע״י רופא נכרי. וכעין מה שכתב בערוך השולחן סי׳ שט״ז סעיף כ״ב לגבי כלב שוטה עיי״ש. ובזה מובנים דברי במשנה ברורה שכ״ח ס״ק ל״ז בשם הט״ז שכתב: אם יש אפילו ספק הצלה ויש סכנה בבירור כל הזריז הרי זה משובח. עכ״ל. לכן אם יש סכנה בבירור מחללים ע״י ישראל, ולא כשהסכנה בספק.

אך אחר בקשת המחילה מכמוה״ר שליט״א אין הנידון דומה לראיה, מה שכתב בערוך השולחן שם כשיש ספק אם הכלב שוטה שאין הישראל רשאי להורגו מספק, היינו כאשר הכלב מהלך כדרכו ועדיין לא נשך, והספק הוא מורכב, מי אומר שהוא כלב שוטה ואפילו אם כן מי אומר שישך, ולכן אין להורגו מספק. אבל כאן מדובר שנחש הכיש ויש ספק אם הוא ארסי או לא, הרי הסכנה בעין, ובודאי מותר לחלל שבת לצורך הנפגע וגם כדי ללכוד את הכלב. וכפי המבואר בדברינו (וכן העיר לי לנכון הגאון רבי בנימין וייס שליט״א, על דברי הגרי״י זילברשטיין שליט״א).

public domain, in order to identify the snake for the purpose of providing the correct treatment.[4]

5. Snakes and scorpions may be charmed on Shabbos to prevent them from hurting people. This is not regarded as transgressing the prohibition of *tzeidah*, trapping.[5]

Scorpion Stings

6. A scorpion's sting is treated like a snakebite.[6] There are various types of scorpions, and specific antidotes exist for some scorpion stings.[7]

Bee or Wasp Stings

7. Those with a family tendency to allergies may develop sensitivity to bee stings. If such a person is stung again, he may have a strong allergic reaction to a second bee sting that is life-threatening. Bee honey may also cause allergic reactions.

   When it stings, the bee injects its stinger through the skin together with a small yellow sack. The sack contains the material that causes the allergic reaction. To prevent an allergic reaction, one must remove the stinger, by pincers or by hand, immediately.

   The signs of a local allergic reaction may include a red patch, swelling, elevated temperature, and other symptoms of inflammation. There may develop symptoms of a general allergic reaction, such as edema of the trachea and respiratory passages, that causes difficulty breathing, a whole-body skin rash and itching, and other signs of anaphylactic shock, such as rapid pulse and low blood pressure. This is an emergency situation.

---

4 עיין בנשמת אברהם הנ״ל.

5 שו״ע שם סעיף מ״ה.

6 עיין בשמירת שבת כהלכתה פרק ל״ב סעיף י״א אות י״ד. ואולם חז״ל במסכת ע״ז דף כ״ח ע״ב כתבו: ״חמימי לעקרבא וקרירי לזיבורא״. כלומר של עקיצת עקרב טוב חימום ולעקיצת דבורה — קירור. שמא נשתנו הטבעים. אולם ברבינו חננאל שם פירש שמי שעקצו עקרב ראוי להאכיל אותו דברים חמים. א״כ אפשר שעל המקום ראוי להניח קר שלא יתפשט העקיצה ולהאכילו בחמין לריפוי.

7 בספר קצות השולחן סי׳ קל״ז בבדי השולחן ס״ק א׳ כתב וז״ל: ובזמנינו נוהגים רפואה למי שנשכו עקרב, צודין את העקרב (כי טבעו של העקרב שאחרי שנשך ופלט ארסו תש כחו ולא יכול לזחול הרבה ולהתרחק ממקומו, ומי שמרגיש עקיצה מחפשין סביבו ואם היה עקרב מוצאין

If there are signs of an allergic reaction, ice should be placed on the site of the sting, and the patient should be brought to a hospital as soon as possible so that he can be given the appropriate treatment.

8. A person who enters a state of shock when stung by a bee or wasp must always carry an automatic injection needle which contains medication for the allergy. He may carry the needle on Shabbos in a public domain, provided that he does so with a *shinui*, in an unusual manner, such as tying it to his hand or leg.[8]

9. In the case of a sting that is definitely not life-threatening, the site of the sting may be washed with vinegar mixed with water, lemon juice, or ice water in order to prevent stinging or itching. However, the site of a sting may not be soaked in the liquid, since such an action is obviously a medical treatment.[9]

10. The stinger of a wasp or bee may be removed on Shabbos.[10]

Mosquito Bites

11. Treatment to prevent mosquito bites on Shabbos is permitted. This involves applying a liquid that prevents mosquito bites, such as a spray, on the exposed parts of the body.[11]

12. Only sprays or other types of liquid may be used to prevent mosquito bites. One may not use ointments or creams.[12]

אותו), ומטגנים אותו בשמן על האש ומשימין אותו על מקום הנשוך, ובמשך שתים שלוש שעות מתרפא לגמרי והיא רפואה בדוקה ומחללין בה את השבת. וכך היו נוהגים בעיה״ק חברון ת״ו שלא היה שם רופא מיוחד על דברים כאלה, וזקני הספרדים בעיה״ק חברון היה להם שימורים של עקרבים מטוגנים בצלוחיות, ואומרים שגם עקרב מטוגן אחר מועיל לרפואה, אבל לא כמו אותו העקרב שנשך. עכ״ל.

8 עיין בנשמת אברהם ח״ד עמוד שט״ז.

9 עיין שש״כ פל״ה סעיף ל״ח.

10 שש״כ שם.

11 בקצות השולחן סי׳ קל״ח בבדי השולחן אות ל״א כתב ז״ל מי שמצוי יתושין בביתו העוקצין ומצערין, ובחול הוא ממרח פניו וידיו בנפט, וריח הנפט מגרש את היתושין, נראה דגם בשבת מותר לעשות כן, ודבר זה ק״ו דהא התירו צידה דרבנן כגון צידת פרעוש בשבת כדי שלא יעקצנו, וכש״כ למרח גופו עם נפט דשרי. עכ״ל.

12 דאף לחולה שאין בו סכנה אסור למרוח משחות על גופו וכמבואר כ״ז לעיל פרק 26 עיי״ש באורך.

13. Also, only bite-preventing preparations may be used, but it is prohibited to use preparations that provide relief from or healing of existing bites on Shabbos.[13] If the preparation acts to heal the existing bites and to prevent new bites, there is reason to regard it as a medicinal preparation, which is prohibited to use on Shabbos. However, a person who does not have any previous bites may use the dual-action preparation for bite prevention.

14. Electric-powered devices for trapping or removing mosquitoes and other types of flying insects may be used only if the device is switched on on Friday and then operates automatically without any human intervention. This applies also to battery-powered equipment. Further study is needed to determine whether it is permissible to ask a non-Jew to switch on such a device in the case of severe distress or when there is a baby on the premises.

Other Types of Bites

15. There are some ant bites or spider bites that cause extreme swelling in the area of the bite. A physician should be consulted to determine whether the situation is potentially life-threatening.

16. If an animal bite is suspected to be life-threatening, Shabbos may be desecrated to treat it. This may include the bite of a donkey or horse and the scratch of a cat or other animals in a place where it is suspected that the animals are rabid. In all these cases, Shabbos may desecrated to treat the bite or scratch.[14]

---

13 דתכשירים המרפאים בשבת יש לאסור בהם מדין גזירה משום שחיקת סמנים.

14 עיין שש״כ פל״ב סעיף י״א אות י״ד.

Chapter 37

Injuries, Fractures, and Dislocations

This chapter discusses treatment of orthopedic injuries, fractures, and dislocations on Shabbos, as well as injuries to muscles, ligaments, and nerves. These include injuries to the upper and lower extremities, the pelvis, skull, rib cage, and the spine.

The chapter is divided into four parts:

a. The type of injury — a fracture or dislocation of bone and injury to a muscle, ligament, or nerve as a result of a fall or as a result of an object falling on someone

b. Intervention — such as X-rays and casts

c. Treatment — bandaging, adjusting straps or belts, and using splints, braces, or other supportive devices

d. Pediatric orthopedics — orthopedic conditions common in children and their treatment

Orthopedic Injuries

1. Injuries caused by a fall may or may not require immediate medical attention. Shabbos may be desecrated if the injury requires treatment.

   These injuries are classified into five categories:

   a. An injury that is life-threatening (due to gangrene, infection, or damage to underlying structures)

b. An injury that endangers a limb (*sakanas eiver*)

c. An injury that is not life-threatening but affects the entire body or causes the person to be bedridden

d. Extreme pain limited to the site of the injury

e. Minor aches and pains that do not interfere with normal functioning

Life-Threatening Injuries

2. A distinction should be made between two types of bone structures: (a) cylindrical bone that has a cavity which contains bone marrow and (b) flat bone, which has no cavity and does not contain bone marrow. There are also different types of fractures. There are fractures in which the whole circumference of the bone is fractured, while in other cases only one side of the bone is fractured. Other types of fractures include comminuted, simple, straight, diagonal, and spiral fractures.

3. In the case of any bone fracture, one should seek immediate medical attention, since a blood vessel might have been ruptured, causing internal bleeding. A compound fracture may also cause infection, which can pose a danger to life. These cases are regarded as life-threatening and warrant Shabbos desecration.

4. A fracture might be life-threatening because, if not treated properly, it may cause permanent damage, pain, gangrene, embolism, or thrombosis and constitute a danger to the heart, brain, and nerves (see also paragraph 16).

5. Fractures of cranial bones, the chest cavity, or spine are considered extremely dangerous because they may damage the internal organs, lungs, brain, and spinal cord.

6. Pelvic fractures are also considered life-threatening because the fracture may cause damage to internal organs (intestines, uterus or ovaries, or urinary tract) or cause significant blood loss. Upon a doctor's recommendation, one may have X-rays taken, blood and urine tests, and ultrasound.

7. If a doctor recommends immediate treatment of a fracture or injury, Shabbos may be desecrated, and even a Torah prohibition may be transgressed to treat it if necessary. This applies in particular where there is suspicion of an infection or blood vessel damage.

8. If a person was hit by a car, he needs immediate medical attention even if he is able to get up and walk, because he may have sustained an internal injury. Blood and urine tests should be taken to check for internal bleeding. Similarly, if a person falls from a high place and hits the ground or, more commonly, if a child falls from a tree or fence, medical attention should be sought. Even if there is no apparent injury and the individual is able to walk, one should verify that no internal damage occurred.

9. All the tests that are conventionally administered to a person who was involved in a car accident or suffered a fall should be carried out on Shabbos to verify that the person's life is not in danger. However, if a doctor states that the individual did not sustain any injury and further testing is not needed, then the tests should not be done until after Shabbos.

Injuries that Endanger a Limb

10. *Sakanas eiver*, danger to a limb, includes localized fractures that could cause malfunction of the affected limb if it is not set in a cast. Since this is not a life-threatening situation, only rabbinic prohibitions may be transgressed to treat such an injury. Therefore, a bone may be set,[1] but a Jewish doctor or technician may not transgress any Torah prohibition to treat the fracture if there is no possibility of infection or danger. In such cases, one should place a temporary cast or splint on the injured limb and postpone molding the permanent cast until after Shabbos.

    If the doctor is a non-Jew, he may mold a permanent cast, since fractures cause severe pain and swelling, which places the individual in the category of a *choleh she'ein bo sakanah*, an ordinary bedridden pa-

---

1 בגמרא מסכת שבת דף קמ״ז ע״ב נאמר: אמר שמואל הלכה מחזירין את השבר בשבת. ע״כ. וכן פסקו הראשונים הרי״ף והרא״ש במקום. וכ״כ הרמב״ם פ״ב מהלכות שבת הלכה י׳ עיי״ש.

tient, or *sakanas eiver*, a person with an endangered limb, and patients in both of these categories may be given all the necessary treatment by a non-Jew.

11. A dislocated bone in any extremity may interfere with its proper functioning in the future.[2] If this is the case, it is considered *sakanas eiver*, an endangered limb.[3] A doctor should be consulted if one is unsure whether there will be permanent damage; he may decide that splinting or bandaging is sufficient until after Shabbos. If the doctor recommends an X-ray for diagnostic purposes, this may be done.[4] The X-ray should be taken by a non-Jew or with a *shinui*, in an unusual manner, to avoid transgression of a Torah prohibition. If a non-Jew is not available and the doctor states that an X-ray is needed immediately, it could be done even by a Jew.[5]

12. If a doctor states that the limb is endangered, and the patient has to be anesthetized while the bone is set, this should be done in a manner that involves only transgression of rabbinical prohibitions, for example, by means of an intramuscular (IM) injection. However, if the patient's life is potentially in danger, such as when a person sustains an open fracture, anesthesia may be administered by any means, even if a Torah transgression is involved.

---

2 שו״ע סי׳ שכ״ח סעיף מ״ז כתב ז״ל: עצם שיצא ממקומו מחזירין אותו ואף שבסעיף ל׳ כתב דמי שנשמטה פרק ידו או רגלו ממקומו לא ישפשפנה הרבה בצונן שזה רפואתו שמשמע שאין לרפאותה בשבת. יש לחלק שבסעיף ל׳ לא נתפרקה לגמרי אלא נקעה במקצת ואילו בסעיף מז׳ איירי בנתפרקה ודעת הרופאים שהוא כסכנת איבר אם לא יחזירה למקומה. לכן שרי להחזירה למקומה. ועוד שפעמים יש בזה גם סכנת נפשות. ועיין במשנה ברורה סי׳ שכ״ח ס״ק קמ״ה שהביא מחלוקת המג״א וספר שולחן עצי שיטים, וסיכם ההלכה בזה״ל: ונראה דגם לדעת המגן אברהם אם הרופא אומר שנפרק בחזקה ויוכל לבוא לידי סכנת איבר שמותר למשוך ולהחזירו למקומו כדרך שעושה בחול עכ״ל.

3 הגדרה זו לסכנת איבר שאם לא יטופל האיבר, יוכל בעתיד להיות מוגבל — זה נחשב לסכנת איבר — עיין בקצות השולחן סי׳ קל״ח בבדי השולחן סס״ק י״ח והובא בדברינו לעיל פרק 28 הערה 5.

4 נשמת אברהם ח״א עמוד ר״ו.

5 בספר נשמת אברהם שם הביא דעת ערוך השולחן סי׳ שכ״ח סעיף ל״ט. דאם רופא אומר שיש בפריקת העצם חשש סכנה דמחללין על פיו, לכן אם יארע ח״ו כזה ידרשו מרופאים ויעשו כדבריהם. ואח״כ הביא מספר שש״כ פל״ג סעיף י״ז שלפעמים יש בזה סכנת נפשות עיי״ש.

Injuries that Are Not Life-Threatening

13. If a person has a sprain or bruising (ecchymosis) that causes extreme pain or weakness, the person is regarded as a *choleh she'ein bo sakanah*, an ordinary bedridden patient, who is allowed to take medicine and painkillers. Similarly, the sprain may be dressed as needed. However, ointments should not be smeared on the injured site (see chapter 26, "Medication for a *Choleh She'ein Bo Sakanah*," paragraph 29, on the use of ointment on Shabbos).

Also, compresses may be placed on the affected area, but the compresses should be prepared before Shabbos. If this is not possible, the compresses should be placed with a *shinui*, in an unusual manner; for example, gauze should be placed on the site and then the water added. If this can't be done, it is possible to be lenient and allow the preparation of compresses. However, care should be taken not to wring out the compress because of the prohibition of *melabein*, cleaning.[6]

Minor Injuries

14. If one has a sprain that does not cause extreme pain, it is considered a minor injury (*michush*). He may wrap it in an Ace bandage to give it extra support or tie it in a sling (using a bow knot).[7]

Treatments and Procedures

15. When visual diagnosis is inconclusive, one may take an X-ray to ascertain the extent and type of fracture.[8]

16. Even though an X-ray may be taken by a Jew in life-endangering situ-

---

6 נשמת אברהם ח״א עמוד ר״ו. ופשוט דאם חש בכאב חזק עד שנחלש כל הגוף חשיב כחולה שאין בו סכנה.

7 שש״כ פל״ח סעיף ל״ה, מהא דסימן שכ״ח במ״ב ס״ק ק״ל ובמ״ב סימן ש״א ס״ק קפ״ב. ובנשמת אברהם ח״א ע׳ קלה׳. והטעם, שאין עושים דברים אלו ע״י סממנים ואין לחוש בזה לגזירת שחיקת סמנים, ולכן מותר. כ״כ בשם הגרש״ז אויערבאך שליט״א. אולם אם חש בכאב חזק דינו כחולה שאין בו סכנה.

8 כתב בשו״ת באר משה ח״ז בקונטרס אלעקטרי ח״ב סימן נ׳, ״עשיית עקסרי (רנטגן) לשבירת יד או רגל בשבת ע״י נכרי מותר, וע״י ישראל אסור. ובמקום שבירת יד או רגל ע״י מכונית, ודאי הוי חשש סכנה ושרי לעשייתו אף ע״י ישראל״. ובשו״ת ציץ אליעזר ח״ד סימן כ״ז כתב דאם האבחנה אינה מחייבת צילום וניתן לדחותו לאחר השבת אין לבצע צילום בשבת. (אולם לא דיבר אם אחרת שרי או לא). וע״ע בזה בשו״ת מנחת יצחק ח״ג סי׳ כ׳.

ations, in the case of a fracture in an extremity, if the injury is in the category of *sakanas eiver*, danger to a limb, then the X-ray should be taken by a non-Jew. If a non-Jew is not available, it may be taken by a Jew provided that it is done with a *shinui*, in an unusual manner.[9]

It should be noted that this applies only to a fracture in the extremities. If the fracture is in the rib cage, skull, or spine, it is considered a life-threatening situation, and a Jew may take the X-ray. Likewise, if the leg or arm fracture may cause ruptured blood vessels or infection or it is a compound fracture, a Jew may take the X-ray in the usual manner.

17. Molding a cast involves transgressing the Torah prohibition of *lash*, kneading, and should be done by a non-Jew. If a non-Jew is not available, the patient should remain under supervision, and a temporary splint should be used. If this is not advisable then the cast may be molded with a *shinui*, in an unusual manner, for example, by first applying the plaster material on the limb and then wetting it.

18. An elastic bandage (Ace bandage) may be placed on a sprained hand or leg. This may be done even if the level of pain does not accord him the status of a *choleh she'ein bo sakanah*, an ordinary bedridden patient. The use of an elastic bandage for easing pain is not regarded as a violation of the prohibition against taking medication.[10]

Orthopedic Equipment

19. In general, when it comes to medical treatment, mechanical devices designed for a specific purpose, even for a medical one, are permitted on Shabbos. The reasoning was explained above, in chapter 2 ("The Ordinance against Preparing Medicine") — anything that cannot be associated with the grinding of medications does not come under the category of healing on Shabbos. Therefore, the use of crutches, supports, orthopedic braces, and orthotics is permitted.

---

9 כיון שבשבר יש סכנת איבר יש להקל — במקום שאין נכרי — לעשות הצילום ע״י ישראל אך ישתדל לעשות בשינוי בכל מה שניתן לשנות. כן יש לבאר ע״פ שיטת הרמב״ן שבסכנת איבר שרי מלאכה מדאורייתא ע״י שינוי כדין גונח שיונק חלב (כתובות ס׳ ע״א) וכנ״ל. אופן השינויים והפעלת הרנטגן יבואר במערכת מכשירים וטיפולים רפואיים בשבת.

10 נשמת אברהם ח״א עמוד ר״ו.

20. Nonetheless, one has to check if there are other halachic problems involved. For example, assembling the parts of the equipment may constitute *boneh*, building. Tying on straps or bandages might involve the *melachah* of *kosher*, tying. The use of electronic devices and pneumatic mechanisms that operate artificial limbs and prostheses may involve many forbidden actions.

21. One is allowed to use Velcro on Shabbos. This is not considered "gluing leather" that the *Shulchan Aruch* forbade (*Orach Chaim* 340:14). (Similarly, one may use Velcro on sandals or shoes without hesitation.)

22. It is advisable to make all the adjustments of trusses and similar devices, including the various connections, before Shabbos and then to only fasten them on the body on Shabbos.

23. Such equipment includes a Taylor belt, Boston brace, Milwaukee brace, CASH orthosis, Jewett orthosis, Xanu brace, corsets, body supports, ankle supports, knee supports, hernia straps, Thomas equipment for prostheses, Thomas equipment for wrist and fingers, elbow pads and cuffs, and other similar equipment.[11]

Slings and Neck Braces

24. Some shoulder fractures do not have a specific treatment other than resting the arm in a sling. This may also be the recommended procedure for a broken arm. One can put on a sling on Shabbos, but the adjustments should be made prior to Shabbos. It is permissible to improvise and use a scarf or a towel as a sling.[12] A double knot may not be tied; rather, one should tie a nonpermanent knot (like that used for tying a tie) or a safety pin.

25. Similarly, one is allowed to put on a neck brace on Shabbos to alleviate pain.

26. One is also allowed to wear elastic or support socks on Shabbos for both the entire leg or a part of it.

---

11 עיין בשו״ת באר משה ח״א סי׳ י״ח.

12 עיין בשו״ת באר משה ח״א סי׳ י״ז אות ה׳.

Prosthesis for Hands and Legs

27. One may attach and detach a foot prosthesis on Shabbos and walk with it even in a public domain, provided that it is mechanically operated.[13] If the equipment is battery operated, it may not be worn on Shabbos.

28. Therefore, a prosthesis below the elbow that is electronically operated may not be used on Shabbos. Only if the entire system is purely mechanical may it be used, attached, or removed on Shabbos.

29. Similarly, modular prostheses for above-the-knee amputations with a mechanical mechanism, but with hinges and electronic controls, cannot be used on Shabbos.

30. One is allowed to enter and walk in a public domain with crutches and medical equipment that are attached to the body.[14]

Orthopedic Conditions in Children

In this section we will clarify some common orthopedic problems associated with babies:

a. CHD — congenital hip dysplasia (dislocation)
b. Congenital club foot
c. Scoliosis (curvature of the spine)

Congenital Hip Dysplasia

31. CHD, when the hip joint does not meet the femur in the proper place, is a congenital hip disorder with various degrees of severity. This may cause limping and other problems. Symptoms include

    a. limited abduction in one or both sides or clicking sound, and
    b. asymmetry in the skin folds.

    The following treatment is usually recommended:

    a. The use of pelvic straps or abduction pillow.

---

13 עיין בשו״ת באר משה ח״א סי׳ י״ז.
14 עיין שש״כ פרק י״ח סעיף כ.

b. In some circumstances, if the straps or pillow don't help, a tension cast is used.

c. In a more severe case, or if treatment is unsuccessful or in the case of a delayed diagnosis, an operation is performed to form a socket.

32. Double diapering treatment is permitted on Shabbos.

33. Similarly, the pelvic straps may be placed on the baby's body provided that the equipment is prepared and adjusted before Shabbos. This is permitted because fastening itself is by means of Velcro strips.

34. Taking pelvic X-rays or ultrasounds are not an emergency in this case and are not permitted on Shabbos or *yom tov*.

35. Likewise, there is usually no urgency to make or remove casts; thus, this activity is prohibited both on Shabbos and *yom tov*[15] unless they are too tight and endanger the limbs.

Club Foot

36. There are several foot deformities that occur in babies:

a. Varus — feet turned inward

b. Valgus — feet turned outward

c. Equinus (plantarflexion) — feet turned upward

d. Calcaneus or calcaneal valgus (dorsiflexion) — feet turned downward

e. Forefoot adductus (FFA) — when the forefront of the foot turns inward

The following treatment is usually recommended:

a. In general, depending on the child's age, either a cast or special shoes are indicated.

b. In certain cases, massage during bathing or after diapering is recommended to cause the sole of the foot to turn to the other side.

---

15 וכ״כ בנשמת אברהם ח״א סי׳ ש״ל ס״ק כ״ב.

37. There is no urgency to take X-rays or to mold casts on Shabbos for such cases.

38. Special shoes may be put on and worn on Shabbos.

39. Likewise, one may massage after diapering to cause the sole of the foot to turn to the other side. This does not involve drugs or medications and thus is not included in the rabbinical decree against healing on Shabbos.

Scoliosis

40. Scoliosis is a disease that manifests in children from the age of twelve to sixteen. The standard treatment for scoliosis of the spine is:
    a. Milwaukee brace.
    b. Alexander's method for strengthening muscles.
    c. Electrical stimulation usually combined with a Milwaukee brace, which causes constant contracture and relaxation of the muscles, strengthening the spinal muscles. This instrument is similar to the heart pacemaker. It emits electrical impulses to the spine and can be operated even at night when the child is sleeping.
    d. Surgical method — fixation by rods.

41. Use of the Milwaukee brace is permitted on Shabbos.

42. Alexander exercise is permissible on Shabbos because it is done daily and doesn't cause sweating. (According to medical opinion, daily treatment is not obligatory, and Shabbos exercise may be skipped.)

43. Electrical stimulation treatment that is required daily is permitted on Shabbos if the equipment runs continuously. It may be attached before Shabbos, provided that no electrical adjustments or connections or disconnections are made on Shabbos. If the equipment needs to operate only for a short time, which involves turning the electricity on and off, it may not be used on Shabbos. It should be noted that according to medical opinion, daily treatment is not obligatory, and one may forgo use of the equipment for twenty-four hours.

Chapter 38
Wounds and Dressings

In this chapter, the following topics will be clarified:

a. The treatment of cuts and wounds
b. Bandaging, including the use of cotton and band-aids
c. Swelling
d. Varicose veins
e. The penetration of a foreign object through the skin

1. The Talmud states that there are several kinds injuries for which Shabbos may be desecrated. They include:

   a. a wound on the dorsal part of the hand or foot;
   b. a deep cut or wound inflicted by a knife or other metal instrument;
   c. animal bites or stings (see chapter 36, "Bites and Stings").

A Wound on the Dorsal Part of the Hand or Foot

2. This includes a wound (that is, an injury, fracture, or inflammation)[1] that is on the dorsal part of the foot or hand (the side where the hair

---

1 כמו שביארו הפוסקים, הובאו לעיל בפרק 7 בביאור דין מכה של חלל.

grows). The back of the hand is the part of the hand from the knuckles (metacarpalphalangeal joints) to the wrist joint. The back of the foot is the part of the foot from the toe joints (metatarsophalangeal joints) until the ankle.[2]

3. If necessary, Shabbos may be desecrated to treat these wounds even if they were not caused by a metal implement. This is because these wounds are considered internal injuries and, if necessary, one may desecrate Shabbos to treat them.[3]

   The reason they are considered life-threatening is that our Sages regarded these as sensitive areas, and they felt that injuries to these places were likely to be dangerous. Even though medical experts today do not regard such wounds as dangerous, this does not warrant disregarding their potential life-threatening nature, and the doubt that still exists permits desecration of Shabbos to treat these wounds. However, pain alone in these areas does not warrant Shabbos desecration.

Injury Caused by a Metal Implement

4. One may desecrate Shabbos as needed for a wound (injury, fracture, or inflammation) caused by a metal implement, even an external one and even parts of the body other than the back of the hand or foot.[4]

5. If compresses are needed to reduce swelling, cold compresses may be prepared on Shabbos. Likewise, if bandaging is necessary, this may be done. Ointment may be applied to the wound and gauze placed as needed.

6. Similarly, a deep cut by a knife or metal instrument, especially if it was rusted (such as a rusty nail), is considered life-threatening, and Shabbos may be desecrated as needed to treat it.

7. When tetanus is suspected, a tetanus shot may be administered on Shabbos. The injured person should be brought to a first-aid station or a hospital with his vaccination records. However, if the injury occurred

---

2 כך פירש בערוך השולחן סימן שכ״ח סעיף כ״ה.

3 שו״ע סימן שכ״ח סעיף ו׳.

4 שו״ע שם סעיף ז׳, ובמ״ב ס״ק י״ח.

close to the end of Shabbos, the shot may be delayed for several hours until Shabbos ends. (The injury, however, should be treated immediately, and quick action in this matter is commendable.)[5]

8. If concern exists that a fracture was caused by a blow from a metal implement, it is permitted to get an X-ray taken, with all that this involves (see chapter 37, "Injuries, Fractures, and Dislocations"), since our Sages regarded a blow by a metal object as life-threatening.[6] It is also permissible to make a cast if a doctor recommends it.

9. A shallow cut caused by a metal object, even coupled with slight bleeding, does not warrant the desecration of Shabbos. This is a common occurrence and can be alleviated by rinsing the site with cold water until the bleeding stops.[7]

Types of Wounds

10. A wound is defined as a break in the tissue or consecutive break in the skin or mucous membrane. The different types of wounds, recommended treatments, and what is permissible on Shabbos are described below.

Scrapes

11. Scrapes are caused by abrasion of the skin or mucous membranes. This type of wound is susceptible to infection. Treatment includes washing the wound in water or antiseptic liquid, removing foreign objects, and applying a sterile dressing. In the case of a face wound, it is usually sufficient to clean and disinfect the affected area. One should also check

---

5 כל זה כתב בספר נשמת אברהם ח״א סי׳ שכ״ח אות כ״א בשם שש״כ.

6 על פי הגמרא במסכת ע״ז דף כ״ח ע״א אמר שמואל האי פדעתא וכו׳. ועיין עוד במסכת סנהדרין דף ע״ו ע״ב אמר שמואל מפני מה לא נאמרה יד בברזל, שהברזל ממית בכל שהיא, ע״ש.

7 כ״כ בקצות השולחן והביאו בנשמת אברהם שם. ובספר ליקוטי הלכות על הלכות רפואה להגאון רבי שבתי שלמה ויגדער שליט״א (עמוד ע״א) הביא בעניין זה מחלוקת האחרונים שהובאה בהגהות הגרעק״א, שהתבואות שור (הלכות טרפות סי׳ מד אות ד׳, הביאו בכפה״ח אות ל״ד) משמע מדבריו דאף חתך קל הוי בכלל סכנה ואילו הכרתי ופלטי פליג עליה דאינו כן, והרב ליקוטי הלכות הנ״ל הקשה על התבואות שור מגמ׳ ברכות דף ח: דאמר רבא שלא לחתוך בשר על גב היד, א״ד משום סכנה א״ד משום קלקול סעודה. ופרש״י משום קלקול סעודה, היכא דנחתך בנחת וליכא סכנה — יש משום קלקול סעודה ע״כ. הרי לך בפירוש דלא כהתבואות שור. עיי״ש.

the injured person's immunization record to see if a tetanus shot is necessary.

12. All of these actions, including cleansing and prevention of infection, may be carried out on Shabbos. An antiseptic, such as iodine or yellow powder, may be applied to the wound to prevent infection or to stop the bleeding. These actions are not included in the prohibition of taking medicine on Shabbos.[8] However, an antibiotic preparation or a medication that causes the wound to close or promotes healing may not be administered on Shabbos.[9] This is because the wound is classified as a tolerable discomfort (*michush*), and thus the rabbinical prohibition of grinding medicine applies. This prohibition, however, does not apply to a person regarded as a *choleh she'ein bo sakanah*, an ordinary bedridden patient, or a child, who is also considered a *choleh she'ein bo sakanah*.[10]

Cuts

13. A cut is characterized by bleeding and is less prone to subsequent infection, provided that there is no evidence of significant tissue damage or penetration by foreign objects. (One should check that there is no damage to ligaments, blood vessels, or other tissues.)

 Treatment involves cleaning the cut with an antiseptic solution such as iodine. If the wound is fresh, less than eight hours old, and it

---

ועי״ע בילקוט יוסף שבת ד׳ עמוד רכ״ב שהאריך בזה ומסקנתו כדברינו, וסיים שם בזה״ל: ברור שאין לחלל שבת על כל שריטה הנעשית בסכין, ובכל דבר שאין רצים על זה לרופא בימי החול אין לחלל שבת על מכה זו עיי״ש.

8 בשו״ע סי׳ שכ״ח סעיף כ״ט כתב וז״ל: מי שניגפה ידו או רגלו צומתה ביין כדי להעמיד הדם אבל לא בחומץ מפני שהוא חזק ויש בו משום רפואה, ואם הוא מעונג אף היין לו כמו החומץ ואסור עכ״ל. מבואר מדברי השו״ע שכל שהמטרה היא הפסקת הדם, ניקיון או שמירה מפני זיהומים — אין זה בכלל רפואה ומותר, אולם תכשיר המרפא וגורם לאיחוי מהיר של המכה — אסור. יצוין שלהלן יבואר דהיינו בפצע המוגדר כמחושים בעלמא דלא שרי ביה רפואה בשבת.

9 עיין בשו״ת באר משה ח״ו סי׳ ל״ח. ועי״ע בילקוט יוסף שבת ד׳ עמ׳ קע״ו. ואולם בשו״ת אור לציון ח״ב סימן ל״ו שאלה ז׳ כתב לחלק בין אבקה ליוד וז״ל: ״אבקה לעצירת הדם מותר ליתנה על פצע בשבת, אך יוד אין לשים אלא לילד או לחולה שנפל למשכב, או בפצע הנמצא במקום פנימי כגון מן השיניים ולפנים״ עכ״ל. וטעמו דלא שרי אלא למניעת זיהום אבל יוד כיון שמרפא ג״כ לא שרי אלא לקטן או לחולה.

10 עיין לעיל פרק 20 סעיף 5 הערה 8 עד איזה גיל נחשב הקטן לחולה שאין בו סכנה.

is not infected, it is closed by sutures, staples, or adhesive under a local anesthetic. A wound of over eight hours should be cleansed and kept open unless on the face or in a younger patient — these sometimes can be closed within twenty-four hours. Secondary closure may be done during the next several days.

14. Treatment on Shabbos involves several considerations:

    a. If the wound is on the back of the foot or hand, or if it was caused by a metal instrument, Shabbos may be desecrated to treat it, as mentioned previously (paragraphs 3 and 4).[11] It is permissible, if needed, to suture the patient under anesthesia.[12]

    b. As mentioned above, in the case of injury to the back of the hand or foot, or injury caused by a metal implement, Shabbos may be desecrated for medical reasons; however, it is forbidden to desecrate Shabbos for cosmetic reasons, such as to prevent scarring (see also note 12). If one requires sutures to prevent scarring, this should be delayed until after Shabbos, or a non-Jewish doctor should be employed.[13]

---

11 כמבואר בבית יוסף בסימן שכ״ח סעיף כ״ט עיי״ש.

12 בספר נשמת אברהם ח״ד חאו״ח סי׳ ש״מ עמ׳ ס״ב דן בארוכה בענין הטיפול בחתכים בשבת, אצטט מה שנוגע לענייננו. חתך עמוק שהפסיק לדמם צריך בכל זאת סגירה כדי למנוע זיהום. וקיימות כמה אפשרויות לסגירת החתך; א׳ ע״י פלסטר רגיל. ב׳ ע״י פרפר. ג׳ ע״י מהדקים. ד׳ ע״י תפירה. ה׳ ע״י נוזל מדביק. מבחינה רפואית הדרך הטובה ביותר למנוע זיהום היא ע״י הידוק טוב של שפת החתך, הן ע״י תפירה והן ע״י מהדקים מתכתיים. סגירה זו גם נותנת את התוצאה הטובה ביותר מבחינת הצלקת. ואצטט בזה דברי הגאון רש״ז אויערבאך זצ״ל השייך לענינינו. ״אדם שנפצע בשבת וזקוק לתפירת הפצע עקב הסכנה ומספיקים חמישה תפרים כדי שיצא מכלל סכנה אך אז תהיה צלקת לא יפה, ולעומת זאת, אם יתפרו שבעה תפרים תיראה הצלקת יפה יותר.״ וכתב וז״ל: לכאורה אין להוסיף תפירות לשם נוי ואין הבדל בין תפירה מעיקרא כשאין סכנה כלל, ובין הוספת תפירות לשם נוי ששניהם אסורים בשבת, אך עדיין איכא למידן טובא. ויותר נראה לי דכמו במילה כל זמן שלא פירש, שפיר מלין גם בשבת וחוזרין גם על ציצין שאין מעכבין את המילה משום טעמא דהתנאה לפניו במצוות, כך גם כאן כמו שהשבת נדחית מפני הצלה מסכנה כך מותר גם לגמור את אשר החל ולהציל את האדם ממום אשר יתבייש ויצטער מזה כל ימיו. וכמו שזה נחשב שם כגמר מילה כך גם כאן היינו גמר הצלת האדם ולא מסתבר לחלק בין הותרה לדחויה. ונוסף לזה גם ראיתי שרבים סוברים דליכא כלל איסור תורה בתפירה שבגוף האדם, אף שלענ״ד כן צריכים לחוש לזה משום דאף אם מוציאים אח״כ את חוטי התפירה אפ״ה התפירה חשיב של קיימא, מ״מ גמר הצלה שאני. ואפשר שגם זה תלוי במה שכתב המגיד משנה (שבת פ״ב ה״ה) דכל מה שרגילים לעשות לחולה שיש בו סכנה בחול עושים גם בשבת אעפ״י שאין סכנה במניעת הדבר ההוא. עכ״ל הגרש״ז אויערבאך זצ״ל.

13 בספר נשמת אברהם הנ״ל הביא את הנדון דלהלן: בחורה שיש לה חתך עמוק בפנים ואין בו כל

c. If the wound is not on the back of the foot or hand or is not caused by a metal instrument, an antiseptic solution may be used to clean the wound, but the wound may not be sutured, glued, or even joined together with a butterfly bandage or band-aid. If it is suspected that a tendon or similar was torn, one may be lenient concerning suturing, gluing together, or joining the two sides of the wound. Otherwise all of these actions are forbidden.[14]

Lacerations

15. A laceration is characterized by jagged edges and, at times, massive bleeding. It may be caused by falling on sharp objects, shrapnel, or dull-object impact. Complications of these wounds typically include hemorrhage, the presence of foreign objects, and adjacent tissue damage. These factors are conducive to rapid onset of infection.

    Treatment includes disinfection and surgical debridement of the wound. It is also possible to do primary closure of the wound if one is sure that there is no internal infection.

16. Treatment of these wounds on Shabbos are subject to the same guidelines laid out in paragraph 14 above.

סכנה, אך עלולה להישאר עם צלקת לא יפה שתקשה עליה להשתדך וזה עלול לגרום לדיכאון נפשי רציני בעתיד. האם מותר לתפור בכה״ג או לא? כתב הגרש״ז אויערבאך זצ״ל שאין לעבור על איסור תורה בשבת משום זה, רק מותר לבקש מרופא נכרי שיתפור את הפצע. עכ״ל. ונראה שיש לזה דמיון קצת לסכנת אבר.

14 נחלקו פוסקי ומאורי דורינו שליט״א אי שרי בשבת להצמיד שני חלקי עור של האדם שנחלקו מחמת פציעה או חתך, האם יש בהידוק והצמדת שני חלקי העור איסור משום תופר, או שאין דין תופר באדם. בספר נשמת אברהם ח״ד סי׳ ש״מ אות ב׳, הביא מספר שמירת שבת כהלכתה (פל״ה הערה ס״ב) ומספר תורת היולדת (פרק ל״ד הערה ל״ח) בשם הגאון רבי יחזקאל אברמסקי זצ״ל שאין איסור תורה של תפירה באדם, ע״כ. ובשם הגרש״ז אויערבאך שליט״א כתב שיש חשש של איסור מדאורייתא של תפירה בכל הטיפולים שמטרתם לחבר את שתי שפות החתך. וכ״כ בשם הגאון רי״ש אלישיב שליט״א שיש בכל תפירה או הדבקת החתך ע״י פרפר או פלסטר וכו׳ ספק איסור מדאורייתא ואין היתר לעשותם אלא במצב של פיקוח נפש, עיי״ש באורך. אח״ז מצאתי בשו״ת ״אור לציון״ למרן הגאון רבי בן ציון אבא שאול שליט״א בח״ב פרק לו שאלה טו שנשאל בדבר זה והשיב בזה״ל: (בביאורים) לשים פלסטר על פצע או חתך מותר ואין בזה משום איסור תופר, שהרי תפירת עראי מותרת בשבת , וכמש״כ בב״י בסימן ש״ז, וכן הביאו הרמ״א שם סעיף ג׳ וכו׳ ועוד שבגוף האדם לא שייך תופר, שאין דרך תפירה בכך (אא״כ תופר ממש את העור) עכ״ל.

Wounds Caused by Penetration of a Foreign Object

17. A puncture wound inflicted by a knife, nail, or any other sharp instrument serves as an ideal site for the development of infection because bacteria are injected deep into the wound. Treatment may include disinfection, extraction of the instrument that inflicted the wound, and bandaging without closure and suturing.

18. This treatment (in paragraph 17) is permitted on Shabbos. However, if a danger of infection exists and a tetanus shot is needed, it is permitted to administer this injection on Shabbos (see chapter 26, "Medication for a *Choleh She'ein Bo Sakanah*," paragraph 13).

Bandages and Medicinal Preparations

19. It is permitted to bandage a wound on Shabbos or to replace a bandage, but without applying an ointment. It is also permitted to tear the paper wrapping of the bandage, if care is taken not to tear any letters — tearing between two letters of a word is permitted. (For the laws that apply specifically to band-aids, see paragraphs 30–32.)

20. It is prohibited to cut a bandage that is too long or to cut it lengthwise to allow tying the ends.

21. The bandage should be tied in a loop or secured with a safety pin or by means of a special bandage clamp. If the bandage is changed daily, it may be tied in an ordinary double knot.

Adhesive Tape

22. It is prohibited to cut adhesive tape into pieces or to apply it to the ends of the bandage in order to fasten it. This prohibition applies even if one end of the adhesive tape is stuck to the skin. However, this may be done if absolutely necessary.

    The reason for this prohibition is that the adhesive tape is removed from the skin rather than from the bandage. This means that the tape will remain attached to the gauze, which is considered a permanent act of *tofer*, sewing. This is similar to tying the band of a *lulav*, which has the status of a permanent knot.

23. It is permitted to use a gauze-coated adhesive tape (such as elastoplast, a type of sticky elastic bandage) to dress a wound, but the gauze must be removed before Shabbos. However, if the gauze is removed before Shabbos and then reapplied, it can be removed on Shabbos if necessary.

24. Adhesive tape used to tighten a dressing should not be removed on Shabbos. However, if it causes the patient discomfort, it may be removed in a destructive manner, even with scissors.

Preparing Bandages before Shabbos

25. As mentioned above (paragraph 20), it is prohibited to shorten a too large bandage or to incise it lengthwise to allow tying the ends. Instead, one should use the entire bandage in dressing the wound. It is similarly prohibited to cut or tear adhesive tape into pieces.

26. Given this, one must prepare before Shabbos all the dressings needed for Shabbos and to cut adhesive tape into the various lengths that may be needed.

27. One should also prepare all the bandages needed for dressing a circumcision wound. If no prepared bandages are available, it is prohibited to carry out the circumcision with the intention of cutting up the bandages thereafter, and the circumcision must be postponed to the next day. However, if one performed the circumcision already and only thereafter found out that the bandages were not prepared, one is allowed to do whatever is necessary, even on Shabbos, because it is regarded as *pikuach nefesh,* a life-threatening situation for the child.[15]

28. Note that in cases of danger (*pikuach nefesh)*, the above limitations do not apply, and it is permitted to do everything necessary on Shabbos without any delay.

Net Bandages (Kerlix)

29. It is permitted to use net bandages to protect a wound dressing.

---

15 נשמת אברהם ח״א עמ׳ רל״ט.

However, it is not permitted to cut these bandages on Shabbos to the required length. These should be prepared before Shabbos in the various lengths that may be needed.

Band-Aids

30. It is permitted to place a band-aid on a wound, whether to protect the wound from abrasion or infection.

31. The band-aid should be unwrapped by asking a minor to tear it open,[16] since this usually involves tearing letters.

32. The band-aid should be put on a finger diagonally so that it will adhere to the finger rather than to the other side of the band-aid.[17]

Cotton

33. The use of cotton on Shabbos involves a number of prohibitions:

    a. Cutting the cotton into pieces.

    b. Immersing the cotton in liquid and wringing it out (squeezing). (The coloring of the cotton by iodine or blood is not prohibited because this is regarded as soiling.[18])

    c. Twisting the cotton into a wick.

34. It is preferable to avoid cutting cotton into pieces on Shabbos. This is because some authorities regard it as the *melachah* of tearing. For this reason, cotton should be cut up before Shabbos into pieces suitable for the expected use.[19]

35. It is prohibited to immerse cotton or lignin (wood wool) in hydrogen peroxide, alcohol, iodine, and other antiseptics in order to clean a wound on Shabbos or to disinfect the skin before an injection, since this involves squeezing the excess liquid from the cotton. One who

---

16 שו״ת באר משה חלק א׳ סימן ל״ו.

17 שו״ת באר משה חלק ב׳ סימן כ״ט.

18 שו״ע הרב מובא בנשמת אברהם ח״א ק״ט.

19 מנחת יצחק ח״ד סי׳ מ״ה אות ב׳. ובשש״כ פרק ל״ה הלכה י״ט כתב וז״ל: ורצוי להימנע מקריעת צמר גפן בשבת. וע״ע בשו״ת ציץ אליעזר ח״ח סי׳ ט״ו פרק י״ד סוס״ק י״א.

does so transgresses the prohibitions of *dash* and *melabein*.

This prohibition applies also when using forceps to apply the antiseptic with cotton. Even though one avoids direct contact with the cotton, the absorbed liquid is nevertheless squeezed out of the material during the procedure.

36. There are two alternatives for disinfection on Shabbos:

    a. using synthetic materials, such as a brush with synthetic bristles, and
    b. dribbling the fluid by means of a dropper onto the site and then wiping it with cotton. Lignin (wood wool) is preferable in this case to cotton.

37. It should be noted that all this applies when there is time and the action can be carried out without difficulty. However, if the time is short and the patient's life is in danger, the alternative means of disinfection should be disregarded. It is permitted then to cut cotton and to dip it in the antiseptic, in the usual manner, without any changes.[20]

38. It is prohibited to twist cotton wool into a wick shape on Shabbos or *yom tov* in order to clean the ears, because this is regarded as making a utensil. However, it is permitted to stick a cotton ball in the ear, because this does not involve creating a utensil.[21]

Swelling

39. Swelling may be caused by a number of factors:

    a. An external injury
    b. Wind or cold
    c. An internal illness or other internal factor

Each type of swelling should be treated on Shabbos according to its source.

---

20 עיין ציץ אליעזר ח״ח סי׳ י״ז אות ל״ג.

21 עיין בשער הציון תקי״ד ס״ק נ״ב.

Swelling Caused by an Injury

40. There is a distinction made between swelling from an injury caused by a metal object, which carries the severity of a "metal-caused wound," and those brought about by other types of injuries.

41. A prevalent practice in treating a person with swelling on the forehead caused by a fall is to place ice on the swollen area in order to reduce the swelling. On Shabbos, this can be done by filling a bottle with ice and placing it on the swollen area.[22]

42. Similarly, if a child fell on his head and it swelled up, it is permissible to compress the swelling with a metal object, such as a spoon or knife.[23] (Doctors no longer recommend this treatment.)

43. If it is suspected that a foot or another part of the body is swollen due to a fracture caused by a fall from a high place, then the injury should be treated as explained above in chapter 37, "Injuries, Fractures, and Dislocations." Otherwise, swelling caused by injury after a fall should be treated, as mentioned in paragraph 41 above, by cold compresses or a bottle filled with ice. Alternatively, pieces of ice may be put into a plastic bag, which should then be wrapped with a towel or another wrap. One should not wet a piece of cloth in order to use it as a compress.[24]

Swelling Caused by Wind or Cold

44. If one's cheek swelled up due to the wind or cold, it can be treated by rinsing the face with wine or warm water that was not heated on Shabbos. (Regarding the use of compresses, see note 24.)

---

22 שו״ת באר משה ח״א סי׳ ל״ג אות י״ח.

23 שו״ת באר משה ח״א סי׳ ל״ג אות י״ד.

24 בכף החיים סי׳ שכ״א אות ה׳ כתב וז״ל: מי שיש לו נפח על אחת מפניו שזה יקרה מחמת קרירות ותרופתו שמטבילין מטלית בתוך השכר ונותנין אותו על הנפח ויתחמם ויתרפא, אם מותר לעשות כן בשבת באופן שלא יבוא לידי סחיטה שהיינו שיהיו נזהרין שלא לשרות המטלית בשכר רק ישפשפו הנפח בשכר היטב ואח״כ ישימו עליו המטלית יבש לשמור חומו. מי נימא דשרי דכיון דליכא סם לא שייכא גזירת שחיקת סממנים, או דילמא כל רפואה נאסרה הגם דלא שייך ביה שחיקה, שמא יעשה רפואה אחרת דשייך בה שחיקה. עיין בפתח הדביר מה דשקל וטרי בהאי עניניא ודעתו להתיר דווקא בדאיכא כל כך צערא דבמקום צערא לא גזור עיי״ש. עכ״ל הכפה״ח.

45. It was once common practice to treat swelling of the hand by bleeding it, which can be done on Shabbos by a non-Jew.[25] Today this practice is obsolete. However, it may happen that a hand may swell because of an infection, which necessitates draining the pus. In this case, if the pus and the infected blood are not drained, the infection may spread, and blood poisoning may occur. This would then be considered an internal wound, which places the patient in the category of *choleh sheyeish bo sakanah*, and therefore it would be permissible even for a Jew to provide treatment.

Swelling Caused by an Internal Factor

46. Swelling may also be caused by an internal factor, such as an internal illness or infection (see paragraph 47 for examples). Such cases require medical consultation and are classified as an internal wound. When such a condition is manifest on Shabbos, and the cause of the swelling is unknown, a doctor should be consulted immediately because the patient's life may be in danger. The matter should be postponed for after Shabbos only if it is not urgent. If treatment cannot be postponed, one should follow the doctor's instructions, even if it involves Shabbos desecration.

47. Examples of swelling caused by an internal factor:

    a. A swollen and red foot may be caused by erysipelas or cellulitis (see chapter 39, "Skin Diseases").

    b. Swollen lymph glands, such as tonsils, or swelling below the bottom jaw are indicative of an infectious disease or a childhood illness.

    c. Swelling of glands near the groin may be caused by various infectious diseases; at times, this may be caused by a hernia.

    In all of these cases, one should consult a doctor to determine that there is no danger to life.

---

25 כפה״ח שם אות קע״ג.

Varicose Veins

48. Varicose veins (swollen veins) is a form of angiopathy and is prevalent primarily in lower limbs. There are several causes of varicose veins, from vascular disease to pregnancy. It manifests itself in local widening of the veins and accumulation of a large quantity of blood. Initially, it appears as blue blotches with soft puffiness. Varicose veins can develop into an inflammation (phlebitis), which manifests itself in local reddening, elevated temperature, sensitivity, and swelling, and danger exists that a clot may form in the veins.

The best way to treat swollen veins is by preventing their appearance — through physical activity, strengthening of the leg muscles, and avoidance of prolonged standing or sitting. Once swollen veins have appeared, it is recommended that one wear elastic stockings that support the walls of the weakened vein. These should be put on in the morning before getting out of bed to prevent veins from filling with blood. Elastic stockings specially designed for the treatment of swollen veins may be worn on Shabbos.[26]

Penetration of a Foreign Object

49. Various foreign objects may penetrate the skin in the course of walking or play. Some of these may be dangerous, whereas others may be removed easily without side effects. These include a thorn or piece of broken glass, a rusted nail, and a broken needle or splinter which can be absorbed into the body.

50. Any action which is certain to cause bleeding, such as scratching sensitive areas of the body, is prohibited on Shabbos.[27] Therefore, if a thorn or a piece of broken glass penetrated the skin, care must be taken not to cause bleeding while removing it. The thorn or glass may be removed with a needle.

---

26 דאין טפול זה נעשה ע״י תרופות — לא שייך בזה גזירת שחיקת סממנים כמבואר לעיל בפרק 2 וע״ע לעיל פרק 37 סעיף 26.

27 מ״ב סי׳ שכ״ח ס״ק פ״ח, ואף דהוא מקלקל — מ״מ אסור הוא לכו״ע ואף דבשחין התירו איסור דרבנן משום צערה הכא כיון שאפשר להוציא הקוץ בלי להוציא דם, אין לעבור איסורה בכדי.

51. However, even if there is no way to avoid bleeding, the thorn or glass may still be removed.

52. It is permitted to pierce a pus-filled wound, boil, or abscess in order to remove the pus,[28] even if the pus is mixed with blood. This is because this is not regarded as inflicting a wound, since the accumulated blood is already out of circulation.[29] However, care should taken not to squeeze the wound in order to cause additional bleeding.

53. In the case of penetration of a rusty nail or a deep scratch inflicted by a rusty iron implement, there exists the strong possibility of infection. Even though small children are usually vaccinated against tetanus, they are not always immune to this kind of infection. For example, if a long time elapsed after the shot, or if not all the shots in the series were administered, the effectiveness of the injection may have decreased. Therefore, the vaccination record should be checked to see when was the last tetanus shot. A doctor should then determine, on the basis of the type of wound and expected protection of the last administered vaccine, whether a booster can be delayed or whether it should be administered on Shabbos. In any case, it is permitted to treat the wound and to apply antiseptic or an antibiotic preparation.

54. A foreign object that has penetrated beneath the skin may cause a serious infection. The object should be removed, and the penetrated area should be cleansed to avoid infection. However, even the smallest foreign object that enters a vein poses a definite danger. Hence, if the possibility exists that this is what has occurred, a doctor should be consulted immediately.

---

28 שו״ע סי׳ שכ״ח סעיף כז.

29 במ״ב שם ס״ק פ״ט.

Chapter 39
Skin Diseases

A Medical Review

The skin is a cellular organ that performs a number of functions:

a. It covers and protects the internal organs from solar and short ultraviolet radiation.

b. It protects the body from injury. For this reason, in injury-prone areas, such as the soles of the feet, the skin is thicker and stronger with more fatty tissues.

c. It protects the body from infection. The keratin layer, the external granular layer visible to the eye, is capable of cell replacement and prevents infection from entering. In addition, sebaceous glands within the skin secrete substances that create an acidic environment to prevent the development of fungi and bacteria. (However, excess secretion by the sebaceous glands or improperly cleaned skin areas serve as sites for inflammation and infection.)

d. It regulates body temperature by means of perspiration and constriction and dilation of blood vessels. When subjected to low temperatures, the skin prevents the escape of body heat by acting as an insulating covering. At high temperatures the skin is cooled by means of sweat through openings in the skin.

e. Fluids are secreted by sweat glands to cool off the skin. In addition, the skin builds the protective protein layer made up of keratin.

f. The sense of touch is vital to a person's normal functioning. Touch is facilitated by the skin, which also provides the facility of feeling. Without this sense, one would be unable to detect changes in pressure and temperature, thereby preventing heatstroke, burns, and other dangers.

The skin consists of three layers: (a) the epidermis, (b) the dermis, and (c) the subcutis.

The *epidermis* is the outer, visible, rough granular layer. It does not contain blood vessels and derives its sustenance from the dermis. The epidermis contains cells known as melanocytes whose function is to produce melanin, a pigment which covers the cells with a brown layer that protects them from solar radiation.

The *dermis* serves as the support and nutrient supplier to the epidermis and also imparts flexibility and elasticity to the skin. The dermis holds a large number of blood vessels, arteries, and veins, and it also holds the hair follicles, which extend to the subcutis.

The *subcutis* contains the sebaceous glands that are connected to the hair and secrete sebum, an oily substance that lubricates the outer layer. (The appearance of an oily substance on the scalp causes inflammation and reddening and can be prevented by keeping the head clean.) The subcutis consists of fatty cells, and its function is to provide additional padding of the skin, particularly in locations under pressure (such as the soles of the feet) or as additional protection for internal organs.

The following are the most commonly known skin conditions:

a. Eczema

b. Fungal infection

c. Erysipelas

d. Diaper rash

e. Heatstroke and sunburn

f. Burns

Eczema

1. Eczema is a skin condition usually caused by contact with an allergen. When this substance comes into contact with the skin, the person develops a sensitivity that manifests itself primarily in itchiness.

   The substance causing the allergy is identified by means of a "rag test." A sample of the substance whose concentration does not cause a direct reaction is applied to the skin for forty-eight hours. The skin is then tested for a reaction, which will consist of heat, itching, and a blister.

2. The standard treatment for eczema is to try to find the cause of the itching. If possible, this is determined by a test. In the case of inflammation accompanied by blistering, the area is moistened, cooled, and bathed. When the swelling subsides, steroid ointment is applied. Antihistamines are given in the case of intense reactions. In severe cases, systemic cortisone is administered.

3. On Shabbos, the use of medications to treat eczema is permitted. However, if possible, this should be postponed until after Shabbos, as long as this will not aggravate the condition.

Fungus

4. Fungus is an infectious disease that is highly prevalent primarily in the summer and particularly in areas with high humidity that causes excessive sweating.

5. Fungus can be prevented at the first stage by rinsing several times a day and keeping the area clean. It can also be prevented by wearing absorptive clothing such as cotton, as opposed to synthetic materials and rubber.

6. Advanced cases of fungal infection can be treated with antiseptic lotions that prevent itching and cause the skin to dry out. Antifungal treatment and caution are required to prevent the development of erysipelas.

7. Antiseptic lotions should not be used on Shabbos. However, it is permissible to wash the feet and even to soak them in water. Also, a kalium

solution or other disinfectant solutions should not be used unless the seriousness of the situation warrants it.[1]

Erysipelas

8. Erysipelas is an infectious skin disease that is usually found in the lower limbs. (Cellulitis is a related skin disease.) It is triggered by cracks in the skin of the feet and by fungi.

9. The symptoms consist of redness and severe swelling, local temperature rise, and pain. The disease is accompanied by elevated body temperature and an overall feeling of unwellness. It may be life-threatening if not treated.

10. Treatment consists of administering high-strength antibiotics and maintaining highly hygienic conditions. It is recommended that the patient lie with the leg elevated.

11. Medicine prescribed for this condition may be taken on Shabbos. It is also permitted to bathe the site with water heated before Shabbos or taken from a solar heater. If necessary, disinfectants may also be used.

    If the need arises to apply a local dressing or an ointment, this can be done on Shabbos, provided that the ointment is only placed on the affected area and not smeared. Massaging the skin with the ointment until it is completely absorbed is also permitted. (The manner in which ointments should be used on Shabbos is described in chapter 26, "Medication for a *Choleh She'ein Bo Sakanah*.")

Diaper Rash

12. Itching in the diapered region is a common occurrence in infants. At times, the child suffers greatly from this problem, and the standard procedure is to apply an ointment to get rid of the rash or to alleviate the itching.

---

1 בספר הלכה ורפואה ח״א במאמרו של הגר״מ הרשלר זצ״ל בענין מחלות עיניים דן את רחיצה במי קאלי כרפואה, ולכן במיחושים בעלמא אין להקל שימוש במי קאלי משום שיש בזה משום רפואה בשבת.

13. On Shabbos, ointment may be placed on the affected area. This is because an infant is regarded as a *choleh she'ein bo sakanah* and can be given medication without limitations. However, care must be taken not to spread the ointment or smooth it out over the affected area.

14. When the ointment is stored in a container, it should be taken out with a stick and placed on the skin without spreading or smoothing. Ointment from a tube is applied by squeezing it out and spreading gingerly over the rash. Subsequent placement of the diaper will complete the application.

15. This law that one should not smear ointment on a rash applies only to ointments. One is permitted to lubricate infant skin with oil or lotion.

Heatstroke

16. Heatstroke and heat exhaustion are highly dangerous conditions. The primary danger stems from the fact that the stricken person, exposed to the sun without liquids and sufficient protection, may suffer from dehydration. This may also cause thickening of the blood and the development of blood clots. This is a potentially life-threatening situation and must be treated with the greatest urgency. A person in such a state should be immediately hooked up to an intravenous fluid supply, and he may be given all the necessary tests.

17. The *Minchas Yitzchak* (5:32) rules that sunbathing on Shabbos is prohibited whether or not sun lotions or creams are used.

18. Sunburns caused by prolonged unprotected exposure to the sun are not included in the category of heatstroke, and none of the aforementioned treatments is permitted (see paragraph 16). No palliative preparations may be applied, even in the liquid state. This is because the situation is not considered dangerous and does not even require bed rest.[2]

    However, it is permitted to pour water onto the painful area and, if necessary, to immerse it in cold water.

---

2 עיין בשש״כ פרק ל״ה סעיף ל״ז.

Burns: General First Aid

When a burn is considered dangerous, one should treat a burn on Shabbos as one would on a weekday. The following paragraphs contain guidelines for dealing with burns in general.

19. A burn may cause damage to one of the constituents of the skin or to all of them. There are three categories of burns:
    a. Superficial (first degree) — injury that is confined to the epidermis.
    b. Partial depth (second degree) — injury to the epidermis and to a part of the dermis but there is still a possibility for regeneration.
    c. Full depth (third degree) — injury to all the layers of the skin, including nerves up to the deepest parts. The main treatment in this case is skin grafting.

20. In the case of a burn, the following should be done immediately:
    a. Move the injured away from the source of the fire.
    b. Extinguish the fire in the injured person's clothing or hair.
    c. Remove all the smoking segments. If the person's clothing is on fire, he should not run or stand, but roll on the ground to smother the fire.
    d. Clothing that adheres to the skin should not be pulled off. The clothing should either be left on the patient, or the part of the clothing that adheres to the wound should be detached by cutting around the wound. The remaining part of the garment may then be removed.
    e. Treat the burn. This involves moistening it and applying a sterile dressing. This will soothe the pain and reduce somewhat the danger of infection. This treatment should not be used for extensive third degree burns. Ice should never be used. No ointments should be applied, the wound should not be cleansed, and blisters should not be punctured.
    f. Cover the injured person with a clean sheet to retain body heat.
    g. Move the patient to a hospital.

21. If the patient is unconscious, suffering from burns on the chest and respiratory passages, or suffering from a blockage of the lungs caused by smoke inhalation, it is important that his breathing passages be kept open. Any discharge from the mouth should be removed, and if the person has ceased breathing, resuscitation should be started immediately. The patient may require an endotracheal tube and a respirator.

    If a person suffers from extensive injuries or is delirious, his head should be turned sidewise to prevent vomiting and suffocation.

    Rings, bracelets, and any other object that might restrain circulation should be removed from a burned limb. The injured limb should be elevated (to minimize edema). If the burn is between the fingers, these should be moved apart to prevent adhesion. However, eyelids should not be separated.

    A person suffering from extensive burns should not be given food or drink.

    If a danger exists that the injured suffers from obstruction of the respiratory tract or of the supply of blood to one of the limbs, this should recorded, and the record should be pinned to the injured in a prominent place.

22. When danger to life exists, all standard treatments should be carried out on Shabbos as on a weekday.

Electrical Burns

23. The passage of an electric current through tissue generates heat that destroys the tissue. The places of entry and exit of the current appear in the form of small entry and exit marks. The external damage caused by electrical burns is relatively minor compared to the damage inflicted on internal tissue. In addition, such burns cause heart rhythm interference.

24. There are two degrees of electrical burns:

    a. Degree C (III) — all the skin layers are affected.
    b. Degree D (IV) — muscles and bones are affected.

25. A fall from an elevated location caused by an electrical shock may cause skull or spinal column fracture. In such a case, the injured must be immobilized prior to evacuation and treatment.

26. Treatment of electrical burns:

    a. Disengage the injured from the source of the current by means of a nonconducting material (wood, cloth, rubber).
    b. Extinguish and remove burning clothing.
    c. Start resuscitation.
    d. Immobilize any fractures.
    e. Immediately move the injured to a treatment facility.

27. At the hospital, the treatment should be the same as with common burns, including copious liquids, standard medical procedures, and monitoring of urine.

Chemical Burns

28. This pertains to a burn caused by a strong chemical agent, either basic and acidic, such as lime, cement, and hydrochloric acid.

29. Immediate treatment includes removing all clothing, and, since damage to tissue continues as long as the agent is in contact with the skin, washing the victim with copious amounts of running water.

30. To prevent injury to the person administering the treatment, he should avoid all contact with the substance by wearing gloves.

    An acid-inflicted burn should not be neutralized by adding a base substance, and, a base burn should not be neutralized with acid. The burn should be treated in the same way as heat-induced burns.

    One should check the patient to eliminate the possibility of inhalation of gases or other poisonous substances.

31. At the hospital, any treatment necessary may be done on Shabbos as on a weekday, since it is a life-threatening situation.

Minor Burns

32. If a person suffers a minor, or first-degree, burn, characterized by a reddened area without blisters, ice should never be applied. Rather, treatment consists of immersing the area in cool water and applying aloe vera. Generally there is marked improvement in twenty-four hours. (Regarding the use of ointments or powders on Shabbos, see chapter 26, "Medication for a *Choleh She'ein Bo Sakanah*.")

Chapter 40
Diseases of the Respiratory System

A Medical Review

The principal function of the respiratory system is to supply oxygen to the body and to aid it in removal of excess carbon dioxide.

The respiratory system is comprised of the upper and lower respiratory tracts. The upper part of the respiratory system consists of the nasal cavity, nasal passages (sinuses), throat (larynx), trachea, and bronchi. The lower respiratory tract includes the lungs and chest cavity.

The lungs are located in the chest cavity. The left lung has two lobes, and the right one has three lobes. The lungs are surrounded by a pleural membrane that creates two sheets, one which surrounds the lungs and the other which touches the chest wall. The space between the pleural sheets is called the "pleural cavity," where a small quantity of fluid is present.

This entire system is coated by the mucous membrane and cilia. The cilia are hair-like protrusions that are constantly in motion and transport excretions and dust particles to the nostrils. The mucous membrane, made of mucous glands, secretes a small but set quantity of mucous substance. The mucous membrane aids in moistening the inhaled air, heating it, and removing infectious substances through the outward motion of the cilia.

The trachea, the tube that leads from the throat to the lungs, branches out into the main bronchi, which in turn branches out into the lobal bronchi (in the lungs). Each lobal bronchus branches out into fractional (segmental) bronchi.

The terminal bronchi open into alveoli. These are coated by a layer of very thin cells. The partition between the alveoli is composed of two layers of such cells, and a network of capillaries passes between these two layers. The walls of the alveoli are so thin that oxygen and carbon dioxide can pass through them. The alveoli transmit oxygen to the blood, which is then transmitted by the pulmonary veins to the heart and then to the circulatory system.

Functions of the respiratory system:

a. *Ventilation of the lungs*. It moves outside air into the lung tissue and back out.
b. *Diffusion*. It moves oxygen from the alveoli to the blood and carbon dioxide from the blood back to the alveoli.
c. *Perfusion*. It ensures a proper supply of blood to the lungs.

The respiratory tract is controlled by a system of nerves and muscles. The inhalation of air into the lungs is brought about by the contraction of the respiratory muscles, increasing the volume of the chest cavity and producing a negative pressure that causes external air to enter the lung tissue.

The exhalation of the air is a passive act and stems from the elastic properties of the lung and chest-cavity tissue. These return to their initial state when the respiratory muscles slacken, allowing air to escape back out.

Respiratory Diseases in Children

1. Children frequently suffer from respiratory problems, mostly stemming from infections. The severity of the disease depends on the severity of the infection, the frequency of the illness, age, weight, the state of the child's immunity, and his general state of health.

Foreign Objects in the Nasal Cavity

2. It is common for children to push foreign objects, such as beads or string, into the nose. An indication that this has occurred is one-sided secretion, at times accompanied by breathing difficulties and uneasi-

ness. When left without treatment, this will develop into an infection.

3. A foreign object should not be removed in an intrusive manner (such as by means of tweezers). If necessary, one should see a nose, ear, and throat specialist who has special tools for this purpose.

4. If the object causes shortness of breath, it is permitted to go by car on Shabbos to the doctor or to a hospital in order to remove it.

Nosebleeds

5. Nosebleeds occur most frequently in children of school age. The bleeding is usually slight and stops by itself. The primary reason for a nosebleed is trauma or penetration of a foreign object. Sometimes there is a family tendency toward nosebleeds. They are also more frequent in the case of infection of the upper respiratory passages. Children with allergies are more prone to this malady.

   Treatment consists of applying pressure to the area. If the bleeding is frequent, the reasons behind it should be checked out.

6. It is permitted to stop the bleeding by applying pressure externally even on Shabbos in the same manner as on weekdays. Usually no medication is needed. Care should be taken not to wipe the blood with a handkerchief because this is regarded as *tzovei'a*, dyeing.[1] Paper tissues or napkins may be used.[2] If nothing else is available, it is permitted to use cloth, but preferably not red-colored.[3]

Upper Respiratory Tract Infections

7. Most upper respiratory tract infections are of viral origin. The common cold, with its associated nasal discharge and other symptoms, occurs most frequently. Children are known to suffer more severely from

---

1 בשו״ע סי׳ שכ״ח סעיף מ״ח כתב וז״ל: אסור להניח בגד על מכה שיוצא ממנו דם מפני שהדם יצבע אותו. עכ״ל ועיין במ״ב שם ס״ק קמ״ו יצבע אותו, ואע״ג דמקלקל הוא ופטור, מ״מ אסור לכתחילה, ובבגד אדום פשיטא דאסור [מג״א]. ובמקום הדחק הסכימו האחרונים דיש להקל דהוא דרך לכלוך.

2 עיין בשש״כ פרק י״ד סעיף י״ט.

3 כמבואר במ״ב לעיל הערה 1.

colds than adults. In infants, the virally induced cold may be complicated by secondary, bacteria-caused infections.

Symptoms include fever, restlessness, and runny nose, which may cause blockage of the upper respiratory passages and may even cause shortness of breath. It is often accompanied by congestion in the ears, which causes ear infection (otitis). Diarrhea and vomiting may also occur. Older children suffer from muscle ache, general feeling of unwellness, and dry throat. Sometimes the nose infection is transferred to the ear or the eyes.

Complications include ear infection, sinusitis, bronchitis, and pneumonia. The frequency of complications decreases in inverse proportion to age.

Treatment consists of prevention and vaccination. It is recommended to try to clear up the nasal passages with nose drops, a vaporizer, and antihistamines. Antibiotics are given only if the situation worsens or if complications develop.

8. On Shabbos, nose drops or saltwater and topical medications may be administered to infants and toddlers without restrictions because children are in the category of *choleh she'ein bo sakanah*, an ordinary bedridden patient (see chapter 20, "The Definition of *Choleh She'ein Bo Sakanah*," paragraph 5). This is certainly true if the condition worsens, because this is a sign that an infection has set in, and an infection of the respiratory system is regarded as an internal wound. The child therefore becomes a *choleh sheyeish bo sakanah* and may be given any treatment necessary.

9. If an adult suffers solely from the common cold without any complications, no drops or saltwater should be administered unless the person is classified as a *choleh she'ein bo sakanah*, an ordinary bedridden patient.[4] However, if the condition is classified simply as a minor illness (*michush*), no medication may be taken.

---

4 עיין שו"ת מנחת יצחק ח"ח סי' ה'.

Acute Pharyngitis (Sore Throat)

10. Acute infection of the pharynx, sore throat, usually occurs in children over a year old and is most frequent in kindergarten-age children. Most of the infections are viral. Symptoms include a general feeling of unwellness accompanied by a rise in temperature, sore throat, and hoarseness. If the infection is bacterial, the situation becomes more severe and the lymph glands may be inflamed. Treatment consists of antibiotics for ten days if the infection is bacterial and supportive treatment (fluids and pain relief) if it is viral. On Shabbos, the treatment is the same.

11. An abscess, a pus-filled wound, that develops in the back region of the throat is one of the complications that arises from bacterial pharyngitis. The symptoms consist of a history of pharyngitis, an abrupt rise in temperature, swallowing difficulties, and loss of appetite. In one form, epiglottitis, the child holds his head backward (hyperextension), his breathing is noisy and becomes increasingly difficult, and a bulge is seen when the throat is examined.

    It is desirable to take a lateral X-ray of the throat in order to help make the diagnosis. An abscess left untreated in the oral cavity may burst suddenly and cause aspiration (entry of food or, in this case, the content of the abscess) into the trachea. In extreme cases, it may cause additional abscesses.

    If detected in time, this condition should be treated by administration of intravenous antibiotics. If the abscess is sufficiently large to interfere with breathing, it is drained by surgical means under general anesthesia. It is best not to touch the abscess, since this may cause it to burst.

12. Since this condition is regarded as an internal wound, it should be treated as needed, even on Shabbos. This includes taking an X-ray of the throat if it is absolutely necessary for proper diagnosis. Antibiotics may be administered intravenously. In severe cases, drainage may be carried out without delay.

Tonsillitis and Adenoids

13. The tonsils are comprised of lymphatic tissue that develops rapidly in childhood and then remains static. Inflammation of the tonsils, or tonsillitis, is bacterial and very frequent at school age. The condition is accompanied by high fever, sore throat, and a general feeling of unwellness. A white discharge or white purulent spots appear on the tonsils. A throat swab may be done in order to establish the nature of the infection. Complications of tonsillitis include kidney infection (glumerulonephritis) and rheumatic fever.

14. Inflamed tonsils are regarded as an internal wound that may be treated on Shabbos.

15. In certain situations, such as recurrent throat infections, removal of the tonsils (tonsillectomy) may be recommended. In general, no urgency exists to perform a tonsillectomy on Shabbos. Therefore, even if indicated, this surgery should be postponed to a weekday.

    Peritonsillar abscesses may also indicate tonsillectomy — a competent *rav* and doctor should be consulted.

16. Adenoids are comprised of lymphatic tissue existing in the pharynx. These adenoids may become enlarged, manifesting in symptoms similar to those of the chronic cold, such as a constantly open mouth, snoring, constantly running nose, recurrent ear infections with fluid accumulation in the ear, and a reduction in hearing — the greatest danger of enlarged adenoids.

17. Treatment may consist of administration of medication, which may be taken on Shabbos. Adenoids should be removed upon (1) reduction in hearing or (2) distortion of the face, where the constantly open mouth changes the shape of the jaw and of the entire face. In general, no urgency exists to remove adenoids on Shabbos. Therefore, even if indicated, this surgery should be postponed to a weekday.

Sinusitis

18. Inflammation of the nasal sinuses, or sinusitis, develops as a complica-

tion in older children because the sinuses attain their final size only at the ages of three to five. In most cases, this is an infection within the nose that has moved upward, where purulent fluid has collected in the nasal cavities. There are four pairs of sinuses; fluid usually accumulates in the maxillary and frontal sinuses.

Symptoms consist of elevated temperature, headache, and local pain. At times, this is accompanied by local swelling and runny nose. Accumulation of fluid in the ethmoidal or sphenoidal sinuses may present with only headaches.

Diagnosis may consist of X-rays of the face in order to detect cavities with fluid within the sinuses. Possible complications are:

a. A breakthrough of fluids in the direction of the brain
b. Orbital cellulitis — infection around the eye
c. Inflammation of the optic nerve, which may cause blindness

Treatment consists of wide-range antibiotics for ten days if it is a severe case. In extreme cases, it is necessary to drain the mucous, which is known as a "second-look operation." This procedure provides relief for a number of years.

19. Ordinarily it is not urgent to X-ray the nasal cavity on Shabbos. However, it is permitted to start antibiotic treatment to treat sinusitis.

Ear Diseases

There are a number of symptoms typical of ear problems:

a. Otolagia, or ear pain, which may originate in the ear or may stem from a problem in the vicinity of the ears, such as the teeth
b. Otorrhea, secretion from the ear, which may be purulent
c. Reduction in hearing, which may be either permanent or temporary
d. Vertigo, or dizziness, since the ear is responsible for balance
e. Nystagmus (involuntary movements of the eyeballs and inability to focus the vision), a condition that causes dizziness during travel
f. Tinnitus, ringing in the ears, which is less frequent in children and is often a side effect of medication

External Otitis — Inflammation of the Outer Ear

20. This condition occurs typically in swimmers who spend long periods of time in the water. It involves a persistent irritation of the auditory meatus (channel) and of the outer ear, which may result in various infections.

    Symptoms include pain in the ear, particularly when the outer ear is moved, redness and swelling in the auditory meatus, mucous discharge, and possibly reduction in hearing. Complications are damage to the cartilage and distortions of the ear.

    Treatment consists of application of antibiotic drops. If infection of the cartilage is suspected, oral antibiotics are also administered, especially in diabetics.

21. In the case of children, oral antibiotics can be given on Shabbos to treat the condition. Antibiotic ointment may also be placed on the area. In the case of an adult, treatment on Shabbos depends on whether or not the patient is regarded as a *choleh she'ein bo sakanah*, an ordinary bedridden patient,[5] in which case medication may be given, or as someone with a minor ailment, for which administering medication is forbidden.

Otitis Media — Inflammation of the Middle Ear

22. Otitis media occurs frequently in children up to school age because the anatomical structure of the ear in children predisposes them to infection. Symptoms include accumulation of pus in the middle-ear cavity, which is located behind the eardrum. Initial symptoms that are not specific to the ears include diarrhea and vomiting, lack of appetite, and high fever. The temperature rises to a high level, and a sense of uneasiness sets in.

    Complications may include breakthrough of the inflammation toward the meninges and perforation of the eardrum. This causes a reduction in hearing and perhaps irreversible damage to the ear.

---

5 הגדרת חולה שאין בו סכנה מבואר לעיל פרק 3 והגדרת מחושים בעלמא מבואר לעיל פרק 31 סעיפים 2–1.

23. Treatment on Shabbos is the same as for external otitis (see paragraph 21). It may be permissible to drip breast milk into an aching ear on Shabbos. (This treatment is no longer practiced today.)[6]

Lung and Bronchial Tube Diseases

Bronchial Asthma

24. Asthma, which manifests itself in spasms of the bronchial tubes and causes shortness of breath, is one of the most prevalent respiratory maladies, particularly in children. Usually it is caused by an allergy to certain substances and increases in the presence of irritants, such as unusual physical effort, smoke, stress, and certain medications.

    The main problem with asthma is the inability to release air accumulated in the lungs. This causes the air to be trapped and prevents proper ventilation of the respiratory system. This situation produces recurring infections and shortness of breath.

25. Treatment of asthma consists of removing the causes of the attack, whether these are environmental or specific allergens. In addition, medication that promotes broadening of the bronchial tubes is administered. The medication may consist of pills, syrups, inhalations, and, in special cases, intravenous injections.

26. Medication taken for this condition by a doctor's orders may be taken on Shabbos. In general, asthma is not a life-threatening illness, and not every attack requires a doctor's attention. However, if it appears that the situation is serious — specifically, if the shortness of breath is severe and the patient does not respond to medication — he should be brought to a doctor or to the hospital.

---

6 בשו״ת יביע אומר ח״ה חאו״ח סי׳ לב אות ז׳ העלה להתיר חליבה מאשה מינקת לצורך רפואה ע״י שניים שעשאוה שתצטרף עוד אשה לחולבת ויחלבו כאחת ובזה הוי איסור מדרבנן ושרי לצורך חולה או לצורך תינוק באינקובטור עיי״ש. גם בשו״ת לקט הקציר סי׳ ז׳ כתב ז״ל: מאן דאית ליה צערא דגופא במיחוש האוזן כי גדל הכאב מאוד ורפואתו תלויה במינקת להטיף טיפת חלב רותח מדדיה תוך האוזן, כתב טל אורות דף כו ע״ב דכיון שהיא מלאכה שאינה צריכה לגופה במקום צערא כהאי גוונא שרי.

Chronic Bronchial Tube Inflammation (Chronic Bronchitis)

27. Chronic bronchitis manifests itself in excess phlegm discharge during most of the day over a long time. It is accompanied by prolonged coughing and wheezing. It is usually caused by smoking, which also aggravates the situation by contaminating the respiratory tract.

28. As with bronchial asthma, treatment should start with eliminating the causes of the disease and avoiding infection of the respiratory tract in order not to exacerbate the problem. The standard treatment consists of antibiotics both for prevention of additional infections and for overcoming the current infection.

29. On Shabbos, antibiotics should be given on a doctor's orders as in the case of asthma above.

Chapter 41

Diseases and Disorders of the Digestive System

A Medical Review

The digestive system is one of the most important and sensitive systems in the human body. Its function is to take in food, and digest it, absorbing those of its components that are important to the body and expelling the waste products. The system is comprised of a number of organs interconnected by a single duct and auxiliary organs located nearby. It starts with the mouth, continues with the esophagus down to the stomach, and from there to the small intestine and large intestine. The liver, pancreas, and biliary system also assist in the digestive process.

The intake of food and the start of chewing trigger the secretion of saliva in the mouth and of digestive juices in the stomach. The food moves through the esophagus to the stomach and ends in the large intestine in a rhythmical wavelike manner known as peristalsis. (This movement can be detected via a stethoscope in order to find changes in the motion or blockage or other problems in the intestinal tract.)

A one-way valve, known as the sphincter, is located between the esophagus and the stomach. It opens to allow the food to enter and closes immediately afterward to prevent the stomach contents and digestive juices from entering the esophagus.

The stomach secretes digestive juices and various acids that assist in digesting the food. These secretions also have the capability to neutralize substances that cause a number of diseases. The food stays for a time in the stomach where it mixes with the different stomach reagents. Then the valve separating the stomach from the duodenum, known as the "pylorus," opens and the food moves to the duodenum.

In the duodenum, the food is additionally processed by substances secreted by the duodenum walls, the pancreas, and the liver and which is stored in the gallbladder. These substances decompose the food into its constituents and assist digestion. The food then continues in its peristaltic movement to the small intestine. There a number of the food's components are absorbed: (a) nutrients (essential food elements), (b) water, (c) various salts, (d) metals, (e) trace elements, and (f) vitamins. After being absorbed, these components enter the blood, which brings them to all parts of the body.

The small intestine is about 12 feet (4 meters) long and terminates at the large intestine. The substance that reaches the large intestine consists of waste products mixed with a large quantity of water. The large intestine absorbs most of the water, leaving a solid mass. The accumulation of solid waste in the terminal part of the large intestine exerts a pressure on the intestine's wall, which gives the sensation that it must be expelled.

Diseases of the Esophagus

1. There are a number of diseases associated with the esophagus:

    a. The esophagus may widen or contract, primarily because of damage to the nervous system that prevents orderly transfer of food to the stomach. This may cause swallowing difficulties (dysphagia).

    b. The esophagus walls can become inflamed due to excessive consumption of alcoholic beverages, which damage the mucosa of the esophagus and cause the appearance of ulcers.

    c. Dysfunction of the valve (sphincter) so that it does not open, as in the case of achalasia, or it does not close properly and the stomach contents return to the esophagus, where the stomach juices cause inflammation and other complications.

d. Abnormal sacs called "diverticulum" may develop in the esophagus and trap food.

2. In all of the above cases, the damage must be corrected both surgically and by medication. At times, surgical intervention is preceded by oral medicine in order to neutralize the nerves of the esophagus or for another purpose. This medicine alleviates the pain of eating and drinking until the surgery is performed.

3. Medication to treat these conditions may be taken on Shabbos, since otherwise the patient could not eat. However, if the patient can be fed liquefied food without difficulties in swallowing, and the medication is needed only to allow him to eat solid food, it is questionable whether it is permitted to take this medication on Shabbos.

Heartburn

4. Heartburn is usually the result of excess stomach juice secretion (however, surprisingly it may also occur in cases of deficiency in stomach juices). Certain people may suffer heartburn from foods that do not affect others in this way. Heartburn may also be triggered by lying on the side and will vanish when one's position is changed. One can alleviate the discomfort by keeping away from foods that cause heartburn.

5. Standard treatment consists of giving the patient antacids. The sodium bicarbonate contained in baking soda also neutralizes stomach acids.

6. One should refrain from eating heartburn-inducing food on Shabbos. Baking soda should not be taken because it is not regarded as an ordinary food but is classified as medicine with its associated restrictions.[1] However, if one cannot eat anything without taking baking soda, it may be permitted to do so on Shabbos.

7. Food or drink that is regarded as standard food, such as cucumber, milk, yogurt, almonds, or soda water may be eaten on Shabbos even if the purpose is to alleviate heartburn.

---

1 עיין לעיל פרק 31 סעיף 3 וסעיף 5 ושם בהערה 9 מבואר באורך איסור השימוש בסודה לשתייה לחולי צרבת.

Stomach Pain

8. Stomach pain may be caused by a large variety of medical disorders, some of them temporary, some serious. It is very important to diagnose the kind of pain, its location, and its cause.

9. Some people place a hot-water bottle on the aching side to treat stomach pain. On Shabbos a hot-water bottle may be filled with preheated water, but the bottle must be dry before it is filled to avoid cooking any cold water that may be present in the bottle.[2]

10. Some people alleviate stomach pain by applying alcoholic beverages, such as arrack or cognac, or olive oil to the abdomen. This is not permitted on Shabbos, since this is not normally done by healthy people.[3]

11. A person with a stomachache may drink tea with lemon or honey or any other kind of tea that was prepared before Shabbos, because these are standard beverages consumed by healthy people.

    Similarly, one may drink alcoholic beverages to alleviate stomach pains or to assist in digestion. For example, one may drink cognac even though it reduces his stomach pains. Since this is something healthy people drink, it is permissible, even though one does so to alleviate one's pain.[4]

12. It should be noted that when the reason for stomach pain is unclear and the pains grow in intensity, there is a danger of *pikuach nefesh*. The pain may stem from an inflamed appendix (appendicitis), ulcers in the digestive system, or various life-threatening blockages. These cases require immediate consultation with a doctor. If a doctor is not available close by, one may call the hospital or the doctor's house in order to consult him. Shabbos desecration is permitted in this case, as for any internal wound.

13. When an infant suffers from stomach pains on Shabbos, the abdomen

---

2 שו״ת באר משה ח״א סי׳ ל״ג אות ט״ו. וכ״כ בשו״ת מנחת יצחק ח״ה סי׳ ל״ב באמצע הסימן.

3 על פי דברי השו״ע בסימן שכ״ז כמבואר לעיל פרק 31 עיי״ש.

4 עיין לעיל פרק 32 והערה 1 בעניין מאכל בריאים ומאכל שאינו לבריאים שהרחבנו בביאור דין זה.

may be massaged with baby oil or olive oil or with cognac. This is permitted since an infant is regarded as a *choleh she'ein bo sakanah*, an ordinary bedridden patient.[5]

14. Abdominal pain in an infant that appears suddenly for no apparent reason and causes the child to be restless calls for immediate medical consultation. There may exist a danger of various types of blockage or of intussusception (where a part of the intestine exerts pressure on another part, blocking blood vessels). These situations are extremely dangerous and require immediately treatment to prevent irreversible damage. Suspicion of such conditions requires desecration of Shabbos to provide treatment.

Diarrhea

15. Many reasons exist for the appearance of diarrhea and sudden and substantive changes in the frequency and variety of excretions. It may be brought about by many factors, including bacterial or viral infections or parasites. Diarrhea may also be brought about by poor absorption (disorders in the mobility of the intestines, frequent in patients with diabetic neuropathy) or chronic inflammation of the intestines, such as Crohn's disease or ulcerative colitis. Additionally, it may be brought about by abrupt changes in the diet, or an illness such as ear problems, psychological disorders, and contagious diseases.

16. Typical symptoms include inflammatory diarrhea, usually accompanied by high fever, general feeling of unwellness, stomach pains, cramps, and at times blood and mucous in the feces. Poor absorption results in prolonged diarrhea with massive feces that float on the toilet water (caused by the high-fat content of the feces), loss of weight, and a general pattern of poor absorption. The cause of a given condition can be determined by means of blood tests, fecal cultures, and tests of the digestive system.

17. The principal complication of severe diarrhea is dehydration.

---

5 כמבואר לעיל פרק 20 בעניין צרכי קטן, ושם מבואר עד איזה גיל נחשב קטן לעניין חולה שאין בו סכנה.

Dehydration from diarrhea sets in very rapidly in children because

a. eighty percent of their body consists of water;
b. the rate of metabolism is much higher than in adults; and
c. a child's kidneys cannot concentrate urine well, and hence dehydration in children is more dangerous.

18. The following treatment is recommended in the case of diarrhea and dehydration:

    a. Calming of the digestive system by reducing food with high-milk content, fats, and products high in cellulose and sugars
    b. High fluid intake
    c. Reducing temperature by standard means
    d. Restoring fluids and electrolytes in order to preserve the cardinal kidney functions and the central venous pressure (CVP)

19. On Shabbos diarrhea should be treated by copious fluid intake and reduction in food intake. It is permissible to take anti-diarrhea medication, as prescribed by a doctor.

20. In severe cases, and when dehydration is suspected, the patient should be driven to a hospital since he may need intravenous fluids.

21. When dysentery is suspected in infants, this may develop into a life-threatening situation stemming from dehydration. The Chazon Ish ruled that rice should be cooked with water on Shabbos for the infant to stop the diarrhea.[6]

22. In addition, fluids should be given in quantities sufficient for preventing dehydration. Therefore, if no boiled water is available in the house or from neighbors, or if a non-Jew is not available for boiling the water,

---

6 עיין בחזון איש מועד סי׳ נ״ט אות ד׳ וז״ל: מש״כ הרמ״א שמותר לומר לא״י לעשות תבשיל לקטן שאין לו מה לאכול וכו׳ שזהו דווקא ברעבון של שעה מועטת, אבל רעבון של זמן שרגילין להקפיד עליו חשיבה סכנה, ובזמננו שמצוי מאוד חולאים מתרגשים בתינוקות, אזי כל שיש ספק שיגרום לו קלקול מעיים לעצור או לשלשל, או גרם כאב מעיים, או חום כל שהוא הרי הוא בכלל ספק סכנה, כי כל קלקול אפשר שיגרום חולי וכל חולי ספק סכנה. עכ״ל.

water must be boiled on Shabbos by a Jew for the infant because this is considered a life-threatening situation.

Constipation

23. Constipation has many and varied causes:
    a. Growths (neoplasms)
    b. Inflammatory processes in the vicinity of the rectum, making defecation painful and causing one to hold it in
    c. Nervous disorders in the bowel movement
    d. Diseases of the bowel muscle
    e. Certain medications
    f. Shortness of time, changes of place, going on trips
    g. Depression or other mental disorders
    h. Inflamed and painful hemorrhoids
    i. Dietary changes

24. Each occurrence should be analyzed, and the underlying causes should be treated accordingly. An attempt should be made to attain regularity of the bowel movement to the point of setting a time for it. One should avoid laxatives, which interfere with softening of the feces in the intestine. Distraction at the time of feces discharge is very helpful.

25. Some alleviate constipation by drinking prune juice or juices of other fruit that have the same effect or by taking various preparations. These may be taken on Shabbos in the case of chronic constipation.[7]

26. A person who suffers pain from constipation is not permitted to use suppositories on Shabbos in the same manner as is done on weekdays; for example, one can insert the suppository widened end first.[8] Care must be taken not to push a suppository in with force to avoid detaching the hair of the rectum.[9]

---

7 שו״ת באר משה ח״א סי׳ ל״ג אות י״א, מורה להקל משום דחשיב קצת מאכל בריאים.

8 כ״כ בקצות השולחן סי׳ קל״ח עמ׳ ק׳ עיי״ש.

9 שו״ע סי׳ שכ״ח סעיף מ״ט, וטעמו דאסר כדי שלא יבוא לתלוש שערות בתחיבת הפתילה, ולכן אם מניחה בנחת מותר, כ״כ במ״ב שם ס״ק קנ״א.

27. It is permissible to administer an enema on Shabbos either to alleviate stomach pains or to empty the bowels. However, only water may be used unless the person is regarded as a *choleh she'ein bo sakanah*, in which case a medicated enema preparation may be used.[10]

Crohn's Disease

28. Crohn's disease manifests itself in a severe inflammation of the intestines. The symptoms include a general feeling of unwellness. The pain occurs primarily in the bottom right part of the stomach. At times, the patient suffers from loss of appetite and high temperature.

29. This disorder is regarded as an internal wound, and Shabbos may be desecrated if necessary. At times, this condition may advance to a state of actual *pikuach nefesh*, since there exists a danger of perforation of the intestines.

    In view of this, a physician should be consulted and his advice followed fully.[11] Needless to say, the patient may take any necessary medication.

Hemorrhoids

30. A person suffering from hemorrhoids may take laxatives on Shabbos (thus preventing itching and abrasion of the hemorrhoids when defecating). This is because this is not done to treat the disorder, but rather in order to prevent discomfort and damage to the hemorrhoids. The medication can be taken after the hemorrhoids disappear in order to prevent their recurrence.

---

10 כתב המגן אברהם סי׳ שכ״ח ס״ק נ״ה אסור לשום פתילה וכו׳ וכ״ש דאסור לעשות קרוסטיי״ר (והוא כלי היורה כחץ שנותנין לתוכו מים ושמן ומכניסין ראשו הדק בפי הטבעת למי שהוא עצור כדי שיצא מבטנו). אפילו הוכנה מאתמול ואפילו ע״י שינוי אם לא בחולה כמש״כ בסעיף י״ז ויזהר שלא יבוא לידי מלאכה מדאורייתא, ואם אפשר יעשה ע״י עכו״ם. ע״כ. וכ״כ במ״ב שם ס״ק ק״נ. עיי״ש. והוסיף באורחות חיים (הובא בכף החיים שם אות רע״א) ואפשר שדווקא בנותן לתוכה דברים המסוגלים לרפואה אסור, אבל במים לבד לצורך פתיחת נקבים במקום צער יש להקל, ובמקום כאב בבטן שקורין קרעמפין בכל גוונא יש להקל. עכ״ל. ועיין מהרש״ם בדעת תורה סי׳ שכ״ח ס״ק מ״ט, שכתב כן, וכ״כ בשו״ת באר משה ח״א סי׳ ל״ג אות י״א.

11 דעת רופא.

According to medical advice, a person who suffers from hemorrhoids should drink paraffin oil or fiber before a meal[12] in order to soften the feces, thus promoting easy defecation and preventing damage to hemorrhoids.

31. A person who had his hemorrhoids removed surgically is permitted to sit in a vessel of warm water heated before Shabbos in order to alleviate his pain.[13] According to some opinions, this is permitted only if the condition affects his entire body so that he cannot function normally.[14]

32. Suppositories may be used on Shabbos in cases of extreme pain. One should insert the suppository with the wide end first.[15] According to some opinions, this is not permitted even in this case.

    When the hemorrhoids are bleeding, it is preferable to wash the area after using the bathroom to prevent coloring the bathroom tissue. However, when water is not available, it is permitted.[16]

Bleeding from the Digestive Tract

33. Bleeding from the digestive tract is a dangerous situation that requires immediate hospitalization in order to locate the source of the bleeding and stop it. Vomiting of blood or blood in the feces may also be indicative of digestive tract bleeding. When the bleeding occurs in the stomach, it causes the feces to take on a black color; if the bleeding is

---

12 עיין בזה בשו״ת ציץ אליעזר ח״א סי׳ ל״ז. וכתב שם דדמי להנפסק בשו״ע סי׳ שכ״ח סעיף כ״ג דנותנין ספוג וחתיכות בגדים יבשים וחדשים שאינם לרפואה אלא כדי שלא יסרטו הבגדים את המכה, ה״נ מה ששותה את השמן פרפין הוא כדי לשמן את היציאה ולהגן על ורידי היציאה שלא יוזקו, ומכיון שאין שתיה זאת לשם רפואה אלא כשמירה שרי. והנה בכף החיים סי׳ שכ״ח אות ל״ה כתב וז״ל: ומי שיש לו טחורים או חמימות בפי הטבעת והוא רוצה לשתות סם הנקרא ראבינ״ט שהוא משלשל, ומקרר הדם אסור, יען כי זה המשקה אינו כ״א לרפואה וכל ששותה לרפואה אסור כמ״ש סעיף ל״ז יעו״ש. רו״ח עכ״ל. ולדבריו נראה דהיינו דדוקא במיחושים בעלמא אך אם גדל הכאב מאוד עד כי נפל למשכב, ודאי שרי כדאיתא התם בסעיף ל״ז. עוד נראה לע״ד שאין דברי הכף החיים והציץ אליעזר נוגדים, דיתכן דאף הכף החיים יודה דבשמן פרפין שרי דכיון שאין בו שום רפואה רק להחליק היציאה, משא״כ סם הראבינט פועל על רכות היציאה ומשלשל, והוי בכלל רפואה. כנלע״ד.

13 שו״ת באר משה ח״א סי׳ ל״ג אות י״ד.

14 עיין בקצות השולחן סי׳ קל״ח עמודים ק׳-ק״ג מה שכתב שם באורך בענין זה.

15 עיין שם בקצות השולחן מה שכתב בזה.

16 במנחת שבת (סי׳ צ״ח ס״ק ל׳) כתב וז״ל: מי שיש לו מורידין (טחורים) המוציאים דם בעת

in the intestines, the feces are red. Rapid blood loss from the stomach may also cause the feces to turn red.

34. In view of this, blood in the feces requires immediate medical attention even if there is no pain. One may desecrate Shabbos for this consultation.

Colostomy and Ileostomy

35. Certain intestinal disorders require that a part of or the entire large intestine be removed. In such cases, an opening is made in the stomach wall to remove the feces, and a bag is connected to the opening. The bag must be periodically replaced; this may be done on Shabbos. One may also go out on Shabbos with the bag, even if it contains feces.[17]

Prostate Disease

36. A patient who underwent a prostatectomy (prostate removal procedure) may need a catheter. Many elderly patients with incontinence have penroses (known in the U.S. as Texas catheters or condom catheters). These have a bag connected to them for collecting the urine. The bags are emptied or replaced as needed. This may be done on Shabbos.[18] It is also permitted to go out into the street with this equipment.

שמפנה את עצמו צריך להחמיר שלא לקנח את עצמו בבגד או אפילו בנייר מפני שהדם יצבע אותם ואע״פ שהוא בדרך לכלוך, ולכן נכון יותר שירחוץ אותו מקום במים, אך אם א״א בעניין אחר כגון שאין לו מים אפשר דיש להקל משום כבוד הבריות, כיון דחומרא יתירה הוא היכא דהוא דרך לכלוך.

17 עיין בזה בנשמת אברהם ח״א סי׳ ש״א ס״ק ד׳.

18 עיין בכל זה בשו״ת ציץ אליעזר חי״ד סי׳ נ״ח שהאריך בזה. הובא גם בנשמת אברהם שם.

Chapter 42
Nonprogressive Chronic Disorders

1. Many people are able to go about their daily business only by taking medication to stabilize a condition or to prevent recurring attacks of a previous illness.

2. It should be noted that this does not refer to diseases where the patient may, at one time or another, be in danger of his life, since in that case he may be treated on Shabbos as necessary. This refers to cases when in the course of recovery or in order to prevent a relapse, it is recommended that the patient take certain medications and follow any medical advice given to help his condition, as Jewish law requires, since a person may not endanger his life.

   However, if the person did not follow medical instructions, and, as a result, he has suffered a relapse which places him in a life-threatening situation, he should be examined. If, as in the majority of such cases, there is suspicion that the situation is life-threatening, everything may be done on Shabbos to help him.

Examples of Chronic Diseases

3. *Heart disease.* People who suffer from heart disorders are classified as belonging to one of four categories: (1) healthy, (2) limited to light

exertion, (3) limited to minimal exertion, and (4) limited to complete rest. The first two categories are included in the definition of chronic disorders discussed in this chapter. This means that these are people who suffer from heart disorders and must take medication in order to maintain a stable lifestyle. Otherwise, they go about their lives like everyone else. The second two categories of patients are in the category of *choleh she'ein bo sakanah*. If the condition worsens, they are classified as *choleh sheyeish bo sakanah*, in danger of their lives. The latter categories are not discussed in this chapter.

4. *Diabetes*. People suffering from diabetes are classified in different categories:
    a. Light diabetes requires changes in diet.
    b. Moderate diabetes requires medication and blood-test follow-ups.
    c. Brittle diabetes requires continuous blood tests and insulin injections to adjust the meal intake with the insulin balance.[1] These injections are given either before the meal or on a specific schedule.

    Diabetes in the last two categories appear outwardly as if there is nothing wrong with them. But they must take medication, either orally or by injection, in order to function normally.

5. *Epilepsy*. Epileptics are regarded as suffering from a life-threatening disease.[2] However, nowadays medication is available to prevent seizures, and they are able to function normally.

6. *Familial Mediterranean fever* (FMF). FMF is a sickness that manifests itself in incidents of high fever, abdominal pain, and arthritis. Sufferers of FMF can function normally if they take medication to prevent attacks. It should be noted that such individuals are not permitted to fast or must at least drink water on fast days.

---

1 השימוש בגלוקומטר לבדיקת רמת הסוכר בדם — לחולי סוכרת בדרגה גבוהה הזקוקים לבדיקה יום יומית או יותר — מותרת בשבת. ופרטי דינים אלו יבוארו לקמן פרק 48 בעניין בדיקות שונות. ואופן השימוש בזריקות מבואר לקמן פרק 46 סעיף 43 בעניין מזרקים וזריקות שונות.

2 כמבואר באיסור והיתר הארוך לרבנו יונה בשם מהר"ם.

7. *Hypertension*. A large segment of the population suffers from hypertension — high blood pressure. This can be controlled by medication.

8. *Stroke.* Someone who suffered a cerebrovascular accident (CVA), or stroke, should be under medical supervision to prevent the formation of blood clots that would cause another stroke and must take blood-thinning medication.

9. *Ulcers*. Ulcer sufferers may reach a point when their life may be in danger and must take certain medications before meals to prevent an attack.

10. *Heartburn*. People who suffer from chronic heartburn, and particularly those with suspected diaphragm hernia, must take medication before a meal.

General Principles

11. Anyone whose life would be in danger if he does not take medication must ensure that all medicines that will be needed are readily available on Shabbos. If the medication could not be obtained before Shabbos, or it was mistakenly thought that the supply is sufficient and it was found on Shabbos that this is not so, it may be permissible to obtain them on Shabbos, subject to conditions that will be enumerated below (see paragraphs 14–16).

12. However, if a person takes medication on Shabbos, but his dependence on the medicine is not critical, he is not permitted to violate Shabbos to obtain the medication.

13. All of this above applies to procurement of medication on Shabbos. However, Shabbos desecration for other needs of a person with a chronic illness is not permitted even when performed by a non-Jew.

Procuring Medication on Shabbos

14. People on maintenance medication should prepare everything necessary before Shabbos. However, if a mishap occurred and the needed medication was not prepared, it may be obtained but one must try to minimize Shabbos desecration as much as possible.

15. The easiest way to minimize Shabbos desecration is to have a non-Jew bring the medication or to purchase it from a drugstore or from a hospital dispensary (see chapter 22, "Permitted Actions on Behalf of a *Choleh She'ein Bo Sakanah*").[3] If no non-Jew is available, a Jew may be sent, preferably on a bicycle.[4] Even though purchasing the medication is only a rabbinical prohibition, it is preferable to purchase it from a non-Jew, first to avoid even a rabbinical transgression[5] and second because ringing up the purchase is a Torah transgression.[6]

16. If the medication cannot be obtained in a manner that will involve only a rabbinical prohibition, one may travel to obtain the medication (see chapter 11 for laws of traveling on Shabbos).

---

3 אמירה לאינו יהודי, נחשבת בלשון חז״ל ל״שבות שאין בו מעשה״, שזו הדרך הקלה ביותר מבחינת איסורי שבת, שעל כן יש להעדיפה על אופנים אחרים. ועיין לעיל פרק 22 פרוט אופני האיסורים ודרגתם חומרתם.

4 רכיבה באופניים בשבת, נאמר בספרי האחרונים ג׳ טעמים לאוסרה מדרבנן. א׳ משום עובדין דחול. ב׳ שמא יסע לחוץ לתחום שבת. ג׳ גזירה שמא יתקן את האופניים אם תקרה תקלה. עיין בזה בשו״ת רב פעלים חלק א׳ חאו״ח סימן כ״ה. ובשו״ת ציץ אליעזר ח״ז סימן ל׳ אות א׳. ובשו״ת באר משה ח״ו סי׳ ט״ז. עיי״ש. עכ״פ זו הדרך הקלה ביותר מבחינת איסורי דרבנן, ומסתבר שבאופניים יותר קל אף מרכיבה על חמור או סוס.

5 מקח וממכר אפילו עם כסף ממש אינו אלא איסור דרבנן גזירה שמא יכתוב, (עיין במ״ב סי׳ ש״ו ס״ק ל״ג) ומשום עובדין דחול (כמבואר בגמ׳ ביצה כ״ט עיי״ש), ולצורך חולה זה יש להקל, ומטעם זה יש להקל נסיעה בתחבורה ציבורית אפילו עם תשלום מנסיעה עצמאית של הישראלי, כפי המבואר לעיל בפרק 11 עיי״ש.

6 בכתיבה אין זה משנה אם כותב ביד או מדפיס בקופה רושמת וכיו״ב, בשני המקרים הרוקח עובר איסור ללא צורך, אך כמובן שכתיבה ביד אסורה מדאורייתא וחמורה יותר כמבואר לעיל פרק 15 הערה 9.

Part 5

Medical Equipment and Procedures

Chapter 43
A General Guide

Below is a list of equipment and the chapter and paragraph where each device is discussed in this book.

Device	*Purpose*	*Chapter*
Apnea cardiometer	Checks a baby's heart function	45:29
Apnea monitor	Checks a baby's respiration rate	45:29
Bed, electric with remote control	Adjusts patient's bed position	47:16
Bed, hydraulic	Adjusts patient's bed position	47:16
Beeper	Communications device	47:27
Bio beam	Speeds healing	46:12
BiPAP	Used for treating sleep apnea	46:42
Blanket, electric	Warms a sick or elderly person	47:36–39
Blood pressure meter, arrow indicator	Measures blood pressure	45:25
Blood pressure meter, electronic	Measures blood pressure	45:26
Blood pressure meter, mercury	Measures blood pressure	45:25

Device	*Purpose*	*Chapter*
Braces	Orthopedic treatment	37:19–25
Breast pump, electric	For expressing milk	47:31–34
Breast pump, manual	For expressing milk	47:28–31
BVM device	Manual breath-restoring device	46:39
Cast	Immobilizes broken bones to allow healing	37:17
Catheter	For incontinence	41:36
Contact lenses	Corrects vision	35:22–23
CPAP	For treating sleep apnea	46:42
CPM device (continuous passive movement)	Physiotherapy after joint surgery	46:11
Defibrillator	Electrical shock device to restore heart function	46:16–19
Dialysis	For patients with loss of kidney function	46:21
Diathermy	Cauterizes blood vessels	46:20
Doppler	Checks fetal pulse	45:19–20
Droplet counter	Regulates the administering of intravenous fluids	46:54, 57
ECG (electro-cardiography)	Checks heart rhythms	45:1
ECG, electrodes	Relates heart's electrical signals	45:3
ECG, electrode gel	Enhances conductivity for checking heart's electric signals	45:3
ECG, holter	Portable ECG	45:7
ECG, telemetric	Allows monitoring of patient's heart rhythms through wireless communication	47:4
Enema	Relieves constipation	46:25–28
Ergometer	Tests heart function under stress	45:17

Device	*Purpose*	*Chapter*
Exercycle	Stationary bicycle for maintaining fitness	47:1
Feeding tube	Tube through which food is administered directly to stomach	46:22
Feeding tube pump	Regulates food administered through a feeding tube	46:23
Fetal monitor	Detects fetal distress	45:27
Glucometer	Tests blood sugar level	48:26–27
Hearing aid	For the hard of hearing	47:17
Heating and cooling equipment	For heating or cooling a patient's room	19:6–11
Holter ECG		See ECG
Impulse vibrator	Physiotherapy device for CF patients	46:13
Incubator	For premature baby care	46:3
Incubator, portable	For premature baby care	46:1–2
Infrared	Speeds healing	46:12
Infusion	System for administering food, medicine, and other fluids intravenously	46:53–57
Infusion pump	For precise measuring of intravenous liquids or medication	46:54–57
Inhalator	For administering medication to the lungs	46:4–5
Injection pump	For administering medication or TPN to infants intravenously	46:58–59
Inner tube	For hemorrhoid sufferers	47:7
Intercom	For communications and hospital orderly alarm system	47:2

Device	*Purpose*	*Chapter*
Interferential device	Electrotherapy for pain	46:9
Intravenous	Infusion for administering medication, food, blood	46:53–57
Lympho press	For accumulation of fluids after lymph node removal surgery	47:14
Mattress, air-pressure	Prevents pressure sores	47:11–12
Mattress, egg-crate foam	Prevents pressure sores	47:10
Mattress, heated	Warms patient	47:25–26
Needle	For injections or administering medication	46:43–46
Ophthalmoscope	Eye diagnostic device	45:12, 16
Orthotics	For orthopedic treatment	37:19–25
Otoscope	Ear diagnostic device	45:9–12
Oxygen, central supply or tank	Provides oxygen for patients with respiratory difficulties	46:24
Oxygen inhalator	For administering medication to the lungs	46:6
Oxygen meter	Measures oxygen in the blood	45:22
Penrose	For incontinence	41:36
Pillow, egg-crate foam	Prevents pressure sores	47:10
Pillow, electric	To alleviate stomachache	47:39
Pillow, silicon or silicor	Prevents pressure sores	47:13
Pressure sleeve	Similar to lympho press (see above)	47:15
Prosthesis	Limb replacement	37:27–29
Public address system	Hospital communications	47:2
Pulse oximeter	Measures oxygen in the blood	45:22–24
Radiographic monitor	Makes a dynamic representation of a patient's internal organs	45:37
Resuscitation devices	To restore breathing	46:38–42

Device	*Purpose*	*Chapter*
Scale, baby	For weighing infants	47:35
Signaling device	For calling for a nurse's aid	47:8–9
Sling	Support for sprained arm or shoulder	37:19–25
Stethoscope	Detects heartbeat and breathing	45:30
Stomic bag	For colostomy and ileostomy patients	41:35
Suction pump	To evacuate fluids or mucous from lungs or other parts of body treatment	46:62–64
Sunlamp	For treatment of pain	46:52
Telemetry	Wireless communication system	47:3–6
TENS device	Electrotherapy for pain	46:7–10
Thermometer, digital	Measures temperature	33:22
Thermometer, mercury	Measures temperature	33:21
Trusses and supports	Orthopedic treatment	37:19–25
Ultrasound	Ultrasonic scan of uterus	45:13–15
Vacuum pump	For vacuum birth	46:60–61
Vaporizer, cold vapor	Restores breathing	46:35–37
Vaporizer, hot vapor	Restores breathing	46:32–34
Volumetric pump	For volume-meter-based infusion	46:57
Walker	Walking aid	47:18
Walking aids		47:18–24
Wheelchair, electric	For handicapped or incapacitated patients	47:22
Wheelchair, manual	For handicapped or incapacitated patients	47:20
Wireless communication (telemetry)	Hospital communications	47:3–6
X-ray	Takes picture of internal organs	45:31–36

Chapter 44
Operating Medical Equipment on Shabbos

It should be noted that everything stated in this chapter concerning alternate procedures or different techniques in using different devices applies only when the situation is not urgent and it is possible to consider one's actions. However, if the situation becomes urgent, these considerations should be dispensed with and everything should be done in the most efficient and speedy manner.

Even though it may be permitted to use a device, such as a vaporizer, inhalator, or breast pump, on Shabbos for medical purposes, care must be taken to plan in advance the manner of its operation in order to minimize Shabbos desecration. The following issues must be taken into consideration:

a. Order of priorities in operating a device
b. Order of priorities in selecting a device
c. Preparations and arrangements before operation

Order of Priorities in Operating a Device

The following actions are permissible in operating a device on Shabbos if it is needed, from the most permissible action to the least:

1. Connecting the device to a timer before Shabbos which is set to the hours when it will most likely be needed.[1]
2. Connecting the device to a timer before Shabbos, but then the need arises to use it earlier, requiring that the timer be reset to the earlier time.[2]
3. Plugging the device into a timer, which was connected to the wall outlet before Shabbos, while the device is off so that the timer will turn on the device.[3] If the timer is not already connected to the wall outlet from before Shabbos, it cannot be used.[4]
4. Asking a non-Jew to operate the device.[5]
5. Asking a child who has not reached the age of *chinuch* to operate the device.[6]
6. Asking a child who has reached the age of *chinuch*.[7]

---

1 עדיפות ראשונה היא פשוטה דהוי גרמה מערי"ש דשרי לכתחילה — נתבאר בדברינו לעיל פרק 4 סעיף 19 עיי"ש.

2 בספר תורת היולדת פ"ה הערה ו' כתב וז"ל: ואם הזמן אינו בהול, ואפשר להזיז את שעון השבת שהוא גרמה, ואעפ"י שעי"כ ידלקו נורות רבות. ויתכן ש"גרמה" קל יותר מכל המנויים למעלה ואף מנכרי וראיה לכך שהרי גרם כיבוי הותר לגמרי במקום פסידא כמבואר בסי' שלי"ד כ"ב ברמ"א. ובביאור הלכה שם כתב דלאו דווקא כיבוי אלא ה"ה כל המלאכות, ואילו האמירה לנכרי לא הותרה לומר לו בפירוש כי אם בדרך רמז, "כל המכבה אינו מפסיד", כמבואר שם סעיף כ"ו, עכ"ל.

3 דזה חשיב גרמה, כיון שבעת הכנסת התקע עדיין לא עובר הזרם למכשיר. אולם לשיטת החזון איש הידועה דהכנסת התקע לשקע חשיב למלאכת בונה גם אם אין כרגע זרם בשקע — אין להעדיף אפשרות זו על האפשרויות האחרות.

4 יש להעיר, חיבור תקע המכשיר לשעון שבת שאינו מחובר לזרם החשמל כלל, וחיבורו של השעון עם תקע המכשיר לזרם החשמל — אסור — דהרי מפעיל בשבת שעון שבת שהיא עצמה מלאכה האסורה בשבת. דהרי שעון מכני שעמד מלכת אסור לעורכו בשבת כמבואר בשו"ע סי' של"ח, ובמ"ב ס"ק ט"ו וע"ע שם בשערי תשובה ס"ק ב'. וא"כ ברור דגם הפעלת שעון ע"י חשמל אסורה כמבואר בשו"ת אגרות משה חאו"ח ח"ג סי' מ"ט. לכן, אם לא חיבר מערי"ש את השעון לחשמל, האפשרות שבידו לחסוך באיסורי שבת — מתחילת מעדיפות רביעית המבוארת, והיינו מאמירה לאינו יהודי.

5 עדיפות רביעית: אמירה לגוי — הוי שבות שאין בו מעשה, דהוא השבות הקל ביותר.

6 עדיפות חמישית: ע"י קטן שלא הגיע לחנוך. כן הוא בשו"ע סי' רס"ו, מבואר בדברינו פרק 4 סעיף 6 וסעיף 7 וסעיף 8, ושם בהערה 10.

7 עדיפות שישית: ע"י קטן שהגיע לחנוך. כמבואר בדברינו פרק 4 סעיף 8. ואם אפשר שהקטן יעשה החלול בשינוי, ודאי קל טפי דהוי שבות דשבות.

7. Operating the device in a nonstandard manner.[8]
8. Two people operating the device simultaneously.[9]

Order of Priorities in Selecting a Device

9. When a non-Jew operates a machine, the type of device is not important. However, if a Jew is operating it, consideration should be given to the kind of equipment that will cause the least violation of Shabbos. As above, all this applies if the circumstance allows such considerations, as in a non-urgent situation.
10. *Mechanical or electronic.* When there is no difference to the patient whether he is treated by a mechanical or electronic device, the former is preferable. For example, a mechanical blood pressure meter is preferred to an electronic one. The same applies to a thermometer, baby scale, and other such equipment.
11. *A display or a graduated circle.* There are devices, such as infusion pumps, that operate with a mechanical graduated circle. These may also have an electronic display. The graduated-circle device is preferable.
12. *With a screen or without.* When there is no medical preference, a device without a display screen should be used.
13. *With or without a printout.* When there is no need to print out the results of the diagnosis, the printout function can be disabled before Shabbos. However, if this will require manually entering the information into the patient's record, it is preferable that the device print out the data and the printout appended to the record.
14. *Main power supply or battery-operated.* A portable, battery-operated device, such as an otoscope for checking the ears, is preferred over a device operated from the main supply.

---

8 עדיפות שביעית: ע״י שינוי. מבואר בשו״ע סי׳ רס״ו סעיף י״א ובמ״ב ס״ק כ״ט דע״י קטן עדיף מגדול בשינוי. ורק אם אין קטן יעשה הגדול בשינוי.

9 עדיפות שמינית: ע״י שניים שעשאוה. אמנם ע״י שינוי וע״י שניים שעשאוה, שניהם דרגה אחת להם באיסורי שבת. אך היות ויש פוסקים שלא בכל מלאכה יש ההיתר של שנים שעשאוה. לכן הבאנו דירוג זה אחר דירוג בשינוי עיין בדברינו לעיל פרק 4 בעניין שניים שעשאוה.

15. For the priorities in which kind of phone to use, see chapter 14, "Using a Telephone on Shabbos."

Preparing a Device before Operating It

16. When operating a device, it is usually necessary to adjust various controls with their associated indicator lights. At times, it is possible to disable unneeded indicators and printing functions.

17. Before operating the device and connecting it to the electrical outlet, all the priorities mentioned above should be considered in order to minimize Shabbos desecration. (See also chapter 9, "Levels of Urgency," where this was discussed regarding a *choleh she'ein bo sakanah*.)

18. For example, before operating an ECG machine, one must attach all the electrodes and adjust them. It is preferable to attach the electrodes to the patient first and then to activate the machine. The same applies to monitors that require cables to be connected. These should be connected before starting up the device.

19. Consideration should be given to leaving certain devices on before Shabbos so that all that has to be done is to attach them to the patient. This will minimize the severity of the Shabbos desecration, provided that leaving the device on does not adversely affect its subsequent operation.

Chapter 45
Diagnostic Devices

Electrocardiography (ECG) Machine

1. An ECG machine is used to determine whether the heart is working properly. It does this by recording the small electric waves that are generated during heart activity. The test determines the state of the atria and ventricles, the contractions of the atria, and the time needed for an electrical wave to move from the atrium to the ventricle. The electric waves are registered by electrodes placed on the body. The results are recorded on grid paper.

2. To set up the test, electrodes are attached to the patient's legs and hands. Another six electrodes are attached to the chest or other parts of the body.

3. There are different types of electrodes that differ in the manner in which they are attached to the patient. Some are attached with adhesive pads, some by suction. The site of the connection has to be moistened to increase conductivity of the electric signals. At times, a special electrode gel is used. A fluid is preferable for Shabbos, but if a fluid cannot be used, the gel may be applied.

4. Mode of operation:
    a. The electrodes are attached to the patient, and the machine is turned on.
    b. The operating rate is adjusted. This can be done before starting the device.
    c. A printout of the results is torn off. This should not be done along the perforation.
    d. The patient's name, date, and time are recorded.

5. On Shabbos, it is preferable to have a non-Jew perform the ECG, in particular the recording of the patient's information. If a Jew operates the machine, it is preferable that he use a preprinted sticker that contains the patient's information instead of entering the data himself.

    This test should be carried out on Shabbos only if there is suspicion of a life-threatening condition. Routine ECG readings should not be performed on Shabbos.

6. Since the electrodes must have direct contact with the skin, it might be necessary to shave the body hair where the electrodes are attached. This should be done before Shabbos. It also may be necessary to do so to prevent hair from being pulled out when the electrodes (especially those attached with adhesive pads) are removed after the test on Shabbos. If the patient was admitted to the hospital on Shabbos, then a non-Jew should shave the patient. When this is impossible, a Jew should do it in an unconventional manner (such as with the left hand).

7. Ambulatory ECG measurements can be carried out by means of a portable device called a holter monitor. This device records the heart's electrical activity automatically. This type of ECG should not be performed on Shabbos.

8. If it is necessary to perform holter ECG measurements on Shabbos, the device should be attached and started up before Shabbos.[1] If it has

---

1 נשמת אברהם ח״ד עמ׳ נ״ח. וז״ל: כתב הגרש״ז אויערבאך זצ״ל שזה נחשב משא ומותר לצאת בו לרחוב בשבת רק במקום שיש עירוב. ועוד דאין בו איסור בעצם הרישום אף אם הוא יתאמץ

to be removed on Shabbos, it should not be switched off until Shabbos is over.[2]

Otoscope

9. The otoscope consists of a flashlight for examining the ear. It is a standard test and used primarily for children. It is usually battery-operated, but otoscopes fixed to the wall by an electric cord are also used.
10. A doctor may use an otoscope on Shabbos to examine a patient. Preferably, a non-Jew should turn on the light, or, if possible, the light should be left on before Shabbos.
11. With some otoscopes, the light intensity must be increased or the focus might have to be adjusted. A doctor may do so if necessary.[3]
12. Some otoscopes and opthalmoscopes recharge between uses when returned to their base. These should not be used on Shabbos unless no other device is available and a medical urgency exists.

Ultrasound

13. The ultrasound machine scans the uterus through sound waves. It is used most often during pregnancy to check on the growth of the fetus, but it is also used to check the uterus for growths, wounds, or other abnormalities or during a procedure. There are three techniques that can be used in an ultrasound scan:
    a. Using a rectangular probe, or transducer, over the surface of the body
    b. Using a microphone-shaped probe over the surface of the body

---

ונגרמים בכך רשומים שונים, כי אין רשום על טייפ נחשב ככתיבה וגם אין איסור בונה כי אין חשיבות למה שנרשם על הטייפ רק באופן זמני ואינו הופך להיות כלי שמשתמש בו תמיד, עכ״ד. דאחרי שהעבירו את הרישום לנייר מוחקים את הטייפ כדי שיהיה מוכן לשימוש חוזר, וידאג שבזמן הרכבת המכשיר, לא יגלחו לו בחזה רק המקום שם עתידים להדביק את החוטים המקשרים בין גופו לבין גוף המכשיר, אלא גם המקומות שם ידביקו את הפלסטרים, כך שבשבת לא יתלשו שום שיער בזמן הורדת הפלסטרים מגופו.

2 נשמת אברהם שם.

3 עיין בשו״ת מנחת שלמה סי׳ י״ב. ובמה שכתבנו לעיל בפרק 21 סעיף 11.

c. Intravaginally

The scan involves turning the device on and off, viewing the display of lines and writing on the monitor, and zooming in or out of a given area on the monitor. The device can be turned on before Shabbos for use.

14. If necessary, a printout may be obtained either in letter or picture form, but at times the picture is not absolutely needed. The picture should be printed out by a non-Jewish doctor or technician.

15. On Shabbos, this scan should be carried out only in life-endangering situations and not as a part of a routine checkup.

Ophthalmoscope

16. An opthalmoscope is similar to the otoscope except that the ophthalmoscope is used for examining the inside of the eye rather than the ear. The laws regarding the otoscope mentioned above (see paragraphs 9–12) also apply here.

Ergometer

17. The ergometer is used for examining people who suffer from heart problems to determine the heart's reaction to physical exertion. It may consist of a mechanical treadmill that forces the person to run at an increasingly higher speed, thus exerting the heart. Alternatively, it may consist of a stationary bicycle (exercycle) that the patient "rides"; friction is continuously added to increase the effort necessary to turn the wheels. As the patient rides the treadmill or bicycle, he is connected to an ECG machine that records the heart's reaction to the exercise to see if he is at risk of a heart attack.

18. In general, it is not urgent to carry out this test on Shabbos, and therefore it should not be performed then.

Doppler Monitor

19. The Doppler monitor is used for detecting problems in pregnancy up

to approximately the twenty-ninth week. When problems with the fetus are suspected, the mother is examined once or twice a day with a Doppler to check the presence of a fetal pulse.

The Doppler operates without a display. It consists of an electrically driven amplifier and a microphone of the kind used in loudspeakers. It operates on the principle of sending out and then receiving sound waves. Since it is more sensitive than ordinary monitors, it is especially suitable for detecting the weak fetal pulse.

20. If the Doppler must be used on Shabbos, it is preferable that it be plugged in by a non-Jew. The testing itself can then be carried out by a Jewish doctor.

Thermometer

21. The laws applicable to the use of a thermometer on Shabbos are enumerated above, in chapter 33, "Fever, Hypothermia, and Measuring Temperature."

Pulse Oximeter (Oxygen Meter)

22. The oximeter is a very important device that provides a precise picture of the blood's oxygen content. It immediately detects any problems so that one may take measures before a situation becomes critical.

23. The oximeter consists of a small monitor that displays the oxygen content of the blood and the pulse rate (some devices provide additional information). The device fits over the finger and looks like a large plastic clothespin. It measures the oxygen level by using infrared waves.

24. Since this device is indispensable to certain patients in order to determine whether they are in need of an outside oxygen supply, it may be turned on during Shabbos. Obviously, if continuous monitoring is required, the device should be turned on before Shabbos. In addition, if there are specific times, such as sleeping hours, when a patient's oxygen level will need to be monitored, the guidelines given above, in chapter 44, "Operating Medical Equipment on Shabbos," should be followed. However, if the need to use the device arises suddenly, the oximeter

may be used on Shabbos in the normal manner.

If possible, the oximeter should be turned on before Shabbos. It should be attached to the finger on Shabbos only when the need arises, as long as this will not interfere with the device's operation.

Blood Pressure Meter

25. There is no halachic problem with measuring blood pressure by a device with a manually inflatable cuff and a mercury and arrow indicator. Such a device may even be used by healthy people, even when there is a medical need.[4]

26. An electronic blood pressure meter should not be used on Shabbos, even in a life-threatening situation, when a manual device can be used instead. If no manual blood pressure meter is available, an electronic meter may be used, but it should be operated by a non-Jew. When no non-Jew is available, the instrument should be prepared *before* being turned on in the following manner:

    a. Adjust the meter to indicate whether the blood pressure of a child or adult will be measured.

    b. Place the pressure cuff on the patient.

    If the printout function can be disabled, this should be done before Shabbos. However, if this will require manually entering the information into the patient's record, it is preferable that the device print it out and then the printout appended to the record.

    The printout should be torn off by a non-Jew. When this is impossible, it should not be torn along the perforation.

Fetal Monitor

27. The fetal monitor is used to detect fetal heart rate and to determine whether there is fetal distress. The monitor has the following components:

---

4 שו״ע סי׳ ש״ו סעיף ז׳, ושם במ״ב ס״ק ל״ו.

a. A tocograph, which records uterine contractions during labor. It has a disc-shaped transducer called a "toco," which is strapped to the woman's abdomen.

b. An ultrasonic transducer, which is also strapped to the mother's abdomen, to check the fetal heart rate.

c. A special ECG electrode which is attached to the fetus's scalp for internal fetal monitoring of the baby's heart rate.

d. A monitor with a display to which the various components (toco, transducer, electrode) are attached.

Manner of operation:

a. The monitor is turned on so that all the data can be displayed on the monitor.

b. The plug of the tocograph and the ultrasonic transducer (or the scalp probe) is plugged in.

c. The controls are set and adjusted to print out data.

d. Controls are adjusted to increase or decrease the volume of the pulse signal.

28. It is preferable to plug the probes into the machine before it is turned on. The machine should preferably be turned on and off by a non-Jew, but a Jew should attach the belts to the patient. When only a Jew is available for operating the device, this should be done in a manner different from the usual, if possible.

Apnea Monitor

29. The apnea monitor is used for babies who are prone to sudden respiratory arrest (leading to crib death, or sudden infant death syndrome). The baby is connected by electrodes to a monitor that displays the respiration rate and signals any significant change in the baby's breathing.

A similar device with the additional feature of heart-function monitoring, known as an apnea cardiometer, is also used when necessary.

The apnea monitor may be used on Shabbos, since its purpose is to prevent a threat to life. If it is needed on a round-the-clock basis, it should be turned on before Shabbos. If it is not needed at all times, it should be connected to a timer that will turn it on at the necessary times. When changes must be made on Shabbos, such as adjusting parameters or disconnecting the alarm, this should be done in a non-standard manner (*shinui*) or by a minor (see chapter 44, "Operating Medical Equipment on Shabbos").

It should be noted that at times infants are born without any apparent respiratory problem, but the parents, because of a previous trauma or because of a SIDS incident in the family, want the child to be connected to a monitor for their peace of mind. A competent rabbi should be consulted in such a case as to what procedure to follow.

Stethoscope

30. A stethoscope does not employ any power or electricity. It consists solely of a hollow tube that transmits specific noises to earphones. It may be used on Shabbos without any restrictions.

X-Ray Machine

31. The X-ray machine provides a picture of various organs. Its power and radiation dosages are adjustable in accordance with its needs. The X-ray laboratory is comprised of several units:

    a. X-ray room
    b. Control panel
    c. Device for printing out patient data
    d. Film development

32. Most of the equipment in the X-ray room is electronically operated. They include:

    a. A large, flat examination table that changes positions.
    b. A drawer under the table which is electronically adjustable. The drawer holds an X-ray film cassette in which the film is placed.

c. A stand-up table for X-raying the nasal cavities or the chest. The patient is positioned near or against a special plate attached to the table.

d. An adjustable overhead telescoping arm that is adjusted for taking X-rays at different angles and varying strengths.

e. A monitor for viewing the X-ray.

33. The control panel is located in a cubicle outside the X-ray room. It is usually glassed in to protect the technician from overexposure to X-rays. The technician inputs information on the X-ray picture to be taken, and then the equipment is directed accordingly from the control panel. The technician activates the machine to perform the actual X-ray from the control panel as well.

34. An ID camera records the patient's data on the X-ray film. For the camera to perform this function, the patient's details must be written on special paper or keyed in. The camera then transfers the data to the X-ray film.

35. Once the X-ray has been taken, the film is removed from the film cassette in the dark room and placed in a development device. The material on which the image is printed out is fed from a roll into the device and removed the same way.

36. An X-ray machine may be used on Shabbos if a life-threatening situation is suspected, but the extent of Shabbos desecration can be minimized in the following ways:

a. The equipment can be operated by a non-Jew.

b. If there are no non-Jewish technicians available, Shabbos desecration can be minimized by, for example, setting all the equipment into the On mode before Shabbos.

c. The ID camera can be dispensed with by using preprinted labels, usually available in the patient's file. These labels can also be placed on the X-ray film envelope rather than writing down the patient's information.

Radiographic Monitor and Image Intensifier

37. An X-ray represents the patient's state at the time the X-ray was taken. However, at times it is necessary to obtain a dynamic representation of the patient's state following the administration of medications. This is done using the radiographic monitor.

    The radiographic monitor has a screen on which the X-ray image is projected. The patient lies on the X-ray examination table, and the technician observes the image on the monitor, intensifies it, and takes an X-ray image if necessary. This machine is used in very special cases and may be operated normally when a life-threatening situation is suspected.

Chapter 46

Equipment Used in Treatments and Procedures

Baby Incubator

1. There are two types of baby incubators: the regular baby incubator and the portable baby incubator. The portable incubator is made to be moved and therefore contains many built-in features:

   a. A mechanical ventilator or respirator which delivers oxygen to the baby

   b. Suction apparatus (for emergency purposes) to evacuate fluids or mucous from the lungs

   c. Light

   d. A heating system and thermostat

   The heating system can be operated from the main power supply or with a built-in battery, and it has a pilot light and thermometer. The light and the suction pump may also be operated from the battery.

2. When it is necessary to move an infant from one place to another, the portable incubator may be used on Shabbos because usually this is done in life-threatening situations.

3. The regular infant incubator is similar to the mobile incubator, but usually there is no built-in suction apparatus and the other systems have backups. The ambient (or air) temperature is controlled by the incubator, and the baby's temperature is automatically monitored as well. The parameters for these systems should be set ahead of time by adjusting the controls before Shabbos. The alarm function should not be disabled because it may detect a life-threatening situation.

Inhalator

4. An inhalator is used to administer medication to the lungs to treat asthma, bronchitis, laryngitis, and other respiratory conditions. It works by converting a solution into a spray, which the patient inhales to clear up the air passages. The electrical inhalator is operated by a compression pump.

   Manner of operation:

   a. The mask is connected to a silicon tube.
   b. The tube is connected to the inhalator.
   c. The solution to be inhaled is poured into the device.
   d. The compressor, which motors the device, is turned on.

   The solution may come in a bottle or in a bag which requires inserting a syringe into it. The assembly of the inhalator does not require any screwing action; rather, each part is inserted into the other with a half-turn. Therefore, assembling the device does not require any *melachah* on Shabbos. The inhalator may be heated, but this is a separate consideration.

   Some authorities rule that the production of the inhalation spray is prohibited on Shabbos. Rabbi Akiva Eiger rules that if water is used, there is no problem.[1]

5. In the case of the sudden onset of a serious respiratory problem on Shabbos, the inhalator should be turned on and operated immediately.

---

1 עיין בתשובות הגאון רעק״א זצ״ל סי׳ כ׳ שדן בארוכה בדין זורה, והסיק דלכו״ע במים אין דין זורה. עיי״ש.

In cases where it is known that inhalation will be needed for a given time period, the inhalator should be connected to a timer. If this was not done, see chapter 44 on operating medical equipment on Shabbos.

Oxygen Inhalator

6. The oxygen inhalator is used to administer medication in the lungs by an oxygen gas-powered device (compressor). The oxygen/air supply system installed in hospitals is usually supplied by a central compressor. This means that there is no need to turn on any device. However, there may still exist the problem of causing the central compressor to run longer. (In some hospitals, the compressors run on demand.[2]) In any case, it is permitted to use compressed air/oxygen even for a *choleh she'ein bo sakanah*, an ordinary bedridden patient.

   As for connecting the external equipment to the built-in compressed-air pump, it is possible to attach the equipment before Shabbos. Then all that has to be done on Shabbos is to open the valve.

   An oxygen inhalator may also be powered by a compressed-oxygen tank with a flow meter. Using such a tank is preferable to using the central compressor. At least some effort should be made to have such a tank available for a patient who will need an oxygen inhalator on Shabbos.

Electrical Physiotherapy (Electrotherapy) Equipment

TENS

7. TENS (transcutaneous electrical nerve stimulator) is one of the most extensively used electrotherapy devices. It is used to relieve pain by sending impulse signals to the nerves. This scrambles the pain messages sent to the brain so that the patient will not sense the pain. Some patients use TENS even for intolerable chronic pain. It is also used in

---

2 עצם השימוש בלחץ אויר מצינורות בית החולים — הוא נידון בפני עצמו, ישנם בתי חולים שמערכת אספקת החמצן וצינורות האוויר פועלות באופן שאין השפעה ישירה בין צריכה בפועל להפעלת הקומפרסור ובזה קל יותר השימוש מבחינת גרם מלאכת שבת. כמובן שאין זה משנה אם יש צורך רפואי אפילו לצורך חולה שאין בו סכנה מותר להשתמש במערכת זו בשבת.

birth to alleviate labor pain. Some TENS units are used to exert mechanical force on temporarily paralyzed muscles with the expectation that this will prevent further muscular degeneration. There are large units for use at institutions and small home-use units.

8. The home-use TENS unit is a rather small device, the size of a beeper monitor. It is worn on a belt, and electrodes are attached to the body with adhesive pads. The unit emits pulses at specified frequencies. If one knows that the TENS unit will be needed on Shabbos, all the controls should be adjusted ahead of time.

9. The interferential TENS unit is similar to the standard TENS device, but has a stronger effect. It is used for a patient who is in extreme pain.

10. Concerning Shabbos use, a physician should be consulted to determine whether skipping a day is detrimental to the treatment. If it is not, the TENS unit should not be used on Shabbos. However, if interrupting the treatment will cause muscular degeneration, it is considered *sakanas eiver*, danger to a limb, for which one may transgress rabbinical prohibitions on Shabbos.[3] It is preferable that the unit be connected to a timer on Friday so that all one needs to do to operate it on Shabbos is to attach the electrodes. Otherwise, the procedures for operating medical equipment on Shabbos discussed in chapter 44 should be followed.

CPM Device

11. CPM stands for "continuous passive motion." It is used for patients who have undergone upper or lower limb joint surgery. These patients must perform exercises to gradually regain use of the joints. The exercises are usually very painful, and the patient therefore has difficulty performing them. The CPM device is strapped to the limb and moves the joint for the patient in accordance with the doctor's instructions. There is usually no need to use a CPM device on Shabbos.[4]

---

3 חשש לאי תפקוד השריר נחשב לסכנת איבר, כמבואר לעיל פרק 28 סעיף 1 ושם בהערה 5 בשם קצות השולחן.

4 ואמנם אם המצב מוגדר כסכנת איבר, בזה יש להתיר איסורים מדרבנן כנ״ל פרק 28, אך אם

Bio Beam and Infrared Device

12. The bio beam and infrared device employ a bulb that radiates at different wavelengths, frequency, and depth of penetration. They are used to heal or accelerate the healing of wounds and for local pain reduction. These devices should not be used on Shabbos unless the doctor says it is necessary.

Impulse Vibrator

13. Sometimes a viscous mucous accumulates in the lungs and interferes with respiration. When left untreated for a long time, this may cause infection of the respiratory tract and breakdown of the lungs. This situation is alleviated by massaging the chest to free the mucous. This can be done manually or by means of an impulse vibrator, which is used particularly for cystic fibrosis patients. There is no urgency in using this device on Shabbos since, if necessary, the massage can be carried out manually, unless a doctor instructs differently.

Shaving a Patient

14. Sometimes a patient has to be shaven in preparation for a treatment or procedure, for example, for an ECG. One must give consideration as to how this may be done on Shabbos.

15. If a patient must be shaved for an ECG, or any other test that requires the attachment of electrodes, it is preferable that he be shaved before Shabbos. The shaved area should include any place where the adhesive pads will adhere to the skin to prevent hair being pulled out on Shabbos when the tape is removed.[5] However, if this was not done, and an ECG must be performed on Shabbos, a non-Jew should shave the patient. If a non-Jew is not available, only the areas where the electrodes will be attached should be shaven.

אין צורך רפואי בכך יש לדלג על פעילות זו בשבת, מה גם שהפעלת מכשיר הסי פי אם כרוך באיסורים מדאורייתא, אלא אם כן ניתן לכוונו מראש ולחברו לשעון שבת כפי המוסבר לעיל פרק 44.

5 לעיל פרק 45 הערה 1 הבאנו בשם הנשמת אברהם, שכאשר מגלחים חולה קודם השבת כדי להניח את האלקטרודות בשבת יש לגלח את כל מקום הנחת המדבקה כדי שבשבת כאשר יוציאו

The same applies when hair in the area of a wound that is in danger of infection needs to be shaved. For example, if the wound needs to be sutured or taped and the area needs to be shaven, it is preferable that this be done by a non-Jew. Most emergency physicians no longer shave the area of a laceration, preferring to leave the site alone to avoid microtrauma, or, in cases where the area is hard to see, scissors are used.

When no non-Jew is available, it is preferable that a hair removal cream be used rather than a razor or electric shaver. A razor is preferable to an electric shaver.

A woman in her ninth month should shave where necessary before Shabbos to avoid possible Shabbos desecration. If this was not done, a non-Jew should be asked to do it.

Defibrillator

16. A defibrillator is used for delivering a closely controlled discharge of electric energy to the heart in order to correct dangerous heart rhythms. This is done in a case of changes in the heart rate (cardiac arrest).

    Manner of operation:

    a. The defribrillator is turned on, and the knob is adjusted for the desired charge.
    b. Two paddles are placed on the patient's chest, and the electric shock is delivered through the paddles.
    c. Electrodes are placed on the patient's body to monitor heart function.

17. This device is used solely in life-threatening situations, and hence its use on Shabbos is not restricted in any way. In the case of stable atrial fibrillation, defribibillation on Shabbos should preferably be done by medication. If electrical shock cardioversion is necessary in a stable patient, a non-Jew should operate the machinery.

את המדבקות לא יגרמו לתלישת שיער עי״ש, יש לציין שבשבת צריך לצמצם בגילוח רק על מקום החיוני להולכה חשמלית טובה (או כאשר יש צורך בפרפר וכיו״ב — את השטח החיוני) אך אין להוסיף בגילוח כדי שבשעת הוצאת המדבקה לא יתלשו שערות, ופשוט. אולם אם הנכרי מגלח בשבת אין צורך להגבילו.

18. There is another kind of defribillator called an "automatic defribillator." The automatic defibrillator is implanted in the patient's body, and it continuously checks the heart rate. If it detects a ventricle fibrillation, it automatically discharges an electric charge to return the heart to normal function.

19. Once implanted (this should not be done on Shabbos), the automatic defribrillator is left to operate, just like a pacemaker, at all times.

Diathermy Device (Bovey)

20. This device is used primarily in the operating room, where it performs two functions:

    a. It serves instead of a scalpel for opening the operation site.

    b. It cauterizes blood vessels during surgery.

    Some diathermy devices include a laparoscope, a miniature camera that is inserted into the body through a minute opening. This presents the operating personnel with a picture of the situation, eliminating the need for a larger incision.

    These devices may be used on Shabbos, even though the same results may be obtained with manual and mechanical equipment. This is because they provide more efficient and infection-free treatment.

Dialysis Machine

21. One of the functions of the kidneys is to remove impurities and poisons from the blood. When the kidneys malfunction, this function is carried out by a dialysis machine to which the patient is connected, usually every third day. The machine is attached through a blood vessel either in the arm or in the abdominal wall.

    Care should be taken not to schedule dialysis on Shabbos. If the doctor insists that dialysis be performed on Shabbos, it is permitted.

Feeding Tube

22. Some patients are unable to eat for various reasons, from a complete lack of appetite brought about by a severe mental disorder to a coma.

These patients are fed via a feeding tube. The feeding tube consists of a silicon tube that is inserted through the nose and leads to the stomach. Food or drink is then administered through it directly into the stomach at set intervals. A feeding tube may be inserted on Shabbos.

Feeding Tube Pump

23. When a patient's food has to be delivered to his stomach in precisely metered portions, the feeding tube is connected to a food-metering pump. On Shabbos, this pump should be used in the same manner as the infusion pump (see paragraphs 53–56 in this chapter).

Oxygen

24. Connecting a person to an oxygen supply does not involve Shabbos desecration because the oxygen moves through a flow meter by virtue of the pressure in the tank and not by an electrical pump.

    It is preferable, if it does not require great effort, to connect the oxygen gas to an oxygen tank instead of to the general hospital oxygen supply. This is because attaching something to a building involves the prohibition of *boneh*, building. However, if a large quantity of oxygen is needed, or if it requires a great deal of effort to bring in an oxygen tank, the patient should be connected to the general oxygen supply. This is certainly true if the patient's condition is life-threatening.

Enema

25. An enema for cleansing the digestive system or to treat constipation may be administered to a patient who is classified as a *choleh she'ein bo sakanah*, an ordinary bedridden patient (see chapter 41, "Diseases and Disorders of the Digestive System," paragraph 27). Medication or liquid soap may be added to the water used in the enema.[6]

26. An enema administered to a healthy person or to one who is suffering

---

6 המדובר בסבון נוזלי או אבקה מסוימת שמתערבת עם המים והופכת לנוזל, אך לפורר שביבי סבון וכיו"ב אין ראוי לעשות בשבת.

from a minor ailment (*michush*) should consist of water only.[7] The water should be warmed up before Shabbos.

27. Extreme caution must be exercised not to detach hair when inserting the enema tube.[8] The enema should be dipped in petroleum jelly or another lubricating substance to facilitate the insertion. However, these should not be smeared on the tube.[9]

28. When an enema is permitted on Shabbos, water that was heated before Shabbos should be used. For a *choleh she'ein bo sakanah*, an ordinary bedridden patient, one may use even water from a solar heater, even though the water that is used is replaced by cold water which will subsequently be heated (see chapter 27, "Bathing and Applying Oils," paragraph 1, concerning washing a bedridden patient). However, the use of water from an electric boiler is not permitted, unless it is needed to treat a *choleh sheyeish bo sakanah*, a dangerously ill patient, or for a *choleh she'ein bo sakanah* by a non-Jew.

Baby Oil

29. Baby oil may be applied to infants on Shabbos.[10]

Plaster Casts

30. Making a plaster cast on Shabbos involves transgressing two *melachos: lash*, kneading, and *boneh*, building. Therefore, a Jew can set a cast on Shabbos only for a *choleh sheyeish bo sakanah*, a dangerously ill patient, and only a non-Jew can set a cast for a *choleh she'ein bo sakanah*. If the patient is not considered a *choleh she'ein bo sakanah*, but it is *sakanas*

---

7 בדרך כלל עשיית חוקן בשבת אינה כרוכה בחילול שבת, משום שהכלים שבהם משתמשים הם כלים מכניים. הן בחוקן המורכב ממיכל עם צינור ומים. הן בחוקן הנעשה עם בקבוק קטן הנקרא "פליט אנמה" והן בטיובות שמחדירים לפי הטבעת. עיקר הבעיה היא אם שייך בזה גזירת שחיקת סממנים או לא. ולכן במיכל וצינור חוקן ושימוש במים שהוחמו מערב שבת בלבד אין חשש לגזירת שחיקת סממנים. אולם עם מי סבון ושאר חומרים או בבקבוק פליט אנמה וטיובה — יש חשש לגזירת שחיקת סממנים, שלכן למיחושים בעלמא אסור הדבר, אולם לחולה המוגדר כחולה שאין בו סכנה מותר.

8 כמבואר בשו"ע סי' שכ"ח סעיף מ"ט ובמ"ב ס"ק קנ"א.

9 כמבואר לעיל פרק 26 סעיף 28.

10 שו"ת באר משה חלק א' סימן ל"ו אות ד'.

eiver (a danger to the limb) if a cast is not set immediately, it should be done by a non-Jew or, if that is not possible, only after Shabbos. Similarly, a plaster cast should not be removed on Shabbos except in a case of urgent medical need.

Vaporizer

31. There are many kinds of vaporizers. Only two of them will be discussed here: the hot vapor vaporizer and the cold vapor vaporizer.

Hot Vapor Vaporizer

32. A hot water vaporizer consists of a container filled with water in which a heating element is immersed. The heating element boils and vaporizes the water, and the vapor is discharged into the air. This restores breathing and induces mucous, if present, to discharge. The container must be refilled every couple of hours to replace the water that has evaporated. Some vaporizers have an automatic switch that disconnects it when there is no water and restarts it when water is added.

33. The operation of the vaporizer involves transgression of two *melachos*: *havra'ah*, when turning it on, and *mevashel*, when the water is boiled. The first problem can be overcome by means of a timer set to the appropriate times. But this does not solve the problem of adding water to be boiled. Therefore, only in a life-threatening situation may the hot water vaporizer be operated in the standard manner, including adding water. In any case, it is preferable to add water that was heated before Shabbos.

34. In the case of a *choleh she'ein bo sakanah*, a Jew may not add cold water to the vaporizer.[11] Some authorities permit adding water that has been boiled before Shabbos,[12] but others do not permit this either.[13] If it is

---

11 דכל צורכי חולה שאין בו סכנה נעשין ע״י עכו״ם אפילו מלאכה מדאורייתא. וע״ע בזה בשו״ת מנחת יצחק ח״ז סימן כ״א. וע״ע בשו״ת באר משה ח״ו סימן נ״א.

12 עיין בתשובת הגאון רבי חיים פנחס שיינברג שליט״א בקובץ אורייתא ח״ז, מאמר ארוך בדין בישול מים במכשיר אדים, והורה להקל בזה עיי״ש.

13 עיין בשו״ת מנחת יצחק הנ״ל.

suspected that the patient's condition will deteriorate, the vaporizer may be activated by a minor if no non-Jew is available.[14]

Cold Vapor Vaporizer

35. A cold vapor vaporizer has no heating element and does not boil the water. Rather, it has a mechanism that vaporizes the liquid into fine droplets and causes them to be discharged through a mouthpiece by pressure. Once the device is operating, there is no Shabbos desecration, but it is not permitted to turn it on or off.

36. Similar to other devices, the vaporizer can be connected to power before Shabbos by means of a timer. As to adding water, this depends on the type of vaporizer it is. If it will keep running even if there is no water, then water may be added. However, if the device shuts off when dry, then adding water causes it to continue operating. Therefore, it is preferable that a non-Jew be asked to add the water. If a non-Jew is not available, a minor should do it (see chapter 4, "*Melachah* Forbidden Only by Rabbinic Law," concerning asking a minor).

37. If a vaporizer used by a *choleh she'ein bo sakanah* was shut off because the water was used up, only a non-Jew is allowed to add water to it.[15]

Resuscitation Devices

38. If a patient stops breathing as a result of shock or a heart attack, the patient has to be resuscitated.

BVM Device

39. The BVM (bag valve mask) device consists of a mask connected to an oxygen tank that is operated manually and serves until the patient is brought to the hospital, where more sophisticated equipment is available (the hospital's BVM is connected to the central oxygen supply). There is no halachic problem in using this device on Shabbos in life-

---

14 עיין בשו״ת באר משה הנ״ל.

15 מבואר בשו״ת מנחת יצחק ושו״ת באר משה הנ״ל.

threatening situations. If assembly is required, or it is not yet connected to an oxygen source, there is a problem of *boneh,* building, and using a tank is preferable for a *choleh she'ein bo sakanah* (see paragraph 24 above).

Hospital Respirator

40. A respirator is used to help a patient breathe. To operate a hospital respirator, tubes are connected to the hospital's central compressed air and oxygen supply. The respirator is then plugged in and the required parameters are set. Parameters include the quantity of air and oxygen pumped per minute and the quantity of the mixture per breath. A mask is also connected to the respirator.

    Since a respirator is usually used in life-threatening situations, one should not spend time looking for a non-Jew to operate it. However, if a non-Jew can be found without causing delay, it is preferable to ask him to operate the respirator.

41. At times, it is necessary to preheat the oxygen-air mixture. This is done by passing the tubing through a canister containing warm water. Here, too, it is preferable to have a non-Jew perform the various tasks involved if he is readily available.

CPAP and BiPAP Devices

42. Certain people suffer from breathing disturbances during sleep. This is known as apnea. The CPAP and BiPAP devices sense such disturbances and are activated automatically to restore breathing. Those in need of these devices may use them on Shabbos. However, it is preferable to connect the device to a timer that will cause it to operate at preset hours (see chapter 44, "Operating Medical Equipment on Shabbos").

Syringes and Needles

43. Four kinds of syringes and needles are currently in use:

    a. A reusable syringe or needle, which can be sterilized and reused

b. A disposable syringe or needle, which is discarded after a single use

c. A disposable syringe or needle that comes in an individual wrapper and is assembled, used, and then discarded while still assembled

d. Preassembled syringes and needles

44. The first three types of syringes and needles are assembled right before they are used. For a patient in a life-endangering situation (*choleh sheyeish bo sakanah*), and particularly when time is short, these may be used without restrictions.

45. In the case of a *choleh she'ein bo sakanah*, an ordinary bedridden patient, the first two types are permissible since the parts are disassembled immediately after use. In the third type, the assembly is permanent and the fact that it is discarded does not make the initial assembly more permissible, even if care is taken to disassemble the unit after use (since this is not the conventional manner of use). The assembly therefore involves a Torah prohibition, and it should not be used for a *choleh she'ein bo sakanah*.

46. The fourth type is preferable for use on Shabbos. However, this type of syringe is more difficult to handle, since sometimes one must use one needle for filling the syringe and another for administering the injection. Still, if it is possible to use the same needle for both purposes, the preassembled syringe is preferred.[16]

Administering an Injection

47. There are three ways to administer an injection: (a) intramuscular, (b) intravenous, and (c) subcutaneous. A patient in a life-endangering situation (*choleh sheyeish bo sakanah*) can receive any type of injection on Shabbos. A *choleh she'ein bo sakanah* may receive an intramuscular or subcutaneous injection, since these do not involve transgressing a Torah prohibition. However, certain authorities hold that since

---

16 עיין בכל זה בנשמת אברהם ח״א סי׳ שי״ג ס״ק א׳ משי״כ בשם מרן הגרש״ז אויערבאך זצוק״ל.

an intravenous injection involves extracting a little blood in order to ensure that the needle indeed entered the vein, this involves a Torah prohibition and therefore may not be performed for a *choleh she'ein bo sakanah*.[17]

48. A diabetic may inject insulin before a meal on Shabbos, since diabetes is a life-threatening condition. (See chapter 42, "Nonprogressive Chronic Disorders," paragraph 6; see also chapter 48, "Tests and Analysis," on the use of a glucometer on Shabbos for measuring blood sugar).

49. Rabbi Shlomo Zalman Auerbach, *zt"l*, questioned whether morphine injections are allowed on Shabbos, since they do not have a therapeutic effect. This is similar to the prohibition of extracting an aching tooth (see chapter 34, "Dental Diseases and Hygiene"). However, an argument can be made that pain can cause a patient's condition to deteriorate and may lead to a life-threatening situation.

50. There is no question that morphine may be injected intravenously in the case of a pulmonary edema (CHF, or congestive heart failure) even if the patient is not in pain, which would prevent a potentially life-threatening situation.[18] Many doctors, however, now feel that morphine serves only to reduce anxiety; nevertheless, it may still be used intravenously for such situations.

51. It stands to reason that an epidural analgesia injection to reduce birth pains may be administered if the medical staff recommends it for a woman in extreme pain. However, no such injection should be administered to a woman who is at the beginning stages of labor and is not yet in extreme pain.[19]

---

17 ובציץ אליעזר (ח״ח סי׳ ט״ו פרק ידי וחי״ט סי׳ י״ז אות ל״ו) ס״ל שזריקה תוך ורידית אינה אסורה אלא מדרבנן. ובחי״ט הביא שכן דעת הגרש״ז אויערבאך שליט״א עיי״ש. ועי״ע בנשמת אברהם ח״א סי׳ שט״ז עמ׳ קנ״ז.

18 נשמת אברהם שם עמ׳ קנ״ד.

19 בחוברת מבית לוי כרך ז׳ דנו גדולי הדור שליט״א כ״ק האדמו״ר מגור זיע״א הגאון רבי פנחס מנחם אלתר זצוק״ל עם יבדל לחי״ט מרן שבט הלוי שליט״א, ומסקנת השבט הלוי שאין ליעץ ליקח זריקת אפידורל בשבת אלא אם במהלך הלידה יש קשיים ויסורים אך לא לכתחילה. עיי״ש.

Sunlamp

52. The sunlamp consists of a special blue- or lavender-colored bulb installed in a semicircular reflector with a handle. It is used to relieve pain by holding it for a time over the painful area. This lamp may be used on Shabbos for a *choleh she'ein bo sakanah*, provided that it is switched on before Shabbos. It may also be connected to a timer (see chapter 44, "Operating Medical Equipment on Shabbos").

Infusion

53. Infusion is used extensively for intravenously administering medication, food, blood, and TPN (total parenteral nutrition) intravenously. The assembly of the infusion device involves various *melachos,* and thus one must do as much as possible to prepare the infusion before Shabbos in order to minimize Shabbos desecration. The following should be taken into consideration when it comes to infusion on Shabbos:
    a. Inserting the needle involves the *melachah* of *dash*[20] and is therefore permitted only in a life-threatening situation or when there is a suspicion that such a situation exists. Thus, in the case of a *choleh she'ein bo sakanah*, the needle should be inserted only by a non-Jew.
    b. The site of insertion should be disinfected by pouring the disinfectant onto the skin and then wiping the area with tissue paper or precut cotton. (In other words, the cotton should not be soaked with the alcohol and then rubbed on the site.)
    c. The infusion unit should be mounted under sterile conditions, which includes opening the bag with the fluids and assembling the tube and needle.
    d. After the needle is inserted, it is fastened to prevent it from slipping out. This should be done using precut adhesive tape (see chapter 38, "Wounds and Dressings").

54. The infusion system's operation is comprised of several steps:

---

20 מבואר לעיל פרק 26 סעיף 15 ובהערה 19 עיי"ש.

a. The infusion is switched on.

b. The droplet counter (which regulates how many drops of fluid flow through the needle per minute) is adjusted by turning a dial manually or electronically by means of a digital display.

c. The viewing port for identifying the number of droplets that flow from the bag is connected at the site where the fluid is discharged from the bag.

d. The infusion tube is inserted through a device that adjusts the pumping of the fluid to the required level.

e. The display is activated.

An infusion unit is usually connected to the main power supply, but it is possible to disconnect it from the power supply and operate it with a built-in battery. There is a pilot light that indicates that the apparatus that stabilizes the tubing and allows accurate supply of medication is improperly closed, and there is a buzzer to indicate a malfunction, such as entry of air into the tube.

55. The purpose of the infusion system is to provide a regulated supply of medication. The patient is connected to the electronically powered infusion system which can administer an exact unit of medication and other fluids.

56. On weekdays the patient may temporarily disconnect the device from the electric supply, such as when he has to use the bathroom. This cannot be done on Shabbos, which will require him to use a bedpan. If the patient is reluctant to use a bedpan in front of others, he may ask a non-Jew to disconnect and then reconnect the infusion device for him. This, however, cannot be done in order to allow the patient to pray with a minyan.[21] Some authorities permit this if the pilot light is not operating on Shabbos.

---

21 נשמת אברהם ח״ד עמ׳ י״ט.

Volumetric Pump

57. Volumetric pumps employ a volume meter in order to deliver the required quantity of fluid in the same manner as the droplet counter of the infusion system. As in the case of the droplet counter, this device should only be used for a *choleh sheyeish bo sakanah,* a dangerously ill patient.

Injection Pump

58. An injection pump is used to administer precise quantities of medication to infants. It is also used for administering TPN or blood. This pump operates according to preset parameters, such as time or quantity per hour.

    A volumetric pump or injection pump may be used instead of an infusion pump because the infusion pump compresses the fluid in the course of pumping, which may damage the blood or medication being administered. Therefore, whenever such damage may occur, volumetric pumps or injection pumps are used.

59. Since injection pumps are usually used only in life-threatening situations or when such a situation is suspected, they may be used on Shabbos. However, if the parameters can be preset before Shabbos and the device can be operated on a timer, this is preferable. But if this will complicate the treatment, and particularly if the parameters vary with time and cannot be preset, the device may be used in the ordinary manner.

Vacuum Birth

60. Sometimes in a birth the baby has to be delivered by vacuum. This involves:

    a. Connecting a cap-topped tube to the device
    b. Starting up the vacuum pump
    c. Adjusting the vacuum pressure
    d. Releasing the vacuum pressure

61. A vacuum pump need not be operated by a non-Jew on Shabbos, since it is used only in emergency cases.

Suction Pump

62. The suction pump is used to evacuate fluids or mucous from the lungs or other parts of the body. The device is comprised of a vacuum pump which can be adjusted for vacuum depth. A tube is connected to the device. The other end of the tube is inserted into the patient's windpipe in order to suction out the fluids.

63. In a life-threatening situation, a suction pump should be operated on Shabbos without delay, unless a non-Jew is readily available. In this case, the non-Jew should start up the equipment, and the Jew should operate it.

    In the case of a *choleh she'ein bo sakanah* who is in need of such a procedure, the equipment should be operated by a non-Jew. If a non-Jew is not available, the priorities enumerated in chapter 44, "Operating Medical Equipment on Shabbos," should be followed.

64. In all cases, the depth of the vacuum of an operating pump can be adjusted by a Jew in the course of treatment.

Ointment

65. The laws applicable to the use of ointments on Shabbos are detailed in chapter 26, "Medication for a *Choleh She'ein Bo Sakanah*," paragraphs 25–34.

Chapter 47

Other Apparatus Used by Patients and Doctors

Exercycle

1. The exercycle is used for enhancing body fitness. Just as in the case of the ergometer (see chapter 45, "Diagnostic Devices," paragraph 17), the exercycle is stationary, and the pedals operate wheels that do not touch the ground. These cycles usually come with mechanical rather than electronic equipment, including the speedometer.

   Those who need this device for health may use it on Shabbos.[1] However, if the speedometer or any associated devices are electronically operated (whether from the main power supply or a battery), or if music or another electronic effect is produced, these devices cannot be used on Shabbos.

Intercom and Public Address (PA) System

2. An intercom and PA system is routinely used in hospitals and other public places to call patients, doctors, or orderlies and to make other

---

1 נסיעה באופניים אסורה בשבת בחוצות העיר, נתבאר דין זה בקצרה לעיל פרק מ״ב הערה ד׳ עיי״ש. אולם טעמים אלו יתכן ואינם שייכים באופני כושר, א׳ אין שייך שמא יצא חוץ לתחום. ב׳ אין שייך כ״כ שמא יתקן שאין זה דומה למהלך בדרך ונתקע באמצע הדרך שם יש חשש גדול שמא יתקן משא״כ באופני כושר, וגם לא כ״כ שכיח שיתקלקלו האופניים. ג׳ דהוי עובדין דחול,

announcements. These should not be used on Shabbos except in life-threatening situations.[2] However, since such communications are vital to the proper operation of hospitals and similar places, provisions should be made to have non-Jews operate the equipment.

Telemetry (Wireless Communication)

3. Hospitals and other medical institutions currently operate stations for communicating with wireless equipment, such as the telemetric ECG and telemetric locators.
4. *Telemetric ECG*. A large number of patients wear an ECG transmitter that transmits their ECG readings to monitors located at nurses' stations or in doctors' offices. This allows continuous monitoring of the patients' condition. These may be used on Shabbos, since these devices are worn only by dangerously ill patients.
5. *Telemetric locators*. Medical personnel wear small battery-operated telemetric receivers. These serve to notify the personnel that they are needed to handle urgent cases.
6. These devices may be worn on Shabbos, and it is permitted to broadcast emergency calls to them.[3]

Inner Tube

7. Some patients, such as those suffering from hemorrhoids (see chapter 41, "Diseases and Disorders of the Digestive System"), have difficulty sitting and use an inner tube to make them more comfortable. The in-

---

אולם מצינו שהתירו חכמים עובדין דחול לצורך כגון מדידה לחש בראשו כמבואר בשו״ע סי׳ ש״ו סעיף ז׳ ובמ״ב ס״ק ל״ו.

2 אם יש צורך לסגור מעגל חשמלי כדי לדבר באינטרקום הרי זה איסור דאורייתא, אך אפילו אם המעגל סגור וניתן לדבר ישירות למכשיר יש עכ״פ איסור מדרבנן של השמעת קול, ויש מחמירים שיש בזה אפילו איסור מדאורייתא בדיבור ברם קול. עיין בשו״ת אגרות משה ח״ג חאו״ח סי נ״ה שהביא ארבעה טעמים לאסור חלקם מדאורייתא וחלקם מדרבנן עיי״ש.

3 עיין בשו״ת אגרות משה חאו״ח ח״ד סי׳ פ״א כתב לענין נשיאת מכשירי קשר לחברי ״הצלה״ וז״ל: ולכן מכשיר קשר קטן שלובשים כדי שישמעו בכל מקום שיהיו לאיזה מקום צריך לילך להציל מותרים לצאת בהם בשבת משום שהוא בחשיבות בגד, עיי״ש. ובנידון שלנו זה לא שונה מחברי ״הצלה״ ואולי אפילו יותר דחוף.

ner tube should be inflated before Shabbos, but if this was not done, it can be inflated on Shabbos.[4]

Signaling for Help in the Hospital

8. There are several devices available so that patients can call a nurse for help. Some of these devices are operated by air pressure. The pressurized air moves a slide that covers a light bulb that is always on, indicating that help is needed. There is no halachic problem with using this device on Shabbos.

9. If the signaling device causes a light to turn on, it may be used only by a patient whose life is endangered or by a non-Jew in the case of a *choleh she'ein bo sakanah*, an ordinary bedridden patient (for example, if a non-Jewish patient is hospitalized in the same room, he or she can be asked to call the nurse). Some authorities permit operating such a signal device even in the latter case if the patient urgently needs help to go to the bathroom to spare him the shame of soiling his clothing.[5]

Pressure-Sore Prevention Treatment

10. Several accessories are available for protecting patients from acquiring pressure sores due to prolonged lying in bed. Some of these devices are simple, such as an egg-crate foam mattress or pillow, and there is no problem with using them on Shabbos.

11. Another type of mattress used to prevent pressure sores is an air-pressure mattress. Two sets of tubing that are built into the mattress are alternately inflated and deflated. This varies the pressure on the body and prevents the appearance of pressure sores. The air supply that inflates the tubes is operated by means of an electronically operated pump.

12. The pump of the air-pressure mattress can be switched on before Shabbos and left operating during the day. If this was not done, it can be operated by a non-Jew. If a non-Jew is not available, see chapter 44,

---

4 ניפוח גלגל בשבת נידון בפוסקי דורנו, עיין מש״כ בספר קצות השבת בסיווגי המוקצה ובהערות שם. אך עכ״פ הכא כיון שיש קצת חולי ומצטער יש להקל לכו״ע.

5 עיין באר משה ח״ז קונטרס אלקטרי סימן מ״ד, ע״י שינוי התיר. אז נדברו ח״א סימן ע״ט.

"Operating Medical Equipment on Shabbos," for guidelines in operating equipment on Shabbos.

13. Similar to the air-pressure mattress, the silicon pillow serves to prevent pressure on the patient's body. Silicon is a very expensive substance, but it is highly effective. Silicor, an imitation of silicon, is less expensive but not as effective, especially in the case of extended hospitalization. Both of these may be used on Shabbos.

Lympho Press

14. Patients who had their lymph nodes surgically removed suffer from an accumulation of fluids in the hand or foot. A lympho press is worn on the affected limb to push the fluid gradually toward the center of the body where it can be drained. There is no justification for using this device on Shabbos, since it can be used either before or after Shabbos.

Pressure Sleeve

15. The pressure sleeve is similar to the lympho press, but it is smaller and less effective. It, too, does not need to be used on Shabbos.

Adjustable Bed

16. The four-way adjustable bed is operated by a remote control that allows

    a. lifting and lowering of the head,
    b. lifting and lowering of the legs,
    c. lifting and lowering of the entire bed, and
    d. moving the bed in a rocking motion.

    The remote control should not be used on Shabbos, but in a case of great need it can be operated by a non-Jew. This does not apply to a bed that is adjustable by mechanical or hydraulic means; these may be used on Shabbos.

Hearing Aid

17. A hearing aid may be used on Shabbos provided that it is switched on before Shabbos. It is permissible to adjust the volume, as long as the adjustment will not cause a filament to redden with the increase in power or to blacken when the power is reduced.[6] It is not permitted to switch on the hearing aid or to change the battery on Shabbos. Hearing aids may be worn outside just like eyeglasses.[7]

Walkers, Canes, and Crutches

18. A person who cannot walk without crutches, whether because of a wound or because his foot is in a cast or because he is physically disabled or paralyzed, may go outside with them. Similarly, an elderly or sick person who cannot walk without a walker[8] or a cane may walk with it on the street.

    However, if a person is able to walk without crutches or a cane, and he uses these only to be able to walk more confidently or with greater ease, may not use them in places that do not have an *eiruv*.[9]

19. Telescoped canes and crutches employ two tubes or a tube and a rod, one inside the other. The larger, outer tube has a number of holes spaced several centimeters apart. The smaller, inner tube (or rod) has a spring-loaded sprocket that fits into the holes, allowing one to adjust the length of the cane. This adjustment is permitted on Shabbos.

---

6 שו״ת באר משה ח״ו קונטרס אלקטרי סימן ט״ו בשם הגרש״ז אויערבאך זצוק״ל, וכן הביאו בשש״כ פל״ד סכ״ח, ובנשמת אברהם ח״א ס״ו סק״ח.

7 ומה שאסרו גדולי הדורות לטלטל ברשות הרבים מכונת שמיעה בשבת, היינו במכונות ישנות שהיו מורכבות משני חלקים, חלק אחד הנתחב לאוזן וממנו יוצא חוט ומחברו לחלק שני היינו הבטרייה המונחת בתוך כיסו, בזה ודאי יש לאסור משום משאוי. אבל במכונות החדשות שהם חלק אחד קטן שנתחב כולו לחלל האוזן או מסביב האוזן, ודאי יש להקל בזה לכל הדעות לצאת בו לרשות הרבים. עיין בספר הר צבי המודפס על טור או״ח סי׳ שמ״ה שהאריך בדין זה. וע״ע בענין זה בשו״ת מנחת שלמה סי׳ ט׳ הערה ד׳. וע״ע בשש״כ פל״ד סע׳ כ״ח. לוית חן אות ל׳. ובשו״ת מנחת יצחק ח״א סי׳ ל״ז, ובח״ב סי׳ י״ז י״ח וקל״ג, ובח״ג סי׳ מ״א ובח״ח סי׳ מ׳. שו״ת באר משה ח״א סי׳ י״ז אות ו׳ ובחלק ו׳ קונטרס אלקטרי י״ד ט״ו. וע״ע בשו״ת ציץ אליעזר ח״ו סי׳ ו׳, ובח״ז סי׳ י״א.

8 שו״ע סי׳ ש״א סעיף י״ז ועיי״ש במ״ב ס״ג.

9 שו״ע שם סעיף י״ז, ובמ״ב ס״ק ס״ד וע״ע בנשמת אברהם סי׳ ש״א ס״ק ח׳ וס״ק ט׳. ובערוך השולחן סי׳ ש״א סעיף ע׳.

There are also wooden crutches comprised of three rods, with the middle rod attached to the two outer ones by a butterfly screw. Increasing or decreasing the length of the crutch requires disassembling this arrangement and moving the rods to a new position until the holes on the three rods match. Then the rods are reassembled. This adjustment cannot be made on Shabbos since it is tantamount to reconstructing the crutch from its constituent parts.

Wheelchair

20. The standard wheelchair may be used on Shabbos. It may also be operated and closed on Shabbos. It is also permitted to insert the foot supports and other parts as long as there is no need to screw anything together.[10]

21. It is permitted to go outside in a wheelchair on Shabbos to any area that has a valid *eiruv*. In this case, the patient may be wheeled to shul or even taken for a stroll by a Jew. When there is no *eiruv*, but the street is not regarded as a *reshus harabim*, a public domain, one may be pushed in a wheelchair by a non-Jew or drive the wheelchair himself.

    In an area that is regarded as a *reshus harabim*, one may be pushed in a wheelchair only under special conditions. For example, he can be assisted by a non-Jew, but simultaneously propel himself forward in a manner that either of them could propel the wheelchair on his own. This can be done provided that the person is being transported to do a mitzvah.[11]

22. An electric wheelchair (whether battery-operated or engine-driven) may not be used on Shabbos.

---

10 דכל גזירת חכמים שמא יתקע המבואר בשו״ע סי׳ ש״ח סעיפים ח׳ ט׳ היינו דווקא בדבר שאין הדרך להכניסו ולהוציאו ובקל, ועוד שצריך תיקון נוסף, אולם בדבר העומד להתפרק ולהתחבר שלא ע״י מסמר או הברגה -שרי, ועיין במש״כ בס׳ קצות השבת פרק ד׳ סעיף כ״ט, ועוד שם באריכות.

11 שו״ת מנחת יצחק ח״ב סי׳ קי״ד ס״ק ג׳, וטעמו דיש להניח שהכיסא טפל לנכה, ושניים שעשאוה הוי תרי דרבנן ובמקום מצווה שרי כמבואר בשו״ע סי׳ ש״ז סעיף ה׳.

Aids for the Blind

23. A blind person who is capable of walking without a walking stick and uses it only to make it easier to walk[12] may not take out his stick on a street without an *eiruv*.[13] However, if he cannot walk at all without the stick, he may use it.[14] This applies if the area where he is walking is definitely a *reshus harabim*. One may be lenient when there is an *eiruv* or if one is uncertain that the area is considered *reshus harabim*.

24. A person who usually goes to shul with a guide dog that he holds on a leash should avoid doing so on Shabbos. But if he cannot walk to shul without the guide dog, he may do so.[15]

    A controversy exists concerning the entry of a guide dog into a shul. Even according to the lenient opinion, the person should sit in the back of the shul with the dog.[16]

Heating Devices

25. Certain patients suffer from cold and have to sleep on heated mattresses. The mattress is heated by hot air that flows through tubes built into the mattress. The air itself is heated by a heating element and forced into the tubes by a blower.

26. If possible, the mattress should be turned on before Shabbos and operated by means of a timer, if needed. Otherwise, the priorities mentioned in chapter 44, "Operating Medical Equipment on Shabbos," should be applied.

---

12 שו״ע סי׳ ש״א סעיף י״ח.

13 כ״כ במ״ב שם ס״ק ס״ח.

14 עיין בנשמת אברהם ח״א שהביא שיטת ערוך השולחן סי׳ ש״א סעיף ע״ב ועוד אחרונים שאם אינו יכול ללכת כלל בלי מקל, דינו כחיגר שמותר לו לצאת במקלו, שמא יפול בבור או ייכשל באיזה דבר. ומילי דמסתברא הוא.

15 עיין שם בנשמת אברהם שהביא דעת שו״ת לב אריה (גרוסנס) שהתיר הליכה עם כלב הנחיה, אולם יש המפקפקים בהיתר זה, לכן לכתחילה ראוי להימנע וכמש״כ.

16 עיין בשו״ת אגרות משה חאו״ח ח״א סי׳ מ״ה, שהאריך בענין זה והסיק שמותר להיכנס עם הכלב, אך יישב סמוך לכניסה שלא להפריע את ציבור המתפללים. ואמנם הרבה אחרונים כתבו נגד פסק זה מכמה סיבות, עיין בשו״ת חלקת יעקב ח״ג סי׳ פ״ז ועוד אחרונים, עכ״ז בשעת הדחק כדאי הוא בעל האגרות משה לסמוך עליו.

Walkie-Talkies and Beepers

27. Communication devices such as walkie-talkies and beepers are used by medical personnel and Hatzalah members who may be called at any time to treat a life-threatening situation. These may be carried and calls received through them on Shabbos. Regarding the dispatcher, if a non-Jew can be employed, this is preferable. However, if there is a possibility that he will not handle the emergency calls with the required speed and urgency, it is permissible to use a Jewish dispatcher.[17]

Breast-Milk Pumps

28. Expressing breast milk on Shabbos is a Torah prohibition.[18] Therefore, even if it is easier for the mother to express her milk into bottles and bottle-feed her baby, she may not do so on Shabbos.[19]

29. Therefore, a woman who is not breast-feeding or who is nursing but suffers from an overproduction of milk may not express her milk into an empty vessel. However, she may relieve the pressure by expressing the milk into alcohol or diluted liquid soap that renders the milk inedible (see chapter 30, "*Choleh B'Miktzas*," paragraph 11).[20]

30. If the baby is unable to feed directly from his mother, either because of weakness (such as a premature baby in an incubator) or because of the mother's poor health (due to mastitis or a similar condition), and the baby is dependent on his mother's milk, it is permissible to use a breast pump to express milk. However, consideration must be given to the type of pump that may be used.

31. There are three types of breast pumps: (a) manual, (b) semiautomatic, and (c) fully automatic. There is no problem with using a manual breast pump on Shabbos. If a woman must express her milk on Shabbos (see

---

17 הגרש״ז אויערבאך זצוק״ל התיר לעניין רופא תורן. ובאגרות משה חאו״ח ח״ד סי׳ פ״א כתב כן לחברי הצלה שמותר לשאת בבגדיהם עיי״ש.

18 שו״ע סי׳ שכ״ח סעיף ל״ד, ובמ״ב ס״ק קי״א.

19 שו״ע שם.

20 עיין בכל הנושא בשו״ת יביע אומר ח״ה סימן ל״ב. ציץ אליעזר ח״ח סימן ט״ו פרק י״ב. תורת היולדת פרק מ״א.

paragraphs 29–30 above), she may use a manual pump with no restrictions.

32. When there is a need to use an electric pump, it should be connected to the power source on Friday by means of a timer set for the desired hours (see chapter 44, "Operating Medical Equipment on Shabbos," for the procedure in operating electrical devices on Shabbos).

33. If an electric pump must be used, it is preferable to use an automatic pump that alternately sucks and stops. A continuously operating pump is much more problematic.[21]

34. The suction rate of an automatic pump may be adjusted on Shabbos.

Baby Scale

35. Many newborns must be weighed often in order to properly assess their state of health and determine if they need to eat more at feedings or more frequently. For this reason it is permitted to weigh infants on Shabbos even though no life-threatening situation exists.[22] However, only a mechanical scale may be used for this purpose. Digital or electronic scales may not be used.

    Similarly, it is permitted to weigh or measure food that is given to a newborn using a mechanical scale, a measuring spoon, or a graduated bottle without any restrictions.

Electric Blanket

36. Patients who need an electric blanket to maintain a comfortable body temperature may use one on Shabbos provided that it is switched on before Shabbos. The blanket should be connected to a timer so that it may be heated at the desired times. Care should be taken that the wire attached to the blanket is long enough so that moving the blanket will

---

21 במכשיר אוטומטי פעולת היניקה נעשית אוטומטית ללא שהאשה פעילה, ואילו במכשיר שהיניקה היא קבועה ועל ידי לחיצה באצבע על שסתום נעשית היניקה והרפיית האצבע מפסיקה את היניקה — יש לחשוש בזה שע״י הפעולה משתנה עוצמת פעולת המנוע.

22 שקילה אסורה בשבת משום עובדין דחול, כמבואר בשו״ע סי׳ ש״ו סעיף ז׳ ובמ״ב שם ס״ק ל״ד. ובמקום צורך מצוה, או במקום צער או צורך גדול מותר.

not cause it to be unplugged.[23] In addition, the controls that allow one to adjust the heating level should be taped over in order to prevent making such adjustments on Shabbos.

37. If one forgot to switch on the electric blanket before Shabbos, and the patient needs it, a non-Jew may be asked to switch it on. If no non-Jew is available, a minor should do it with his left hand. If the patient is very uncomfortable, a *chinuch*-age child may be asked to switch it on with his left hand.[24]

38. For a *choleh she'ein bo sakanah*, an ordinary bedridden patient, if a non-Jew or a minor is not available and there is a danger that being cold will cause the patient's condition to deteriorate, an adult Jew may turn on the blanket with his left hand.

39. Placing an electrically heated pillow on the stomach can alleviate certain stomachaches. The pillow used for this purpose should be switched on before Shabbos. If this was not done, and the patient cannot function normally and is weakened because of the pain, the pillow may be switched on by a non-Jew or by a minor below *chinuch* age.

---

23 עיין בשו״ת אגרות משה או״ח ח״ג סימן נ׳ שהאריך לבאר שאין זה בכלל מוקצה ומותר להשתמש בזה בשבת אפילו למוגדר כבריא. עיי״ש. וע״ע בשו״ת חלקת יעקב ח״ג סימן קפ״א. ובשו״ת באר משה ח״ו קונטרס אלקטרי סי׳ כ׳.

24 שו״ת באר משה ח״ו קונטרס אלקטרי סי׳ כ׳.

Chapter 48
Tests and Analysis

Blood Tests

Blood tests have three aspects:

a. Taking blood for analysis
b. Analysis in the lab
c. Reporting and receiving results

Taking Blood

1. Blood may be taken from a vein or from a finger on Shabbos only in the case of a life-endangering illness. This may be done even if the result of the analysis will not become known until after Shabbos. The blood test is permitted if (a) the test has to be taken close to a certain event (even if the analysis itself is to be carried out only after Shabbos) or (b) when there is a time factor of lifesaving importance in obtaining results.

   It is likewise permitted to analyze blood by means of an instrument that simultaneously performs several analyses (auto-analysis) even when not all of them are needed in the given case. However, an effort should be made to take all the blood needed with a single needle rather than from several places.

2. It is preferable to take blood with a preassembled syringe (see chapter 46, "Equipment Used in Treatments and Procedures," paragraph 63).

3. Blood may also be taken automatically (known as a vacutainer). For this procedure a needle is inserted in a vein, and the other end of the needle is inserted in a test tube. The blood fills the tube to capacity, and then the tube is detached and another one substituted to be filled. This type of blood taking involves a more serious transgression and is permitted only in life-endangering cases even according to opinions (quoted in *Magen Avraham* 328:52) that permit taking blood on Shabbos from a *choleh she'ein bo sakanah*.[1]

4. In general, it is forbidden to cause bleeding on Shabbos.[2]

The Laboratory

5. The clinical laboratory plays a crucial part in the diagnosis and analysis of disease, and it is therefore very important to keep it operating on Shabbos. There are, however, certain factors to consider:

   a. The kind of test that must be carried out on Shabbos
   b. The specimen (full blood, plasma, serum, urine, LP) being analyzed
   c. The manner in which the analysis is carried out
   d. The analytic equipment used
   e. The person who carries out the analysis

6. It is impossible to resolve all the questions pertaining to medical analysis in this book. There is a vast amount of analytic equipment used for this purpose, and the types of equipment used change frequently. We will only discuss the most commonly used equipment and present a number of recommendations on avoiding desecration of Shabbos in the laboratory.

---

1 נשמת אברהם ת״א קנ״ב.

2 במגן אברהם סי׳ שכ״ח ס״ק נ״ב על מה שכתב בשו״ע סעיף מ״ב ז״ל: אסור להניח בגד על מכה שיוצא ממנו דם שהדם יצבע אותו. ואסור להוציא דם מהמכה וכו׳, כתב המג״א וז״ל: ואסור

Blood Specimens

7. Blood is made up of three kinds of cells: (a) red blood cells (erythrocytes), (b) white blood cells (leukocytes), and (c) platelets (thrombocytes). The term *blood* refers to whole blood, which contains water, protein, nutrients, and blood cells. Blood consists of two elements that the doctor may want to test:

    a. The cell portion, which includes the red blood cells, white blood cells, and platelets

    b. The fluid portion, which is called "plasma" or "serum"

    Plasma is mostly water, but it also contains minerals and proteins. It is obtained by separating the liquid portion of unclotted blood from the cells. *Serum* is the fluid that remains after the blood has clotted. It contains no cells and, unlike plasma, no dissolved proteins.

    Whether plasma or serum is used for a blood test depends on the type of blood test ordered. For technical reasons, most biochemical analyses are carried out with serum, although the concentration of various reactants in both fluids, serum and plasma, is similar.

Test Tubes

8. Samples may arrive at the laboratory in different kinds of test tubes:

    a. A glass or plastic test tube without an anticoagulant, usually used for routine testing

    b. A test tube with fluoride ("sugar blood")

    c. A test tube with anticoagulant to test the clotting characteristics of the blood sample

---

להוציא דם. רש״י פי׳ סוף עירובין דה״ל חובל והוי אב מלאכה. וכך כתב בהגהות מיימונית פרק כ״א דהמניח דבר המושך דם וליחה הוי מפרק. ומלשון רש״י משמע שדווקא כשמהדקה בגמי הוא דהוי אב מלאכה דהוא עביד מעשה, אבל כשמניח עליה דבר המושך דם לא הוי אב מלאכה דאיהו לא עביד מידי, וא״כ כ״ש כשמעמיד עלוקה שקורין ניגליי״ן דשרי לחולה כמש״כ סעיף י״ז דשרי שבות. אבל בזבחים דף י״ט משמע דכשנתכוין להוציא דם אפילו אין מהדקו הוי מלאכה. ובסנהדרין דף ע״ח שהשיך בו נחש ר״מ מחייב משום דהוי כתוקע סכין בבטנו ולאו גרמא הוא שהרי כלי משחיתו בידו ע״כ ואפילו רבנן דפטרי היינו דס״ל דארס מעצמו מקיא אבל גבי עלוקה הוי כעושה בידיים. והמוצץ דם בפיו אסור דהוי חבורה (רש״י פי״ט) וא״כ אסור למצוץ דם שבין השיניים ואפשר דהוי אב מלאכה. ועיין סי׳ ש״ד סעיף א׳.

d. A test tube with EDTA or any other substance that absorbs calcium ions and prevents blood coagulation, usually used to obtain the standard blood count (RBC, WBC, and PLT)

Laboratory Personnel

9. If it is possible to employ expert non-Jewish laboratory technicians, this is preferable, particularly since often the need arises to perform blood analysis for patients who are not regarded as being in a life-threatening situation, in which case a Jew may not perform the analysis.[3]

10. It should be noted that it is permissible to ask a non-Jew to carry out an analysis if the results are needed on Shabbos. If the results will not be needed until after Shabbos is over, the non-Jew may not carry out the analysis. Therefore, even though it is recommended that hospitals employ non-Jewish laboratory technicians, they are not permitted to carry out non-urgent analyses for a Jew.

Analyses that May Not Be Carried Out on Shabbos

11. When patients arrive at the hospital, it is sometimes necessary to perform certain tests before treatment can be determined. These patients are then given medications, and the tests are repeated several days later to determine the suitability and/or effectiveness of the medicine. When there is no medical urgency to perform these tests on Shabbos, they should not be carried out then since the results are usually needed a day or several days later.

12. No tests should be done on Shabbos that are not needed for that day, even if they are needed for surgery that is to be performed on Sunday. However, tests that must be performed every few hours for a specific time period to monitor the patient's condition may be carried out on Shabbos.

---

3 שהרי בדיקות אלו כרוכות באיסורי תורה רבים, ובחולה שאין בו סכנה ולא חשש סכנה — אין היתר לישראל לעבור על איסורי תורה כדלקמן פרק 21 סעיף 4 וסעיף 22.

Reporting Results

13. Laboratory results may be sorted in the laboratory itself for delivery to the different departments where they are needed in order to speed delivery to each department. However, once they reach the department, the results may not be sorted or placed in each patient's chart. The only permitted way of distribution is for the doctor to insert the results into the file of the patient as he checks each report.[4]

Laboratory Equipment

Centrifuge

14. One type of equipment that is used in the laboratory is a centrifuge. The centrifuge separates substances or particles of different weights present in a solution into different layers.

    There are different types of centrifuges. Table-type centrifuges are used for separating blood components, sedimentation of urine, and for other such analyses. The capillary centrifuge checks the hematocrit (the ratio of the volume of blood cells to the volume of blood).

    A capillary centrifuge operates as follows: Blood is placed into a slender glass tube (capillary) that is plugged on one side. The centrifuge turns at 1,500 rotations per minute. This causes all the blood cells to move to one side of the tube, while the plasma remains at the other side of the tube. This device may be used to check the bilirubin level of newborn infants.

15. Certain analyses must be performed only with the blood fluid (serum), which requires separating the blood into its components. However, there are analyses that can be performed either with whole blood or with blood that was separated, and the result is the same in both cases. In such a case, it is preferable to perform the analyses with whole blood on Shabbos in order to avoid using the centrifuge, which involves at least two *melachos*.[5] It should be noted that when several analyses are needed,

---

4 ששי״כ ס״מ סעיף ל״ה.

5 השימוש בצנטריפוגה, מורכב משני איסורים מדאורייתא, א׳ הפעלה חשמלית. ב׳ מלאכת בורר, והיינו ברירת והפרדת סרום מפלסמה.

some of which require centrifuging and some do not, it is not necessary to divide the blood into separate tubes to avoid unnecessary centrifuging, since it can all be done in a single operation. But if the sample is already in different tubes, only the sample that needs to be separated should be centrifuged.

Analyzer

16. Analyzers are automatic devices that perform comprehensive blood analyses of hematology, coagulation, chemistry, and blood gases. Some of the analyses can be performed from the capillary tube, and some directly from the syringe that contains the blood sample or from the test tube, and others must be performed on separated blood components (plasma or serum).

    Most of the automatic devices with a digital display require depressing various digital keys or inputting directions into a computer when inserting the sample into the device. (A large number of modern devices are currently operated by bar codes.)

    The majority of these devices employ various reagents,[6] most of which can be prepared before Shabbos. This requires that the state of integral reagents (those that are supplied automatically to the device by tubing) be checked before Shabbos. External reagents needed for carrying out standard analyses should also be prepared and checked before Shabbos.

17. A hematological analyzer operates with whole blood. The device draws automatically all the reagents needed for the analysis by way of permanent piping. All that has to be supplied is the patient's blood sample. This sample can be taken either by means of an automatic sampler, a vacuum test tube, or regular test tubes. With test tubes, the plug that seals them must be opened in order to obtain the blood sample. If an automatic sampler is available, it is preferable to use it on Shabbos.

---

6 ראגנט — הינו חומר כימי שעם פגישתו עם הדם מפרקו ובודק את הפרמטרים הנדרשים.

Chemistry Analyzer

18. Chemistry analysis can be carried out by the dry chemistry method, such as KODAK, or by the wet method. The principal difference between the two methods is that with wet chemistry the device is connected to water and all the tests are carried out in the aqueous medium. Therefore, the device draws clean water in the course of the analysis and discharges the spent test medium into a waste flask.

    These two methods also differ by the kind of reagent they use. The dry method employs pretreated slides that are specific to each test.[7] In the wet method, the reagent is a solution, which is at times supplied ready to use, whereas at other times it has to be prepared in the laboratory.

19. Most routine chemistry analyses are carried out with blood serum, which requires centrifuging the sample before analyzing it.

20. All the chemistry analyzers perform routine chemistry analysis. The most up-to-date devices also perform additional medical tests.

21. There are devices that can be preprogrammed to print out the results on paper without additional human intervention. Stapling the printout to the patient's file is preferable to copying the results from the computer screen (which also prevents human error that comes with writing down a large quantity of data). The printout should be torn off by hand, without using the toothed cutter.

Various Analyses

22. There are devices that check for blood gases with internal reagents. This device uses whole blood in a test tube with an anticoagulant (heparin). No centrifuging is needed. All the parameters can be preset, including the patient's identification and the desired analysis; the device receives blood directly from the capillary tube. If the blood is delivered by a syringe, the device does not draw blood automatically; the techni-

---

7 סלייד — הינו חומר מוכן כמין ראגנט שמוכנס למכשיר על כל בדיקה ספציפית.

cian must depress the syringe in order to introduce the blood into the testing port.

23. A device that analyzes electrolytes — primarily the level of salts and sodium in the blood — is capable of analyzing both whole blood, directly from the test tubes or from capillary tubes, or blood that has been centrifuged. Since the analysis can be carried out on whole blood, the blood should not be centrifuged on Shabbos.

24. Analysis of bilirubin level involves identification of color without resort to a reagent. The blood has to be pre-separated with a capillary centrifuge. The results are displayed on the device's screen.

    It is not permitted to check bilirubin level on Shabbos even for permitting a circumcision on that day. Such a test is permitted only for purely medical considerations (to determine whether the bilirubin level is dangerous to the infant's health). It goes without saying that such a test cannot be carried out on Shabbos to determine whether the infant can be circumcised the next day.

25. Determining blood type requires centrifuged blood. There are two steps to carrying out this analysis:

    a. Serum typing (back typing)
    b. Red blood cell typing (front typing)

    To determine whether blood is type A, B, or O, the analysis is carried out both on the basis of red blood cells and on serum or plasma. The results of the analysis includes the testing of blood cells using standard anti-A and anti-B antibodies and of the serum with standardized A and B blood cells. Rh (D) typing is carried out with an anti-D reagent. Matching all the results together gives the blood type.

    All the results of this analysis must be recorded. A computer printout is preferred to a manual recording.[8]

---

8 עיין לעיל בפרק 15 סעיף 10 וסעיף 13 שביארנו שיש להעדיף שימוש במחשב על פני כתיבה ביד, עיי"ש.

Measuring Blood Sugar

26. People who suffer from diabetes must check their blood sugar level several times a day. This is done with a glucometer. The test requires the following:
    a. A finger is punctured and a drop of blood is extracted.
    b. The blood is placed on a test slide.
    c. The device is reset, which causes it to display a digital countdown (the numbers on each device are different). When a certain number is reached, the device beeps to indicate that the slide should be inserted into the test slot.
    d. The slide is inserted into the slot.
    e. The device reads the color produced by combining the blood with the sensing substance. It then displays the blood sugar level.

27. The glucometer operates with codes that depend on the kind of test slide. Different test slides are produced by different companies, and each slide has a code that is identified by the device. These parameters have to be input before the glucometer can be used. This preparation should be carried out before Shabbos.

28. One should check whether the test slide can be inserted before the beep sounds.

29. Diabetics must measure their blood sugar content before injecting insulin, whether the insulin is injected automatically with a device attached to the body or whether the insulin is injected manually. The blood sugar level determines the quantity of insulin that needs to be injected.

30. Everything that is needed to determine the blood sugar level may be done on Shabbos. However, it is preferable to carry out these operations by a device connected to a timer if possible.

31. If this test does not need to be carried out daily, every effort should be made that it should not be performed on Shabbos.

Urine Analysis

32. Urine analysis is essential for every patient who is admitted to the hospital or undergoing a physical examination. It is a useful indicator of the patient's state of health.

33. The glucose level in urine can be measured with a dipstick test. The dipstick has been impregnated with chemicals that react with specific substances in the urine to produce color-coded visual results. The depth of color produced indicates the concentration of the substance in the urine.

34. The *general urine analysis* is an important test that provides an overall picture of levels of ketones, leukocytes, proteins, bilirubin, and other substances. The results are based on changes in the color of the test strip that point to different levels of these substances. Ketones may appear in the urine in large quantities before their level rises in the blood.

    This test is very important in cases of lack of appetite and of abnormal metabolism when there is a shortage of carbohydrates and other constituents or a danger of dehydration.

35. The presence of large quantities of white blood cells (leukocytes) in the urine is indicative of a urinary tract infection. Together with bacteria in the urine, it is an important indicator, among others, of infection in the lower urinary tract, such as cystitis or urethritis. This is determined with the dipstick test.

36. Nitrite in urine is also checked in the general urine analysis using the dipstick method and serves to detect various bacteria in the urinary tract.

Punctures

37. The drawing of fluids from the body cavities, such as the chest (lung cavity), stomach, or the joints, is not the same as taking blood and is permitted by Torah law. However, if it is possible to postpone the test until after Shabbos, this should be done. If a life-threatening situation

is suspected, and the test is carried out to determine whether an emergency exists, it may be performed.

38. Therefore, lumbar puncture, for drawing fluid from the space between vertebrae, which is done for a precise diagnosis of such illnesses as meningitis and cerebral bleeding, is permitted. This test is usually performed in cases when a life-threatening condition is suspected and thus is certainly permitted. Since the diagnosis of multiple sclerosis is rarely an emergency, however, it is better to put off testing by LP until after Shabbos.

Index

The reference numbers refer to chapter and paragraph numbers respectively.

זכרון לפניך בשחק לעד בספר יוחק

In memory of the esteemed philanthropist
a patron of yeshivot and charity organizations worldwide

MR. REFAEL EDMOND EZRA SAFRA
BEN YAAKOV AND ESTHER
who passed away on 24 Kislev 5760

May his memory be for blessing
and may the Almighty remember
his philanthropy and generosity.

And to
MRS. LILY SAFRA

A true woman of valor
who continues in her husband's path
of *chesed* and charity

May she be blessed with a good and long life
and may the merit of her *chesed*
stand by her and her children
both in this world and in the World to Come.

To

NURI, SHLOMO, AVRAHAM, AND MOSHE MAHADAV הי"ו

and their wives and families

May they be blessed with success in all their endeavors, good health, and a long life filled with joy and fulfillment.

In memory of their father

YOSEF BEN GRAS ז"ל

who passed away on 23 Shevat 5744

May his soul be bound to the Source of eternal life.

And for the success of their mother

MRS. RACHEL SHULI שתחי'

A true woman of valor

To our dear friends, supporters of Torah and its scholars

The **Yad Yossef** congregation of the Syrian Jewish community of Brooklyn, New York, under the spiritual leadership of our esteemed friend, who is so dedicated to Torah education

RABBI DAVID OZERI שליט"א

And to our dear friends and supporters of Torah and its scholars

DR. YIZHAK MAHADAV
and his family

May they be blessed
with success in all their endeavors,
good health, and a long life filled with
joy and fulfillment.

To our dear friends, supporters of Torah and its scholars

MR. SHLOMO GAD
and his family

May they be blessed with success in all their endeavors,
good health, and a long life filled with joy and fulfillment.

In memory of their righteous wife and mother

MRS. SHOSHANA BAT MOSHE AND ESTHER VARDI
who passed away on 10 Cheshvan 5761

May her soul be bound to the Source of eternal life.

To our dear friends,
supporters of Torah and its scholars

MRS. SHIFRA GAD
and her sons
Nissan Michael and his wife, **Rina**, and their family
and **Yosef Gad** and his wife, **Venecia**, and their family
and her daughters
Leah and her husband, **David**, and their family
and **Pircha Fiji** and her husband, **Moshe**, and their family

May they be blessed with success in all their endeavors,
good health, and a long life filled with joy and fulfillment.

In memory of
their husband and dear father
a pursuer of charity and *chesed*
a supporter of Torah and its scholars
NAFTALI GAD BEN NISSAN AND LEAH
who passed away on 21 Tevet 5759

May his soul be bound to the Source of eternal life.

To our dear friends,
supporters of Torah and its scholars

MR. YAAKOV (JACK) AVRAHAM הי"ו
and his wife **Nora** תחי'
and their children **Chava Eve, Daniella, Yitzchak Isaac** הי"ו
and their daughter **Nicole Devora** תחי'
and her husband **Zvi Kitt** הי"ו
and special blessings to
their mother **Sarah** תחי'

May they be blessed with success in all their endeavors,
good health, and a long life filled with joy and fulfillment.

In memory of

SHALOM BEN DAVID AND YOCHEVED ז"ל
who passed away on 25 Shevat 5736

May his soul be bound to the Source of eternal life.

To our dear friends,
supporters of Torah and its scholars

HaRav Yaakov Nesirov הי"ו
Rabbi of the **Anshei Shalom** Congregation

***

Mr. Gavriel Aharon הי"ו
and his family

***

Mr. Avraham Mor הי"ו
and his family

***

Mr. Meir Batzal הי"ו
and his family

***

Mr. Emanuel Eliasaf הי"ו
and his family

***

Mr. Ilan Siman-Tov הי"ו
and his family

***

Mr. Yissachar Cohen Ambalo הי"ו
and his wife, **Tamar** 'תחי
and their dear children
Ofer Refael, Rani, Dana, and **Sharona Rachel** הי"ו
and their dear grandchildren
and for the success of their mother
Rachel 'תחי
May she be blessed with good health.

In memory of his father
Meir ben Mordechai Cohen ז"ל
May his soul be bound to the Source of eternal life.

To our dear friends

MR. YISSACHAR COHEN
and his wife, **Penina**
and their children **Ariel, Rachel,** and **Sarah**

In memory of his father **Azaria ben Yehuda Cohen** ז"ל
who passed away on 28 Av 5744

and his mother **Rachel bat Leah** ז"ל
who passed away on 3 Shevat 5765

and his father-in-law **Eliyahu ben Sarah** ז"ל
who passed away on 18 Tevet 5753

May their souls be bound to the Source of eternal life.

To our dear friends
MR. ELIYAHU BETZALEL and his family הי"ו
MR. EFRAIM BETZALEL and his family הי"ו
MR. MORDECHAI BETZALEL and his family הי"ו

May they be blessed with success in all their endeavors,
good health, and a long life filled with joy and fulfillment.

In memory of their father
Binyamin Zev Betzalel ז"ל
ben Rav Agagon Elisha and Rachel
May his soul be bound to the Source of eternal life.

And for the success of their mother **Pircha** תחי'

To our dear friends, supporters of Torah and its scholars
the **Ohel Simha** congregation
of the Bukhara Jewish community
in Queens, New York,
under the spiritual leadership of
our esteemed friend,
who is so dedicated to Torah education

RABBI YIGAL HAIMOFF שליט"א

and his wife
MRS. EFRAT HAIMOFF תחי'

and their family

May they merit to continue their tremendous *chesed* and
hachnasat orchim in good health and peace.

To our dear friends,
supporters of Torah and its scholars

Mr. Asher Zamir הי"ו
and his family

In memory of his father
Yitzhak ben Asher Zamir ז"ל
May his soul be bound to the Source of eternal life.

***

Mr. Gyora Dabrayov הי"ו
and his wife **Hagit** הי"ו
and their children
Dorom, Daniel, Sarit, Mishael,
and **Yonatan** הי"ו

***

Mr. Yorik Shamsayof הי"ו
and his family

***

Mr. Haim Aharonov הי"ו
and his family

***

Mr. Avraham (Albert) Ksherim הי"ו
and his family

***

Mr. Moshe Ksherim הי"ו
and his family

May they be blessed with success in all their endeavors,
good health, and a long life filled with joy and fulfillment.

To our dear friends
supporters of Torah and its scholars
the **Shaarei Tzion** congregation
of the Syrian Jewish community
of Brooklyn, New York
May they be blessed with success in all their endeavors, good health, and a long life filled with joy and fulfillment.

In memory of
RABBI BARUCH BEN HAIM זצוק"ל
the esteemed pillar of Torah in New York, a renowned genius and great scholar, who was devoted to our congregation
May he rest in peace.

He was very pleased with this *sefer*, which he reviewed during the various stages of its editing and greatly encouraged us to publish it. Unfortunately he did not live to see the finished work.
May he continue to pray from Heaven for his beloved family, congregants, and the entire Jewish nation, and may his soul be bound to the Source of eternal life.

ויבולע המוות לנצח ומחה ה' דמעה מעל כל פנים

To **RABBI SHAUL KATZIN**
Rabbi of Shaare Tzion
and his family

In memory of his father, **HaRav HaGaon Yaakov S. Katzin** זצוק"ל
and his mother, **Mrs. Mazal Katzin bat Sara**
a true woman of valor
and his dear brother, **Rabbi David Katzin ben Mazal**

May their souls be bound to the Source of eternal life.

To our dear friends, supporters of Torah and its scholars,
of the **Ateret Torah** congregation
of the Syrian Jewish community
of Brooklyn, New York
under the spiritual leadership of our esteemed friend who is so dedicated
to Torah education
Rabbi Yosef Raful שליט"א

and to the health of
Rabbi Avraham Moshe Chai Raful שליט"א
ben Rabbi Aharon and Rachel

And especially
RABBI MOSHE BUSO שליט"א
and his family הי"ו
grandchild of the holy Rabbi Ishak Abihatzera זצוק"ל
For his encouragement and dedication to seeing this book translated.

and to the health of
Gras bat Flores
May she have a complete and speedy recovery.

May they be blessed with success in all their endeavors,
good health, and a long life filled with joy and fulfillment.

To our dear friends, supports of Torah and its scholars

MR. MORDECHAY SHEM TOV
and his wife, **Elka** הי"ו
and his family

and to the health of their sister
Gras bat Flores הי"ו
May she have a complete and speedy recovery.

In memory of his brother
Victor Chaim ben Sarah Nina ז"ל
who passed away on 21 Shevat 5765
May his soul be bound to the Source of eternal life.

To the esteemed doctor,
great philanthropist,
and supporter of Torah and its scholars,
who so kindly volunteered to review this book

DR. YOSEF HADAD הי"ו
and his family

May they be blessed with success in all their endeavors,
good health, and a long life filled with joy and fulfillment.

And to **Itsak ben Adil** and **Esther bat Eliza**
May they have a complete and speedy recovery.

And to
MR. YAAKOV (JACK) FALAH הי"ו
and his family

and a *refuah sheleimah* for **Salha bat Klir**

*****

And to
MR. ELI HAMAWI הי"ו
and his wife and family

May they be blessed with success in all their endeavors,
good health, and a long life filled with joy and fulfillment.

To our dear friends,
supporters of Torah and its scholars

the **Beit Shaul VeMiriam** congregation
of the Syrian Jewish community
of Brooklyn, New York, under the spiritual leadership of
Rabbi David Cohen שליט"א
who is so dedicated to Torah education
and who contributed to the success of this book

*****

With special appreciation to
our dear friends, supporters of Torah and its scholars
MR. YEHEZKEL SHAHADROZ הי"ו
and his wife **Sara** תחי'
and their children **Moshe, Aaron,** and **Yosef** הי"ו

and

MR. ESHKOL SHAHADROZ הי"ו
and his wife **Denise** תחי'
and their children **Dorit, Tzipora, Shlomo,** and **Miriam** הי"ו
And to the success of their parents, **Mr. Elazar** and **Homa**

May they be blessed with success in all their endeavors,
and may they be granted *nachas* from their children and
grandchildren in good health and a long life
filled with joy and fulfillment.

To our dear friends,
supporters of Torah and its scholars

The Mashhad community of Great Neck
under the leadership of
Rav Eliyahu Ben Chaim and **Rav Yosef Biton**

And especially
MR. AGAGUN (SHMUEL) NASIMI הי"ו

May he be blessed with success in all his endeavors,
good health, and a long life filled with joy and fulfillment.

And to his wife
Esther bat Yitzhak תחי'
May Hashem send her a complete recovery.

In memory of his father
Mashiach ben Shmuel ז"ל
who passed away on 17 Kislev 5765

and his mother
Esther ז"ל
who passed away on 8 Av 5765

and his daughter-in-law
wife of Mr. Avraham Nasimi הי"ו
Hana Laleh bat Reuven Haviv ז"ל
who passed away on 8 Shevat 5765

May their souls be bound to the Source of eternal life.

To our dear friends,
supporters of Torah and its scholars

MR. SHIMON CHIZKIYAH הי״ו
and his wife **Hana** תחי׳

and their dear sons, **Simcha, Moris,** and **Albert** הי״ו
and their families
and their daughters, **Diana** and **Alice** הי״ו
and their families

May they be blessed with success in all their endeavors,
good health, and a long life filled with joy and fulfillment.

In memory of their daughter
Malka bat Hana ז״ל
who passed away on 13 Adar I 5765

May her soul be bound to the Source of eternal life.

To our dear friends,
supporters of Torah and its scholars of the
Shirah Hadashah congregation of the Mashhad Jewish community in Long Island under the spiritual leadership of our esteemed friend who is so dedicated to Torah education

Rabbi Shlomo Shuv שליט"א

Mr. William Mordechai Achdut
and his family

Moshe Sulimani ben Nehemia ז"ל

Mr. Yaakov Shmulian
and his family

Yitzhak ben Shmuel ז"ל

Mr. Mashiah Dil
and his family

Mr. Gadi Levian
and his family

Mr. Moshe Zarnigian
and his family

Mr. David Chizkiyah
and his family

Mr. Efraim Namdar
and his wife **Maya**
and their daughter **Natalie**

Tzadok Halevi
and his sons, **David, Danny,** and **Ido**
and his family

Mr. Avraham Tzioni
and his family

Mr. Aaron (Babak) Avdul Zada
and his family

Mr. Michael Kordipor
and his family

Mr. Yehuda Kordipor
and his family

Mr. Yaakov Aziz
and his family

Mr. George Dilmani
and his family

Mr. Daniel Zer
and his family

May they be blessed with success in all their endeavors, good health, and a long life filled with joy and fulfillment.